In Defense of Men, and Civilization. (Doyle's War)

Common Sense Realities on Gender

In the year of our Lord 2020

Copyright © October 2020

By Poor Richard's Press, Forest Lake, Minnesota

ISBN—978550080757

"Girls are made of sugar 'n spice 'n everything nice.
Boys are made of snips 'n snails 'n puppy dog tails."
"It's Tommy this and Tommy that, an chuck him out, the brute;
But its savior of his country when the guns begin to shoot..."
From Rudyard Kipling's poem, *Tommy*
"Whether 'tis nobler in the mind to suffer the slings and arrows of
outrageous fortune or to take arms against a sea of troubles, and by
opposing end them."
From *Hamlet* by William Shakespeare

Contents

Introduction

Society is engaged in several cultural wars to the detriment of humanity, this book addresses the one against men, a Cri de Coeur against the evils of misandry [fn1]. Both men and women should take it as seriously as other cultural wars. We are in trouble, not just in terms of gender, but also politically.

This book is divided into six parts: Part 1, The War on Men, identifies at length the two main sections of this war. It concerns blatant sex discrimination directly affecting men and families, and causes and results of this War. It identifies mindsets and professions involved.

Examples of anti-male prejudice in divorce and crime punishment are old news (as are some citations herein) and well-addressed in earlier versions of this book. Students of history or sociology, victims already well aware of these problems, or anyone believing that cited examples are anecdotal may want to proceed to derivative theses or arguments — issues that are more controversial, by skipping this lengthy Part. Check the Table of Contents, below, to find other subjects of interest to you.

Part II Sex and Gender includes sex differences, characteristics, confusions, occupational inclinations, social issues, morality, marriage and health. Part III identifies areas in desperate need of reform and proposes defenses and realistic approaches. Part IV examines the men's movement, such as it is. Part V the Annex addresses civilization itself and tells the author's story.

Male perspectives are emphasized throughout. Lord knows, those of females have been examined and broadcast exhaustively almost universally. Susan B. Anthony created a magazine titled *The Revolution* whose masthead read "Men their rights and nothing more; women their rights, and nothing less." It may have been appropriate in its time; however in these times it is necessary to transpose the genders. In the last several generations of our feminized, unmanned, lawyered-up society, the position of men has deteriorated significantly. In hot pursuit of women's rights, society has looked the other way regarding men's interests. In the past, many prejudices favored men over women (sometimes with good cause). Today that situation is reversed. An analogy illustrates the historic reversal of sex favoritism from men to women: Luther once compared humanity to a drunkard who, after falling off his horse on the right, remounts and falls off again on the left.

In the great "to do" about the alleged problems women encounter by virtue of their sex, the problems of men, especially fathers, receive little

---

[1] hatred—or at least denigration—of men

attention. Traces of discrimination against women may remain, but that which exists against men is vastly greater. There are few expectations of women, and many of men. Disparate views and treatment are especially flagrant in domestic relations, crime punishment, image and health. That famous phrase from George Orwell's Animal Farm is apropos: "All animals are equal, but some are more equal than others." Discrimination is pervasive; the double standard extends into nearly all areas of law and society, a collective idée fixe is taken for granted, institutionalized and unexplainable but provable. This is one among many elephants in the room that nobody notices, or pretends not to notice; even dogs in the street know it.

Society has lost its sense of proportion. In early 2012, certain matters caused feminists to declare existence of a "war on women." As Professor Amneus [fn2] would say, that out-chutzpahs chutzpah! The axiom that women are more discriminated against than men in Western society is the greatest hoax going. Those who believe it are deluded. Feminists believe it. I will leave it to readers to complete the syllogism. If women were treated as are men in many situations, the screams would be audible on the moon. Martin Luther King said, "Injustice anywhere is a threat to justice everywhere." These ideological blinders and the metastasizing of feminism have severely damaged society.

Men's sorry situation results largely from combinations of indiscriminate chivalry, misandry, and political correctness. These universal zeitgeists override the principle of natural justice. Our social conditioning reflexively rejects questioning chivalry in liberals and conservatives (whatever those are) alike, nixing even consideration of the evidence. The whole question of anti-male prejudice, of which there is copious empirical evidence, is one that society would rather sweep under the rug. To most people it is inconvenient, embarrassing or confusing. Certain subjects are offensive to many who would prefer not to face them, but their airing might prevent consequences worse than ruffled feelings.

I intend to prove the thesis that men are more sinned against (largely by themselves) than are they sinners. True, some women have suffered abuse, sometimes horrible abuse, mostly in foreign countries, but not on the same scale as have men. Here, women have the entire legal establishment oriented to help them, so we should be no more overly concerned with their problems, however legitimate, than the NAACP is with white people's problems. This advocacy has been compared to tilting at windmills; but civilization's enemy is not Don Quixote's windmill — it is an honest-to-goodness many-headed dragon.

---

2 Regarding this good man, see the Dedication sub-section, at end.

One should not take lightly the emasculation of the Western male or the ruin of thousands of men, children, and families.

The other side of the saving manhood coin is saving womanhood. It should be self-evident that gender justice will benefit women and children as well as men. Decent women, though they may read this with one eyebrow raised, do not want sons, brothers and loved ones to suffer, or the institution of marriage to disappear. Children deserve a family — father and mother — an environment free from prejudice, and a country safe for marriage.

A dissenting voice to the feminization of the West, this look at the perceived battle of the sexes, though it can't hope to completely reverse sex favoritism, should give "think tanks" something worthwhile to think about. Nor is it intended to drag women down to the level of treatment accorded men, but to bring men up to that accorded women. My purpose is to rescue men, not to denigrate women. Opposition to prejudice is not reverse prejudice, although one must be on guard against that. Defending men does not infer attacking women, even if some wrongly assume it to be thus. Thoughts expressed herein have been mischaracterized as hate speech. Not so. No battle of the sexes should be necessary.

A problem with assertions can be dishonest use of data. I trust my references here, from reliable sources, are accurate. Some may be old, but as valid now as ever and indicative of ongoing situations and changing reality; facts are facts and stubborn things. From the numerous facts and examples gathered, composed and presented here piecemeal, nitpickers are bound to find something argumentative to criticize and will take many things out of context. Without benefit of teams of researchers, an error or two, like obsolete references, may occur (some situations cited could change between this writing and time of publication), and on that basis critics may condemn the entire book, ignoring its overall statistical accuracy; no one has yet articulated sensible objections. On the other hand, some claims may prove to have been understated, but of course, critics will be mum on them. They may consider situations mentioned to be mere anecdotes. If anecdotes are sufficient in number, they become probative statistics. There are so many real instances of situations referred to herein it is impossible to cite them all, but common sense reveals the actuality. Critics of previous editions lost sight of the forest — the essential message of anti-male discrimination — while criticizing some of the trees. The unfortunate situations of many men described, however real, are difficult to comprehend and relate to by anyone who has not experienced them. Hence, they may be received with skepticism. Almost any divorcing man or jailed innocent will concur that these are the ugly reality. In the words of Elie Wiesel writing of Jewish extermination camp prisoners: "Knowledge can be shared, experience cannot."

Critics have maintained that this thesis is not 'balanced.' It is not intended to be balanced; it is intended to restore balance, and to question those forces fundamentally opposed to equal rights for males. It raises issues that most people are unwilling to consider, and suggests considerable changing of mindsets. Elitists on PBS roundtables will not touch them. The very idea of men's rights is unpopular and shocking. It stokes multiple snobberies among academics, feminists, anti-male males, etc. It is somehow discourteous, disrespectful or misogynous to defend men. But history teaches us that all great truths began as heresies. Defending one's country internationally is important, but strengthening the country internally is equally important, hence this book. I think most sensible people will agree with most here. This book is long, but the subject is extensive.

Demanding equal rights and dignity for men, criticizing unreasonable perquisites for women, seeking to preserve families, are ideas whose time has come. My often-harsh observations and perceptions are logically defended. Some politically sensitive persons will not be able to stomach them. Some women will clutch their pearls. The book opens formerly sacrosanct subjects to debate. Speaking truth to power and deflating pretensions, these writings restate the obvious — or what should be so. Almost everyone's ox will be gored, and should be. Politically and socially correct this book is not! It may outrage chivalrous instincts, but such instincts are largely responsible for society's problems.

Like hitting a hornets' nest with a stick, and with all the subtlety of a Panzer division, I wade into such no-fly zones as homosexuality and narrowly defend with logic a (gasp) sexual double standard — in Part II, to the chagrin of certain elements. To those with an agenda much will be called "hate speech" because it offends feminists or others. Frankly, I don't give a damn, having long ago given up trying to please all. Offensive? Yes. How else can one deal with offensive subjects? The fairness principle — if nothing else — demands airing of these views. If feminists, male wimps, religious prudes, or other ultra-sensitive types are offended, screw 'em. One must break eggs to make an omelet. To state the truth is not bigoted; to deny truth is bigoted. No apologies. Let the book-burning commence (thus stimulating sales).

Criticizing both sides of the political divide, this book introduces an unusually realistic perspective on politics. Its approach is classically liberal and socially conservative. At risk of displeasing some of liberal and even libertarian bent, I prefer the old liberalism of Madison and Tocqueville, not the type seeking a narrow view of 'social justice,' focusing on diversity and identity politics or the artificial segmentation of Americans into antagonistic groups organized along ethnic, racial and sexual categories. These divisions are tearing America apart.

Not just a voice for angry white men, this book addresses a much larger constituency. It is time — beyond time actually — to speak for men without the time, talent, or inclination to sit behind desks manipulating facts and statistics favorable to our cause as our more glib opponents and detractors do, to speak for guys like Joe Sixpack — blue collar, common guys working on a farm, in a factory, in a garage, driving a truck, laying bricks, fishing the Bering Sea, military grunts, motorcycle riders — the lumpen proletariat, but not excluding the elite. Unfortunately, few of my target audience read serious books like this.

This is not a polished, professionally written Ph.D.-level tome; full of trendy jargon. A 'populist' screed, in the true sense of the word. it contains plain English that would appall professor Amneus. Other better-educated persons may sneer at it, but I believe wisdom is composed of common sense and life experience as well as education. Think street level reality. The wise Thomas Jefferson said," State a problem to a plowman and a professor. The plowman will decide it often better than the latter, because he had not been led astray by artificial rules." Adam Smith maintained "... 'Knowledge' has its roots in the imagination and the passions, and in the use of intellectual powers we acquire through habit, custom, education and the experience of common life." It will become apparent how politics affect gender/sex issues and vice versa. I seek to recognize and define ideal philosophic and old school normality. This book is informed by decades of research, by interviewing noted professors and habitants of skid row, by conducting divorce counseling, doing organizational work and by culling the thoughts of better men than I. Among the saints and philosophers whose insights were harvested was Omar Khayyam writing nearly a thousand years ago — well before his advanced Persian culture nosedived. [fn3] Wisdom from workingmen friends of mine was also informative. No Facebook philosophy here.

Because of the danger of immorality, not just in personal relationships but in society itself, there is a strong moral aspect. Many matters can be viewed in terms of right or wrong (good or evil if you will), or some mixture of both. I approach issues, not from a religious viewpoint (nor opposed to those views), but from a commonsense viewpoint. [fn4] This is a rearguard defense of men and traditional families, resurrecting old school concepts and examining their conflict with law and behavior. Thomas Jefferson said, "The greatest principles of right or wrong are legible to every reader; to pursue them requires

3 They call him "the tentmaker," but he was much more than that

4 Admittedly a term open to interpretation.

not the aid of many counselors." Sir William Blackstone, the central legal mind that the post-1787 U.S. courts looked to for guidance, wrote, "The primary and principle objects of the law are RIGHTS and WRONGS." Who or what is to be the deciding authority as to what is right and what wrong is up to the reader.

The U.S. Constitution prohibits laws that limit the free exercise of religion, yet in numerous legal situations mentioned throughout the book secularism overrides, if not prohibits, moral and religious considerations. Some readers may object to inclusion of morality. That issue is germane to saving the males because immorality is inimical to marriage and family. Intact families are foremost concerns of most men, their raison d' être — or should be.

The subtitle "Doyle's War" in this title, not an ego thing, is an adaptation of the name of a TV series, "Foyle's War," a Masterpiece Mystery feature show. Writing it has been a never-ending task; this current version has been revised, corrected, expanded and refined several times. It is self-published because its subject matter is so unpopular with the entire publishing industry including agents. I must apologize for the lack of odd-number pages, and blame the Microsoft Word program for that. New issues are necessitated by fast-evolving subject matter.

Earlier poorly-written versions received little attention in the West; however scholars in Doha, Qatar [5] appreciated them, and invited me at the expense of the Qatar Foundation to moderate their 'Men in marriage' seminar in April of 2014. I presented several ideas there regarding the position of men in families. Check endnote 1 for a brief summation of my presentation.

---

5 Qatar is a politically schizophrenic but highly astute oil-rich little country in the Persian Gulf in the heart of the Arab Muslim world. I still have jet lag, and can blame subsequent mistakes on that — but got some great pictures

Part I. The War on Men

Chapter 1. Domestic Relations
Divorce Amerikan Style
The Twilight Zone

Long-time married couples normally have too much of themselves (not to mention money) invested to even consider divorce. The underlying assumption is that divorce is a bad thing, though that is not always true. This section applies somewhat, but only somewhat, more to traditional marriages than to modern marriage. Here is an important statistic: most divorces are initiated by, and granted to, women. [fn6] Shere Hite says the wife is the instigator in seven out of eight divorces. [2] Alan M. Parkman of the University of New Mexico finds a somewhat smaller percentage; he correctly blames No-fault divorce laws. The following sections are written in full understanding that divorce often adversely affects both sexes, and that both partners usually share blame for the death of their marriage.

While women can walk out of marriage at the drop of a whim, men are expected to stoically bear all sorts of faults in their wives. An unholy alliance of the divorce system with feminist philosophy has been instrumental in relieving women of marriage obligations, while assuring them of its advantages and denying advantages to men.

Perpend Amneus: The husband's major contribution to the marriage is irrevocable. It cannot be removed retroactively; he has supported his wife, paid her bills, given her a home, and raised her standard of living by 73 percent. [3] But the wife's major contribution to

---

6 Lenore Weitzman, The Divorce Revolution: The Unexpected Social and Economic Consequences for Women and Children in America (New York: The Free Press, 1985), p 460: 'These researchers [Robert Schoen, Harry N. Greenblatt, and Robert B. Mielke] report that "78 percent of all divorce petitions in California were filed by wives...." p 147 (quoting attorney Riane Eisler), "By social convention, the vast majority of divorces were filed by women." p. 174, "In California, in 1968, under the adversary system, over three quarters of the plaintiffs—those who initiated the legal divorce proceedings—were wives filing charges against husbands." According to David Chambers, Making Fathers Pay (Chicago: University of Chicago Press, 1979), p.29, "the wife is the moving party in divorce actions seven times out of eight." According to Joan Kelly, author of Surviving the Breakup, "Divorce is sought about three to one by women" (cited in Joint Custody Newsletter, January 1988). According to Christopher Lasch, NYRB, 17 February 1988, three-quarters of divorces are granted to women. According to Elsie Clews Parsons's The Family: An Ethnographical and Historical Outline (New York: G. P. Putnam's Sons 1906, 331), (Continued next page)   "A large majority of divorces are obtained by women." According to court records in Marion, Howard, Hancock, Grant and Ruch counties in Indiana in 1985, of 2,033 dissolutions granted, 1,599 (76.6%) were filed by wives, p. 474 (23.3%) were filed by husbands (National Congress for Men Network, Vol. 1, No. 3). According to Shere Hite (Women and Love: A Cultural Revolution in Progress New York: Alfred A. Knopf, 1987, p. 459), "ninety-one percent of women who have divorced say they made the decision to divorce, not their husbands.' NY Review of Books 2/17/66

the marriage, the gift of a family, is removed retroactively in over half of marriages and threatened with removal in all. She never really gave him the family which was the quid pro quo for his supporting her. The husband discovers in the divorce court that what motivated him to get married and to labor during the years of the marriage had no permanent existence; it was not a gift but only a loan backed by a woman's promise, and un-backed by the law. He discovers that the law which must enforce contracts interprets this most basic contract as not binding on his wife, only on him; and therefore deems it just to deprive him of his most precious possession, his children — probably also of his home and his future income.

Although domestic relations laws are generally fair on their face, the administration of them — that is, their application and interpretation under color of law — varies primarily with the sex of the litigants. For divorcing men there is no 'due process', no 'equal protection.' All citizens have rights and responsibilities — legal and moral. Nevertheless, divorce courts generally enforce men's responsibilities, but not their rights. Conversely, they generally enforce women's rights, but not their responsibilities. Any semblance of justification has become a national joke, unfunny to victims.

Actual picture of a man begging his wife not to divorce him. Chicago divorce court 1948

The treatment of men has always been Kafkaesque. Out of some misbegotten sense of chivalry "Up the woman is the unstated major premise. Court customs and practices, regardless of the criteria in use, outrage not only traditional principles of justice, but basic human rights transcending laws of the land. There are all sorts of legal sophistries and sufficient legal precedent on either side of most issues to justify any decisions judges choose to make, even contradictory ones — anything to favor women. Ordinary men are held in a legal headlock from which there is no escape. A man is like a solitary pawn, face-to-face with the queen on a chess board. Like a black man in the South competing for a job 70 years ago, he must be superior just to be considered equal. Hear this statement from the Canadian National Association of Women and the Law: "Courts may treat parents unequally and deny them basic civil liberties and rights, as long as their motives are good." Gadzooks! Orwell saw this coming a long time ago.

Players in these hackneyed charades include the female plaintiff — damsel in distress; the plaintiff's lawyer — her champion; the judge —

ostensibly the force of righteousness, wisdom, and impartiality, but more often her champion's advocate; the male defendant — the villain; and the defendant's lawyer — the devil's advocate.

Disputed proceedings are often conducted in the spirit of the Star Chamber or the Inquisition. In brutal violation of common sense and decency, domestic courts dignify the double-think satirized in the book Catch 22 into logic and law. Incredible and even contradictory judgments right out of <u>Alice in Wonderland</u> are the rule, not the exception. These Kabuki dances can be so stylized that only occasional, limited variations of issues and circumstances occur.

A Texas District Attorney asked Clara Harris why she repeatedly ran over and killed her husband for having an affair, when she could do "like every other woman — get his house, car, kids, and make him wish he were dead." In State v. Oakley, Wisconsin's Supreme Court upheld a lower court ruling that placed restrictions on an alimony/support obligor's right to procreate and attached criminal sanctions to the fathering of a child. There's more; a Wisconsin law ordered divorced men not to remarry without permission of ex-wives and the court (That law was reportedly rescinded). The U.S. Supreme Court refused to review the constitutionality of Georgia statutes allowing alimony for women only. Yet federal courts have eagerly entered domestic matters for the sole benefit of women. [4]

Marriage is a contract, and it is the responsibility of the legal system to enforce contracts. That is what judges are paid for; but with this, the most important contract, that is what they refuse to do. Domestic relations commissars routinely demolish twenty-year marriages and put asunder children. Judicial overlords may deliver in cold blood their sentences of death to families with less time and attention than they devote to contemplating their lunch menu. Divorce court judges wield awesome power to enhance or wreck the future of children of divorce. They claim to be following dictates of society; yet, as Amneus suggests, their anti-male rulings may be inspired instead by what they see other judges living in legal silos do. Such practices undermine the institution of marriage.

Received wisdom is that many fathers "desert" families. Writer George Gilder quaintly assumed that most marital breakdown results from "powerful men" abandoning the wives of their youth and lusting after their young secretaries. [5] A moment's reflection would convince him that there are not that many powerful men, and that high status men have a lower divorce rate than most other males. The sometimes mistaken former Fox News's conservative Bill O'Reilly jumped aboard this bandwagon, blaming poverty on "fathers abandoning their children." [6] It's called the myth of the absconding father. Terming these fathers "runaways" merely adds insult to injury. It is like stabbing a man in the back and accusing him of carrying a concealed weapon.

Deployed military personnel find it extremely difficult to contest divorce, custody and or paternity claims and unfair rulings, perhaps contributing to the high suicide rates among them. The Men's Defense Association's 'Sad Stories' file got so large we discontinued adding to it. It had enough heart-wrenching letters to sober a judge. Though we closed the MDA counseling and attorney referral service over 35 years ago I got letters for well over 20 years from divorced men and prison inmates with pitiful stories begging for help.

This double standard is quasi-legally possible because divorce courts are "courts of equity," wherein 'judgment' is the primary basis of issue determination as opposed to 'courts of law,' where law, sometimes statute — sometimes case, is the primary basis of issue determination. Therefore, protection of law is largely absent, and judges can do nearly as they wish, supported by no higher authority than that of their own rhetoric. Appeal is a costly exercise in futility, and usually amounts only to availing oneself of a pool of prejudice. A dozen wrong men — all part of the same establishment and tradition — produce as little justice as one.

Article VII of the Amendments to the Constitution provides that, "In suits at common law where the value in controversy shall exceed $20, the right to trial by jury shall be preserved." Try to get a divorce-related jury trial in most states of the union. Presently the workload is so great that the right to juries is seldom recognized. In the few jurisdictions where a pretense is made to honor this portion of the Constitution, it is restricted to certain narrow issues only.

The divorce problem is like the weather; many talk about it, but no one does anything about it. The 'fix' is too sensitive. Most people prefer to remain anonymously uncommitted. Their credo is, "We don't want to get involved." There is a veritable sea of public apathy, if not outright hostility, and one can drown in it. How long can the world close its eyes, pretending that it just does not see? Amneus opined,

If the genders were reversed, women would not submit to what men now submit to. If judges did to women what they routinely do to men — if they deprived them of their children, their homes, their property, their role, and compelled them to work and share their income with their ex-husbands, those judges would be torn to pieces by mobs of frenzied women.

Lest any skeptic think that these statements are exaggerations, or believe the contention that things are much better now, let him go to the local courthouse, listen in on these sad dramas, and smell the stench of some of the rulings. Most women are fine with the situation, until years later when their sons and grandsons suffer.

Previous versions of this book contained dozens of examples of outrageously anti-male divorce orders. Citations could go on ad infinitum. To save space, I cite below only four, but they are exemplary of, not hundreds, not thousands, but millions of similar cases. Current ones can be read in the papers every day.

Navy submariner Matthew Hindes from Washington State was given permanent custody of his daughter Kaylee in 2010, after she was reportedly removed from the home of his ex-wife, Angela, by child protective services. While Hindes was serving on submarine duty thousands of miles away in the Pacific Ocean, a judge ordered him to appear in a Michigan courtroom immediately or risk losing custody of his 6-year-old daughter, and having a bench warrant issued for his arrest. [7]

Colonel Bob Stirm was a POW long imprisoned in North Viet Nam. *People* magazine featured a Pulitzer prize-winning picture of Bob meeting his family after his release. Unbeknownst to Bob, his wife had dissipated all of his salary while he was a POW and was planning divorce, having agreed to marry at least three different men while Stirm was a POW — including attorneys in Texas and California and a Naval officer in California. Divorced at this writing she still drew 42% of his retirement pay. The irony of this situation was stated most poignantly by Colonel Stirm during an address to the American Retirees Association national convention, "During my six years as a prisoner of war, I was able to survive for one reason... by strong faith in God, my country and my family" [8] Mat Eytan a famous San Francisco attorney agreed to use the Stirm case in arguing, in the U.S. Supreme Court, to overturn the practice of awarding large portions of military pensions to divorced wives. I am unaware of the Strim matter outcome at this writing. The law allowing this outrageous practice has harmed military women also.

Thumbing their noses at the law, women violate domestic court orders far more often than men do — and get away with it. The case of a former all-conference football star from the University of Kansas is an example. This gentleman, whom I met while working at Charlie Metz's America's $ociety of Divorced Men in Elgin Illinois, and whose name I forget, developed a terminal disease — lateral sclerosis — whereupon his wife filed for divorce. She openly refused to comply with judicial instructions to honor the visitation portion of the divorce order, left the jurisdiction of the original court, and moved to Topeka, Kansas. The dying and immobile man spent thousands of dollars in unsuccessful attempts to see his children. The Illinois and Kansas courts refused to enforce their own orders against the fugitive mother. Kansas Chief Judge Prager, an equine posterior, declared that it would be best for all if the man would hurry up and die. [9]

A woman took her children to Germany, prevented visitation, agreed to reduction of support for that inconvenience, then when her third mate couldn't help her supplement the reduction, obtained increased support on the contention that the biological father could afford it because he bought a motorcycle. Another ex-husband was held in contempt of court for not paying $26,700 support on a child who was spirited away to Holland for eight years. [7] What do such practices say to a wife getting bored with her husband? What do they say to a young man contemplating marriage and creation of a family?

Every man is but a guest in his own home.

Evictions. The folly of wrecking families by expelling fathers and then holding them responsible for their own victimization is readily apparent. Do so-called "deadbeat dads" walk away or are they expelled? Mostly the latter. In truth, a very large percentage of absent fathers have been evicted, either directly or indirectly. Every man is but a guest in his own home, living there only at the forbearance of his wife. He is evictable at a moment's notice if she tires of him and/or makes even unsubstantiated allegations of abuse. At the passing of a whim or a hot flash, a married man can find himself removed from his home and literally imprisoned, sometimes at police gunpoint. Mere allegations of abuse set in motion boilerplate ex parte (one-sided) orders that summarily and routinely evict husbands and 'domestic partners.'

Many of these allegations are patently bogus; faults are magnified. Most violations of restraining orders are non-violent, such as placing a telephone call about a sick child. True, abuse or the fear of it must be alleged but that is often a subterfuge. Such orders also require removed husbands to continue supporting wives and pay their attorneys — all without opportunity to protest.

Some years ago, and probably to this day, in New Hampshire the eviction process was so routine a form was used upon which the clerk stamped a judge's name. Ipso facto, the deed was done. An example of judges doing the Limbo on men's constitutional rights is this: New Jersey Municipal Court Judge Richard Russell at a judge-training session said, "Your job is not to become concerned about all the constitutional rights of the man that you're violating as you grant a restraining order. Throw him out on the street, give him the clothes on his back and tell him, 'See ya around.'" If that is due process of law, I'll eat my hat.

Massachusetts courts issue around 40,000 domestic restraining orders each year. Researcher Steve Basile extensively documented the anti-male bias therein until feminists in the legislature, prevented further research. Attorney Elaine Epstein, former president of the

---

[7] Efforts are underway to strengthen a now-toothless International Convention on Child Kidnapping.

Massachusetts Bar Association, wrote, "The facts have become irrelevant. Everyone knows that restraining orders...are granted to virtually all who apply... The Massachusetts Supreme Judicial Court has acknowledged the problem by writing that we must "resist a culture of summarily issuing and extending these orders." Beware! It could happen to any married man reading this book — or not reading it. The more one examines the situation, the clearer it becomes that viable marriages exist as much in spite of the system as because of it.

Samples of Criticism from within the Court System:

Florida Circuit Court Judge Balaban said:

"Divorce courts handle domestic relations in meat-cleaver fashion — dispense meat-axe justice; the handling of children's welfare is the slaughter of the innocents." As Chauncey M. Depuy, Chairman of the Pennsylvania Bar Association's Family Law section understates it, "To tolerate these conditions one must have an elastic conscience."

Attorney Samuel G. Kling, a Maryland divorce attorney for over thirty years: "The whole approach to divorce in America is uncivilized. There is no branch of law more fraught with hypocrisy, chicanery or fraud than divorce laws and procedures." Domestic abuse has become "an area of law mired in intellectual dishonesty and injustice," according to the Rutgers Law Review.

The Minnesota State Bar Association's (MSBA) Family Law Section conducted a survey of its 830 members (including both public and private sector attorneys.) [10]

Two-thirds of the respondents stated directly, or clearly indicated, that there was gender bias present in the application of the law to family law cases. The most common remarks addressing bias had the stated perception that women received more favorable results... Again, common points raised in the responses were that women are generally receive [sic] better outcomes on the issue of custody, Orders for Protection...

Dr. David R. Mace, of the American Association of Marriage Counselors:

America's divorce statutes should be torn up, and more worthwhile employment should be found for the nation's divorce attorneys ... Everybody is utterly sick of the divorce laws in America. They are a travesty of law, shot through with deception and dishonesty.

Editor Gaeton J. Fonzi, in the *Philadelphia Magazine*:

Pennsylvania's divorce laws and the administration of them here reek with inconsistencies and asininities. They corrupt the courts, foster hypocrisy and cynicism and just about demand fraud and perjury. Of all the areas of law, none is so free of dignity and majesty of justice as that which concerns itself with the dissolution of marriage. The divorce system itself is an expensive, legally condoned network crossed with lies and misrepresentations; degrading and insulting to those who are forced to use it and a blotch on the judicial system that implements it.

Stewart A. Newblatt resigned his Michigan judgeship, saying:

"I can no longer apply an archaic and cruel divorce law that prevents a court from properly performing in the best interests of the parties, the children, and the public. We leave kids with the mother when they ought not to be, because we have glorified the mother." [fn8]

Unnamed Canadian-Ontario Family Court Judge, Ottawa Courthouse, Courtroom 22, July 2006:

"We Judges know that women lie and deceive in family court about issues related to the father in order to gain legal advantage, but we accept that as part of the process."

Dr. Leon R. Koziol, Esq presented comprehensive criticism of the system at the Moreland Commission on Public Corruption Commission Hearing. 11 For the latest expose on the divorce racket, read Divorce Corp. 12

The judicial mentality

The Know Nothing era.

If a child wants to live with his mother, however irrational the choice, his rights as a citizen to do so are usually upheld. If he wants to live with his father, they are often denied. There are plenty of appropriate precedents to cite in defense of any chosen position. According to most interpretations, "Ordinarily where parents are divorced, the mother should have custody of children as against the father." 13 This latter "Bull" (in the ecclesiastic sense) is the regnant official canon or party line, as exemplified in Nye v. Nye 14 and many similar citations. Florida has a law requiring courts to give fathers equal consideration in custody; yet that state's courts like others, impervious to evidence, apply their own prejudice or case law giving mothers preference, even if the mother is so bad she has to live with her parents and share custody with them in order to qualify. 15

Usually lip service is paid to justice, then the axe falls. Digest this:

We agree with the defendant's argument that under the modern and realistic trend of the law, the mother has no absolute or invariable right to be awarded the custody of the children; and that the father's rights and interests are entitled to equal and just consideration. (Then 30 seconds later) "We think there is wisdom in the traditional patterns of thought that the roles of the mother and father in the family are such that the children should be in the care of their mother...; and that this may be true even where the divorce is granted to the father. 16

---

8 Actually, it is judicial practice, not law, that prevents proper performance.

Momism is practically a judicial religion, rendering many judgments indefensible. For example, consider this verbal flatulence equally worthy of a legislator:

What a mother's care means to her children has been so much romanticized and poetized that its substance has sometimes been lost in the flowers of rhetoric, in the aureole of song, and in the vivid color and glistening marble of painting and sculpture. A mother's care means instruction in religion and morals, it means the inculcation of patriotism and love of country, it means the maintenance of a clean heart, it means the imparting of lessons on duties in citizenship, courtesy and good will to one's fellow-man, it means the practical things of preparing healthful food and the mending and repair of clothing, it means ceaseless vigil and the balm of the healing, and when fever visits and the virus strikes—it means all these things and a million others, from all of which the child grows up resolved that he may never be unworthy of the lessons learned at the knee of his most loving companion, his best teacher, his most devoted defender, and his greatest inspiration for this and the life to come, his blessed mother. [17]

(Such drivel. Your turn to puke.)

The supposition by the legal system in the U.S. and other western societies is that it ought to go along with mother custody because it is more "natural," a fiction of its own creation. Prof. Amneus comments on a case referred to by reformer Sonny Burmeister (RIP):

A Georgia superior court judge named Robert Noland always gave custody of children to the mother when he tried a divorce case. He explained, "I ain't never seen a calf following a bull. They always follow the cow. So I always give custody to the mamas." The reason Judge Noland never saw a calf following a bull is that cattle don't live in two-parent households. If we want to live like cattle, he has the right idea.

He did only what he had always done and what most other judges do. He saw that the biological link between the mother and the offspring is closer than that between the father and the offspring and that therefore the mother is the natural custodian of the children.

He's right in a sense. Patriarchy is artificial like everything about civilization, a shaky structure only five thousand years old, built on the firm base of a two-hundred-million-year-old mother-headed reproductive unit shared by cattle. The cattle enjoy the blessings of nature. Judge Noland thought, as Margaret Mead thought, that the female role is a biological fact and that fatherhood is a social invention, man-made, artificial and fragile. When the social props it requires are withdrawn society reverts to matriarchy, the pattern of cattle and the ghettos. Because other judges think as Judge Noland thinks and because they nearly always create female-headed households in place of father-headed households when they try divorce cases, the larger society, as Senator Moynihan said, is coming to take on the pattern of the ghettos.

The tobacco-spitting Judge Nolands of the world who systematically and spinelessly relegate children to the clutches and fathers to the bondage of unfit mothers scorn morality, family and the welfare of children — the very principles they profess to uphold. Unable to differentiate between diseases and symptoms, and impervious to evidence, they piously agonize over the breakdown of society's moral fabric and the disintegration and disorganization of families, ignorant of the fact that these problems are merely symptoms of a disease that they themselves helped cause.

King Solomon's custody solution could be no worse than the judgments of some divorce courts. It must be a psychiatrist's nightmare to see judges, not qualified to diagnose a common cold, much less a neurosis, routinely place the lives, future, and fortunes of children, if not entire families, at the disposal of immature and/or incompetent women.

Judges evicting fathers, simply following tradition, are obviously ignorant of the Hippocratic Oath: *First, do no harm.* Giving custody of children to unfit mothers is child abuse — worse, at least quantitatively, than the celebrated child sex abuse by clergy. Moral — if not legal — criminals, divorce court judges have ruined more children than Doctor Spock, [fn9] and enabled countless aspiring divorcees. They should be tried for high crimes against humanity, and punished under Sharia law. Giving judges this authority, as someone said in another context, is like handing a Stradivarius to a gorilla.

In Barron County Wisconsin, Angela Carroll had split custody of her son with his father, Timothy Miller, neither paying child support. After Judge Michael Bitney accepted a Facebook friend request from Carroll, Bitney ruled that Miller had abused Carroll and gave Carroll sole custody and physical placement of their son and ordered a review of Miller's child support obligations. In New York, a domestic relations court wisely gave custody of two four-year-old twin girls to their father because their mother had previously coached them to falsely accuse their father of sexually molesting them. The more traditional Appeals Court over-turned the lower court's ruling, proclaiming that the "appropriate response to the mother's unacceptable conduct" was not to transfer custody away from her but to "treat her condition." [18]

Misguided women's advocates often claim that fathers usually win custody when they pursue it, and that the reason few fathers have custody is because few of them want it. That is patent nonsense. Feminist psychologist Phyllis Chesler claimed in her book <u>Mothers on Trial</u> that fathers win 70% of custody battles. This widely cited factoid

---

9 His son committed suicide.

was based on a biased, pre-selected sample of 60 women who had been referred by feminist lawyers or women's aid groups because they had custody issues. *Boston Globe* columnist Cathy Young, a rare rational feminist, examined the research upon which these claims are based, and concluded that they belong in the 'Phony Statistics Hall of Fame.' For fatuous minds, facts do not matter. Many divorcees want custody of their children for such base reasons as to have a meal ticket, because it is expected or to spite the ex-husband.

True, few men fight for custody, not because they don't want it, but because of — in addition to social expectations — the overwhelming odds against winning, and because of the prohibitive costs. Benny Hill said, "Just because no one complains doesn't mean all parachutes are perfect."

Access (Visitation)

A 1991 Census Bureau study found that about half of fathers receive no court-ordered visitation. One judge in Belvedere, Illinois, granted newly divorced Homer Von Behran three times as much visitation as the average ex-husband gets. It was to visit with a dog that had been awarded his ex-wife. One might think children deserve as much consideration as a dog does.

Divorce orders usually allow access to fathers, but it can be reluctant. Conservative Judge Robert Bork, dissenting in Franz vs. United States, blazed new trails of misandry with this:

There is no substantive right to so tenuous a relationship as visitation by a non-custodial parent. ...I cannot agree that the Constitution of its own force establishes any such right for a non-custodial parent. [19]

Hear Richard Hutter, former chief judge of the New York County [Manhattan] Family Court, with enough humbug to blot out the sun:

You have never seen a bigger pain in the ass than the father who wants to get involved; he can be repulsive. He wants to meet the kid after school at three o'clock, take the kid out to dinner during the week, have the kid on his own birthday, talk to the kid on the phone every evening, go to every open school night, and take the kid away for a whole weekend so they can be alone together. This type of involved father is pathological. [20]

Despite the undisputed fact that fathers are necessary in children's lives and despite the clamor for "responsible fatherhood," divorced fathers have been jailed for merely trying to contact their kids: Queens, New York Judge Duane Hart sentenced John Modica to 30 days in jail because Modica peacefully approached the judge in a parking lot asking for a continuance to attend his son's soccer game. [21]

Englishman Mark Harris, involved in a bitter divorce, was ordered not to have contact with his daughters. In 2001, he was sentenced to ten months in prison for contempt of court [fn10] for driving past their house to catch a glimpse of them. Later, he was jailed for standing outside his former house to wave at them. He went on hunger strike for two weeks.[22] A Melbourne Australia father of three named "Mick" was jailed 9 days for sending a birthday card to his daughter. [23]

If a divorced man or non-custodial parent lives with a woman not his wife, he will normally be prohibited from having overnight visitation in his home; on the other hand, custodial mothers with live-in boyfriends (or lesbian girlfriends) seldom have such restrictions. Rockdale County, Georgia Judge Sidney L. Nation, an admitted sexist, required that a female be in the house when a father (guilty only of being male) has visitation with his 8-month-old child. [24]

It is often claimed that 'enlightened' U.S. child custody philosophies have evolved. Perhaps in a few sensible jurisdictions they have. Letting extraordinary fathers have custody or reasonable visitation sometimes is pretty weak gruel. However, in general, plus ça change, etc. Florida State Senator Tom Lee, together with House sponsor Representative Ritch Workman and other Republicans submitted bills (SB 668) for several years that would permit access by children of divorce to both their parents. To the great acclaim of Florida Democrats and Barbara DeVane of NOW, feminist-pandering Republican Governor Rick Scott vetoed the bill. [25]

Even when fathers do receive court-ordered access to their children, the provisions are usually only as good as the inclination of mothers to comply. Those who ignore the orders usually go unpunished. Joan Berlin Kelley and Judith Wallerstein, in Surviving the Break-Up, [26] found that almost half of all mothers see no value in fathers' contact with their children following separation or divorce. Sanford Braver, a University of Arizona psychologist, confirmed that up to 40% of mothers interfere with the dad's relationship with his kids.

"Mentoring" by non-custodial fathers is widely advocated, but deplorable when actual fathers are available. The function of Big Brothers Inc. is to stand in for dispossessed fathers. Divorced mothers have been known to make radio pleas for male mentors for their sons whose fathers they evicted. It would be preferable to let fathers stand in for themselves.

Child custody

One might reasonably assume that the right to the care and proximity of one's own children is among our 'unalienable rights.' Indeed, these rights go beyond the Constitution; they are God-given. That sentiment does not square with the facts. Available figures show that around 90 percent of child custody awards are to mothers. The

---

10 It should be honorable to be in contempt of a contemptible court.

last time I checked, Minnesota courts granted moms sole custody of children 94 percent of the time.

While there are exceptions to every rule, law and public policy doggedly oppose significant father involvement with children. An actual father-phobia prevails. The prevailing idolatrous preference for maternal custody in divorce results from an unexamined major premise, a holy maxim that women are ipso facto superior human beings, regardless of reality.

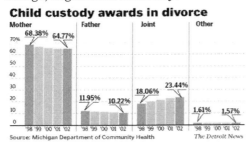

Child custody awards in divorce

Source: Michigan Department of Community Health

The Detroit News

Michigan statistics

Despite Michigan's figures (left), Professor Stephen Baskerville of Patrick Henry College says family courts fail to keep records on the sex breakdown of custody awards "because judicial interests lobby to prevent such records from being kept." Feminist interests do likewise.

Roughly, between one and three million children lose their fathers in the U.S. every year. In 1960, there were 10 million father-deprived homes in the US. According to the Census Bureau, three out of five children born today will spend part of their childhood in a single parent home. In 1993, 24 million children lived without their real fathers. [27] In 2002, Maggie Gallagher said "This Father's Day, some 24 million American children will sleep in (father-deprived) homes." [28] By 2003, this figure had climbed to 25 million. Another source claims there are 60 million divorce orphans (presumably including some who are mother-deprived) in the US. [29] Dr. Wade Horn, former Assistant Secretary of Health and Human Services, Children & Families, former Assistant Secretary of Health and Human Services, Children & Families, said, "Fathers have become viewed as optional to parenting, kind of like a sunroof on a car. They are nice to have around sometimes, but they aren't really necessary." He claims between 20 percent and 30 percent of households are father-deprived. [30] The National Fatherhood Initiative said, "Almost 40% of America's children will go to sleep in a house where their biological father does not live. Seventy one percent of today's youth cannot qualify for military service. Of course not all are fatherless, but I am betting that a disproportionate number are so. Japan, amazingly, is even more misandric regarding custody than is the U.S.

Attorney Thomas James J.D of Cokato, Minnesota, a Minnesota domestic violence expert, informed me that:

[E]arly custody decisions were based on marital fault. Marital fault was supplanted by the 'Best interests of the child' test during the latter half of the 19th century. The Hauteville case, circa 1843, is the first one of which I am aware in which a court officially abandoned the marital fault principle in favor of the 'best interests' test. From there, it was only a short hop, skip and a jump to the maternal preference doctrine (the presumption that best interests are served by placing children with their mothers.)

The most popular rationale used in favor of exclusive maternal custody and exclusive paternal support is that mothers are more available to care for children. This is stereotypical nonsense; most hire baby-sitters, go straight to work, and become part-time parents, which is the ostensible objection postulated against paternal custody. In the year 2000, 62.8 percent of U.S. married women were in the work force. [31] The following old citations are from a Labor Department study, *Children of Working Mothers:* Seventy-three percent of divorced working mothers have children between the ages of 6 and 17. Almost 27 million children in the U.S. had mothers who were working or seeking work in March 1974. A Roper poll shows 70 percent of women work outside the home, or plan to, and those holding full time jobs have doubled since 1970.

The judge's knowledge that the father is more likely to pay is another reason he gives custody to mothers. If he gave custody to fathers, the mothers would contribute little or nothing, but with mother custody the children have a parent and a half because most fathers will continue to subsidize Mom.

Thomas Paine said, "The greatest tyrannies are always perpetrated in the name of the noblest causes." Theoretically, judicial decisions in matters regarding children *should* be made in their best interests. The courts and social services agencies are forever congratulating themselves on their concern in this area. In fact, an unbelievable amount of sin has been committed under the best interest of the children guise. Phyllis Schlafly (RIP) said "The courts pompously assert they are invoking 'the best interest of the child,' but how can it be in the best interest of children to make them forfeit one parent?" Custodial discrimination can hurt women as well; many grandmothers have been cut off from grand-children they loved.

Problems with Maternal Preference

Lawmakers and judges get things backwards: they suppose that a biological fact — motherhood — requires their support, and a social creation such as fatherhood does not. They seem to have scant sense of cause and effect. This bribe is no doubt the greatest single external divorce-causing factor. It is causing women to initiate about eighty percent of divorces. Their mistake is largely why we have a fifty percent divorce rate, why our families are in ruins.

The crucial correlation that never seems to have been noticed is the increase in the number of divorces following the switchover from automatic father custody to virtually automatic mother custody, plus the indiscriminate assurance to divorcing women of other fruits of marriage, including financial sustenance (or the spoils of war).

The old shibboleths about motherhood must be exposed. Contrary to romantic lore and electioneering principles, motherhood, per se, is a mere biological accident undeserving of categorical blessing. The current clamor for abortions and childcare centers ought to dispel many of the myths. Leatrice Brewer, of long Island New York, called police claiming she killed her three young children. Police said the children were drowned, poisoned, and one's throat was cut. Brewer had six arrests — two felonies and four misdemeanors — on her record dating to 2000. The children's fathers said they had fought in vain to obtain custody from Brewer.

Danger: Divorce, though usually portrayed as a protection against child abuse, is far more frequently a contributing cause. The amount of abuse increases enormously when the mother becomes single. Betty Rollin, Senior Editor of *Look* magazine, said, "The realities of motherhood can turn women into terrible people. And, judging from the 50,000 cases of child abuse in the U.S. each year, some are worse than terrible." In Milwaukee County in 1989, there were 1,050 reported cases of child abuse. Eighty-three percent of these cases occurred in households receiving AFDC, in other words in mostly female-headed households. [32] Professor Urie Bronfenbrenner (RIP), speaking before a Congressional committee on child abuse, said, "The most severe injuries occurred in single-parent homes and were inflicted by the mother herself." According to Patrick Fagan [33] and William Fitzgerald, the person most likely to abuse a young child is the child's own mother. Likewise, Maggie Gallagher says, "The person most likely to abuse a child physically is a single mother.

The person most likely to abuse a child sexually is the mother's boyfriend or second husband. The most dangerous place for a women and her child is an environment in which she is cohabiting with a boyfriend who is not the father of her children. The rate of child abuse may be as much as 33 times higher." [34]

Male animals often kill their current female mates' offspring who are not fathered by them. Newspapers are rife with instances of this phenomenon in the human species.

The most dangerous place for a women and her child is an environment in which she is cohabiting with a boyfriend who is not the father of her children.

An Eagan Minnesota man accused of fatally beating his girlfriend's foster child after having to change the boy's diaper was sentenced to 25 years in prison. Charles Wayne Homich, 28, was sentenced by Dakota County District Judge Christopher Lehmann in connection with the 2017 death of 3-year-old Zayden Lawson. Zayden was a foster child in the care of Homich's girlfriend, Zeporia Dionn Fortenberry, [35]. Most recently also in Minnesota, Adam Michael Peter Travis, [22], was sentenced to 57 months in state prison for the fatal abuse of his 2-year-old stepdaughter. Travis was charged with five felonies, but four were dismissed as part of the plea.[36]

In Onslow County North Carolina, Adolphus Earl Kimrey II is accused of murdering 3-year-old Mariah Woods, daughter of his girlfriend and housemate Kristy Woods. An autopsy revealed the girl died of chloroform toxicity. Alex Woods, Mariah's biological father, had been in a custody dispute with Kristy over Mariah and her two brothers. Woods alleges that Kimrey sexually abused Mariah and physically abused the two boys. Police believe the girl died from "unnatural causes," and that Kimrey killed her and concealed her death and body. Kimrey was held at the Onslow County Detention Center on a $1million bond facing the death penalty. Woods said, "It's unreal. It's a nightmare."

Derion Vence, lived with Maleah Davis and her mother Brittany Bowens in Sugar Land Texas. Vence has been arrested for the abduction and probable murder of Maleah.

Kimberly Dawn Trenor, and Royce Clyde Zeigler II, the mother and stepfather of little Riley Ann Sawyers — "Baby Grace" — were arrested on charges of killing Riley Ann. The mother admitted the girl was beaten with leather belts, had her head held underwater in a bathtub and then was thrown across a room, her head slamming into a tile floor.

William A. Warr, Sha'Reese Miller's boyfriend, beat her 4-year-old son Key'ontay Miller Peterson to death. [37]

Manuel Garcia of Racine Wisconsin was sentenced to 40 years in prison for killing, by "blunt trauma," his girlfriend's 23-month-old Jovani Martinez. [38]

More recently, Devioun Johnson, live-in boyfriend of Tawanna Chizelle, and involved in a 2013 child protection complaint, was charged with murdering Chizelle's three-year-old son. [39]

Milwaukee resident Nicholas Fuchs put his girlfriend's 4-year-old daughter in the clothes dryer and turned it on. [40]

Brazilians Roborto Carlos Magalhaes the stepfather and Angelina dos Santos the mother stuck a series of needles in her 2-year-old son in a murder attempt that made headlines. [41]

I've noticed many such articles in local papers. [42] On February 12th 2015, Mike Meak sexually assaulted and brutally murdered his girlfriend's 18-month-old daughter while babysitting her in Maplewood Minnesota. [43] Meak was sentenced to 25 years. More recently Quran Jabari Mitchell, 21, beat his girlfriend's toddler to death in the Minneapolis suburb of Crystal. Jonathon Wierstad, 29, was sentenced to 25 years in prison for beating to death his fiancee's 16-month-old child Blake Holmquist.

A jury convicted a St. Paul man of raping his girlfriend's 4-year-old twins and giving them both a sexually transmitted disease. [44]

The same situation exists in England:

The fact is that files of relevant government bodies are bulging with evidence that broken homes mean more battered children. Research has shown that it is 20 times more dangerous for a child if the natural parents cohabit rather than marry. It is 33 times more dangerous for a child to live with its natural mother and her boyfriend than with the natural parents in a marriage relationship. [45]

Consider this: Sixty-two percent of child-killers are men. While very few of them are fathers, the media frequently lumps these ordained villains in with mothers' boyfriends and other caregivers, thus supporting arguments in court for mother custody. [46] Ah so!

Joint Custody. "Joint Legal Custody" is gaining in popularity, but is largely meaningless, a sop to make fathers think they have an equal say in the care of their children. It is a Hobson's choice: take it or take nothing. Only joint residential custody is worthy of the name.

A Colorado Court of Appeals gave a non-biological lesbian "psychological parent" 50-50 joint custody with her former partner of a young adopted daughter. [47] How then can actual biological dads who were in married households deserve less?

For five years Army National Guard Spc. Joe McNeilly of Grand Ledge, Mich. had had a 50-50 custody arrangement for his 10-year-old son with his ex-girlfriend Holly Erb. When called up to go to Iraq, he gave her temporary full custody while he was overseas. While he was gone, Erb persuaded a family court to make her full custody permanent. When McNeilly protested, he was told that his year-long absence constituted abandonment and produced custody "points" against him. State Rep. Rick Jones (R-MI) became interested in this injustice. When he contacted the Judge Advocate General's office, he discovered that there were 15 to 20 similar cases in Michigan and it is a common problem all over the United States.

The Financial Part:

The Road to Serfdom

Only the very rich and the very poor can afford divorce. It is most costly to the vast middle class. The wealthy can write it off taxes if they know how, or are able to afford it. The poor have nothing to lose. In the U.S. a few years ago, "the average divorce costs around $50,000, and ... $175 billion was spent annually on divorce, mostly on litigation." [48]

Divorce is an immense engine for transfer of wealth, moving more funds in America than will and probate. Redistribution of wealth, generally frowned upon except by leftists, is widely accepted in divorce — from male to female, and is one of the biggest mischiefs governments engage in. The Communist philosophy applies, "From each according to his ability; to each according to (her) needs." The whole transfer concept ignores the fact that the financially superior status of males that once justified it has all but evaporated.

The popular cliché, "feminization of poverty," coined to justify the transfer of male-earned funds to women, is misleading because women already own approximately 70% of this nation's wealth, [49] and because with child custody awards go house and financial packages designed to maintain mothers and children, but not fathers, at or near their former level of affluence. Female poverty, where it exists, results chiefly from the feminization of custody.

Alimony,

Money greases the wheels of divorce; women require it for themselves after divorce, and attorneys become involved for the fees. Alimony's purpose before emancipation was to support destitute, incapacitated ex-wives. Subsequently it became corrupted into the notion that an ex-wife "has a right (in the words of one judge) to continue to live in the manner to which she has become accustomed" (by her husband). It is considered to be "in the nature of a pension." Like automatic custody awards, automatic alimony awards are nails in the coffin of marriage.

Divorce courts operate on the assumption that men's sole function is to be a financial base upon which ex-wives can live and amuse themselves. Not having women's immunity from responsibility, men are judiciously enjoined, under penalty of jail, to perform functions only implied in the marriage contract. Upon dissolution of marriage, men's obligations continue to be enforced; yet no judge has ever ordered a woman to cook, clean and sew for her ex-husband, not to mention an existing one. (OK, sewing is an anachronism and the others increasingly so.) A famous old judge said, "Alimony drones neither toil nor spin."

Hear Professor Amneus on alimony:

Imagine an employee quitting her job and demanding to be paid for doing so... Why is the woman entitled to a pension? For bearing the man's children and giving him a family? ... She would have been entitled to a lifetime pension for maintaining rather than undermining his connection with his children and for preserving his family. This is the idea of marriage — why it is a lifetime contract.

So she is not giving him children and a family, she is taking them away from him — depriving him of most of what gives his life meaning. And for this, she imagines herself entitled to a lifelong pension from the man she victimizes.

An argument for alimony is that husbands owe money to wives for 'services rendered.' This post facto service charge is, as the anachronistic saying goes, "the screwing you get for the screwing you got." The claim that women give men the best years of their lives is nonsense. It's a horse apiece; men give the same and don't ask for stud fees when it's over.

Eulogies have been prepared purporting to list the monetary value of a wife to a husband. According to Reuters Limited, an informal study conducted by Web site Salary.com, years ago, showed that stay-at-home moms would earn an average of $131,471 annually including overtime if they received a paycheck. Ridiculous, considering that her actually-working husband may earn only $60,000 a year! Such preposterous claims assume that all the alleged benefits somehow accrue to the husband alone, an insult to the greatest recipients — women and children. Wives' costs are not listed. Including reserve for alimony, it should come out about even. A great many are liabilities, not worth their salt.

The difficulty of housework is greatly exaggerated. A competent housewife without kids can do normal daily tasks in a couple hours, with kids — a little longer, and have the balance of her time to lie around watching soap operas, reading *True Romance*, coffee-klatching, eating bon-bons, and complaining of overwork. The fact they live longer demonstrates that women have life easier. Before my wife died I was nurse, cook and housekeeper, in addition to the usual outdoor and office chores. I considered the housework part a pleasant occupation.

Husbands' services, including on the job, usually exceed in value those of wives. Looked at realistically, an average father raises his wife's and children's standard of living by 73 percent. His marriage motivates him to do so.

Shortly after its introduction, the Equal Rights Amendment was interpreted by a presidential panel as safeguarding women only (excluding equal rights for men, therefore), and as justifying increases in alimony. Feminist Lenore Weitzman justified alimony by declaring, based on contrived 'studies' that an ex-husband's standard of living skyrockets by 42%. This myth has been disproved by the scholarly attorney, Jed Abraham, JD, [50] and by Professor Amneus in <u>The Case for Father Custody</u>. Two New Jersey Appellate Division cases cited one-week apart decided that if you are a woman, your education doesn't count towards imputing your income, but if you are a man, it does. [51]

Alimony often discourages women from the formality of legalizing new unions and, believe it or not, in some states does not necessarily terminate if they do. According to an Oklahoma appellate court, it is not necessarily terminable by death. It has even been awarded in voided marriages. California laws, which say alimony ends when a former spouse remarries, mention nothing about homosexual relationships. [52] An Orange County California judge ordered Ron Garber to continue paying alimony to his ex-wife — even though she was in a registered domestic partnership with another woman and used the other woman's last name.

Although separation agreements making no provision for alimony to husbands are legal, the New York Supreme Court for New York County held that separation agreements making no provision for alimony to wives was "contrary to public policy," therefore illegal. [53]

The principle that assets owned prior to marriage are not divisible in any subsequent divorce often does not apply if it would be to the advantage of the wife to divide them. [54] Although women routinely receive greater property divisions than men because of lesser earning ability, a Texas Court of Appeals held that the reverse is illegal. [55] Husbands' earnings in community property states, except Texas, remain community property; wives' earnings generally are their separate property. Despite the "community property" law, women in California find it very easy to retain their separate assets. This principle is applied de facto in all states.

Even prenuptial contracts can be dishonored to favor women. A wife can sign a document acknowledging her husband's ownership of property, later claim she did not know what she signed, and invalidate the document. Donna Austin and Craig Austin were married in May 1989, each for the second time, and divorced after 12 years. Despite a prenuptial agreement in place containing a waiver of alimony and despite hundreds of thousands of dollars that Donna realized in the division of property assets, an Appeals Court overturned the alimony waiver.

Paul and Theresa Taylor were married for 17 years. He was an engineer for Boston's public works department, while she worked in accounting at a publishing company. They had three children, a weekend cottage on the bay and a house in the suburbs. In 1982 when they divorced, the split was amicable. She got the family home; he got the second home. Both agreed "to waive any right to past, present or future alimony." But more than two decades after the divorce, Ms. Taylor, 64, told a Massachusetts judge she had no job, retirement savings or health insurance. The judge ordered Mr. Taylor, then 68 and remarried, to pay $400 per week to support his ex-wife. [56]

Alimony has achieved nosebleed levels at times. When Jeff Bezos, primary owner of Amazon, and his wife McKenzie divorced, she received $35.6 billion (with a B) in Amazon stock plus 4 percent of the company's outstanding common stock, making her the third-biggest shareholder at the company. Alimony has been awarded to women with considerably greater assets than the husbands ordered to pay it. Oil billionaire Harold Hamm offered ex-wife Sue Ann Arnall a $975 million divorce settlement. She rejected it, demanding more. [57] One New York judge, incensed about a man's pre-marital promiscuity, ordered alimony payments in the amount of 105 percent of his income despite alimony's non-punitive intent.

On the bright side, a Kentucky court allowed as how, "Such conduct of the ex-wife as shooting and killing the husband's second wife, however, may be amply sufficient to warrant his refusal to make any payments from which she might in any way derive benefit." [58] Another: Golden, Colorado, district Judge Roscoe Pile — a brave and unusual man — jailed Mrs. Virginia Ealy for defying a court-ordered property settlement in a divorce case.

Colleagues in socialist Canada tell me that, "What's hers is hers and what's his is hers too." Hear Dr. Charles Corry on Canadian legislation being introduced:

In the fall of 2000, legislators in Ottawa, Canada introduced Bill 117 that provides that any woman could have a man restrained, imprisoned, and his property transferred to her all in the same day without any pretense of due process. Writing for the *Ottawa Citizen*, columnist Dave Brown noted, "The new legislation is based on the premise women in abusive relationships can't escape because they are economically dependent. The intent is to correct this by making it possible to immediately transfer all property to her.

Written into the scheme are ex-parte applications. The alleged abuser does not have to be present when the order seizing his property is made. Application for an Intervention Order can be made by anyone in a one-to-one relationship, including dating... It will take precedence over any acquittal, dismissal or withdrawal of a criminal charge, or any order under any statute, including the Divorce Act.

'Child Support'

Because the word 'alimony' has fallen into justifiable disrepute, courts are avoiding the distaste by disguising it as 'child support' in divorce decrees, often doubling or tripling (or more) the actual cost of raising children; hence my use herein of the dual term alimony/support and the use of quotation marks around the term.. Such de facto alimony, a howling injustice, is worse than actual alimony because the obligation continues regardless of need until the children are emancipated. Child support payments accrue to the legal custodian, even if the child is living with the other parent, and continue until the court decides to modify the meaningless decree and order otherwise. Probably thousands of fathers who did not know this have paid double, been held in contempt, or jailed for non-support.

Dias Griffin, divorcing wife of Illinois' richest man Ken Griffin, is worth $50 million and asking a million a month for 'child support.' [59] Former glamour model Heather Mills sued former Beatle "Sir" Paul McCartney for divorce. To fund her daily needs, such as 24-hour bodyguards and two full-time nannies for their young daughter, Beatrice, Mills wanted as much as $160 million of McCartney's $1.6 billion empire, most of which was earned decades before they got married in the summer of 2002. McCartney reportedly offered Mills a lump sum between $20 million and $40 million, in addition to annual payments of $5 million until Beatrice would turn 18.

Diane Richie, aspiring ex-wife of Lionel Richie, filed for separation in October 2003 and divorce in January the next year, citing irreconcilable differences. In March of '04, she asked for $300,000 a month in child and spousal support to maintain the extra-ordinary extravagant lifestyle the couple had during their nearly seven years of marriage.

NHL goalie Martin Brodeur must pay his ex-wife Melanie DuBois $500,000 a year alimony/support until 2020. [60] In May 2014, a Swiss court awarded Elena Rybolovlev $4.7 billion from Russian billionaire Dimetry Rybolovlev's assets. In Sacramento, California, the wife of a police detective, tried to hire hit men to kill her husband. After getting out of prison, divorced, she was awarded half the couple's $70,000 property. [61]

On December 7th, 2012, a New Jersey newspaper, the Hunterdon County Democrat, reported that John Waldorf, had been in county jail for 7 weeks due to inability to pay $2,000 a week in alimony to his ex. That amounts to $104,000 a year. In addition, he was ordered to pay $3,300 in child support. The problem is that Waldorf took home only about $90,000 a year on average. He also owed about $100,000 in legal fees. It appeared Waldorf lost his job because of his jailing. [62] On December 17th, the NJ Supreme Court ordered Waldorf's immediate release, that he must pay $1,000 per week in alimony, and if he lost his job that he find one within 30 days.

Stuart, Georgia attorney Willie Gary must pay $29,100 a month for 16 years, a total of more than $5.5 million, to Diane Gowins, an Atlanta woman, for the twins he fathered out of wedlock. In Kansas, Craigslist sperm donor William Marotta was forced to pay child support to a lesbian couple — despite giving up parental rights to the baby girl before she was born. [63]

TMZ.com reported NFL football star Matt Leinart was in "a raging legal fight" with ex-girlfriend, Brynn Cameron, over the couple's toddler son Cole. According to sources close to the case, Brynn wanted Matt to hand over more than $30,000 per month! The sources said Leinart was not happy about this — "having already bought her a car, as well as voluntarily giving her around six grand a month."

James Richards was ordered to pay $208,000 in support arrears for his girlfriend's daughter plus $2,281 a month until the girl turned 18, which at the time was five years away, despite conclusive DNA proof that he was not the father. The Tennessee Court of Appeals later stopped the monthly payments, but ordered Richards to pay $98,108 in back support because he had acknowledged paternity, [64] deceived though he was.

Geoffrey Fisher of Auburn, Maine had a brief relationship with a woman and believed her when she got pregnant and told him he was the father. He began paying child support but fell behind over time. The girl was placed in foster care at age 3. When Fisher pushed for custody, the state ordered a paternity test, which proved he was not the father. In the summer of 2001, the Department of Health and Human Services took him to court because of delinquent payments. A District Court judge ruled that he no longer had to pay child support for a child that was not his. Later, the state sent him a letter seeking $11,450 in child support, even though officials knew that DNA tests proved he was not the father of the child in question. The court ordered him to pay up, and the state had his license suspended under the "deadbeat dad" law. It's crazy; one branch of the human services department told him he could no longer see the girl because he was not the father, while another said he owed over $10,000 and couldn't have a driver's license because he *was* the father. [65]

In the early '90s, Bobby Sherrill was a Lockheed employee and divorced father working in Kuwait when Iraq invaded. Sherrill was held captive by the Iraqis for five months. Upon his return to North Carolina, he was arrested for non-payment of $1,425 in alimony/support that accrued while he was held hostage. Aaron O'Connor, a soldier from Oneonta, New York on leave from active duty in Iraq, was arrested for not paying alimony/support despite the fact that his payments were automatically deducted from his Army pay. [66]

Deployed Oklahoma National Guardsman Brian Whitlock went to the state child support enforcement department to get a modification of his child support, since his income was going to decline. Instead of the downward modification, he got an unexplained increase, and the Department of Human Services seized all of his and his wife's bank accounts. A lien was placed on all assets — meaning every penny Whitlock was paid while in Iraq could have been seized. [67]

On December 9, 2012, Stephen Schmidt, 70, of Jonesboro, Ga., was pulled over for a traffic violation. The trooper ran Schmidt's driver's license and found a warrant for unpaid alimony/child support — dating back to 1975. Schmidt was taken to jail on that 36-year-old warrant. The ex-husband of Toni Anderson, a North San Diego County woman, absconded to Canada in the early 1970s without paying alimony/support. Because there was no statute of limitations on child support, with accrued interest of 10 percent a year, what would have been a total payment of some $30,000 became more than $170,000 for their now 53-year-old daughter. Anderson sued her ex for that amount. At a private hearing in Vista Court he settled for $150,000 (Moves are afoot across the country, one in the Minnesota Legislature, to do away with all statutes of limitations).

The State of Michigan ordered Detroiter Carnell Alexander to pay tens of thousands of dollars, or go to prison for default on a 1987 child support order for a child that DNA testing proved was not his, and that his "ex" admitted was not his. [68] A child support court in Houston Texas ruled that Gabriel Cornejo owes his ex-girlfriend $65,000 support for a child she had 16 years ago because, she claims, there was no way he wasn't the father, and he didn't object when support payments started coming out from Cornejo's paycheck. Cornejo took a DNA test proving the child his ex-girlfriend had 16 years ago was not his. However, Texas' family code, chapter 161 states, 'even if you're not the biological father, you still owe child support that accrued before a DNA test proves you're not the father.' Cornejo's lawyer maintains he was never served with court orders in 2002 when the actual paternity petition was filed against him. [69]

Although the age of majority is 18 in most states, many courts force ex-fathers to continue supporting offspring until age 21, reasoning that age 21 was considered to be the age of majority at the time the divorce order was written. The logic is convoluted from that permitting 'No-fault' states to destroy without cause marriages entered prior to passage of No-fault legislation. An Italian court ordered a middle-aged father to keep supporting his 28-year-old son through university, after he turned to the law to try and force his offspring to get a job. A court ruled that the son's "personal aspirations" must be paid for by his father. The son completed a degree in literature, taking several years longer than expected to finish the course, and enrolled on a post-graduate course in experimental cinema in Bologna. The case was just one of 8,000 similar disputes that end up in Italian courts each year, with adult children demanding an allowance from their parents. The country's spoilt "big babies" who refuse to leave home and instead sponge off their parents are termed "bamboccioni."

Men's subsequent families have no standing regarding obligations to their first one, and support obligations can continue even after death of the father. In Nebraska, Don Harriman died leaving second wife Debra, their 14-year-old daughter and two other daughters by a previous marriage. Up until his death, Harriman never missed a child support payment to his previous wife. Enter Nebraska statute 43-513.01, which states, "A judgment for child support shall not abate upon the death of the judgment debtor." The government intercepted $1,867 of Debra's tax refund, and was after more. Debra's protests were in vain. Harriman had no assets, no property and no life insurance, so the state was attempting to collect from income after his death.

Professor Amneus analogized the argument that women and courts use to justify giving large alimony/support awards to divorcing women with the "Mutilated Beggar" phenomenon. In some large cities of the East there were begging rings headed by rascals who kidnapped children and mutilated them for use as beggars. The more pitiable and grotesque the mutilations, the more the beggars earned. The alms went to the owners of the begging rings.

For some men behind in alimony/support, their choice is jail or a vasectomy. In Kentucky, Family Court Judge D. Michael "Mickey" Foellger gave that option to several men. Beth Wilson, executive director of the American Civil Liberties Union in Kentucky, said the policy is questionable. Foellger said he had considered offering women accused of multiple instances of abuse or neglect the option of having a tubal ligation; but he rejected that saying it's an invasive procedure that could have unknown consequences.

Chivalrous courts exist beyond U.S. boundaries as well. For 16 years in the UK, James MacLetchie, an infertile man, fought the government's demand for Child Support. A legal quirk prevents DNA testing for parentage without the mothers' agreement. This, MacLetchie's ex-wife refused. [70] A Quebec Superior Court of jurisdiction ordered this Canadian father to pay child support to his ex-wife despite results of DNA testing that found three of the four children he helped raise are not biologically his. [71]

In order to justify increased alimony/support awards, the Agriculture Dept. artificially bumped up the costs of raising children by an accounting trick called "proportional accounting," which uses per capita costs instead of marginal costs. This scheme determines the total cost of a household, and then divides by the number of persons therein. This is illogical because the adults therein incur most of that cost with or without children, who add only marginally to the cost.

Child support enforcement in the U.S. was originally federalized to recover welfare costs, since no constitutional provision mandates federal involvement. Yet shortly after its creation in 1975, the machinery was dramatically expanded, with no explanation, to include all child support cases, including the vast majority not on welfare. Today, welfare cases — consisting mostly of unmarried parents — account for just 17% of all child-support cases, and the proportion is shrinking. The remaining 83% are non-welfare cases consisting largely of involuntarily divorced middle-class fathers with pockets to mine. The support collection procedure, refined and federalized under Title IV-D of the Social Security Act, has been broadened to also include collection of alimony. [72] The exiled male does not even get to claim head-of-household tax status, although financially maintaining the household. Talk about taxation without representation!

In 1986, the Bradley Amendment (authored by former Democrat Senator Bill Bradley from New Jersey), signed into federal law, requires state courts to prohibit retroactive reduction of child support obligations. This ill-advised, ironclad prohibition has caused great hardship including prosecution and imprisonment of indigents, deprivation of driver's licenses, revocation of passports and entry into poverty. Victims have had difficulties holding jobs, maintaining bank accounts or having any kind of meaningful access to the economy. By prohibiting obligors from retroactively reducing arrearages, the amendment has had the unintended consequence of preventing non-custodial parents from reaching a point in which they can satisfy the obligations imposed on them.

Nationally-known attorney Jeffrey Leving said "Child support orders cannot be retroactively modified, no matter how mistaken, misguided or ridiculous. Even men who fell behind on their child support because they had heart attacks, broken legs or cancer cannot have their arrearages eliminated." Phyllis Schlafly (R.I.P.)penned a brilliant criticism of the Bradley Amendment in Townhall.com on February 27, 2006.

Nevadan Anthony Fernandez once earned between $500,000 and $4 million a year in the stock market. When that market tanked, he ended up earning $3,000 a month selling cars, approximately the same as or less than his ex-wife's income. District Court Judge Cheryl Moss denied Fernandez's petition to modify child support payments. [73]

Few seem to know or care if fathers can even afford to pay. The Office of Child Support Enforcement published a series of reports titled *The Story Behind the Numbers*. The first in the series, *Who Owes the Child Support Debt?*, points out that the vast majority (70 percent) is owed by non-custodial parents with reported incomes of less than $10,000 per year, and 42 percent of the debt is owed by debtors with no reported income. [74] Federal Child Support Director Sherri Heller acknowledged, during a meeting for African-American groups in Washington in August 2004 that "about two-thirds of the [child support] debt is owed by people who earned less than $10,000 the previous year According to state officials in New York, at least 35 percent is owed by men with income of $12,500 or less. Less than 4 percent is owed by men with incomes of more than $40,000. Even Office of Child Support Commissioner Margot Bean admitted, "A federally-funded study shows most arrears are highly concentrated among a relatively small number of non-custodial parents, and most arrears are owed by non-custodial parents with no or low reported wages." [75] In other words, it appears that most of the debt is owed by extremely poor debtors.

Former Washington political analyst Stuart Miller explained:

> Of the 30% of child support payments not collected, a significant number are owed by fathers who are imprisoned. A high percentage of prisoners have child-support obligations, and as many as one-third of the inmates in many county jails are there in the first place because of child support noncompliance.

> Many of the other delinquent fathers are addicts, alcoholics, disabled, mentally incapacitated, unemployed, or otherwise unable to pay pre-set child support amounts. [76] The General Accounting Office found in 1992 that as many as 14% of fathers who owe child support "cannot afford to pay the amount ordered." Others do not even exist.

Divorced father, Dr. Amir Sanjari, an Iranian-born British citizen, went on hunger strike March 26, 2011 the day he was arrested for an alimony/support debt. Sanjari and his ex-wife shared equal custody and had similar incomes, yet he was ordered to pay $1,000 a month alimony/support. When he lost his job and applied for a reduction, it was denied. He says his ex-wife won sole custody of the children by lying about him while he was out of the country. Sanjari says the system has been "playing dirty" with him, and "is a conspiracy, a fraud" (imagine that). [77]

Some protests can be humorous: an East Chicago fireman, denied visitation for a year and a half, was brought into court on contempt charges when he made a $175 support payment in the form of pennies packed in grease.

Responsibility is not reciprocally applied. Non-custodial mothers are rare, and if ordered to pay child support at all, it is usually in only token amounts. The federal Office of Income Security Policy found in 1991 that less than 30% of custodial fathers receive a child support award, whereas almost 80% of custodial mothers do. In Missouri in 2000, about 6% of divorced custodial fathers were awarded child support; mothers were awarded child support in 72% of the cases, and no support was awarded in 21% of the cases. Such support provisions are usually only as good as the inclination of mother obligors to comply. About 47% of them totally default on their obligation; Census figures show only 57 percent of mothers required to pay child support pay some or all of the money they owe. That compares with 68 percent of dads who pay up. [78] If a woman is arrested for non-support, it makes the news. It's not news with fathers.

An argument for reliving mothers of child support obligations is that raising children burdens mothers enough, so they should not be obliged to share in the costs. Nonsense! From my experience, most fathers would love to be so burdened; and many if not most of those forgo receiving support to have custody.

The collection Gestapo
"Ve haff vays of making you...."
der prozess, as Kafka would put it.

"Men must support their children, and be forced to do so if necessary." That sounds good if you say it fast. Snorting and frothing about non-custodial parents not paying ordered alimony/support is immensely popular politically; it gets the boob vote. As Civil war era clucking about runaway slaves (unlawful under the Fugitive Slave Law) postulated the planted axiom that slavery is acceptable (lawful), so too does the uproar over "deadbeat dads" postulate the false premise that child support orders are reasonable and that the whole process is fair to men who have been deprived of their children.

Alan Keyes, an otherwise astute political thinker, proclaimed that alimony/support debtors "should be horsewhipped." "We will find you; we will make you pay," threatened former President William Jefferson Clinton. "The government will say to absent parents who aren't paying their child support: 'If you're not providing for your children, we'll garnish your wages, suspend your license, track you across state lines and, if necessary, make some of you work off what you owe.' People who bring children into this world cannot and must not walk away from them." Clinton's denouncement of such parents during his State of the Union Address met with the loudest cheers of any of his proposals that evening.

In From Courtship to Courtroom, attorney Jed Abraham describes the child support collection machinery as "Orwellian." If all you have is a hammer, every problem looks like a nail. Overly aggressive enforcement and draconian seizure methods are employed against men unable to meet alimony, palimony and child support orders. Men lose assets, including unemployment compensation, pensions, and even disability annuities. Pictures of these debtors are sometimes put on pizza boxes and billboards. New York Senate bill 2292 would make non-support a felony.

An entire bureaucracy has grown up around the collection of domestic relations obligations. Government agencies, local and national are the largest overall pursuers. They have turned into giant collection agencies for divorcees; it is one of county governments' largest functions. Legions of drones have been employed in this pursuit. Male-sympathetic writer Wendy McElroy said, "For almost 30 years, an army of civil servants and government officials have spent billions of dollars to track these debtors down." Additionally, commercial collection agencies are tracking the debtors.

ACFC's Professor Stephen Baskerville says, "The federal government is up to its ears in family law by its funding for child support enforcement, domestic violence programs, and child abuse 'prevention.'

By padding their roles with millions of middle-class parents, state governments found they could collect a windfall of federal incentive payments. Federal taxpayers now subsidize state government operations through child support. They also subsidize family dissolution, for every fatherless child is an additional source of revenue for state governments.

To collect these funds, states must channel not just delinquent payments but current payments through their criminal enforcement machinery, subjecting law-abiding parents to criminal measures. While officials claim their perennial "crackdowns" on "deadbeat dads" increases collections, the "increase" is achieved not by collecting arrearages of low-income fathers already in the system but simply by pulling in more middle-class fathers."

H.L. Mencken observed, "There is always a well-known solution to every human problem — neat, plausible, and wrong." Alimony/support enforcement advocates are like old-time bloodletting doctors; when patients worsened, they maintained they didn't take enough blood. When their methods failed, collectors doubled down on them. Albert Einstein defined insanity as doing the same thing over and over again, and expecting different results. Traditional debt collection measures are ineffective, no matter how aggressively they are enforced.

The welfare agency charged with the task of collecting alimony/support debts is the Office of Child Support Enforcement (OCSE). It operates under the guise and provisions of Title 4-D of the

Social Security laws. The fraudulent and predatory nature of the child support system has been documented in peer-reviewed publications by the Independent Institute, the National Center for Policy Analysis, the American Political Science Association, and repeatedly in *Society* magazine. Whistleblowers, including Carol Richards, former Michigan Family Court officer, explain the nefarious ways in which the federal law, Title IV-D works, in a video. [79] Through Enron-style creative accounting, the Office of Child Support Enforcement claims to collect $3.95 for every $1 it spends. The reality is they collect an estimated 20 cents for every $1 spent. Alimony /support collection costs were $17.8 billion in the year 2000. [80] (Another source claims $4.5 billion for child support only.) [fn11]

Robert Franklin, Esq. says, the United States government spends over $499 for child support enforcement for every $1 it spends to enforce access and visitation by non-custodial parents. That's the news from a document entitled *Payments to States for Child Support Enforcement and Family Support Programs* issued by the Department of Health and Human Services' Administration for Children and Families. [81] True, some money has been spent on 'demonstration programs' for access, but they wind up being anti-father and putting limits on access.

In response to a suggestion that it might be appropriate to include interests of the non-custodial parent as well, Paige Biava of OCSE defines a "family" as the custodial parent and children. She said the National Child Support Enforcement Strategic Plan 2005-2009 lists "our customers, partners, and stakeholders (include) children, custodians, child support enforcement agencies, courts, law enforcement agencies, employers, financial institutions, hospitals, departments of corrections, attorneys, prosecutors, interest groups, churches, and legislatures." The list does not include non-custodial parents.

Welfare agencies do investigate themselves, but that's like a fire department showing up after a house burns down, and shouting "Fire." Back in 1984, OCSE paid The Urban Institute to perform a pilot study, called the *Survey of Absent Parents* (SOAP), on why 'absent parents' (code word for fathers) were "abandoning their children." This study was to be expanded nationally; but when the study showed that fathers were not abandoning their children, and most child support wasn't paid because the fathers didn't have a job, hence the money — the study was abruptly cancelled with no explanation. OCSE has never attempted a similar study since. The SOAP study is an example of 'results-oriented analysis,' where a special interest group performs a study to validate

---

11 A Missouri child support auditor found that 27% of the state's 240,000 child support cases have incorrect balances. Some of the errors have gone unfixed for nearly a decade, and have led to enforcement action against innocent men.

their good work. Failure is presented as success. If it shows otherwise, they cancel the study.

When implementing the Social Security program, Congress pledged to the American people that Social Security numbers would never be used for police purposes. Yet national and local governments use them to track down ex-fathers for alleged violations of support laws under URESA (Uniform Reciprocal Enforcement of Support Act). Benjamin Franklin's words are coming back to haunt us, "Those who would give up essential liberty to purchase a little temporary safety deserve neither liberty nor safety." Not surprisingly, 'secret' government records have never been used to track down mothers absconding to frustrate the father's (equally legal) visitation rights.

Due to national security concerns, demand is increasing for a "National Security Card." Congress enacted the so-called *National Intelligence Reform Act of 2004* (S.2845)—also called the *Intelligence Reform and Terrorism Prevention Act of 2004* or *"Real I.D."* to the tune of $4 billion. The danger therein lies in its probable corruption of purpose to assist in tracking alimony/support debtors. The Transportation Security Administration (TSA) has implemented *Computer-Assisted Passenger Prescreening System II* (CAPPSII) to enhance airline security. TSA admits that, unlike with early broken promises about Social Security, it *will* be used for purposes other than detecting jihadists (namely looking for alimony/support debtors). [82]

In *Society*, Bryce Christensen writes, "The advocates of ever-more-aggressive measures for collecting child support... have moved us a dangerous step closer to a police state and have violated the rights of innocent and often impoverished fathers." Research by the Urban Institute, a think tank in Washington, found that aggressive collection of these debts played a crucial role in pushing low-income black men ages 25 to 34 out of lawful employment, the opposite effect policy makers might have desired. It should come as no surprise that some seek alternate incomes in order to live even a partially decent life. Child support will be further addressed in Part III.

Jailing for Debt

And we criticize the old Soviet Gulag! Human bondage is not dead; it simply has a new look. Marriage is the only civil contract wherein unpaid debts result in imprisonment. Men are routinely jailed for alimony/support debt — a profoundly un-constitutional practice. Thomas Paine observed generations ago, "and if being bound in that manner is not slavery, then there is not such a thing as slavery upon earth." Justification of such measures requires feats of high-level metaphysics that medieval era theologians would be proud of. The legalistic rationale for these jailings is a subterfuge known as "Orders to Show Cause why the accused should not be held in contempt of court." Under it, a man can be jailed until he does what the court orders him to do (pay the debt). In a Clintonese type parsing of words, courts justify the practice by claiming the jailings are "non-criminal," and are for "contempt of court," a distinction without a difference. Calling it punishment for disobeying an order is simply camouflaging it. This is like putting lipstick on a pig. You can paint a turd pink but it's still a turd; it doesn't pass the smell test. According to University of Michigan law professor David L. Chamber, speaking at the National Dist. Attorneys Assn. Child Support Enforcement Conference in Arlington, Va. Oct. 1, 1975, such jailings *are actually for debt,* [83] and probably a violation of the presumption-of-innocence principle.

Thousands of victims are in illegal debtors' prisons for inability or refusal to pay — thrown in simply to see if they can or will pay. [84] New York's version of debtor's prison (formerly at 434 W. 37th St.) has been widely known as alimony jail since the '20s. To relieve jail overcrowding in Georgia, a sheriff and judge proposed creating detention camps specifically for "deadbeat dads." The Pittsburgh City Planning Commission considered a proposal "to convert a former chemical processing plant ... into a detention center" for "deadbeat dads." Such workhouses should have signs over entrances: "ARBEIT MACHT FREI."

How many male prisoners are locked up for defaulting on alimony/support? Even such basic and easily collected data is difficult to find." Government figures on that category do not exist. Are officials too embarrassed to collect the information? According to K.C. Wilson, author of Male Nurturing, The Multiple Scandals of Child Support and other e-books on family and men's issues, there are an estimated 15,000 fathers in jail at any one time (100,000 a year) for this non-crime. The group, *Hunger Strike for Justice*, estimated the figure to be 250,000. According to an AP report, more than 130 alimony/support debtors were rounded up on Fathers' Day 2007 in Cook County Illinois for failure to pay their debts.

Philadelphia attorney H. Beatty Chadwick was imprisoned in 1995, jailed nearly a decade and a half for failing to obey a judge's order in a nasty divorce battle. Delaware County Judge Chad F. Kenney Sr. ruled that Chadwick owes his ex-wife $4.2 million. Chadwick set a Pennsylvania record for the longest time a person was imprisoned on a civil contempt charge. Chadwick underwent treatments in prison for a recurrence of non-Hodgkin's lymphoma, a potentially fatal cancer. His petitions for release because of his health were ignored. His doctor said he was on borrowed time. His attorney Michael Malloy said, "Even murderers go out on an electronic bracelet sometimes, and this guy can't get out. He can't get work release. He can't get a Christmas furlough." Chadwick was released on July 10, 2009 after serving 14 years — a U.S. record for contempt of court. [85]

Charles Gillam, a 34-year-old South Bend Indiana man, was sentenced to serve nine years in prison, and placed on probation for 15 years upon release, for not paying over $120,000 in alimony/support. News reports did not indicate if this man had the means to pay the debt. [86] George J. Chiconine spent five years in the Windsor, Vermont, maximum security prison for not paying his ex-wife. He was sentenced without a jury trial. [87] A Chicago dentist was accosted by police in his patient-filled office, handcuffed and thrown in jail until he posted a huge bond to assure alimony. Why? Because his ex-wife told her lawyer, falsely, that he was going to Germany. Reportedly, he then abandoned dentistry and studied law. One husband was actually sentenced to life imprisonment for failure to post alimony bond. [88] Frank Hatley spent a year in jail for being a deadbeat dad. But there's one problem — Hatley doesn't have any children. [89]

In Knox County Illinois, Judge Harry Bulkeley found Berwick resident Douglas Alexander guilty of not paying alimony/support. Bulkeley thundered "If it were up to me, I think I would have the word "deadbeat" branded on your forehead so that everybody would know what a louse you are," and ordered Alexander to spend 364 days in jail, serving the time every weekend for the next 3½ years.

For a $68,000 alimony debt, Dennis Kern, 51, of Kosciusko, MS was sentenced to 10 years in prison with two years to serve and eight suspended. He was also sentenced to supervised probation and ordered to make restitution. [90] According to a Milwaukee newspaper, 57-year-old John L. Brayshaw of Washington County in Wisconsin owed $347,000 in alimony/support. The Washington County Sheriff's Department requested charges of 18 counts of failure to pay support over 120 days. If convicted, he could have faced a maximum prison sentence of 90 years.

In Florida, Francisco Rodriguez was accused of fathering a woman's child, and ordered to pay child support. A DNA test proved he was not the father, and the mother later admitted she lied about him being the father. Orders were issued for Rodriguez to appear in court, but never delivered to him. Consequently, he was jailed for non-support. Three judges and five hearings later, he was still in jail. [91]

A hapless Mississippi man who missed two $100 support payments due to illness was found guilty of criminal child neglect and sentenced to two years in the pen, commuted to five years' probation. John Hansen, a former Men's Defense Assoc. member, was a road equipment operator whose wife kicked him out to make room for a paramour. Because his work was dependent upon the weather, he was often unemployed and unable to meet alimony/support payments. Whenever that occurred, Stearns and Morrison County, Minnesota Judges Willard Lorene and H. M. Braggans took delight in clapping him into jail until he borrowed enough money to ransom himself. The former judge told him to rob a bank if necessary. Finally, in utter frustration (and to get a little publicity on the matter), this writer issued a public challenge to Judge Lorene for a fistfight. He didn't accept. That was many years ago.

Lest you imagine these practices have gone the way of the Colonial-day stocks, New Jersey resident Ari Schochet was jailed at least eight times for missing, due to economy-related income reduction, lifetime alimony/support payments that total almost $100,000 a year ($78,000 in alimony alone). Bankrupt auto mogul Denny Hecker was jailed in Minnesota in 2010 for failure to pay alimony.

John Murtari, a divorced ex-Air Force pilot, a fathers' rights hero/activist (founder of AKidsRight.org) and associate of this writer has been repeatedly jailed in a New York prison for peacefully demonstrating against divorce injustice. In February 2010, he was again incarcerated for chalking a protest on the Old County Courthouse in Lyons, NY. Murtari went on a hunger strike for nearly 4 months, force-fed through a feeding tube. All previous divorce reform hunger strikes by others have been terminated either voluntarily or by force feeding.

Jailing of alimony/support debtors actually does more harm than good. [92] It is an inconvenient truth that these jailings prevent even partial payments. Because of prison overcrowding, the Ohio House of Representatives approved a bill that, if enacted, would sentence most alimony/support offenders to community programs instead of jail. [93]

Paternity Fraud

One of the most significant, albeit seldom-mentioned, scandals in society concerns paternity fraud. This abomination is a disservice not only to alleged fathers, but also to the children involved. Somewhere between 10% and 30% of children born in the U.S., and maybe all of the western world, are not the biological progeny of the presumed father. Even the *NY Times Magazine* (Nov 17, 2009) acknowledged the severity of the paternity fraud problem.

A study by the American Association of Blood Banks found that "the overall exclusion rate [of paternity on tested men] for 1999 was 28.2 percent for accredited labs." [94] The British Child Support Agency has had to refund hundreds of thousands of pounds in maintenance payments to more than 3,000 men after DNA tests revealed that mothers in paternity suits had wrongly named them. One in six men who took a DNA test to challenge claims by women that they were the fathers of their children were cleared by the results, according to official figures disclosed by the agency. [95] These figures are undoubtedly higher than what would be found in a random sample of the general population, as men who request tests already have reason to question paternity. No one knows the real number.

Across the country, many courts have ruled that men must pay child support for children demonstrably not their progeny. The "Lord Mansfield" rule, applicable in most states, proclaims (in effect) that every child born to a married woman is fathered by her husband. Therefore, he must support that child in event of divorce. Countless men have thusly been ordered to pay child support for children probably or demonstrably not theirs. As Mr. Bumble opined in <u>Oliver Twist</u>, "If the law supposes that, the law is a ass — a idiot." The famous California case of Herschensohn vs. Carol D. is an example.

Courts in Texas, North Carolina, and Pennsylvania have ignored the Mansfield Rule; the latter stating that it "lacks a basis in good sense or in social policy." California paternity fraud victims are finding relief under a landmark 2004 court decision and a law that went into effect in 2005. Gov. Arnold Schwarzenegger signed a paternity fraud law called AB 252, which allows un-married men to challenge established child support orders under limited circumstances. "In just the past few weeks, I have overturned seven [men's support orders]... They're off the hook," Santa Ana, Calif., lawyer Linda S. Ferrer told *The Washington Times* in January of '05.

Decades ago, a New York court ruled that a Hauppauge man is legally responsible for at least one of the four children his wife conceived while he was serving 9 1/2 years in state prison for a robbery conviction, and according to prison officials had never been visited by his wife. The man sued for divorce from his wife on grounds of adultery, but another judge denied the divorce, saying that the evidence that he had been in jail all the while, "did not rule out the many possibilities of access." In other words, he did not prove that his wife had not managed somehow to get into the jail, so there was still a possibility that the children were his. During his confinement, he said he kept getting news of his wife's pregnancies. "Right along, I was finding out. Then her mother wrote and told me — while I was in prison." He tried to file for divorce while in prison, but regulations prevented him from doing so (the old "Catch 22" again). After the man's parole in April 1972, he was denied Legal Aid assistance. Two lawyers, who felt sorry for him, agreed to take his case pro bono. Because of a five-year statute of limitations on adultery, the first three births could not be counted as valid grounds. That left the last birth in 1971 to be contested. Despite letters submitted by the warden to the court that the wife never visited the man during his entire confinement, the divorce was denied. The wife did not appear at the hearing to oppose the divorce. By telephone, the wife, later living in North Carolina, admitted that while her husband was in prison, she "did have kids — they're going in his name, but they're not his."

Carnell Smith of Atlanta Georgia was fraudulently led to believe he was father of his then-girlfriend's child. He supported this child emotionally and financially for eleven years until a DNA test proved he was not the father. Smith appealed his case all the way to the U.S. Supreme Court. On June 10, 2002, those worthies announced refusal to hear the case, demonstrating typical judicial indifference to the rights of men. Gulf War veteran Taron James, with the help of NCFM attorney Marc Angelucci, fought a paternity fraud case in California regarding a child proven to be not his.

In Australia, Liam Magill's unfaithful wife Meredith falsely claimed two of their three children were his. Magill sued, and was awarded $70,000 in damages and costs by the Victorian County Court in November 2002. With strong financial backing from Australian feminists, the former Mrs. Magill appealed the decision and won, obtaining a settlement of $40,000 from Liam. Justice Frank Callaway sophisized that there was no evidence on which the County Court judge could find Mrs. Magill *intended* her husband to rely on the birth certificates to establish his paternity. His book is available. [96] Anti-paternity fraud advocate Cheryl King informs us via Australia's *Endeavour Forum* that Magill's lawsuit would be reopened. See www.justice4Liam.com.au.

One in five British fathers was wrongly identified by mothers in Child Support Agency claims in which paternity was resolved through DNA testing. Since DNA paternity testing figures began to be collected in 1998-99, 4,854 paternity claims turned out to be false after DNA testing (Many, many more by now). Though it is a criminal offence to make a false statement or representation, these false identifications resulted in no prosecutions for the mothers. [97]

Despite clear wording of the U.S. Constitution to the contrary, 42 U.S.C. section 666(a)(5)(I) mandates that states deny jury trials in paternity actions. Failure to so violate the Constitution would make a state ineligible for the federal dole in TANF block grants by the Office of Child Support Enforcement (OCSE). Attorney Thomas James J.D. informs me that the website of the Legal Services of North Dakota contains the following statement, "There is no right to a jury trial for paternity cases in North Dakota."

Mr. James also pointed out the consequences of signing a Recognition of Paternity form (ROP):

> For example, a man who signs a ROP gives up the right to challenge paternity and demand blood tests, the right to an attorney, and so on. In return, he gains the right to start paying child support. The state will file a lawsuit to get him to start paying child support retroactive to the day the child was born. The state is not legally permitted to ask the court to enforce his right of access to the child however. That right will not begin unless and until the father rounds up enough money to hire a private attorney, file a lawsuit and persuade a judge that it would be safe to let him see the child. Meanwhile, the very same government funds public service ads urging unwed fathers to maintain strong relationships with their children.

A not-so-funny joke circulated around the Internet follows:

Today is my daughter's 18th birthday. I'm so glad that this is my last child support payment. Month after month, year after year, those payments! I called my baby girl to come over to my house, and when she got here, I said to her, "Baby girl, I want you to take this last check over to your momma's house; you tell her that this is the last check she's ever going to get from me, then I want you to come back here and tell me the expression she had on her face." So my baby girl took the check over to her. I was so anxious to hear what the witch had to say and what she looked like. As my baby girl walked through the door, I said, "Well now ... what did your momma have to say?" "She told me to tell you that you ain't my daddy."

Illinois, Georgia, Maryland, Ohio and other states have enacted legislation that allows putative fathers adequate time and judicial flexibility in challenging paternity findings. The governor of Missouri has signed into law a bill that allows men two years after they've been adjudicated to be a child's father to contest the matter in court via genetic testing. If a test proves the man is not the biological father, he would be excused from previous child-support debt and would have criminal nonsupport convictions removed from his record, under the Missouri law. [98]

DNA testing is extremely accurate. New technology permits rapid, inexpensive testing. Carnell Smith, the paternity fraud victim mentioned earlier, formed a company, 4TRUTH Identity Inc. for the purpose of protecting families from fraud through DNA testing. His web site is 911DNAtest.com. Jeffery Leving, the attorney that represented Carnell Smith, and 'Idgentigene,' the DNA identification company that aided Smith in determining that he was not the biological father of the child in question, have stressed the need for legislation to protect men against paternity fraud. Smith tells me that the number of legislative bills (passed and pending) designed to prevent paternity fraud increased from 19 in 2001 to approximately 48 in 2004. NOW objects. Hmmm! Wonder why.

Almost everyone Jared Rosenthal does business with has a secret or a suspicion, something they hold close and keep confidential and do not share even with those nearest to them. Mr. Rosenthal is or was the owner of two trucks, each emblazoned with a slogan as blunt as it was effective, posing a simple question: "Who's your daddy?" The trucks — recreational vehicles that have been converted into rolling laboratories offering on-the-spot DNA testing — invariably attract stares and questions when they appear around New York City. Over the years, he said, he has brought long-lost siblings together and told others that they were not, in fact, related. He has told men that the children they raised were not biologically their own. He has told others they were the fathers of children they never knew they had. His charge?: $400. [99] DNA test kits are available at Myheritage.com (A discount code: fox) [100]

Though it was not designed to assist accused fathers, legislation was submitted in Minnesota to join three or four other states in taking DNA samples from all arrestees, much to the consternation of the ACLU. Pelle Billing an M.D. who writes and lectures about gender/sex, also suggests DNA test of all newborns. [101] "Privacy" advocates and even many conservatives oppose such testing. Republican state Senator Steve Johnson of Colorado sponsored a bill, now law in that state, that forbids the use of DNA testing after a separation or divorce has been filed. For personal reasons, I wish the technology had been available in Minnesota decades ago.

Demonstrating bipartisanship, reform proposals cause demagogues of both political persuasions to wring hands, wail and gnash teeth. Democrat Senator Sheila Kuehl from the 23rd District of California told that state's Senate Judiciary committee she supports laws that force falsely-identified men to pay alimony/support, based on past practices and "best interest of the child."

Some fathers want these kids. In a Kentucky case, thanks to Judge Virginia Wittinghill, Ren Hinshaw fought for and won custody of a 8-

year-old boy his ex-wife had fooled him into believing was his biological son. An appeal went before the state Supreme Court.

The theory that de-facto parenthood should take precedence over biology was pioneered in Minnesota in the 1960s by Charlie Metz, and later articulated by Professor Amneus. I greatly respect these gentlemen, but don't understand their reasoning.

Causes of Divorce

Very few of the princesses or princes we dreamed of at age 17 ever materialize. There is an old adage, "Marry in haste; repent at leisure." How true! Bad marriages lead to trails of destruction. This great American dream is often a nightmare. While the returns of marriage are great, many are not able to pay the price. It can be difficult to live with another person. Marital unhappiness is far more prevalent than commonly realized. A ten-year study by Dr. Clifford R. Adams revealed that only 17 percent of married people are really happy with each other. Like the tip of an iceberg, divorce statistics reveal only obvious terminations. Many are technically wed, but emotionally divorced. These were once passionate love affairs. Such a massive hemorrhage of good will is a shocking proposition. For every 100 U.S. marriages, 49 are aborted by divorce.

Marriage partners are akin to a team of horses. If they are well-matched, they can pull a tremendous load. But if one hangs back, the other has to pull not only the load but the laggard horse as well. It takes two to make a marriage work, but takes only one to destroy it. Lincoln said, "A house divided against itself cannot stand." When the contributions of one partner in terms of functions and responsibilities exceed those of the other partner, the under-contributor is somewhat more drag than lift to use aeronautical terms.

University of Wisconsin sociologist Professor Ersel E. LeMasters claimed that women are boss in most contemporary families (she-who-must-be-obeyed). This seems a good place to throw in a Scottish proverb, "It is a sad house where the hen crows louder than the cock." Shakespeare wrote of taming shrews. They are better avoided. The man who marries a shrew may deserve her, just as citizens deserve their corrupt officials. A man would be foolish to marry such a woman, even though he may fancy himself "in love."

It must be acknowledged that marriage, as presently constituted, is a risky venture for both but maybe mostly for men, financially and otherwise. The financial pressures are enormous. In some ways families are becoming more a liability than an asset. In old rural America, wives and children helped produce. In this new urban world, they mostly consume. Marriage is no longer premised on female dependence, lifetime expectations, fidelity and mutual economic advantage. Grandma considered it security. Today's bride, often as not, considers it collateral with husbands a mere economic and social convenience.

If some marriages are made in Heaven, others are made in Hell. Observations of old bards, below, are relevant to many situations:

"The female, not the male, determines all the conditions of the animal family. Where the female can derive no benefit from association with the male, no such association takes place." —Robert Briffault
"Man is for woman but a means" —Nietzsche.
"He that takes a wife takes care." —Ben Franklin.
"Marriage is a trade union of women." —George Bernard Shaw.
"No man, examining his marriage intelligently, can fail to observe that it is compounded, at least in part, of slavery; and that he is the slave." — H. L. Mencken.
"The wedding is never otherwise than a tragic event, and all present should be clothed in black. and upon the wedding bell should be written 'A day is coming when one of these hearts shall break.'" —Mark Twain.
"By all means, marry. If you get a good wife, you'll become happy; if you get a bad one, you'll become a philosopher." — Socrates

Internal Causes: Immaturity, Marital Disloyalty, Low Moral Standards, Greed

Immaturity: Young often equates with foolish; as they say, "Youth is wasted on the young." Growing up can take a very long time. Youthful lack of maturity and wisdom, combined with hormones coursing and crashing through the system, is a recipe for disaster. Stupid, youthful mistakes haunt us through life, and can live on after us — with cascading, burgeoning effects in our progeny.

Little girls can be the essence of sweetness. The fly in the ointment is that they physically mature, with a high probability of taking their turn at the altar of human sacrifice. Other than "sweetness," much the same can be said of males. Normal men desire to mate with beautiful women (likewise, normal women desire to mate with rich, powerful men). One must admire the Creator's handiwork, however there are pitfalls. Pretty women without the intelligence to handle their looks are like kids with loaded guns — very dangerous. Beauty is only skin-deep and we men are fools for it. I tended to tip a pretty waitress more than my wife did. It is what is on the inside not the outside that counts. Women getting by on looks alone seem to have escaped the need to develop intelligence — perhaps giving rise to the "dumb blonde" jokes. Abercrombe & Fitch had a line of girls' T-shirts emblazoned with, "Who needs brains when you have these?" Marilyn Monroe was a perfect example.

Marital Disloyalty, Low Moral Standards
The games people play

Immorality destroys marriage. The family and sexual liberation cannot co-exist. They are mutually exclusive. People who do not believe in a set of rules dictated from a higher authority drop in and out of marriages on whims. "Faithfulness has disappeared; the word itself is banished from their speech" – Jeremiah 7. Jeremiah was born about 650 BC. This timeless quote could have been written yesterday, with reference — far beyond the transient Hollywood couplings — to the games people play. No longer is a person reasonably safe in assuming that marriage means fidelity. Adultery is no longer a crime in Colorado, or realistically nearly anywhere.

Romance died the day easy sex was born. In days of yore, men would do a Herculean amount of work, like hewing timber in creation of a farm, to win a woman's rare sexual favors. Now, many men still work prodigiously, even though many women dispense those favors randomly. The sexual revolution was hugely promoted by a sexual psychopath Alfred C. Kinsey posing as an academic researcher. [102] In recent decades, moral standards have dropped like a prom dress. That horse broke out of the barn big time in the 1960s. CDC reports for the second year in a row that 40.7 percent of the babies born in the United States were born to unmarried mothers. [103] Who would want to marry a woman who has slept with half the guys in town? Party with them maybe, but marry them?

Many liberated housewives think an affair will brighten up their humdrum existence. It may, but it may also destroy their marriage. Linda Wolfe, in preparing her book, <u>Playing Around</u>, interviewed 67 women having extramarital affairs. After a follow-up survey she reported, "Their marriages were more often destroyed than enhanced." Sociologist Robert Bell of Temple University estimates that the number of married women having extramarital affairs is 40 percent. This figure is almost as high as is Dr. Alfred Kinsey's estimate for men, and is climbing rapidly. [104] One survey showed that more young wives than young husbands are committing adultery. [105] A nine page spread in *Newsweek* (July 12, 2004) described, not un-approvingly, the epidemic of adultery by wives. Such women sacrifice the good of their children to satisfy their lust — as do men but usually with lesser consequence. Ashleymadison.com promoted infidelity on the internet, advertising "Life is short; have an affair." Ashley Madison described itself as the "World's leading married dating service for discreet encounters." [106] To quote Dostoyevsky, "If God does not exist, everything is permitted."

The incidence of infidelity of military wives while husbands are deployed overseas is staggering. I am told that Navy ships returning from sea duty earlier than expected would lay offshore until the expected arrival date, in order that the sailors would not catch their wives in compromising situations. Adultery is bad enough, but that committed by or with the wife of a G.I. serving overseas during time of war is beyond the pale.

I come down heavier on women in this section because they report most marital unhappiness, they initiate divorce more and their unchastity is much more damaging. The lowering of moral standards and sexual disloyalty in females is more destructive to marriage, incomparably more threatening and damaging to civilized society than men's philandering. Double standard, you say? Definitely. I have dedicated an entire sub-chapter to justification of just that. See *Chivalry Trade-Offs; the Double Standard Justified* later, under *The Phenomenon of Chivalry.* In Part II, Chapter 2.

Greed: Greed is another important cause of divorce. Boston divorce lawyer Joyce Kuffman is quoted in the *Washington Post* as stating, "One of the benefits of marriage is divorce." Most women would not divorce without the incentives of custody, property awards and subsidization by an ex-husband. However, one should not put too much blame on low mentality women who are offered these incentives on a silver platter by judges and lawyers like Kuffman.

External causes: law, modernism, peer pressure, sex favoritism, welfare

Divorce and its pathology arise primarily from personal failings, but external factors also come into play. Shere Hite says the wife is the instigator in seven out of eight divorces. [fn12] Alan Parkman of the University of New Mexico finds a smaller percentage; he correctly blames No-fault divorce laws.

The times they are a-changing; fast-paced, centrifugal forces of modernism are loosening the social, economic and religious bonds that once held society and families together. Relationships are more easily made and broken than ever before. In a never-ending pursuit of "The New," everything is disposable, from food containers to families, even human life — not just in abortion. The serial polygamy commonly accepted these days is killing the traditional marital concept. Only 22 percent of households constitute traditional nuclear families. Families today are composed of his kids, her kids, their kids, and Lord knows whose kids. Single-parent families are portrayed as "alternative life styles."

Welfare — enemy of men and marriage.
Its connection to divorce and social devastation.

---

12 Shere Hite, Women and Love (New York, Knopf 1987) 459, and many other sources cited herein.

From time immemorial, before welfare, women and children were naturally dependent on men for food and shelter, not on society. This dependency was reciprocal; men received in-kind benefits. That arrangement, unlike today's, made sense. It is a fallacy that charity preserves families; that kind of charity can *destroy* families. This section will address personal welfare only — leaving aside the ill-advised connection to business and agriculture. [fn13] The divorce connection is its availability, its promise and incentive. In his excellent book <u>Men & Marriage</u>, George Gilder stated family dissolution in the modern world leads to "a welfare state to take care of the women and children, and a police state to handle the teenage boys." But it's a chicken and egg situation; which comes first? Both divorce and welfare cause each other at different times, and both adversely affect men disproportionately.

Menken described the U.S. federal government as a "milch cow with one hundred twenty five teats." We devote far more resources than many other countries to social spending using 126 programs and feeding 38 million Americans. Twenty one and a third percent of Americans were on the dole prior to the Covid-19 pandemic. Robert Rector of the Heritage Foundation claimed federal and state spending on means-tested programs would rise to $1.2 trillion per year (probably understated because of nominally non-welfare programs such as Social Security. Then there is state spending, earned Income and Child Tax Credits, etc., etc., amounting to $257 billion annually. Over 30 separate handouts commenced in the 1960s. The Grace Commission identified 963 federal programs that redistributed wealth. Here's one egregious example: New York's publicly funded Medicaid program paid more than $63,000 for erectile dysfunction drugs and other sexual treatments for 47 sex offenders, despite laws banning such expenses.

Over $60,000 is spent annually per household on "Entitlement" programs constituting 60 percent of federal government spending. The "War on Poverty" ($5.4 trillion) cost more than the U.S. spent fighting World War II. Since LBJ's Great Society's beginning, the government spent $15.9 trillion, in inflation-adjusted 2008 dollars, on all means-tested welfare, more than twice the cost of fighting all major wars in U.S. history. Curiously, "entitlement" spending is greater than defense spending even in this era of increasingly dangerous enemies. The money would be better spent to counter China's growing threats than on welfare.

---

13 Amazon gets $ billions

At this writing, the federal debt has surpassed $27 trillion according to data released by the Treasury Department. And it is rising, driven largely by Social Security, Medicare (from which my wife and I greatly benefited), Medicaid, growing numbers of illegal aliens and costs stemming from increasing military requirements and the Covid virus.

The demographics of an aging population exacerbates the problem. It has been called 'the most predictable economic crisis in history. The annual deficit will forever remain above $1 trillion, barring major structural reforms to government, according to the latest budget and economic outlook from the Congressional Budget Office (CBO). [107] Independent forecasters now expect this year's budget deficit to nearly quadruple the pre-coronavirus estimate. That amount of red ink in a single fiscal year would dwarf the deficit peak of $1.4 trillion during the Great Recession and approach levels not seen since World War II. Even Republican politicians, including President Trump and past administrations, share the blame. But most Democrat politicians — those who don't simply ignore this problem — propose to solve it with utterly impractical and arithmetically impossible solutions.

The Aid to Families with Dependent Children (AFDC) program commenced in 1936 as a charitable effort to aid widows and women whose husbands had abandoned them — in theory a noble concept. Former President Johnson termed it a "safety net." But "The best-laid schemes o' mice an 'men gang aft agley" (Apologies to Bobby Burns). As with many such good intentions, the safety net gradually became more of a hammock, relied upon when dismissed ex-husbands or boyfriends could not or would not (bless them) subsidize their women. In practice, by guaranteeing comfort to mothers, AFDC underwrote divorce. It took the onus of support off the parents, and turned many single mothers into parasitic 'brides of the state.' It is like the 1976 Swine Flu vaccine that caused more death and illness than the disease it was intended to prevent.

Roughly half of the spending is on households with children mostly headed by single mothers, providing employment for social "workers." Divorced and unmarried mothers, laying up on welfare, remain the largest group of recipients. Ronald Reagan referred to them as "Welfare Queens." An attitude of entitlement develops in recipients. One homeless woman with 15 kids said, "Somebody needs to pay for all my children." Hello "Octomom." We might see an HEW pamphlet entitled, "Raising Children for Fun and Profit." This website takes you to a radio call from a woman making a rational case for taking welfare: http://safeshare.tv/w/csrqsTAmSx

According to researchers Lowell Galloway and Richard Vedder of the Univ. of Ohio, fifty percent of the increased divorce rate between 1964 and 1970 can be traced to incentives provided by welfare growth. Welfare has become a device for the elimination of fathers in all demographics and especially blacks. In 1984, Charles Murray demonstrated in <u>Losing Ground</u> that welfare programs hurt many who need help the most.

Walter E. Williams, a black George Mason University economist and author aptly argues that welfare has done more damage to black society than slavery or Jim Crow. Another black educator, Thomas Sowell, PhD, concurs. Former President Reagan's *Task Force on the Family* recognized welfare as hugely responsible for breakdown of the family.

Some aspiring professional athletes can benefit from the largess: well-fed youthful gladiators of all colors, with absent fathers and mamas laying up on welfare, have little to do other than pump iron and shoot hoops. Those who do make the pros, not always paragons of virtue, may show appreciation for this largess by kneeling during the National Anthem, others may become the toughest guys in prison. Welfare has often tilted — and practically ruined — amateur and professional sports. Whatever fun was left in sports is gone after both this racial dominance and the pink colors (See Part II, Chapter 2, Health) and racial messages now seen on uniforms.

Welfare reform was supposed to save money, discourage unmarried childbearing and encourage marriage and two-parent families; but figures show that it has failed from the standpoint of the family. Throwing ever-increasing resources into father-substitute schemes reflects the triumph of hope over reality. Though Wisconsin Republican legislators attempted to introduce reforms to the food stamp program, over the objection of Democrat legislators, [108] there was no coherent national strategy to alleviate the problems. The combination of easy availability of welfare benefits and the "no-fault" divorce criteria sent the divorce rate skyrocketing[108]. Given these bribes, in effect, girls and women no longer need husbands to support them and children. They can marry Uncle Sam, which encourages and subsidizes illegitimacy.

Advocates of indiscriminate handouts wrongly blame poverty and lack of education funding for social problems. These two straw men are associated with the problems, but do not *cause* them. Father-deprivation and institutional chivalry are much more important causes, occurring in two major — often overlapping communities — divorced households and never-married households. Once family status is controlled for, neither race nor income has effect on social problems. Half of America's seven million poor families are so because of divorce, separation or out-of-wedlock births. In contrast, of America's 50.4 million intact families, only 7% are poor. Almost 75% of children in single-parent families will experience poverty before the age of eleven, contrasted with 20% in two-parent families.

Welfare has a just and noble place in society: feeding the aged, infirm and kids is fine, but call most of its programs what they are — charity. There's an iron law of economics, but some politicians seem immune to the evidence: *Subsidize something, such as divorce, you get more of it.* We reap what we sow.

The racial perspective of this subsection cannot be overlooked. Our old slavery sins have brought modern chickens home to roost. U.S. racial and ethnic minorities accounted for all of the nation's population growth during the last decade, according to new Census Bureau estimates. The data underscore the nation's growing diversity and suggest that the trend will continue as the white population ages and low birth rates translate to a declining share. Non-Hispanic whites declined to 60.1% of the populace in 2019 and their number shrank by about 9,000 from the 2010 Census to slightly more than 197 million. Reportedly, the 'Black National Anthem' is being played at football games.

Divorce's ill effects on men, women, children, families, and society will be addressed in Chapter 4 of this Part — *Effects of the War on Men*. Welfare reform and its impact on society beyond divorce will be addressed in Part III. Less monetary, but equally foolish, efforts to compensate for old slavery sins are exemplified by Associated Press capitalizing the word 'Black' but not the word 'white' when referring to people.

Chapter 2. Crime & Punishment.
Disparate treatment.
"Crimes" too often are defined not by their statutory illegality but by ideology.

Treatment of men
In General
In <u>Darkness at Noon</u>, Arthur Koestler wrote of the nightmarish world of Stalinist show trials of the 1930's, wherein all accused were guilty and protestations of innocence were acts of subversion. Koestler describes how secret police used their power to extract confessions, and how perfectly innocent men were manipulated into publicly declaring their crimes and guilt. As prosecutors say, "You can indict a ham sandwich." NKVD head Laurentiy Beria said, "Show me the man, and I'll show you the crime." This was exemplified in a minor way by the indictment on a charge of tampering with government records of

abortion opponents who made undercover videos of a Planned Parenthood official discussing that outfit's selling of fetal organs.

It is a basic principle of U.S. law that a person is presumed innocent until proven guilty. However, there is an a priori presumption to the contrary regarding males as opposed to females. If charged, however innocent, males are more often found guilty and suffer the consequences. According to F.B.I. statistics, and the Institute for Juvenile Research, there are nearly as many actual, if not adjudicated, crimes committed by women as by men; yet ninety-four percent of prison inmates are male. [109] A Pasco County, Florida, jail inmate report for the month of February through March 12, 1974, which is probably typical, showed an average of 85.5 male prisoners and an average of three female prisoners. According to a BJS report, one of every 109 men is living in prison or jail (Another report states the figure is one of every 75 men). For women the figure is one in every 1,613. If 94 percent of prison inmates were female, the problem and the injustice would receive far more attention.

Hear Robert Franklin, Esq.:

> We've known for some time that, all things being equal, women tend to receive more lenient sentences than do men when they're convicted of criminal wrongdoing. Last year, two University of Washington researchers studied criminal sentencing in cases in which the only penalties were monetary (fines, restitution, etc.). They found that, when all normally-considered factors were equal, the sentences assessed men were harsher than those assessed women. And this study published in the *Journal of Law and Economics* found that, in the U.S. federal system, the benefit of being a woman compared to a man was the same as the benefit of being white compared to being African-American.

> But in the United States, we still prefer to either pretend that the discrepancy in sentencing women doesn't exist or simply ignore the fact. We still like to maintain the pretense that justice is blind to things like race, sex, class, etc. We know the pretense is flagrantly wrong, but we're more comfortable with make-believe than with reality. Not so the British. A referenced article here tells us that judges are now *being trained* to give more lenient sentences to females convicted of crime than to their male counterparts. [110]

That there are a great many wrongful convictions (of males) was exposed on CNN TV, July 15, 2012. A study by University of Washington Sociologists Katherine Beckett and Alexes Harris for the *State of Washington Justice and Minority Commission* confirms what many have long thought — that criminal courts discriminate on the basis of race and sex in the sentences they hand down. The study, conducted spanned four years and looked at 3,366 cases. [111]

Bills have been introduced in the Minnesota Legislature, which would eliminate the statute of limitations for sex offenses. Men are assumed to deserve capital punishment because they are perceived to have less value than do women. Between 1930 and 1995, 3,313 males had been executed and only 30 females. Since the Supreme Court allowed capital punishment to resume in 1976, 13 women have been executed in the U.S. In that same time period, more than 1,300 male inmates have been executed nationwide [112] (more by now). Additionally, male defendants are assessed significantly higher fees and fines than female defendants.

A substantial percentage of all convicted male prisoners are actually innocent, scapegoat victims of ambitious, man-hating or feminist-pandering prosecutors and judges, and of execrable laws and Potemkin trials. This Chapter will detail some of these.

A large proportion of our population consists of low life people. They appear in both sexes, many of them not from ghettoes. A great many men *are* slobs deserving of judicial punishment; newspapers are rife with examples and pictures of them. The San Francisco police stopped releasing mug shots of arrestees to avoid racial "stereotyping." [113]

Examples:

Wilbert Jones languished in a Louisiana prison, convicted for the kidnapping and rape of a Baton Rouge nurse. Forty-six years later State District Judge Richard Anderson overturned Jones' conviction, saying the prosecution withheld "highly favorable" evidence that probably would have led to his acquittal. [114]

Lewis Taylor was sentenced to 28 consecutive life sentences, one for each murder count leveled against him for starting a horrific hotel fire. He spent 42 years in prison before it was realized that this indigent black youth was in all probability innocent. It took 6 attorneys to free him in a plea deal. [115]

Ricky Jackson, 57, and Wiley Bridgeman, 60, were released after 40 years imprisonment, some of the time on death row, for robbery and murder based on testimony of a 12-year-old who now admits he was coerced by detectives. The Ohio Innocence Project said Jackson was the longest-held U.S. prisoner to be exonerated. [116]

Michael Morton spent 25 years in prison for the murder of his wife wherein the prosecutor, Ken Anderson — now a judge, had concealed exculpatory evidence. Barry Scheck's Innocence Project got Morton released and a 2 million settlement from the State of Texas. By law, Anderson is immune from prosecution. [117]

Joe Salvati and Peter Limone were incarcerated for three decades for crimes the FBI knew they did not commit. A federal judge excoriated the agency for withholding evidence of the men's innocence, and ordered the government to pay a record $101.7 million to their families and those of two other men convicted with them who died in prison. [118]

Tony Sanborn, was convicted of killing his girlfriend, 16-year-old Jessica Briggs. Hope Cady testified that as a 13-year-old she was pressured by police and prosecutors into identifying Sanborn as the killer. Cady said she had juvenile charges against her at the time, and the authorities threatened to send her away for years, "They basically told me what to say."

The execution of Hank Skinner, accused murderer of his girlfriend and her two adult sons, is under "stay" at this writing. A succession of Texas District Attorneys had opposed requests from Hank and his lawyers for DNA tests. After a decade of denials, the request was granted in April 2013. Hank has been on death row since 1995, and has steadfastly professed his innocence. Since his conviction, the star witness against Hank has recanted her testimony, and others have implicated another man as the killer. Citing new DNA evidence, a Durham NC judge threw out the double-murder conviction of Darryl Howard. The 54-year-old Howard was convicted in 1995 on two counts of second-degree murder, and served 21 years in prison. [119]

DNA tests have cleared a thousand people that spent over three thousand years in prison for crimes they did not commit. [120]

Michigan State University sports doctor and former USA Gymnastics team doctor Larry Nassar put his fingers into the vaginas of 10 young girl athletes and touched the breasts of 3 of them. Nassar was sentenced to 40 to 175 years in prison, essentially a life sentence. Imagine similar punishment if the sexes were reversed.

Orville Lee Wollard, a 53-year-old husband and father is serving twenty years for a crime in which no one was injured, no property taken. He fired a warning shot into the wall of his house after his sixteen-year-old daughter's boyfriend refused to leave the house and approached Wollard in a threatening manner. The boyfriend had scuffled with Wollard earlier in the day and left Wollard's Florida home after having torn Wollard's stitches from recent surgery. When the boyfriend returned later, he was angry enough to pound his fist through a drywall. Had Wollard shot the boyfriend, he might have been spared prison under Florida's "Stand Your Ground" law, but this discharge of a firearm was punished under Florida's mandatory sentencing requirements: 20 years. [121]

Kharon Davis of Dothan, Alabama was arrested in 2007 suspected of murder. After 10 years without a trial Davis sought release citing lack of a speedy trial. [122] For perhaps the worst such miscarriage of justice, see *The Last Victim, National Review*, Sept. 10, 2018 pg. 29.

Matthew Charles, a Tennessee black man, was sent back to federal prison after two years of freedom when an appeals court ruled he had been released in error. Charles was released early from federal prison in 2016, having served 21 years of a 35-year sentence for selling crack to a police informant. Federal prosecutors then appealed, arguing that, because Charles had been originally been classified as a "career offender," he was ineligible for the retroactive sentencing reductions put into place during the Obama presidency. Charles found religion in prison, became a law clerk and GED instructor, helped illiterate inmates decipher court documents, and served 21 years of hard time without a single disciplinary infraction. After his release, he held down a steady job and volunteered every Saturday at a food pantry. Despite a request from a federal judge asking prosecutors to drop their appeal, citing Charles' "undisputed rehabilitation," the U.S. Attorney's Office pressed on. A federal appeals court ruled that, by the letter of the law, Charles should never have been released from prison.

Stewart Parnell knowingly sold contaminated peanuts, unintentionally killing some victims. His prison sentence was 28 years. Illinois sought a life sentence for mechanic Michael Allison for recording police officers' brutality, though an Appeals Court ruled such recordings legal. [123] Public pressure got the case thrown out. California's "three strike law" has incarcerated men (exclusively men, for all practical purposes) to 25 years to life, with over half (57%) of its subjects guilty of non-violent offenses. In one case, Santo Reyes was sentenced to 26 years to life for trying to take the written portion of a driver's license test for his illiterate cousin.

US District Judge Richard D. Bennett sentenced William Edward Wray II of Crespatown, Maryland to 50 years in prison, followed by a lifetime of supervised release for two counts of sexually exploiting minors to produce child pornography, after Wray plead guilty.

Many situations are, as the cerebral and wryly humorous writer/philosopher Charles Krauthammer observed, "scandals in search of a crime."

Unknown to Jeffrey Williamson, his son Justin skipped church. Police arrested Williamson for child endangerment. He faced up to 6 months in jail and was fired from his job as a result of gender biased news coverage.[124]

Seventy-year-old Roy Chuster was confined for 30 years in a New York hospital for the criminally insane because he complained about jail corruption. U.S. Appeals Judge Irving Kaufman called it a "shocking story." Stephen Slevin was driving across country in 2005 and was thrown into a New Mexico jail in solitary confinement for DWI. Psychologically confused, he was all but forgotten there for nearly two years. After release, he sued and won $15.5 million in one of the largest prisoner civil rights awards in U.S. history. [125]

This writer obtained the release of a perfectly normal man who was locked in a Minneapolis psychiatric ward at the request of a wife from whom he wanted a divorce. His "abnormality" was having a girlfriend.

The wife coaxed him to a purported marriage counselor, actually a psychiatrist, who, deeming his behavior to be "inappropriate," signed commitment papers. One call from the Men's Defense Association to that psychiatrist, and the man was released.

Floridian Jerry McCallam, who had 92 dead and sick cats in his home, was convicted of felony animal cruelty and misdemeanor animal abandonment, and sent to prison for three years. [126] Women who commit similar transgressions are almost never punished. At the Will County Courthouse in Joliet, Ill., Clifton Williams stretched and let out a ill-timed yawn during his cousin's trial. Circuit Judge Daniel Rozak sentenced Williams to six months in jail for the indiscretion the maximum penalty for criminal contempt without a jury trial. [127] There's no pursuit of happiness for this Long Island man: local cops busted Robert Schiavelli for laughing too loudly in his own home. He was slapped with two summonses because his next-door neighbor complained that he could hear his laughing across the driveway. Each summons carried a $250 fine or 15 days in jail. Alabaman Dale Peterson was taken to jail after he ate a handful of cashews from a jar at a Sam's Club store and then returned the nuts to a shelf after deciding not to purchase them. Former Breitbart reporter Michelle Fields physically harassed Donald Trump at a rally. Trump's campaign manager Corey Lewandowski pushed her out of the way, and was charged with battery.

Santaluces, Florida high school teacher Andrew Foster had a sexual relationship with a 16-year-old female student. He was held without bail. [128]

Minnesota Vikings' Adrian Peterson whipped his son leaving welts. It seems the child was an unmanageable brat like so many others raised by single mothers. Mad at him, his wife or girlfriend — unclear which — took pictures of the marks. The goalposts were moved for Peterson, as politicians and local sportswriters lined up to grandstand. Despite the old adage about sparing the rod, nationwide media and public outrage exceeded that when mothers *murder* their children. The NFL suspended Peterson without pay for the 2014 season. Talk about overkill! Florida State University quarterback De'Andre Johnson and a woman argued in a Tallahassee bar. She punched him, and he responded in kind. Johnson was dismissed from the team. No mention of a penalty to her. I'll stop here rather than go on forever with like instances.

Undeniably and unexplainably, some men have escaped punishment for murder, child rape and other transgressions. Sometimes skin color may have been a factor: O.J. Simpson and Maurice Clemmons [129] for instance. Other times, they are just plain screw-ups. But such cases are rare and receive widespread and deserved publicity.

The Supreme Court has noted that, because of sex differences, adolescent brain anatomy can cause "transient rashness, proclivity for risk, and inability to assess consequences," thereby diminishing "moral culpability" and, more importantly, enhancing "the prospect that, as the years go by," offenders' "deficiencies will be reformed." Hence "a lifetime in prison is a disproportionate sentence for all but the rarest of children and those men whose crimes reflect 'irreparable corruption.' " This reveals the problem with mandatory minimum sentences.

Child Abuse, sexual and otherwise

A man can hardly speak to, or touch or appreciate the beauty of children without accusatory glares. False claims of child abuse against men have increased dramatically. The 1980's and 90's witnessed an epidemic of Salem witch-hunt cause célèbres where child "protective" services with empires to build and maintain ran amok. From Jordan, Minnesota to McMartin [130] in California, to Kelly Michaels in New Jersey, to Amirault in Massachusetts, to Little Rascals in North Carolina [fn14] and to Wenatchee in Washington, et al, America witnessed a feeding frenzy of false accusations. It brought out the pitchfork brigades. No other field provides greater opportunity for politicians to grandstand.

Feminist prosecutors dove to the bottom of that slope, whipping up public invective against parents they jailed yet knew to be innocent. Gerald Amirault spent 15 years in prison although every sentient person knew he was innocent. Nevertheless, Martha Coakley, then Middlesex district attorney, lobbied Gov. Jane Swift to keep him in prison to further her political ambitions and show that she was a take-no-prisoners prosecutor, who "stood up for the children." As a result, Gov. Swift denied clemency for Amirault who sat in prison another three years.

Prosecutor Nancy Lamb in North Carolina acted similarly. Janet Reno made her reputation (such as it was) and landed her position as Attorney General of the U.S. under President Clinton through questionable prosecutions of alleged child abusers in Florida.

Prosecutors hooked men up to penile plethysmographs, [131] devices to measure tumescence, in the expectation (naturally) that a positive reaction will occur while watching pornography, giving them an excuse for prosecution. It is very much like dunking accused witches to see if they survive, in which case they were considered witches. Imagine hooking women up to similar devices. The very idea is repugnant. Why is it not equally repugnant regarding men?

It is becoming common for mothers to accuse fathers of child molestation to doubly ensure maternal custody or to deny visitation. Judges and other officials take these allegations seriously, often

---

14 For perhaps the worst such miscarriage of justice, see 'The Last Victim', National Review, Sept. 10, 2018 pg 29.

removing or punishing men under the rationalization that even if their actions are wrong they prefer to "err on the side of caution," evidently one of the few places that error is permitted. [132] Douglas Besharov Ph.D. of the American Enterprise Institute and former director National Center for Child Abuse and Neglect reports that 67% of all child abuse claims are unfounded. Most experts claim the percentage is much higher in divorce situations. Estimates are that between 90% [133] and 77% [134] of child abuse reports — over 700,000 in America each year, mostly divorce related — are untrue. Hear Dean Tong, forensic legal consultant and author of the book Elusive Innocence: Survival Guide For The Falsely Accused [135]:

Without a doubt, the most devastating issue to men and fathers over the past 35 years has been that of false abuse accusations... The SAID (Sexual Allegations in Divorce) Syndrome has been coined 'divorce's atomic bomb' — the ultimate weapon. Typically, men and fathers are on the recipient end of SAID allegations, and because child sex abuse is such a reprehensible crime, when it does happen the same are presumed guilty... Of the 2.9 million reports of alleged child abuse and neglect in 2002, approximately 2 million of the same were unfounded or without foundation.

The *Child Abuse Prevention & Treatment Act* (CAPTA), also known as the Mondale Act, charged CPS (the Child Protective Services) to investigate anonymously made complaints and even reports made in bad faith. This is an open invitation to malicious slander. CAPTA immunized government child protection agencies from being sued for monetary damages, claiming sovereign immunity under the 11th Amendment.

In Florida, House Bill 77, misleadingly entitled the 'Keeping Children Safe Act,' went into effect in 2007. This Constitutionally dubious legislation provides for parental (read paternal) visitation to be automatically stopped once a telephone report is made, essentially from any source, alleging sexual abuse. No questions asked. The caller may remain anonymous. Visitation continues to be interrupted until the court has a hearing about this, at which point the court may allow visitation to resume. It constitutes an implicit presumption of guilt versus one of innocence. At the hearing, the accused must prove by clear and convincing evidence (the highest of legal thresholds), that the safety of the child would not be threatened by continued visitation.

In Victims of Memory, Mark Pendergrast shows how the recovered memory hoax destroyed families, ruined lives, and sent innocent parents to prison. Former Vancouver, Washington police officer Clyde Ray Spencer spent nearly 20 years in prison after he was convicted of sexually molesting his son and daughter. Later, the children admitted it never happened. Matthew Spencer, 9-years-old at the time, told a judge he made the allegation after months of insistent questioning by now-retired Clark County sheriff detective Sharon Krause just so she would leave him alone. Matthew's sister, Kathryn Tetz — 6-years-old at the time, said she doesn't remember what she told Krause back in 1985, but she said that when she finally read the police reports she was "absolutely sure" the abuse never happened. "I would have remembered something that graphic, that violent," Tetz said. Both children said that while growing up in California they were told by their mother, who divorced Spencer before he was charged, that they were blocking out the memory of the abuse. [136]

Hear Freud's skepticism of women's reports of father incest:

Almost all of my women patients told me that they had been seduced by their father. I was driven to recognize in the end that these reports were untrue and so came to understand that the hysterical symptoms are derived from fantasies and not from real occurrences. [137]

Some incest obviously occurs (maybe 2% of the allegations). In the hundreds of divorces I have dealt with, two men admitted to sexually abusing their daughters, a couple more were not sincere enough in my estimation. Those few actually guilty individuals provide misandrists with fuel to fire the anti-male image, to tar most men with the same brush. The herd instinct takes over. Full of righteous indignation, politicians jump on the stump, shaking fists.

Liberal laws and applications label men, more than women, as criminals; e.g., men can be jailed for making drunken passes at women and for patting one on the ass.

There are a few lowlifes, the ilk of John Evander Couey who in 2005 killed little Jessica Lundsford, and also of convicted sex offender Joseph E. Duncan III who later that same year killed four in Utah in the process of abducting 8-year-old Shasta Groene and several illegal aliens. But only one percent of alleged child abuse involves serious assaultive behavior the public regards as truly abusive. [138]

Actual guilt

According to the National Child Abuse and Neglect Data System, women are the most common abusers of children. Women are more likely than men to abuse children, especially boys and the elderly, throughout history — not merely since receiving the preponderance of custody. [139] The nasty, unmentioned truth is that 62 percent of child abusers are mothers. [140]

According to Ronald Tansley, "In Oregon in 1994, 33 children were killed as a result of child abuse. Mothers were killers in 27 of these cases." [141] A Minnesota study of physical child abuse in 1967 showed the ratio of mother guilt to father guilt in such cases to be seventeen to seven. An analysis of the data in the U.S. Dept. of Health and Human Services child maltreatment reports from 2001—2006, shows that:

• 70.8% of children killed by one parent are killed by their mothers!
• 70.6% of children abused by one parent are abused by their mothers!
• 60% of the victims are boys!

Though the vast majority of those who seriously mistreat young children are female, ninety seven percent of people incarcerated for doing so are male. The fiction that fathers are the principal child abusers is promoted not only by mothers, feminists, the media and politicians seeking the feminist vote, but also by otherwise respectable scholars. Thus, Richard Gelles compares mothers, not with fathers but with all males, lumping fathers with the second greatest abusers (after mothers) — boyfriends of the mothers (who may become stepfathers): "But males, although they spend less time with children and have less overall responsibility for child care, are more likely than females to injure or kill children..." Note Gelles' skillful subterfuge. Later he admits, "A child's mother is more likely to kill or injure him than his stepmother is. Male offenders tend to be more distantly related to their victims. A child's stepfather or the boyfriend of his mother is more likely to kill or injure him than his father is." [142.] The papers are full of such instances. Such is the source of "fake news" stories.

Male offenders, in other words, tend not to be fathers — fathers tend not to be offenders. Gelles says (if the reader takes the trouble to winkle out the meaning) that the biological father is the child's best protector, not only against the stepmother but against the mother, who is far more likely to abuse or kill the child than the father, and who is especially abusive and murderous if she becomes single — i.e., if she and the judge exile the child's best protector, the father.

Actual perverts are habitual; so unless there are substantiated previous or subsequent complaints such allegations are probably lies. Unfortunately, few states mete out penalties for promulgating malicious false child abuse accusations.

Violence perceptions

Like reversing magnetic poles, individuals of opposite sex seem to attract, then repel — sometimes violently. Practically every time a man and woman get into a physical fight, regardless of who is the aggressor, the man is blamed. When it comes to 'He said/she said,' 'she said' usually wins. It is a feminist mantra that inter-sex violence is a one-way street — something men do to women, fodder for bumper stickers. Perception becomes reality. Society, officialdom and the media are profoundly indignant regarding violence against females — only.

People assume that all men "have the potential for violence and sexual aggressiveness," says Peter Stearns, a George Mason University professor. [143] The public perception, like the legal one, must be that women can't commit violence. The general perception is that Tiger Woods' wife may slug him with a 9-iron for his infidelities, but he mustn't slug her for hers. How do people typically react when hearing about or witnessing a woman-hits-man situation? Other than presumptively asking, "What did he do?" they don't seem to care.

Twenty-year Seattle family law attorney Lisa Scott explains:

> From top to bottom, the current domestic violence system won't let women be anything but victims and can't see men as anything but batterers. And from the moment a 911 call is made there is practically no such thing as an innocent man. It doesn't matter that you're actually innocent. Or that she attacked you first. Or that you both went over the line and that both of you want to put it behind you and work it out. The system will prosecute you and persecute you until you've confessed your sins — even if you've none to confess. And you're not cured until they say you're cured — even if you were never sick to begin with.

Gender violence figures are overblown and ill-defined. According to Robert Franklin, Esq., domestic violence can now be defined as a pattern of abusive behavior in any relationship that is used by one partner to gain or maintain power and control over another intimate partner. Many women are prone to call the cops to teach a lesson to men they are mad at. "Domestic violence" (DV) laws allow men to be arrested and prosecuted for "violence" that is not violent.

Each of the following constitutes violent behavior under the definition of the Office for Violence against Women: under-mining your partner's "sense of self-worth, making repeated attempts to get your wife to stop buying so many pairs of shoes, putting to sleep a terminally-ill pet. Slamming the door can be considered violence. Shooting your husband in the head with a shotgun while he sleeps? Not necessarily. The federal Center for Disease Control (CDC) conflates "violence" with "abuse," and then defines "abuse" to include being stared at angrily by your spouse/partner. DV can include verbal, mental, and emotional, "name-calling and constant criticizing, insulting, and belittling the victim, blaming the victim, ignoring, dismissing, or ridiculing the 'victim's' needs." The term "psychological battery" now includes "acts of lying, humiliation, withholding information, and refusing help with child care or housework."

The Obama Administration defined domestic violence very broadly, such as alleged economic, emotional, or psychological abuse. Practically speaking, this sex-based massive expansion of federal police power addressed crime against women only. Under it, a woman could get her husband thrown in jail for 10 months because he "disrespected" but did not hit her. [144]

In England, "controlling behavior" by husbands will be a jailable offence. Theresa May, while British Home Secretary and with the assistance of Women's Aid, published proposals designed to criminalize men who "bully, cause psychological harm or deny money to their partners." Exact terms of the offence are yet to be defined, but it could involve humiliating, frightening or intimidating a partner, keeping them away from friends or family or restricting their access to money. There would have to be a "pattern" of abuse to trigger a prosecution. Violence would not be necessary. [145] In response to lobbying by feminists, a French law banned 'psychological violence' within marriage and cohabitation. Offenders could face a fine, restraining order or even jail. [146]

Nottinghamshire England has officially recognized misogyny as a hate crime, but not misandry. Examples include unwanted or uninvited sexual advances, verbal assault, unwanted or uninvited physical or verbal contact or engagement, use of mobile phones to send unwanted or uninvited messages, and taking photographs without consent. It will be the duty of Sue Fish, Chief Constable, to train her underlings in arresting the guilty.

Prosecutors waste jurors' time with ludicrous, politically motivated, evidence-free domestic violence prosecutions against men. Each year about 780,000 persons are wrongfully arrested for "domestic violence" in the U.S. [147] Many women will take advantage of domestic-violence laws and procedures, knowing that if a man they assault retaliates calling the police will generally result in the onus being placed on him. [148] An allegation of domestic violence is made in approximately 25% of divorces. Such allegations are more common in relationships involving children.

Arrested on Sept. 21, 2007, Donnell Bonney of Albany New York was sentenced to 24 years in prison after being convicted in a domestic abuse case. [149] Twenty-four years for domestic abuse? Come on! Prosecutors claim Michael Wiley, a triple amputee "attacked" his wife, by shoving himself into her and causing her to knock over a lamp. Division Director Mike Halkitis has said he will push for the maximum sentence of five years for Wiley. [150]

Mess with the bull and you get the horn. It is especially unwise to attack a high strung, highly intense athlete when both are drunk, thinking they can get away without retaliation in kind. A seemingly endless media firestorm has ignited over violence between NFL players and wives or girlfriends. Like Adrian Peterson, mentioned earlier, players have been kicked off teams and maybe out of the NFL. Three are mentioned below. They lost $millions in endorsements; jersey sales were suspended. In its own defense, the NFL hired a "social responsibility" team consisting of 4 female sex abuse activists to inform its guidelines.

Baltimore running back Ray Rice's girlfriend slugged him in a hotel elevator, and he stupidly responded by decking her. A video camera captured the event. This triggered ESPN's popular host Stephen A. Smith to remark about women's responsibility for domestic violence thusly: "We also have to make sure that we learn as much as we can about elements of provocation. Not that there's real provocation, but the *elements* of provocation." Consequently, ESPN said it would remove Smith from programming for about a week. [151] The "victim," later Rice's wife, deplored the whole fuss. The normally goofy Whoopie Goldberg made sense by coming out with a logical defense of ESPN's Smith on *The View*, saying "No woman should be surprised if they make the decision to hit a man and the man hits back." Of course, Whoopie didn't suffer Stephen Smith's punishment.

After a night of drinking, Minn. Vikings football player Chris Cook physically restrained his girlfriend Chantel Baker, leaving bruises on her, after she violently assaulted him. Angry, Baker called police, blaming Cook for assault. At Cook's trial, nearly a year later, the sober Baker testified she had lied in blaming him. Nevertheless, Hennepin County Prosecutor Sarah Hilleren refused to accept her retraction, and proceeded with the trial. [152] In July 2014, Arizona Cardinals Jonathan Dwyer was arrested for aggravated assault on a girlfriend who later denied his guilt.

In How Feminists Tried to Destroy the Family, Erin Pizzey outlines how the issue of domestic violence was co-opted by radical neo-Marxist feminists (redfems). In line with their agenda of re-engineering society to fit their theories, feminists have brought about an expansion of the definitions of violence, abuse and rape. The whole hullabaloo is part of the war against masculinity itself.

Official figures have revealed that record numbers of men are reporting domestic abuse by their partners to police, while the proportion of women victims turning to police has fallen. [153]

Violence against Women Act and Similar Legislation

The Violence against Women Act (VAWA), passed in 1994 embodied the fem/lib political agenda. Talk about virtue signaling! Presidential aspirant and plagiarist Joe Biden initially sponsored the Act. Former Republican presidential candidate Sam Brownback was a strong supporter. Like so many other laws and judicial practices, this Act was influenced by the moral fallacy that the ends justify the means. Lacking a clear, appropriate definition of violence against women, the Act has probably caused more harm than good.

Steve Chang and Gordon Smith are two fathers from Delaware who were falsely accused under VAWA and had their lives destroyed. They filed a class action lawsuit in Washington DC on behalf of all taxpaying, law-abiding loving parents nationwide.[154] Ironically VAWA came back to bite Biden in 2019 when he was accused of sexual improprieties for brushing up against Democrat politician Lucy Flores [155] and staffer Tara Reade.

Plaintiffs are qualified to receive free legal assistance from VAWA, though defendants are not so qualified, despite the Sixth Amendment which states: "In all criminal prosecutions, the accused shall...have the Assistance of Counsel for his defense." Arrests are funded by Section 102, titled "Grants to Promote Arrest and Enforce Restraining Orders." This section not only permits officials to trample Bill of Rights protections, but also prohibits police from "asking or requiring an alleged victim of an alleged sex offense to submit to a polygraph examination as a condition for proceeding with the investigation of such an offense."

VAWA enables agencies to systematically alter, conceal, or manipulate the results of scientific research in order to continually renew funding for this legislation, and provides generous financial incentives for them to do so. According to news reports, the Obama Administration leaned on the military to waste funds on related witch hunts, funds that would have been better expended elsewhere.

Attorney Lisa Scott said:

What we really have is MAWA: Men Annoying Women Act. The government seems unable to define gender bias except as 'bias against women.' The program holds male victims of domestic violence responsible for women's violence, even where the man is a saint. Any modern man not terrified of being in a relationship with a woman has not been paying attention.

Trudy W. Schuett, an Arizona-based former contributor to *The Liberator* writes about DV:

(Family violence) is a complex human issue; it cannot be addressed by any political ideology or simplistic government program. Ten years out, there is no evidence that (it) and its myriad programs has been of benefit to anyone beyond those municipalities, organizations and individuals who are recipients of VAWA funding, or employed by VAWA-funded agencies. Once in the program, she is bombarded with feminist ideology about being 'empowered' by her victimhood, signed up for whatever government programs are available, and helped to apply for an

Order of Protection against her presumed offending spouse or significant other. Divorce is presented as the ultimate solution to her problems.

Phyllis Schlafly said:
During the Clinton Administration, the feminists parlayed their hysteria that domestic violence is a national epidemic into the passage of the Violence Against Women Act. This created a gigantic gravy train of taxpayers' money, known as feminist pork that empowers pro-divorce, anti-male activism.

On the 18th anniversary of VAWA, former Obama Attorney General Eric Holder profusely praised it. On March 8, 2010, as part of the Justice Department's year-long commemoration of the 15th anniversary of VAWA, and to assist feminists in propagandizing students, Associate Attorney General Tom Perrelli kicked off a nationwide college campus tour by top department officials to "raise awareness of violence against women."

Billions of dollars have been spent to create this fat, bloated bureaucracy. VAWA is funded with an obscene $3.9 billion (with a "b") to finance feminists' goals, 156 plus a billion taxpayer dollars a year. Professor Stephen Baskerville asks, "Why is $4 billion in taxpayers' money required to outlaw something that is already against the law?" The 2/20/2011 Phyllis Schlafly Report said it costs $20 billion a year to support VAWA's single parent, welfare-dependent "families," and at least $100 billion a year for all federal poverty programs connected with family fragmentation and fatherlessness. The VAWA bureaucracy asked for even more money. Minnesota's Dakota County sheriff's office was awarded a $450,000 federal grant to gather evidence of domestic and sexual violence and stalking-related electronic crimes. The funds were sought by the Minnesota Coalition for Battered Women.

Not satisfied with several billions from the U.S. Treasury, 67 feminist and liberal organizations supported a lawsuit to try to get private allegations of domestic abuse heard in federal courts so they could collect civil damages against men and institutions with deep pockets.

Billions of dollars have flowed from VAWA to the states to finance private victim-advocacy organizations, private domestic-violence coalitions, and the training of judges, prosecutors and police. fn15 This tax-funded network is, of course, staffed by radical feminists who teach the presumption of father guilt. ... Judges saddle fathers with restraining orders on the wife's say-so without any investigation as to whether it is true or false.

---

15 This mindset is so ubiquitous it's termed the "Duluth" model of training judges, largely founded by feminist Ellen Pence.

Hear men's activists Mike McCormick of ACFC and blogger Glenn Sacks on December 11, 2007 discussing this assault against men:

When it comes to domestic violence legislation, the road to hell is paved with good intentions, and Senator Joe Biden (D-Del) owns an asphalt company. Biden's latest domestic violence bill is the National Domestic Violence Volunteer Attorney Network Act (S.1515), which amends Biden's Violence Against Women Act to create an extensive network of volunteer attorneys to help abused women. The attorneys would provide free legal help in forging divorce or separation agreements and in winning child custody.

According to Biden, S.1515, which will be heard by the Senate Judiciary Committee and is co-sponsored by Senator Arlen Specter (D-PA), will enlist 100,000 volunteer attorneys. The bill is supported by the American Bar Association, the Family Violence Prevention Fund, and the National Organization for Women, which is currently running a campaign in support of the bill.

In 2007 the Women's Edge Coalition, in partnership with Amnesty International USA and the Family Violence Prevention Fund, developed and campaigned to introduce to Congress the International Violence Against Women Act (I-VAWA). The purpose is to export radical feminism to many foreign countries via the World Health Organization and various U.N. feminist NGO's. I-VAWA provides a $1 billion blueprint to create global-feminist socialism and destabilize the family. Analyst David Usher says, "I-VAWA would create a 'legal brigade' — an army in excess of 100,000 lawyers trained to act as clones of the infamous Duke prosecutor Mike Nifong." I-VAWA specifics: Senate Bill: S. 2982, House Bill: H.R. 4594. Sponsored by Senators John Kerry, D; Barbara Boxer, D; Olympia Snowe, R; and Susan Collins R.; House members Bill Delahunt, D; Ted Poe, R; and Jan Schakowsky D, with the assistance of Senator Biden. [157]

Besides sponsoring VAWA and I-VAWA, Biden introduced the National Domestic Violence Volunteer Attorney Act. This equally execrable act would farm out $55 million to the American Bar Association to sign up legal "volunteers" so they can harass men. In July 2010, the General Assembly of the United Nations further demonstrated its gender bias by voting to create the UN Entity for Gender Equality and the Empowerment of Women. [158] VAWA reform will be addressed in Part III — *Defenses: reformation, dammit!*

VAWA was reauthorized in 2000, 2006 and on March 7th, 2013. Re-authorization was sponsored by Patrick Leahy (D) and Mike Crapo (R). It last passed the Senate Judiciary Committee on a straight party line vote — Democrats prevailing. This, despite the fact that the rate of sexual violence fell 64 percent in the last decade. [159] Wikipedia says, "The Act's renewal was fiercely opposed by conservative Republicans..."

Trump's Attorney General Jeff Sessions voted against it while a Republican senator. Although the exact date is unclear, the act has expired years ago.

Media RADAR reported that Rep. Lucille Roybal-Allard (D-CA) and Ted Poe (R-TX) introduced H.R. 739, the Security and Financial Empowerment (SAFE) Act. The bill creates four new entitlements for alleged victims of domestic violence: lifetime employment, health insurance, 30 days annual emergency leave, and unemployment insurance. The first two entitlements have no means-testing, verification of need, or time limits. These entitlements represent a substantial unfunded government mandate to be subsidized by companies with 15 or more employees. The law would spur growth in false allegations of domestic violence. RADAR's analysis of the SAFE Act reveals it will substantially harm the financial well-being of employers and may create severe dislocations in the American economy, for three reasons: It will require employers to hire millions more employees than needed. It will make it far more difficult to terminate workers. It will render the American economy less robust"[160]

In Canadian schools, the "Black eyed Susan" program used to brainwash children is an example of the success that the anti-father movement has achieved. This program begins its indoctrination in kindergarten, and feeds teachers with the same statistics as Canada's National Judicial Institute feeds judges. By making children play-act the role of victimized mother and abusive father, authorities send subliminal messages about male violence against women. Canadian columnist Barbara Kay at a Real Women conference said:

Domestic violence is worth lingering over because it is the single most effective propaganda tool feminists have found for entrenching misandry in the general population. The truth is that domestic violence affects perhaps 7% of the population, is initiated in near-equal proportion by men and women, and results in Canada in about 70 intimate partner deaths a year. Yes, more women are killed than men, but the overall figure is so nugatory in a country of 35 million people that clearly individual dysfunction accounts for all of it; and no possible generalization about the nature of one sex or the other can be drawn from it.

To fixate on and endlessly keen about violence against women only, and not on the equal or greater violence against men requires a perverse form of sophistry. Sen. Reid (D. NV) said, "Men don't have jobs. Women don't have jobs either, but women aren't abusive... Men when they're out of work tend to become abusive." [161] The *London Daily Mail* reports that the Archbishop of Canterbury, Rowan Williams, backed a Church of England report that claims viewing the Creator in masculine terms can validate "overbearing and ultimately violent patterns of behavior" in intimate relationships and "contributes to domestic abuse."

Hear Professor Stephen Baskerville:

Special "integrated domestic violence courts" presume guilt and then, says New York's openly feminist chief judge, "make batterers and abusers take responsibility for their actions." They can seize property, including homes, without the accused being convicted or even formally charged or present to defend himself. Lawyer Walter Fox describes these courts as "pre-fascist": "Domestic violence courts ... are designed to get around the protections of the criminal code. The burden of proof is reduced or removed, and there's no presumption of innocence."

According to a Harvard researcher writing in the Aug 7, 2007 *New York Times*, the mandatory arrest laws enacted over the last 20 years have proven counterproductive, significantly increasing the number of murders in those states. A Harvard study of these laws in 15 states found they increased partner homicides by 57%. The state of Maine has a mandatory arrest law in domestic violence cases. Buttressing that is a law, LD 1039, which requires law enforcement agencies to adopt a "process to evaluate and determine who the predominant physical aggressor is in a domestic violence situation." This combination will lead to the arrests of many innocent men because, according to reformers McCormick and Sacks:

When police officers respond to a domestic disturbance call, they are instructed not to focus on who attacked whom and who inflicted the injuries, but instead consider different factors which will almost always weigh against men. These factors include comparable size, comparable strength, the person allegedly least likely to be afraid, who has access to or control of family resources (i.e., who makes more money), and others. Given these factors, it is very difficult for officers to arrest female offenders.

A bill passed by the New York state Senate provides that any person who receives an order of protection must wear an electronic dog collar (OK, so it's actually an ankle bracelet). No exceptions. This is a device that allows a person's location to be monitored 24/7 by law enforcement personnel. Not a peep out of the ACLU. The device, sold by Omnilink Systems, costs nearly $4,000 per year per wearer. Massachusetts Lieutenant Governor Kerry Healey (Republican) has proposed an "Act Relative to Enhanced Protection for Victims of Domestic Violence." Under this bill, any violator of a domestic restraining order could be required to wear a satellite tracking device similar to an electronic dog-collar.

Alaska Governor Sean Parnell proposed house bill 298: Anyone who has ever committed any type of crime involving sex, including urinating in public... is labeled a child kidnapper or sex offender, and not even allowed to attend church! Illinois State Representative Robert Pritchard proposed a database of domestic violence "offenders" similar to the "Sex Offenders Registry." Lynn Rosenthal, Obama's Domestic Violence Czar, Director of the National Network to End Domestic Violence, a vicious anti-male feminist, supported male castration.

Imagine the additional weapons false accusers would have if these measures pass.

Ontario Judge Justice Judith Beeman, Ottawa Court House, Courtroom 32, on July 27th 2008 said, "Luckily in Canada we don't need evidence to have a man charged with domestic violence." Men's advocate Glen Sacks said that Costa Rican law automatically jails men on allegations of violence, and that women in that country are fleecing innocent expatriate Americans by threatening to invoke the law. Writer Carey Roberts says Mexico passed a law that could put a man in jail simply because he became jealous.

Fortunately, the Department of Justice in the Trump Administration has sensibly clarified the meaning of domestic violence to include only conduct that would be a felony or misdemeanor if charged as a crime.

Marital infidelity understandably causes men to lose temper. By their very nature, it outrages husbands more than it does wives. Dr. Charles E. Corry of the Equal Justice Foundation said:

> At least 40% of the married men who contacted us about false allegations of domestic violence were charged after they found evidence their wives were having an affair. So, the unintended consequence of draconian domestic violence laws is that they provide a perfect weapon for adulteresses. Today we punish the husband for his wife's adultery. Curiously, in the few cases we have heard of, the husband's anger was primarily directed towards his wife's lover.

I too am mystified by the misdirected anger of cuckolded men toward their wives' paramours. They almost invariably take revenge on the guy instead of the one who hurt them far more, the unfaithful wife. 'Lover boy' didn't vow fidelity to him — wifey did. The implied assumption that women are not intelligent or responsible enough to behave is demeaning.

As a matter of self-protection, no man should ever let himself care enough about a woman to let her unfaithfulness drive him to violence. No marriage or woman is worth the repercussions in this day and age. This reaction is foolish because another lover always crops up, and the injured husband cannot contend with every horny man. Wasn't it General Beauregard who opined that it was impractical to shoot his entire staff?

GIs returning from overseas assignments to unfaithful wives and the prospect of losing their children — the very things they fought and sacrificed for — can be forgiven for harboring thoughts of murder. In

August 2002, four GIs returning to Fort Bragg from combat in Afghanistan did more than harbor such thoughts. They actually did the deed. Well aware that divorce courts reward — not punish — infidelity in wives, the Ft. Bragg soldiers evidently felt they had no choice but to take matters into their own hands. The counseling that the military provides to wives of GIs should include warnings of the possible consequences of infidelity. Veterans losing families in the service of their country ought to be compensated, just as if they had lost an eye or a limb. Most men would rather have lost an eye or limb.

Youthful targets of prejudice

Prejudice is directed even to boys. In February 2007, Cory Mashburn and Ryan Cornelison, both 13, were arrested and taken in handcuffs to a juvenile detention facility, spending five days there after they were caught running down the halls of Patton Middle School, in McMinnville, Oregon slapping girls on the rear on "slap-butt day." "It's like a handshake we do," one girl said, according to the police report. The boys were initially charged by District Attorney Bradley Berry with five counts of felony sexual abuse. The boys faced 10 misdemeanor charges of harassment and sexual abuse, with a maximum of up to one year in juvenile jail on each count. It is highly unlikely they will ever serve that much time; but if convicted, the boys could still face the possibility of some jail time or registering for life as sex offenders. [162]

12-year-old Floridian Cristian Fernandez is a troubled youth with an extremely unfortunate life. Two forensic psychiatrists concluded that he was "emotionally underdeveloped but essentially reformable despite a tough life." In January 2011, he was rough-housing with his 2-year-old brother, David and accidentally broke David's leg. Another time he pushed David against a bookcase, and David sustained a head injury. Their mother waited six hours before taking David to the hospital. David eventually died. Prosecutor Angela Corey, Chief Prosecutor in the Trayvon Martin murder case, charged Cristian with first degree murder — as an adult — and wanted to make sure he would never leave jail. [163] A plea deal got him off with 5 years.

Police charged an Andrews SC high school student with third-degree assault and battery after he threw a paper airplane that struck a teacher. [164] Eighteen-year-old Walter Charwood picked up a rifle that accidently discharged, killing his best friend. An Itasca County Minnesota District Court sentenced Charwood to one year in jail and 15 years' probation. [165]

Nine-year-old Emanyea Lockett suffered a two-day suspension from Brookside Elementary School in Gastonia, North Carolina, after he told his friend that he thought his teacher was cute. Speaking to the local

WSOC news, Emanyea said, "I was talking to my friend and I said Miss Taylor was cute. That's all I said." It wasn't even Miss Taylor who reported the incident. Having overheard Emanyea's remark, a substitute teacher informed the principal, who then issued Emanyea a two-day suspension for "sexual harassment. [166] This incident had a happy outcome: The principal was later forced to retire because of his attitude.

D'Avonte Meadows, a first-grader at Sable Elementary School in Aurora, Colorado was accused of sexual harassment and suspended from school for three days because he told a girl "I'm sexy and I know it," a line from a popular song. [167] Amid a tidal wave of negative publicity, a Colorado school system let a 6-year-old boy return to school, and said it won't classify his kissing a girl on the hand as sexual harassment. The story of first-grader Hunter Yelton made national news and spurred outrage after word spread that his school near Colorado Springs suspended him for the kiss and accused him of sexually harassing the girl. CNN affiliate KRDO reported that Canon City Schools Superintendent Robin Gooldy met with Hunter's parents. The superintendent then changed Hunter's disciplinary offense from "sexual harassment" to "misconduct." [168] A 13-year-old Pikesville, Maryland boy was charged with second-degree assault for kissing a 14-year-old girl on a dare. Police became involved.

A Hercules, California 6-year-old boy was accused of brushing his friend's leg or groin while the two were playing at Lupine Hills Elementary school. He was kept in the principal's office for two hours, suspended, and a sexual battery charge was placed on his permanent school record (Removed after his parents contacted an attorney). [169]

An 18-year-old boy in Maine got a job at a carnival. His job was to buckle the kids in, lying on their bellies so they don't fly out. One girl told her mother, "He touched my bottom! The boy's description of his job constituted a confession. Thus convicted of "Indecent Assault and Battery on a Child," he went to jail for nine months and was put on the Sex Offender Registry for life.

His younger brother was at the urinal in the school bathroom when a girl too young to read burst in. He yelled at her to "Get out! Get out!" She started crying, left and told her mom who called the police, who asked if he was in the men's room with a girl? That much he admitted, but not touching the girl. However, his admission got him convicted of "Visual Sexual Aggression against a Child — the crime of having a child see his genitals. He got six months in jail and placed on the Sex Offender Registry for the next 10 years. His mother put it well: "We're all just one accusation away from the sex offender registry." [170]

Much of the evidence used to charge and convict children can be unreliable. The Center on Wrongful Convictions of Youth (CWCY) – a joint project of the Center on Wrongful Convictions and the Children and Family Justice Center – was created to address the unique problems faced by wrongfully accused youth.

Sex crimes, non-crimes and punishments

Sex offenders, even unproven ones, are modern day lepers of society. Elizabeth Cady Stanton and Susan B. Anthony wanted rapists executed. A handful of states, responding to public outcries about sex crimes against children, have amended their death penalty statutes to make the rape of a child a capital offense. State Senator Josh Penry (R) wants Colorado to join the five other states that already have the death penalty for this crime. It doesn't have to be rape; Richard Davis was sentenced to death on Dec. 12, 2007 for sexually molesting a 5-year-old girl (Citation lost).

Mark Wayne Rathbun raped 14 women around Long Beach California from 1997 to 2002. None died or were seriously physically harmed according to newspaper accounts. In September 2004, he was sentenced to 1,030 years plus 10 life terms.

Examining "Rape"

Prof. Neil Gilbert of the Univ. of Calif., Berkeley has shown that exaggeration is rampant and definitions of the term, "rape," are highly dubious. [171] In Acworth, Georgia, three boys, ages eight to nine, were charged with raping, kidnapping, false imprisonment and sexual assault of an 11-year-old girl they had been playing with. [172] Either they are extraordinarily, if not impossibly, mature, or the definition of rape has been incredibly stretched. It has.

The FBI sought to change the definition of 'rape'. An agency panel voted on Dec. 6, 2011 to change the narrow definition then in use: "Carnal knowledge of a female forcibly and against her will." The panel removed the word "forcible," along with several other amendments. "It's a great victory," said Eleanor Smeal, president of Feminist Majority Foundation, which launched the campaign. [173] The Center for Disease Control (CDC) has also radically expanded its definition.

Rape does not always live up to its involuntary connotation. Eighty percent of sentences are for statutory, not forcible, rape. A Philadelphia study by Menachem Amir, reported in the *University of Chicago Press*, found no violence in 87 percent of rapes. Prior and subsequent sexual liaisons between "victims" and the accused bear on the likelihood of consent.

A woman can define a sexual event by how she *feels* about it later. She can call it "rape" or not, and her word usually is determinative. Where it is a man's word against a woman's, the woman's is usually believed. There is one important caveat to this: as with the Chris Cook violent assault case a few pages back, if the 'victim' later rethinks the incident *and recants*, which often happens, then her word is seldom determinative and prosecutors go for a conviction whether the complainant wants them to or not.

Until recently, it was customary in rape prosecutions for the judge to read Sir Matthew Hale's admonition that the jury ought to "view the woman's testimony with caution. Rape is an accusation easily to be made and hard to be proved and harder to be defended by the party accused though never so innocent." No more, the legal system suppresses Sir Matthew Hale's commonsense admonition. See The Rape of Justice, by Prof. Baskerville, a modern day successor to Professor Amneus. In the words of Dr. Warren Farrell, "Laws against date rape with broad definitions are like 55-mile-per-hour speed limits — by making everyone a violator, they trivialize those who are real violators." U.S. Senate Bill 590 would encourage and support unfounded accusations. Former Republican presidential candidate Marko Rubio supported that bill.

"People can be charged with virtually no evidence," says Boston former sex-crimes prosecutor Rikki Klieman. "If a female comes in and says she was sexually assaulted, then on her word alone, with nothing else — and I mean nothing else, no investigation — the police will go out and arrest someone." "A defendant who can absolutely prove his innocence ... can nonetheless still be convicted, based solely on the word of the accuser," write Stuart Taylor and K.C. Johnson in Until Proven Innocent. In sexual assault, and in no other crime, Federal Rule of Evidence provides that "in a criminal case in which the defendant is accused of an offense of sexual assault, evidence of the defendant's commission of another offense or offenses of sexual assault is admissible, and may be considered for its bearing on any matter to which it is relevant."

On page 18 in his book, The Tyranny of Tolerance, Missouri Circuit Court Judge Robert H. Dierker, Jr. wrote:

> For every ill perceived by the gender and justice commissions, they demand special "training" of judges and lawyers. Such training was a thinly veiled effort to reeducate judges and lawyers to toe the femifascist line in every case, but especially in domestic violence, sexual assault and similar cases. Judges were to "encourage" prosecutors to pursue rape cases to trial, regardless of the merits of the case, and regardless of the proper role of the judge as neutral arbiter in an adversary system.

Some lesbian feminists consider all heterosexual intercourse to be rape. Even criticizing this kind of absurdity creates a "hostile environment" for women according to Hunting Ground filmmakers.

Despite claims that as high as 37 percent of women have been "raped," only 1/10 of one percent of women has actually reported rape. [174] The 1990 'National Women's Study,' in a survey of 4,008 women, claimed the incidence of rape is 683,000 per year. In actuality, the U.S. Dept. of Justice, Bureau of Justice Statistics (NCS) reported 130,000 rapes in one year, and the FBI Uniform Crime Report for 1990 claimed 102,560.

While less than 2% of the male population commits 100% of the actual male-on-female rapes in America, exaggerated allegations precipitated widespread rape shield laws which, combined with questionable — actually illegal — interrogation methods, have unjustly convicted many men. These laws and language encourage false accusations and convictions, and war with the presumption of innocence. As in all accusations by women against men, the burden is on the man to prove innocence, which is exceedingly difficult, and contrary to basic rights. Men accused of rape (spousal or otherwise), brutality or 'sexual harassment,' are routinely denied due process, not permitted to properly defend themselves because it might insult female complainants, regardless of truth.

Under military law, the maximum penalty for rape is life in prison without the possibility of parole and a dishonorable discharge. [175] A little harsh, don't you think? President Obama called for dishonorable discharge for military members found guilty of lowered standards of sex "crimes."

Robert Shibley, executive director of the Foundation for Individual Rights in Education (FIRE) says, "Once an accusation has been made, it's somehow up to the accused person to prove they did have consent. What that means is that they're guilty until proven innocent.... The person who's accused is left with effectively no defense." Blogger "Abusegate Bob" says, innocent Americans spend half a billion dollars each year to defend themselves against false accusations of domestic violence.

Specific cases:

A federal jury found that two D.C. homicide detectives framed Donald E. Gates, an innocent man, for a 1981 rape and murder by fabricating and withholding evidence. Gates was imprisoned for 27 years. [176] Luis Diaz spent 26 years in a Florida prison for rapes that DNA testing proved he did not commit. [177] Dallas black man Michael Phillips spent nearly a quarter of a century in prison for a rape he didn't commit including time for failing to register as a sex offender. He was freed when DNA tests exonerated him. [178] Henry McCollum and Leon Grown were convicted of killing an 11-year-old girl, and spent three decades on death row. Nine months after DNA evidence cleared them they were freed and given $45 each, but may be eligible for up to $50,000 each. [179]

At age 17 James Bain was sentenced to life in prison for a rape he did not commit. His repeated pleas for DNA testing were rejected until the Innocence Project [fn16] of Florida got involved in his case. Bain was released on December 17, 2009 holding the longevity record. A Florida statute makes him eligible for more than a million in reparations, $50,000 for every year he spent wrongfully incarcerated. Before Bain, the longest-serving inmate exonerated by DNA was James Lee Woodard of Dallas, who was released after spending more than 27 years in prison for a murder he did not commit.

Kenneth Ireland of Wallingford Connecticut spent two decades in prison before DNA testing showed he could not have committed the crimes. [180] William R. Strong, Jr. has been in a Virginia prison for a decade on false charges of "wife rape." Mr. Strong has been trying to get a DNA test, confident that the semen in the prosecution's test is not his but that of the lover of his unfaithful wife. Prosecutors, ignoring their obligation to protect the rights of the innocent, argue that he has no right to the evidence, under the sophistic rationalization that Strong was convicted prior to the advent of DNA testing.

A "psychologically unstable woman with 3 criminal convictions related to dishonesty, including false information to police, and check forgery" accused Don N. Conley of putting his hands inside her pants in a St. Paul, Minnesota elevator. A female judge sentenced Conley to 10 years and 8 months in prison. [181]

In violation of Constitutional prohibitions against cruel and unusual punishment, Minnesota male sex offenders have been kept in prison indefinitely after their sentences are served, in case they might re-offend. 700 Minnesotans were in this situation when this came to my attention. [182] At least 19 other states do likewise. Federal District Judge Donavan Frank ruled the Minnesota practice unconstitutional, and ordered the state to remedy the situation. [183] A federal Appeals Court stayed that lower court ruling, thereby permitting indefinite imprisonment. Former Democrat governor Dayton also resisted Donavan's ruling.

Rape is uncivilized and must be severely punished — when proven. Minds at the time and memories later are often numbed by alcohol. As with adultery, the urge is natural but succumbing to it is unacceptable behavior. Watch pious critics take the following passages out of context. Without in any way condoning actual rape, it must be said that it usually involves no physical harm and far less mental harm than that suffered by many men in divorce. I titled a previous book The Rape of the Male because, to any reasonable person, being literally raped in the back seat of a car, as happens to very few women, is far

---

16 The Innocence Project is a non-profit legal clinic affiliated with the Benjamin N. Cardozo School of Law at Yeshiva University and created by Barry C. Scheck and Peter J. Neufeld in 1992. The project is a national litigation and public policy organization dedicated to exonerating wrongfully convicted people through DNA testing and reforming the criminal justice system to prevent future injustice. As a clinic, law students handle case work while supervised by a team of attorneys and clinic staff. info@innocenceproject.org

preferable to being figuratively raped in divorce court, as happens to many men. The mental damage from rape cannot begin to compare with that suffered by men whose children are torn from them and alienated in divorce.

Al-Qaeda member Ahmed Ressam attempted to smuggle explosives into the U.S. in a plot to bomb Los Angeles International airport. Caught and found guilty, he received a sentence of 22 years and will be out in 10. On Dec. 21, 1988, Abdel Baset al-Megrahi's bomb killed 270 passengers on Pan Am Flight 103 over Lockerbie Scotland. He served some eight years of a life sentence, and was let off in a shady political deal. Contrast these times served to those for "rape."

False accusations.
Hell hath no fury... "He's mad that trusts in... a whore's oath."
— Shakespeare, King Lear

People often resort to calumny to blacken the name of former husbands or lovers. False charges are self-generating; some people are eager to believe anything negative about others. As the saying goes, if a story is worth telling, it's worth embellishing. Some women cry 'rape' to provide an alibi, to gain sympathy, to explain a pregnancy, if they didn't get paid, etc. Society is conditioned to take anything a woman says at face value, and feminists are furious at the suggestion that a woman might lie.

Susan Shapiro Barash, author of Little White Lies, Deep Dark Secrets: The Truth About Why Women Lie, published by St. Martin's Press, said, "Women lie as a survival technique, but also to get what they want." "Women lie every day," says Ottawa Judge Dianne Nicholas. Linda Fairstein, former head of the sex-crimes unit for the Manhattan District Attorney, estimates that half of all reports are unfounded. Careful, this kind will call the cops on you for no good reason.

Consider the following facts. Between 27 percent and 60 percent of rape allegations are false. [184] A 1994 study conducted by Purdue University professor Eugene Kanin, Ph.D. found that 41% of forcible rape allegations made during a multi-year period were false. The Royal Canadian Mounted Police found 80 percent of rape complainants who took lie detector tests were lying. A few years ago, the Orlando Florida police said false reporting had reached an epidemic level.

Morning-after remorse precipitates many false rape accusations, as seemed to be the case with Kobe Bryant's accuser. When the marriage of Woody Allen and Mia Farrow broke up, Farrow, embittered about Allan's extramarital affair, convinced her daughter Dylan that Woody had "sexually assaulted" her when she was seven-years-old. The allegation and denials have continued ever since, including in Op-Ed letters to the *New York Times*.

The earliest false rape charge was reported in Biblical times. Potiphar, the Egyptian potentate to whom the Ishmaelites sold Joseph (Gen. 39:1), was 'Captain of the Guard.' Joseph, though a foreigner, gradually gained Potiphar's confidence, and became overseer over all his possessions. Potiphar's wife attempted to seduce Joseph. When it failed, she accused him of rape. Believing the false accusation that his profligate wife brought against Joseph, Potiphar cast him into prison, where he remained for several years.

Joseph's story has been repeated innumerable times throughout the ages. In Michigan, an Air Force veteran's wife ran off with a low-life boyfriend, leaving her husband (I'll call him Will) with the children. When he filed for divorce and she realized he would obtain custody, she and her mother concocted a scheme to defeat him. She returned, feigning reconciliation, and persuaded him to go to bed with her, whereupon she jumped up screaming "rape." An ambitious prosecutor obtained the first conviction under that state's new feminist-inspired 'wife rape' law. With his money impounded by the divorce court, poor Will was unable to hire counsel, yet denied a public defender because technically he had money. Talk about a Catch 22 situation!

The prosecutor offered to ask the court for no further jail time than already served if he would plead guilty. Being innocent, Will refused and pled 'not guilty.' The feminist-pandering judge, Thomas Yeotis, then sentenced him to 15 to 30 years, twice the guidelines, declaring he was "sending a message" to wife-rapists.

I spoke to famous liberal attorney Alan Dersowitz about the case (Got through to him by phone while his gatekeeper was otherwise occupied. He probably won't recall it). He would not get involved — there was no money in it for him — and was peeved at the request. After he was also falsely accused by Virginia Giuffre of sex crimes he discovered how Will must have felt. Phyllis Schlafly became interested — also at my request — but was not able to wangle a pardon out of the Michigan Governor, who was not of her political persuasion.

For many years, a feminist on the parole board was instrumental in blocking Will's release, despite his failing health. Finally, after over twenty-two years and with liver cancer, on October 15, 2009 a parole was granted. Now, released with a record of a "sex offender," he can't get public housing, visit his grandchildren or obtain a decent job. The last time I talked to Will he told me this blight on his record prevents him from collecting veterans' benefits and climbing out of poverty.

Even if Will were guilty, the sentence was far too long. Most murderers who actually did the deed, certainly female ones, receive far lesser sentences. A crime *was* committed, not by him, but by the State of Michigan in so persecuting this man. Every citizen in Michigan ought to be ashamed that this travesty was committed in his or her name. Every day since hearing of his plight, I thought of Will and the unspeakable injustice done to him. Would that he had joined the Men's Defense Association before his trial, instead of after (Hold my beer a while; I'm getting so damn mad I'm shaking).

In an apparently identical case, Marine Corps Sgt. Brian Foster won custody of his children in a hotly-contested divorce. His vindictive ex-wife then hired a feminist attorney specializing in women's rights and accused him of marital rape and domestic violence. Being innocent of the charges, Foster refused to cop a plea to relatively minor "non-judicial" punishment. However, after a military crocodile court-martial trial, Foster was convicted and sentenced to 17 years in prison. His lawyers filed appeals which eventually proved his innocence. Foster served nine years, two months and 17 days of the sentence, most of it at the maximum security United States Disciplinary Barracks at Fort Leavenworth, Kansas, for a crime he did not commit. [185]

Falsely accused Vladek Filler, is a father and small business owner. On January 15, 2009, Mr. Filler was convicted on three counts of assaulting his former wife who has proven to be a violent criminal, a liar who has been caught in false allegations against her husband, and a physical and emotional abuser of her husband and children, and had a history of severe psychiatric problems. [186] Twenty-one months later the Maine Supreme Court ordered a re-trial on the basis that ADA [assistant district attorney] Mary Kellett had sought to exclude key evidence that would have served to establish Filler's innocence. [187] The organization Stop Abusive and Violent Environments (S.A.V.E.) sent a Complaint for the Disbarment of Prosecutor Mary Kellett to the Maine Board of Overseers for the Bar.

Another witch hunt occurred in Maine's Hancock County. Prosecutors Michael Povich, and Mary Kellett (mentioned above) have "criminally charged men in the community with rape, and for such alleged crimes as splashing water on their wives, spitting, 'terrorism' due to offensive song lyrics, visual aggression, etc. With exculpatory evidence blocked, these accusations were widely publicized along with pictures and identities of the men. Stating she does not believe women lie about rape, Kellett treated all accusations made against the men as truth, and coached the accusers through the process. After their accusations were proven false, the female accusers were not named and continued to live in obscurity. The prosecutors acted with full immunity for their actions.

Army Brigadier Gen. Jeffrey Sinclair had a consensual relationship with his mistress, an Army captain, who broke it off after three-years. Upset that Sinclair wouldn't leave his wife, she accused him of rape and numerous other charges most of which aren't criminal in the civilian world. However, politics dictate extraordinary attention in military situations including court-martial. Facing a penalty of 15 years in prison, dismissal from the Army and inclusion on the sex-offender registry, Sinclair pleaded guilty to lesser charges, and was probably reduced in rank and pension.

Police officers have been victims of false accusations by women they arrested; in Minneapolis, a woman filed rape charges against two. Fortunately, high tech equipment exonerated them. After a GPS device in the squad car showed it moving and at a different location at the time alleged and a medical exam showed no evidence of rape, she was charged with filing a false report. Feminists were apoplectic.

Persons who knowingly make false allegations are almost never subject to legal sanctions. The Washington State Supreme Court ruled that an order restraining an ex-wife from making false allegations is unconstitutional. [188] Casey Gwinn, a San Diego prosecutor and national authority on domestic violence, admits, "If we prosecuted everybody for perjury that gets on the witness stand and changes their story, everybody would go to jail." [189] Check out the Amazon book Arrest-Proof Yourself, especially chapter 22, titled "When Girls Tell a Tale That Sends You to Jail."

Liars *have* been punished: To cover an indiscretion, New Yorker Biurny Peguero Gonzalez falsely accused William McCaffrey of rape, sending him to prison for nearly four years. Later she recanted her story after new DNA evidence proved she'd been lying. Manhattan Supreme Court Justice Charles Solomon said, "What happened in this case is one of the worst things that can possibly happen in our criminal-justice system," as he sentenced her to one to three years for perjury.

U of Minn. Law School professor, Francesco Parisi, won a nearly $1.2 million defamation case in Hennepin County against former lover, Morgan Wright who had falsely accused him of rape.

Some haven't been punished: In 1955 in Tallahatchie county Mississippi, a white girl, Carolyn Donham, claimed Emmet Till made sexual advances toward her and grabbed her hand. The allegation was evidently untrue; however, the claim inspired the brutal murder of Till. His mutilated body was found in the Tallahatchie River. Now, a book by author and historian Timothy B. Tyson a Duke University scholar The Blood of Emmett Till says Donham told him a decade ago in an interview that she was not telling the truth with her claims of sexual advances. Till's cousins, Wheeler Parker and Deborah Watts who witnessed the incident, also denied the allegation, though Parker admitted Till did whistle. Donham's first husband and his half-brother were acquitted of murder in the killing, but both subsequently claimed responsibility in a paid magazine interview. At age 83, Carolyn Donham lived in Raleigh, N.C.

I'm aware there are dangerous, lying men, possibly as many as there are dangerous, lying women. However, this book is intended to "save the males." Examples of anti-male prejudice in crime could fill many books this size. If the prevailing atmosphere were unusual, the men's movement would have less reason to concern itself with unfairness and could stick to its original concerns about discrimination in divorce. But such outrages are happening in courts across the land every day.

The *Partner Abuse State of Knowledge Project* (PASK), comprising almost 2,700 pages of information including tables, is by far the most definitive study on the subject. Its purpose is to bring sound scientific methods to the field of DV research. The Law Offices of Michael S. Discioarro, has opened a website to assist those falsely accused of domestic violence. A student organization, SAVE (Stop Abusive and Violent Environments), was formed to defend against false sexual accusations.

The Collegiate Atmosphere
Consensual and perhaps non-consensual trysts

Background: Title IX is a 1972 federal law that has spawned the misnamed Offices of Equal Opportunity and Affirmative Action at colleges throughout the nation. These inventions have literally made federal cases of alleged campus "rapes."

Former President Obama falsely claimed, "An estimated one in five women has been sexually assaulted during her college years." In a 2011 "Dear Colleague letter" the Obama administration threatened to cut off funding to a college or university that the Office of Civil Rights determined was unable or unwilling to enforce that administration's interpretation of Title IX. The letter recommended schools provide "holistic and comprehensive victim services" (counseling, etc.) to accusers, and stipulated that colleges must apply a "preponderance of the evidence" standard to its proceedings rather than the higher "clear and convincing" standard or even the highest "beyond a reasonable doubt" standard used in criminal cases.

Sexual assault policy at many schools has become downright ferocious, inverting the principle of "innocent until proven guilty." College campus kangaroo courts considering allegations of, and determining punishments for, rape — or what is often defined as rape — are usually utterly devoid of due process. Traditional defenses are prohibited under the curious authority of Title IX and the Education Department's Office of Civil Rights. Such considerations are motivated by the prospect of funding under ever-increasing governmental control

In December 2013, Amherst College imposed its first major sanction under a new get-tough sexual misconduct policy, expelling a 21-year-old senior after a disciplinary board concluded that he had forced a female classmate to perform oral sex during an alcohol-infused encounter nearly two years earlier. The senior said he had blacked out and doesn't remember the events. Four months later the expelled student presented new evidence in his defense — text messages the woman sent, one admitting she had initiated the incident, and another inviting the alleged perpetrator for a repeat performance which resulted in another sexual encounter. When presented with said evidence Amherst declined to revisit its decision to expel the student, whereupon the expelled student filed a lawsuit in US District Court in Springfield, Mass. No further information. [190]

In November 2014, catering to the habitually offended crowd, *Rolling Stone* published a made-up story titled "A Rape on Campus" by Sabrina Rubin Erdely, which described a brutal gang rape of a woman named Jackie at a University of Virginia fraternity house; and the school's alleged indifference to other instances of alleged sexual assaults. Rape activists on campus supported the allegations. The story generated worldwide headlines; but later fell apart, inasmuch as no one was ever charged or interrogated. *Rolling Stone* apologized for its participation in the farce. [191] Phi Kappa Psi, the fraternity at the center of the article, and three members have sued *Rolling Stone* over the hyped-up story.

Occidental College is a small college in Los Angeles with a feminist faculty and administrators (Barack Obama is a former student). A drunk freshman boy (John Doe) met a drunk freshman girl (Jane Doe) in the school's dorm. Neither knows who initiated the sex, but she asked him if he had a condom, and proceeded to perform oral sex on him. [fn17] Subsequently, perhaps somewhat troubled by the incident, Jane discussed the matter with two radical lesbian professors, admitting consent and saying "it didn't feel like rape." During discussions, Professor Danielle Dirks told Jane that John fit the profile of other rapists. Evidently Gloria Allred was a legal advisor to Dirks. Jane then decided she would report the incident to both the campus and criminal authorities. This caused administrators to expel John and make the record available to other colleges. When another college wouldn't admit John, in February 2014, he filed suit with the L. A. Superior Court to ask for a Writ of Mandate (aka "Mandamus"), which would overturn the college's decision and clear John's record on grounds that he didn't receive a fair hearing. John's lawyer then filed a Title IX complaint against Occidental with the Office for Civil Rights in

---

17 Seems like I went to college 60 years too soon

mid-October. The Office of Civil Rights receives many complaints but only commits full investigations to a fraction of them. [192] At this writing there were three John Doe vs. Occidental cases and more on tap.

HBO star Lena Dunham claimed in a book that she was raped by a conservative guy named Barry at Oberlin College. But after publishing the book, Random House disavowed it. [193] Emma Sulkowicz, aka Mattress Girl, walked around the campus of Columbia University carrying a mattress to protest the university's attitude to her alleged on-campus rape by Paul Nungesser. Nungesser was cleared by the university's inquiry into the allegations, but Sulkowicz was allowed to carry her mattress through her graduation ceremony without interference from school officials. Nungesser filed a gender bias lawsuit against Columbia, saying it failed to protect him. The school settled the suit on undisclosed terms. Evidently her stunt was a hoax to publicize a college thesis she wrote. [194]

Kevin Parisi was kicked off Drew University campus in Madison, N.J., accused of forcing a female student to have sex with him. His world collapsed. The school's action stems from a bizarre interpretation of the Title IX provision in the Education Amendments of 1972. After several months Parisi was found "not responsible" in a campus disciplinary proceeding. He is one of at least 30 men who are striking back against campus rules on sexual assault that deny them due process by assuming their guilt. Their ranks have quadrupled since 2011. Another lawsuit alleged 52 rapes in four years by Baylor football players. [195]

The University of Georgia requires consent to be 'imaginative' among other things. A new policy approved by the board of trustees at East Carolina University announced neck rubs could be declared to be sexual battery under their interpretation of Title IX. [196] With fanfare from the Duke Women's Center, Duke University instituted a "sexual misconduct" policy that can render a student guilty of non-consensual sex simply because he or she is considered "powerful" on campus.

A Hofstra University student alleged she was gang raped by five men inside a dormitory bathroom. Four of the accused were placed under arrest, and incarcerated until the accuser admitted to making the entire story up. All charges were dismissed; however, as of this writing, Nassau County D.A. Kathleen Rice has not decided whether to press charges against the woman. [197]

See *The Campus Rape Frenzy: The Attack on Due Process at America's Universities*. [198] This atmosphere, write Weiss and Young, "make(s) it easier to send someone to jail for failing to get an explicit nod of consent from an apparently willing partner before engaging in sex." California Senate bill, SB 967 would have colleges and universities adopt a standard of unambiguous consent among students engaging in sexual activity under a proposal passed by state lawmakers. Such policies would be required at all public colleges and other institutions that receive state funds for student aid. Students engaging in sexual activity would first need "affirmative consent" from both parties. [199] Reformers are in favor of replacing the old standard of "no" means no with "yes means yes."

Apple made available a consensual sex app "Good2Go" that prompted those considering sex to record their willingness. Later, Apple pulled that app off the market. Years earlier, the National Center for Men in New York and Dr. Roy Schenk devised "consensual sex contracts" to protect men from women who after having consensual sex decide to charge their partners with rape. The *Weekly Standard* magazine printed a comprehensive article on this subject. [200]

Believing that too many students have been treated unfairly as colleges complied with Obama's policy on handling sexual assault, President Bush's Education Secretary Betsy DeVos, re-appointed by President Trump, accused the prior administration of creating kangaroo courts by weaponizing guidelines that prod colleges and universities to aggressively investigate sexual assaults with a policy that schools must use a standard known as "preponderance of evidence" when weighing sexual misconduct cases. She vowed to replace the "failed system" of campus sexual assault enforcement to ensure fairness for both victims and the accused.

On November 16, 2018, DeVos proposed a major overhaul to the way colleges and universities handle sexual misconduct complaints, adding protections for students accused of assault and harassment and narrowing which cases schools would be required to investigate. Her plan would scale back important Obama administration rules while adding mandates that could reshape the school disciplinary systems that schools developed. Under the new plan, colleges would have to investigate complaints only if the alleged incident occurred on campus or in other areas overseen by the school, and only if it was reported to certain officials. By contrast, former rules required colleges to review all student complaints, regardless of their location or how they came to the school's attention. DeVos's overhaul adds several provisions supported by groups that represent students accused of sexual misconduct. Chief among them, it says accused students must be able to cross-examine their accusers, although it would be done through a representative to avoid personal confrontations. The proposal effectively tells schools how to apply Title IX. Not curiously, the left wing ACLU opposed the De Vos reforms.

Students Defending Students is a subsidiary of the Ohio University Student Senate. They say, "We are dedicated to upholding students' rights and advising students through the process of Ohio University

Community Standards and Student Responsibility." Occasionally justice prevails: Nikki Yovino got a year in prison, for falsely reporting that she was raped by two football players at Sacred Heart University. Her target, Malik St. Hilaire, lost his scholarship and dream of continuing to play football and is in debt $30,000. [201]

Horny athletes and camp followers

In April of 2006, the Duke University Lacrosse team hired Crystal Gail Magnum, a stripper with a criminal record, to appear at a team party. Drunk, she passed out and falsely accused several partygoers of raping her. In line with their policy of concealing the names of even false accusers of rape, most of the mainstream media refused to publish her name until much later.

An overeager and politically ambitious prosecutor, Mike Nifong required the entire 46 Duke team members to submit to DNA testing, an action which violated hell out of Constitutional prohibitions against self-incrimination as well as of state statutes. Nifong was obviously trying to force a plea bargain. Later documents proved he and police withheld hordes of exculpatory evidence in seeking indictments. [202] Meanwhile, the coach was fired for his innocent connection. Though all DNA tests proved negative, and that Mangum had bedded others just before, a racist mob demanded Grand Jury indictments of the all-white team, and got two. Reminiscent of the Tawana Brawley fiasco, professional black charlatans Jessie Jackson and Al Sharpton [fn18] joined left-leaning Duke Professors righteously condemning the boys.

Despite all the chatter, over a year later on April 11, 2007, charges against the boys were dropped. Mangum was not tried because "She thought it might have happened." Ann Coulter said, "Stripper lied; white boys fried." Whoopi Goldberg made sense in demanding Al Sharpton apologize to the players (Whoopee!).

The situation was so flagrant the North Carolina Bar Assn. charged Nifong with violating a rule requiring prosecutors to "refrain from making extrajudicial comments that have a substantial likelihood of heightening public condemnation of the accused," and with engaging in conduct involving dishonesty, fraud, deceit or misrepresentation and conduct prejudicial to the administration of justice. The North Carolina Attorney General called him a "rouge prosecutor." Nifong was disbarred after being found guilty of a battery of ethics violations in the matter. [203] Subsequently, he filed for bankruptcy. Unfortunately, most other prosecutors get away with it.

Dorothy Rabinowitz, in the Wall Street Journal wrote:

> There is little that is new or strange about Nifong. We have seen the likes of this district attorney, uninterested in proofs of innocence, willing

---

[18] Sharpton was "ordained" a preacher at age nine or ten.

to suppress any found, many times in the busy army of prosecutors claiming to have found evidence of rampant child abuse in nursery schools and other child-care centers around the country in the 1980s and throughout most of the '90s.

If the lads did not have the collective resources to fight this travesty, they might now be in the jailed company of so many other falsely accused males. The players sued the University, the city of Durham and several school and police officials for fraud, abuse and breach of duty for supporting the prosecution. I hope they include Mangum (in case she ever comes into money), the newspapers, TV stations and anyone else involved. Subsequently, Mangum was slapped with a $190,000 defamation lawsuit. In a follow-up to the story, she was arrested on February 17, 2010 on charges of arson, attempted murder of her boyfriend, providing a false identity and resisting arrest. [204] Her victim died from her stab wounds.

Reminiscent of the Duke University lacrosse team scandal, the University of Minnesota jumped aboard the same anti-male bandwagon. A 22-year-old female student attended a party with 10 black players from the football team. Drunk, she had sex (to say the least) with two of them. Others, admittedly as stupid and guilty as she, began to participate and make video recordings of the activity. The recordings showed the woman to be conscious and in control of herself. Sober the following day, she claimed her participation was not altogether consensual, and asked that the players be barred from the stadium because she worked there. The Hennepin County attorney's office twice decided not to press charges against the men for obvious reasons, but did admit that their behavior (not the woman's, of course) was "deplorable." The progressive atmosphere infecting the school dictated that 5 players be suspended, making them ineligible to play against Indiana State, Colorado State and Penn State. As usual, only the males were named in published reports while the woman involved was widely referred to as "the victim." Later — just prior to the Holiday Bowl game in San Diego, California — the school's Office for Equal Opportunity and Affirmative Action suspended 10 of the players. One of them "was found to have violated the student conduct code for being present outside the bedroom at the time." [205] Yet no penalty seems to have been assessed against the woman who was IN the bedroom.

Justifiably angered by the situation, the entire team refused to engage in any athletic activities until the suspensions were lifted. Tracy Claeys, the team's good coach was severely criticized for supporting the boycott and demanding due process. Later, the team suspended the boycott, played the game short-staffed, and presented Claeys with an impressive win despite being 10 point under-dogs. The University fired Claeys (necessarily including his entire staff) costing the school a cool $5 million. He understandably vowed never to set foot on school grounds again. After investigation, the university decided to "support the student and protect her right to privacy." [206] Four of the players were expelled and two suspended. The players sued the school in U.S. District Court, alleging the U. denied them due process and discriminated against them on the basis of race and sex. They demanded compensatory damages and that the expelled players be reinstated with clean discipline records. Plaintiffs' attorney David Madgett said that President Eric Kaler and Title IX Coordinator Tina Marisam saw an opportunity to show what they were doing to address sexual violence on campus. These statements are from published reports.

A female student at the Naval Academy went to a party, got drunk and had sex with 2 or 3 (she isn't sure) Navy football players. When she found out later about the sex, she complained, resulting in court-martial for the players, but not for her. [207]

A UNC-Chapel Hill wrestling coach C.D. Mock was critical on social media of how universities handle sexual assault allegations that do not go through the courts is out of a job. After 12 seasons as head coach of the UNC wrestling program, Mock was "relieved of his duties" by UNC athletics director Bubba Cunningham. Mock had questioned whether the due-process rights of the men accused were being trampled. [208] Mike Poplardo, an economics teacher at Fox Lane High School in Bedford, New York showed his students a Fox News documentary titled *The Truth about Sex and College* as part of a lesson plan to prepare them for college. He said, "All people (male and female) are at risk of being a victim of sexual violence and are at risk of being accused of sexual violence." He was suspended for telling the truth.

Camp followers may be even more prevalent in professional sports. Many years ago I saw a woman grab a Minnesota Vikings coach by the crotch in the MSP airport terminal building as the team returned from winning a distant game.

Prostitution

Prostitution is another example of the double standard. Logically, one might expect the prostitute to be a more socially undesirable creature than her customer. Evidently not, it is the only transgression in which the buyers of an illegal commodity are considered more culpable than the sellers — because they are male. Robert Kraft, billionaire owner of the New England Patriots, faced charges of soliciting a prostitute at a shopping-center massage parlor in Florida. As usual, there was no mention of charges against the prostitute. Extending the logic of this nonsense would make buyers of stolen goods and of drugs as culpable as the fences and pushers. Canada makes it legal to sell sex but not to buy it.

In a 15-month study, men were defendants in 63 percent of prostitution cases prosecuted by the St. Paul, Minnesota City Attorney's Office. [209] The Minneapolis city attorney's office brought prostitution charges against a male pimp, a former assistant county attorney, and male "clients," but declined to charge the prostitutes. [210] Several years ago the Minneapolis police dept. posted pictures of prostitutes' customers on the internet (johnspics.org), but not pictures of the prostitutes; it might have embarrassed them. North Dakota cops arrested "Johns" in oil field areas, but not the prostitutes. [211] In Sweden. clients of prostitutes are prosecuted, but prostitutes are not. Ditto with San Francisco. Young prostitutes were put up in shelters in Minnesota, and called "victims." Ponder this convoluted logic: years ago, Minnesota prostitution laws were held unconstitutional by Judges Ledbodott and Riley because they discriminate against women. Yet other state laws which explicitly punished only males for non-support have been held to be constitutional. [212]

Entrapment

Police officers around the country have dressed as women or used policewomen to entrap men, then arrested those who responded. Entrapment defenses may work for would-be terrorists, but not for men caught in prostitution stings. It might be interesting to attempt citizen's arrests of policewomen shills for soliciting. Manatee County Florida prosecutors charged two 93-year-old men with soliciting an undercover officer during prostitution stings. [213] Migod, they should have been given awards!

In May of 2007, a woman, sunbathing topless in Berliner Park in Columbus Ohio, flirted with firefighter Robin Garrison. In response, Garrison dropped his pants to expose himself. Arrested, he was fined and sentenced to probation. The unnamed (of course) sunbather was not charged. [214] In an undated web article on *Lew Rockwell.com*, respected journalist Paul Craig Roberts said of the incident:

Take heed, ye red-blooded American males. The police are operating a new sting designed to destroy your life. The police are planting attractive women half-naked in parks. They entice passing males, engage them in conversation, lay back, spread their legs and rest their feet on the men's shoulders. After being as friendly and suggestive as possible, they ask to see your penis. Don't show it to them. You are being filmed by police. If you show your penis, you will be arrested as a pervert.

Revenge Porn. Pictures of ex-girlfriends naked and/or having sex are being uploaded onto 'revenge porn' websites by former boyfriends, causing 26 states to enact Revenge Porn Laws (against the men). Timothy James Brandt's girlfriend allowed him to take a photo of her topless. After a breakup, Brandt posted the photo on his Facebook account, resulting in his being charged with a felony

Harassment Claims

Practically anything a man does in relating to women — even simple flirting — can be considered sexual harassment, and can get him in big trouble. There has been an epidemic of men railroaded by "huntresses" with the power to ruin careers for pointing fingers at them. A gullible majority populace, is eager to accept accusations, however dubious, of women against men. Sheer repetition of allegations are often considered to be proof of guilt.

Women have filed preposterous claims and won outlandish court awards or settlements for minor insults or leers. Due process is seldom extended to the accused. Overheard jokes and private pin-ups have constituted harassment. A man who told two women they were extremely beautiful was arrested on charges of harassment. Denver Police said 32-year-old Jeff John Hergert approached the women and "expressed interest in them." He told each woman that she was extremely beautiful and that she should consider modeling. Hergert was held on two counts of harassment with a $10,000 bond. [215] CNN's Erin Burnett publically condemned a guy who sent nude pictures of a young girl over the internet, but she did not condemn the girl who posed for the pictures.

Feminist attorney Lisa Bloom tried to line up big paydays for women who were willing to accuse President Trump of sexual misconduct during the final months of the 2016 election, according to an explosive report. [216]

" THOSE OTHER WOMEN ARE SUING YOU FOR SEXUAL HARRASSMENT! I'M SUING YOU FOR DECRIMINATION !"

The hype began with Lin Farley's 1978 book, Sexual Shakedown: The Sexual Harassment of Women on the Job. Later the book Sexual Harassment of Working Women (1979) by Catharine MacKinnon defined sexual harassment as a legal issue. Ellison v. Brady introduced the "reasonable woman" standard into law. Conduct was no longer analyzed from the perspective of a "reasonable person," but of a "reasonable woman," from the perspective of the complainant, not of the defendant. The grievance industry went into high gear.

In 1991 Anita Hill accused the patently decent Clarence Thomas of talking dirty to her quite evidently hoping to deprive him of a slot on the Supreme Court. Toward the end of 2017 such accusations have exploded, some allegedly occurring very many years before. To go into detail on them would take too much space here; news reports have covered them only too well. A great deal of piling on and hypocritical outrage occurred. Pastor Franklin Raddish of the Capitol Hill Independent Baptist Ministries, a nationwide church, told AL.com that the spate of accusations against men in politics, Hollywood and elsewhere constituted a "war on men."

A harassment policy proposed for the Minnesota legislature provides, "Supervisors will be directed to "take a broad view of what may be harassment" and "err on the side of promptly reporting" any complaint they receive. Everyone is advised "you should report any concern," even if you were just a bystander or witness. [217]

Ivanka Trump said there should be a special place in Hell for people who prey on children (referring to older men relating to young girls). I suggest that there should be a special place in Hell for false accusers and those who give them credence. It is this writer's opinion that speculation is unreliable, and that allegations MUST be proven and immediately reported, or else they probably should be considered false.

Simple attraction is not harassment or abuse, however modern political life may make it necessary for men to suppress natural instincts in order to evade criticism. One must always be careful lest some innocent remark be misconstrued. The bar for social shunning has been lowered to the point where men are now afraid to shake a woman's hand. Granted, some allegations may be wholly or partially true. It can be hard to distinguish between actual victims and enablers. Many encounters are probably consensual or mutual. [fn19] Both sexes instinctively know when a person of the opposite sex is interested in them. Men will very seldom make advances to women unless they are, or seem to be, receptive.

In March of 2020, the ailing 67-year-old movie mogul Harvey Weinstein was sentenced to 23 years, essentially a life sentence for a man of his age, for what some accusers have called rape. Aspiring actresses dive into the beds of guy's like Weinstein, or at least lead them on. Most such so-called "victims" probably have naively shown receptivity or not shown objection. Powerful men like them are sorely tempted in the sexual area by the same juices and motivations that made them powerful. This is not to excuse boorish behavior, but maybe to explain it. Many powerful men ARE oversexed, causing masses of women to initiate complaints; no doubt some are justified, while others

---

[19] As much as I dislike defending Al Franken, I do wonder why Leeann Tweeden had her mouth open during a stage kiss rehearsal, then years later complained that he had thrust his tongue into her mouth.

just aspire to cash in. Professional feminists need Harvey Weinstein types for business purposes.

"OFFICER, THAT MAN IS STARING AT ME !"

After dressing for attention, some women scream bloody murder when the wrong men pay attention. If one is curiously attired, or unattired, it follows one is going to be the object of curiosity. For that reason, flirtatious women who go about in public only partially clothed, whether or not in "style," have little cause to complain about yobos leering after them, or unwanted sexual advances, even vigorous ones. A Toronto police officer's flippant comment that women should avoid dressing like tarts to avoid being raped sparked an international series of protests known as SlutWalks, the heterosexual equivalent of "gay pride" parades. Tennis star Serena Williams was excoriated for truthfully saying a 16-year-old rape "victim" "shouldn't have put herself in that position." Stage icon Angela Lansbury said, "We have to own up to the fact that women, since time immemorial, have gone out of their way to make themselves attractive; and unfortunately it has backfired on us. When John Kasich advised women to avoid booze parties, a Democrat National Committee flack accused him of blaming victims.

A "study" by the American Association of University Women found that "nearly two-thirds of college students experience sexual harassment at some point during college." The AAUW's definition of sexual harassment is, "unwanted or unwelcome sexual behavior that interferes with your life." Guidelines from the Justice Department and the Education Department's Office for Civil Rights on how colleges should handle sexual harassment cases are even more insane: including verbal conduct, propositions, spreading rumors, etc. It could be dangerous to even ask for a date. [218]

The Appalachian State University Women's Center website claims that 'telling racist, sexist, homophobic jokes that demean people because of their protected class membership' is sexual harassment." In an e-mail to feminists there, Writer Mike S. Adams hoisted them thusly: "According to the examples of sexual harassment listed on your website, you have clearly sexually harassed me and, in fact, every other man who has logged on…" Adams — probably all of us — could sue!

A University of New Hampshire school flyer was distributed indicating women students gained 10 to 15 pounds in their 1st year. In response, student Timothy Garneau posted a flyer urging overweight freshwomen to lose weight by walking up stairs instead of using the elevator. For his troubles, Garneau was evicted from his dormitory, forced to undergo psychological counseling and write a 3,000 word paper reflection about the counseling. The penalties were reduced somewhat after Garneau contacted the Foundation for Individual Rights in Education (FIRE). [219]

A University of Minnesota graduate student Stephanie Jenkins' accused a colleague, U.S. Fish and Wildlife scientist Ted Swem, of sexual harassment. Evidently her case was very weak, inasmuch as she was awarded just one dollar. However, U.S. District Judge John Tunheim ordered Swem to pay $305,000 in fees to attorneys.

In Nottinghamshire England incidents like harassment, verbal abuse and taking photos without consent are considered gender-based hate crime, and female parliamentarians demand extension of the policy throughout the country.

A step toward sanity in workplace harassment charges occurred when the U.S. Supreme Court ruled in Pennsylvania State Police v. Suders, "It is a valid defense for employers to demonstrate that a complainant failed to use whatever reasonable system existed for the reporting of sexual harassment." A poster appeared in the cubicle of a female Nortel engineer: "In this cubicle, sexual harassment will not be reported, but it will be graded." That gal had a sense of humor.

In the military

Numerous complaints of sexual harassment in the military are occurring. The climate has gotten so crazy that sailors talking like sailors in the presence of delicate female navy personnel ears is a court martial offense, as Navy Lt. Bryan Black discovered. Black used "salty language" in the presence of female midshipmen, and immediately apologized. That did not appease "fire-breathing feminist" lieutenant commander Shelly Whisenhant, who conducted her own investigation, and intimidated the U.S. Naval Academy into ordering a court-martial for Black. Militarycorruption.com reports that Black went unpunished, thanks to Rear Admiral Terrence McKnight, the Commandant of the Naval District of Washington. In another case, even though an investigating officer recommended only administrative action, the U.S. Naval Academy ordered a court-martial for a faculty member who made a "crude" remark in the presence of female midshipmen (In other words, talking like a sailor).

Consider the "Tail hook" incident. Horny women cavorting with horny Navy fliers at a drinking party, like strippers performing before athletic young bucks, should know exactly what to expect. Such is to be expected of testosterone-driven (thankfully) troops. In September 2011, former Secretary of the Navy John Lehman, bitingly accused Navy officials of sinking the storied naval air branch into a sea of political correctness over the Tail hook issue. [220]

The General Accounting Office, now the Government Accountability Office, in the early 1990s and the Service Academy *2005 Sexual Harassment and Assault Survey* listed behaviors that amount to sexual harassment: derogatory comments, jokes or nicknames, comments that standards have been lowered, comments that women did not belong, offensive posters, signs, graffiti or T-shirts, derogatory letters or messages, mocking gestures, whistles or catcalls, unwanted horseplay or hijinks, unwanted pressure for dates and unwanted sexual advances, offensive remarks about appearance, body or sexual activities, gestures or body language of a sexual nature that embarrass or offend, offensive sexist remarks; unwanted attempts to establish a romantic sexual relationship, continued requests for dates, drinks.

The military has become so soft [221] and politically correct now that only atheists, Muslims and homosexuals are protected. If we eliminate alpha males in the military let's hope we don't get into another war.

CIA officer Robert Baer's memoir, *See No Evil*, illustrates one of the idiocies. When he asked for Farsi speakers in Afghanistan, he was offered a sexual harassment team instead. During Hurricane Katrina, Indiana firemen went to Atlanta to rescue victims. Federal bureaucrats instructed them to attend courses on sexual harassment and equal employment opportunity — then hand out flyers.

Treatment of women

On the other hand, being female is obviously an extenuating circumstance in consideration of crime punishment. Where women are at fault there is a great closing of eyes and opening of hearts —legality be damned. Females are favored from decision to arrest, to amount of bail required, to guilt or innocence in judgment, to severity of sentence, to physical conditions of imprisonment, to release on parole. Women are charged fewer times than men for violent crime, convicted less when guilty of the same crimes as men, and are given shorter sentences or simply receive probation. Judges are reluctant to jail women; while men are arrested 4 times as often, they are imprisoned 24 times as often. Crying is an effective defense; it works as well with judges as it does with men in general.

Having a license to kill, women can murder men and often receive less punishment than men who cannot pay their alimony or who urinate in the street. Acquittal, token punishment or forgiveness of them signals open season on men. Women who kill husbands premeditate over half of the domestic murders they commit, and yet half of them claim self-defense quite successfully. Even while not in immanent and immediate danger, they need only murmur "brutality" and hearts bleed. No rebuttal is possible; the victim is dead. Such women are convicted of between 15 and 26 percent of the homicides in this country, but suffer less than 1 percent of the executions, proportionately 50 times less than men in relation to their murder conviction rate. They serve an average of 6.2 years in prison, while men who kill their wives serve an average of 17.5 years in prison. It happens so often the Men's Defense Association ceased keeping files on it.

Mary Winkler is a Tennessee woman who fatally shot her preacher husband in the back in March 2006, pulled the phone cord out so he could not call 911, abducted their three children and fled to Orange Beach, Alabama. Despite the well-known gentleness of her dead husband, this murderess was able to sell the jury the usual story about suffering years of verbal and physical abuse. [222] She was released in August 2007 after spending a total of 143 days in jail plus seven months in a Tennessee mental health facility where she was treated for depression and post-traumatic stress disorder. She lost custody of her three children when charged with murder, but regained custody Sept. 19, 2008. [223] 32-year-old Amber Cummings of Belfast, Maine shot and killed her sleeping husband, later claiming "abuse." No mention in the newspapers of her reporting same to police. Chivalrous Judge Jeffrey Hjelm handed her a suspended sentence. [224]

Barbara Sheehan of Queens, New York killed her husband, using two guns to fire 11 bullets inside the couple's home, and claimed the "Battered Woman" defense. New York's self-defense law justifies the use of lethal force when a threat to a person's life is deemed immediate. Mr. Sheehan had been shaving before he was killed, his body found on the bathroom floor — the faucet still running. Nevertheless, on October 6th, 2011 a jury acquitted Barbara of murder. [225]

Jilted actress Claudine Longet, who killed live-in lover Spider Sabitch in 1976 because he found a new girlfriend, was convicted and sentenced to 30 days, the same sentence a young Wisconsin lad served in 1984 for playing hooky, and a Cheyenne, Wyo. boy for violating a local ordinance by fishing with a worm instead of a fly. [226] Cops re-decorated the cell for her.

Christine Spillane severely stabbed Josh Denenberg, of York, Pennsylvania with a kitchen knife while he was holding their baby. Not calling it domestic violence, police charged her with aggravated battery. Judge JoAnn Teyral let her out of jail on $5,000 bond and issued an order of no contact against her. Jill Ann Miller-Cooper of Farmington, Minnesota rammed her husband with her car, drove a half mile with him clinging to the hood, and suddenly stopped, throwing him to the road where he suffered a fractured knee. The county attorney's office filed a criminal complaint against Miller-Cooper, but refused to term it "domestic violence."

According to the Department of Justice's Office on Violence Against Women (OVW), [227] such incidents are not considered domestic violence —

because only males can commit that crime, just as blacks cannot be guilty of racially motivated hate crimes. An OVW briefing used the catch-phrase "violence against women" four times, but that office does not recognize violence against men.

According to the prevailing vision, which manifests itself regularly in Canadian family courts, it is understood that when female allegations of domestic violence color the narrative, even if unsupported by evidence, social-justice considerations may supersede the principle of equality under the law. [228] Nicole Doucet Ryan, a high school teacher in southwestern Nova Scotia, was arrested in March 2008 and charged with soliciting an undercover police officer to kill her husband, Michael Ryan. [229] Eight of the nine Canadian Supreme Court Justices accepted the unproven contention that Doucet "was the victim of a violent, abusive and controlling husband," and that "she believed that he would cause her and their daughter serious bodily harm or death and that she had no safe avenue of escape other than to have him killed."

While drinking, Canadian Mary Lisa Joyce Carrier attacked her boyfriend, with a frying pan. He ran outside, but she grabbed a kitchen knife and stabbed him to death; didn't spend a minute in prison. Judge Tonning (1st name missing) gave her a six-month conditional sentence followed by a year's probation. Tonning admitted that if the sexes were reversed the sentence would not be as light: "More likely (a man) would be incarcerated for a significant period of time," he said. [230] The infamous murderess Jodi Arias who shot her boyfriend, stabbed him 27 times and cut his throat was found guilty of 1st degree murder. Her claims of being an "abused woman" were actually taken seriously. She did not get the death penalty usually applied in such cases due to a female jury holdout and the sympathy normally attaching to attractive women.

Under a new law, British women who kill abusive partners in cold blood could escape a murder conviction if they prove they fear more violence. They will be punished for the lesser offence of manslaughter, sparing them a mandatory life sentence. They must establish only that they were responding to a 'slow burn' of abuse. [231] The BBC informed us that Doris Keningale of Risca, South Wales, in the U.K., stabbed her husband to death with an eight-and-a-half-inch knife blade. She told Judge John Griffith Williams QC, of Cardiff Crown Court that the knife "accidentally entered her husband's chest." The chivalrous jurist sentenced her to three-years of community rehabilitation. On July 5, 2011, in a case that captivated the nation, a patently guilty Casey Anthony was found not guilty of murdering her 2-year-old daughter Caylee, due to a prosecutorial miscalculation.

Andrea Yates and Susan Smith murdered their children by drowning (Yates — five children, Smith — two). They each got one life sentence. Incredibly enough, on January 6, 2005, a 3-judge Appeals Court panel overturned Yates' conviction because the prosecution's psychiatrist was confused regarding an episode of TV's *Law & Order*. A Texas jury later ruled Yates to be not guilty by reason of insanity. Yates was committed by the court to the North Texas State Hospital, Vernon Campus, a high-security mental health facility in Texas where she is currently receiving medical treatment and sharing a cell with another woman who committed filicide. She should be out in a few years, along with Smith (Maybe they are out by now). Both Yates' husband and Smith's ex-husband chivalrously came to their defense; the Stockholm Syndrome?

Two women were not as lucky as Lizzie Borden. A Mississauga, Ontario, Canada woman was convicted of killing her mother and sentenced to 10 years for first-degree murder in the deliberate and planned drowning of her mother in the bathtub. She was let out of prison after 4 years, and allowed to move to a halfway house so she can do online university studies. [232] Sarah Mary Catherine Purcell strangled her disabled mother to death because she was "(expletive) pissed at her." Purcell was sentenced to 30 days in jail followed by 3 years on probation. [233]

Child custody provides an even greater exculpatory benefit to mothers than it does financial benefit; it provides immunity from prosecution. In February 2005, Carisa Ashe, a 34-year-old Atlanta woman who had 8 children by 8 different men, pled guilty to brutally killing her five-week-old daughter. Fulton County District Attorney Paul Howard agreed to a plea bargain that would allow the woman to avoid a murder trial and possible prison sentence if she would agree to be surgically sterilized. Such agreements are not uncommon. [234] Georgians initiated a move to recall Howard from office.

The number of newborn babies murdered by their mothers will never be known. In Canada, Katrina Effert gave birth to a baby boy, strangled the child and threw his body over the fence into a neighbor's yard on April 13, 2005. A jury found Effert guilty of second-degree murder, but the highest court in the province decided that the jury had made a mistake, overturned the conviction and replaced it with a lesser charge of infanticide. She received a three-year suspended sentence by Judge Joanne Veit, who determined that her actions were no different from an abortion. If Effert abides by the court's conditions for the next three years, she will not spend any time in jail.

A Minneapolis day care provider accused of hanging a toddler in her home admitted she acted with intent to kill the 16-month-old boy in her care and to severely injuring three other people the same day. Her excuse was that her husband inflicted physical and emotional abuse on her. Citing 'extreme mental illness,' the judge sentenced her to 10 years' probation.

A Yuba City California woman who drove across a centerline in the Yuba County foothills and collided head-on with a North San Juan motorcyclist, killing him, was sentenced to the two days in jail already served; Amanda Danielle Driggers had trace amounts of marijuana and Vicodin in her system after the accident that killed 51-year-old David Michael Beaver. [235] Heather Hulsey was a drunk driver who collided with and killed Dr. Ronald Shlensky. Superior Court Judge Frank Ochoa recalled Hulsey's sentence of six years and four months in state prison, and instead gave her five years of probation because she is pregnant. [236]

"Reality Show" star Nichole Ritchie was given a mild 4-day sentence for driving under the influence of drugs. She was released after 82 minutes without even getting behind bars. On the same day, another celebrity Lindsay Lohan, charged with seven drunk-driving and cocaine infractions, was sentenced to 1 day in the slammer, a fine and probation. [237] Paris Hilton was released from jail on January 7th, 2007 after serving only three days of a 23-day sentence, evidently because she was "upset" about confinement. The outcry caused subsequent re-confinement. Compare these sentences with the 48 days actor Kiefer Sutherland spent in a California jail for drunk driving.

Heiress Patty Hearst joined the Symbionese Liberation Army in 1974, become a gun-wielding revolutionary called Tania and held up banks. She was sentenced to 35 years imprisonment, later commuted by President Carter to seven years. Hearst was released from prison on February 1, 1979, having served 22 months, and granted full pardon by President Clinton on January 20, 2001. "Sister Soulja," AKA Sara Jane Olson, part of the infamous Weatherman murder gang, caught after being on the lam for 24 years was let off after serving only 6 years of a puny 12-year sentence. Another revolutionary "terrorist," Susan Rosenberg, was pardoned by President Clinton. Bobbi Parker left her family and ran off with escaped convict and murderer Randolph Dial, helping him hide for 10 years. Parker received no penalty, because she was initially coerced.

A Twin Cities woman, Holly-Ann Collins stole her two children from their father after he was awarded custody, and fled to the Netherlands for 14 years. Collins returned after being turned in by a neighbor who saw a FBI poster on her. Hennepin County District Judge Margaret Daly dropped a charge of parental abduction and sentenced her to 40 hours of community service for this felony. The message to divorcing women: disregard the law, alienate your children from the father, make allegations of abuse, get the support of domestic abuse advocacy groups, and hide out. In the end, you will win.

Sandra Bathke robbed an Elysian, Minn. Bank to the tune of $7,800. She plea-bargained for 15 years' probation and a fine of $1,500. [238] In March of '06, U.S. Representative Cynthia McKinney (D. Ga.) slugged a House of Representatives guard who had asked her for her credentials, then accused him of assaulting *her* because she's a black female. A chivalrous Grand Jury declined to indict her.

Thirty-five-year-old Mary Kay Letourneau was sentenced to serve six months in county jail and enroll in a three-year sex offender treatment program for repeated sex with a 13-year-old boy, and released early for "good behavior." Twenty-five-year-old "Playboy pretty" Tampa Florida schoolteacher Debra Lafave pleaded guilty to repeated instances of sex with a 14-year old boy. Her lawyer argued that she was too pretty to go to jail. Charges were dropped when the boy refused to testify. [239] Forty-three-year-old Pamela Diehl-Moore, a middle school teacher, had sex with a 13-year-old male student. New Jersey Superior Court Judge Bruce A. Gaeta slapped Diehl-Moore's hand with five years of probation, and all but suggested that sentence was too harsh. In a more recent case, U.S. District Judge J. Thomas Marten in Kansas also questioned whether sex with kids (meaning boys) was really bad. [240] Thirty-three-year-old Rebecca L. Noonan, the girls soccer coach for Champlin Park Minnesota High School plead guilty to fourth-degree criminal sexual conduct for having intercourse with a 13-year-old boy. Her sentence included a "stay of adjudication," meaning her case will be dismissed if she meets all requirements demanded of her while on supervised probation for up to 10 years. [241] Dozens of these 'pederastette' teachers are listed at website http://www.wnd.com/?pageId=39783. We could almost fill a book with such as them.

In Omaha, one mother had sex with her 15-year-old son on a nightly basis. She lost custody, but news reports mentioned nothing about jail time [242] It seems the boy personifies a common ghetto expression that starts with an M and ends with a R).

In 1997, female B52 pilot Kelly Flinn committed adultery with the husband of an enlisted woman, lied to her superiors and refused to follow orders. She was allowed to resign from the Air Force instead of being court-marshaled as would have been the fate of any male officer.

A 17-year-old Little Falls, Minn. girl was texting while driving. She ran a red light, hitting a van carrying Charles Maurer of Becker and his daughter Cassy, killing both. Her sentence? Probation and 240 hours of community service. [243]

The "Pain-capable Unborn Child protection Act" banning abortions after 20 weeks, law in 13 states, provides severe penalties for abortionists (mostly male), but not for the parties equally responsible (the mothers). Women who damage their babies during pregnancy by fouling their bodies with poisons (nicotine, alcohol, dope, etc.) are seldom prosecuted. This happens to about one fifth of babies born in West Virginia. [244]

Oxford University student Lavinia Woodward stabbed an ex-boyfriend in a drug-fueled frenzy (and stripped naked with Oxford pals in support of the university's LGBTQ society). At court, she wept and dabbed her eyes with a tissue, complaining she can't go clubbing without being recognized. Judge Ian Pringle said he would not jail her for the stabbing because a custodial sentence may be "too severe" and could ruin her medical career. Her family told her to keep her "head held high." She retreated to her family's $2 million villa near Milan. [245]

At one university, a slut had consensual sex with a group of football players, then claimed innocence because she was too drunk to give consent. Let some male driver claim that defense if he kills a woman while drunk. BTW, the football players were severely punished. These camp followers are a pretty disgusting lot.

Sometimes these types get what is coming to them: Nikki Yovino got a year in prison, for falsely reporting that she was raped by two football players at Sacred Heart University. Her target, Malik St. Hilaire, lost his scholarship and dream of continuing to play football and is in debt $30,000. [246]

Girls on Spring Break have a proclivity to bare their breasts at parties. TV producer Joe Francis photographs them with their permission. He was jailed in Panama City, Florida — not the girls. A topless woman was arrested for indecent exposure at a Twin Cities soccer game, but the charge was dismissed. [247]

Treatment of both sexes in similar situations
Women do the crime; men do the time

Considering the intense media coverage of male sexual predators victimizing female children, one might expect a stiff prison term, accompanied by a withering rebuke when the sexes are reversed. Not so. The contrast in punishment may be most apparent where defendants of different sexes were in identical or similar situations. Some of these "reasonings" rise to the level of Cirque du Soleil contortions.

If a man is caught looking into a home in which a woman is undressing, he will be arrested for voyeurism. If a woman is looking, again the man will be arrested, this time for indecent exposure. It happened; the Mississippi Supreme Court rationalized the verdict, as did courts in Delaware County Pennsylvania and Portsmouth, Virginia.

14-year-old, Caril Fugate and her 19-year-old boyfriend, Charlie Starkweather, went on a killing spree in Nebraska and Wyoming in 1957-58 that claimed the lives of Fugate's mother, stepfather, 2-year-old sister and eight others. Starkweather was executed, while Fugate left prison in 1976. [248]

In October of 2005, Lynndie England of Abu Ghraib fame was sentenced to 3 years for mistreating prisoners, and served a year and a half. Her equally guilty male co-operative Pvt. Charles Graner Jr. was sentenced to 10 years in Leavenworth.

In June 26, 2001, Kari Engholm left her baby daughter in a car when temperatures were near 90 degrees. The girl died from overheating. In December that year, Judge Paul Huscher claimed Engholm "did not consciously forget about her child" and found her innocent of involuntary manslaughter and neglect, describing the death as a "heartbreaking, tragic accident. The court cannot hold the mother accountable, even for reprehensible conduct." [249]

On March 14, 2004, Antonio Balta, left his daughter Veronika in a sweltering hot car while he worked at a Florida racetrack. She died from the heat. Circuit Judge Ilona Holmes declared Balta's actions "totally callous" and sentenced him to 20 years. [250]

On Aug. 23, 2007, Brenda Nesselroad-Slaby, left her 2-year-old daughter Cecilia strapped into a car seat for about eight hours while she was at work at Glen Este Middle School in Ohio. The child died as temperatures outside reached about 100 degrees. Clermont County Prosecutor Don White said leaving the child in the car for the workday was "a substantial lapse of due care," but it did not meet the definition of reckless conduct necessary for prosecution. He declined to file charges.[251]

Kamilyn Kartchner Hadley caused the death of her infant son by leaving him outside in an oven-like car. The car was parked in the driveway in direct sunlight on a day when outside temperatures ranged from 86 to 89 degrees. Police said the temperature inside the car may have reached 120 degrees. The boy died at a hospital three days later. Police said Hadley was "visiting a friend" while the baby sweltered outside in the sun. District Judge Michael Allphin ordered her to obtain counseling with LDS Family Services.

Jana Gailey left her 18-month-old son Myles Gailey in the back seat of a vehicle after a trip to the grocery store, as temperatures hovered around 80 degrees. Later, Gailey called paramedics who pronounced the boy dead. No charges were filed against Gailey.

In May 2017, Texan Cynthia Marie Randolph left her 2-year-old daughter and 16-month-old son in a hot car to teach the girl a lesson while she went back into the house, smoked marijuana and took a nap for two or three hours. The children died. Randolph was arrested on two counts of causing serious bodily injury to a child. Like Balta she was sentenced to 20 years. I'm taking bets on who gets our sooner.

In battered baby cases, guilty fathers are fined heavily or jailed. Mothers, guilty of more and worse cruelty, are usually put on probation and ordered to get help. In other words, if the father does it, he is a criminal; if the mother does it, she is mentally ill and needs help.

Alba Ingrid Scarpelli, of Germantown, Alabama, was convicted of multiple counts of child abuse for tying up and torturing her 5-year-old stepson, Richard. Her sentence: 18 months on work release. The boy's father, Alan Lee Holmes, merely stood by while girlfriend Scarpelli committed the abuse. Montgomery County Circuit Court Judge DeLawrence Beard sentenced Holmes to eight years in prison. Beard's "justification" — Holmes was the father; he had a "higher duty" to protect his son. Quoth Beard, "You are going to receive a substantially more severe sentence because you were substantially more culpable... You were in a superior position to intervene and stop this." [252] Beard pointed to Holmes's job as a volunteer firefighter and certification as a medical technician as reasons the father should have seen the signs. Misandrist Judge Beard also presided over the Ashe outrage (mentioned earlier in the Treatment of Women section). Feminists did not object that he, in effect, proclaimed men to be more sensible than women.

Joy Anne Schwartz pled guilty of cruelty to a 6-month-old boy whom she bruised and whose wrists she fractured as punishment. She was sentenced to nine days on home monitoring and anger management classes. Contrast that with Minnesota Vikings' Adrian Peterson's punishment at the beginning of this Chapter. [253]

If a man kills an unborn child against the mother's will, he has murdered a human being. If an abortionist does it, it is the mother's "right" and the "fetus" loses human status, even if mostly or completely out. A glaring, example of this is the conviction and life sentence of 18-year-old Gerardo Flores of Lufkin, Texas. His pregnant 16-year-old girlfriend, Erica Basoria, tried unsuccessfully to induce miscarriage then asked Gerardo to kick her in the stomach, causing the death of their twins. Basoria was not charged. [254]

Another example is the murder of Laci Peterson and her unborn son, Connor. Her husband Scott was convicted of killing both — of 1st degree murder of Laci and of 2nd degree murder of Connor. Scott received the death penalty. Yet Laci and an abortionist could have killed Connor without danger of conviction.

In Will County, Illinois, near Chicago, forty-four-year old Fred M. Flynn and his thirty-four-year old wife Rita were convicted of selling their twelve-year-old daughter in 1972 for marriage to a wealthy man for $28,000. Although they both pled guilty to the identical charge, the man got a five-month jail sentence and the wife got probation. In

Texas, a man and woman violated a local ordinance by swimming in the nude; police arrested only the man.

Colo. Judge Stephen Schapanski sentenced Richard and Mayumi Heene, parents of the "Balloon Boy," to jail by for concocting the costly and much-publicized stunt. Richard got 90 Days and Mayumi 20 Days. Ho hum. [255] A man stealing thousands of dollars is a felon. A woman defrauding the welfare department of the same amount is winked at.

Actress Lori Loughlin and her husband Mossimo Giannulli bribed the University of Southern California $500,000 to get their daughters into school as rowing recruits. Loughlin is facing two months in prison and a $150,000 fine. Her husband is facing five months in prison and a $250,000 fine.

Hillary Clinton, General David Petraeus and other military men [256] leaked classified government information. In July 2016 the general got 2 years' probation and a $100,000 fine. Clinton skated. The concept of 'intent' convicted these guys, but did not apply in Clintons' case.

Most of the remainder of this book addresses indirect or tangential connections to misandry.

The Prison System

We have the highest incarceration rate in the world, even higher than strongly authoritarian countries. Senator Jim Webb (D. VA) deplored the fact that the U.S. imprisons far more of its citizens (mostly men) than does the rest of the world, a larger percentage of population than Iran or Syria. This country, inhabited by only 5% of the globe's population, accounts for fully 25% of the world's prisoners, [257] some for just smoking a joint or two. In *Thinking About Crime*, Michael Tonry, a distinguished American law professor and director of Cambridge University's Institute of Criminology, reports that of any country on earth the US has the highest percentage of its population in prison. The US incarceration rate is as much as 12 times higher than that of European countries. Prisons represent our 35th largest state. We have more people in prison than live in Nevada, West Virginia, New Mexico, Nebraska, Maine, Idaho, New Hampshire, Hawaii, Rhode Island, Montana, Delaware, South Dakota, North Dakota, Alaska, Vermont, or Wyoming.

The U.S. prison system is one large Gulag Archipelago, the "tombs of modern society" Chuck Colson called it. It would make Stalin's mustache twitch with envy. The federal system is 40 % over capacity. The prison population is growing 13 times faster than the general population. The U.S. Dept. of Justice states that over 7 million people, one in every 32 adults, were incarcerated in federal or state prisons, local jails or on parole as of December 2005. [258] On 03/02/2009, Pew researchers claimed the number is 7.3 million, or 1 in every 31 U.S. adults, terribly overcrowding the system. Thirty some years ago, the rate was 1 in 77. Most observers fail to notice that a large number of these prisoners are men who cannot pay their alimony/support or have offended women in one manner or another. The inmate population continues rising despite a fall in the crime rate and despite many states' efforts to reduce some sentences, especially for low-level drug offenders. [259] [fn20] These large numbers attest to the blatant indifference toward justice for men, and the haste of prosecutors, judges and juries to convict men.

Incarcerating men is big business. Prisons have to be fed with inmates in order to maintain an industry providing employment for system 'workers.' The term "reformatory" is deceptive. Jailers are seldom interested in rehabilitation or education of prisoners. Perpetuation of jobs is a larger concern. Modern methods of imprisonment and rehabilitation neither precisely punish nor adequately rehabilitate. Few people give a damn about male prisoners. More than 4,300 federal inmates were kept in prison beyond their scheduled release dates from 2,009 to 2,014, some for a year or more. [260] In one study involving thousands of cases, a strong prediction of paroles granted was how long it had been since the judge had eaten.

Conditions in some men's prisons are themselves crimes as great as those committed by the inmates (except for the luxurious new Cook County jail in Chicago). Guards in a Michigan prison watched while mentally ill Timothy Souder thirsted to death. [261] Criminal charges were brought against seven Milwaukee County jail staffers in the dehydration death of Terrill Thomas on April 24, 2016. Souder went without water for seven days. [262]

The prison atmosphere reduces to the lowest common denominator. A Justice Dept. special report revealed that almost one in eight youths reported being sexually assaulted while imprisoned. [263] Although only a sick SOB would want to screw another man, in prison or out, men in jail are more likely to be raped than women on the outside. It is done brutally, often, and sometimes permitted by prison authorities as a means of controlling the prison population — and condoned by the silence of society. One never hears rape crisis center sob sisters decrying male rapes in or out of jail. More umbrage is shown over the treatment of jihadists in Gitmo.

The previously mentioned John Murtari, discussing his prison conditions, said, "I am happy to report the local sheriff is an Equal Opportunity Employer. They have a lot of female guards. They walk through our cage any time, even when we are using the litter box!

---

[20] I am amused by "experts" pretending that addiction is a disease instead of a weakness in order to remove the stigma and lessen the burden on conscience.

They are even there when we are taking a shower." He formed a divorce reform organization. 264

Former NYPD Commissioner Bernie Kerik agreed that incarceration is not appropriate for low level, non-violent offenders, but they are treated the same as violent ones. On the other hand, some prisoners are savages and in need of being caged. Actual sex offenders ought to be isolated and harshly treated; seven states allow castration. I have no objection if the subjects are guilty of something very serious. I would like to see "BTK" killer Dennis Rader subjected to the same tortures he inflicted on his female victims. Same with the sick KKK bastards that brutally murdered poor Emmett Till.

Twelve states don't bother to financially compensate wrongly incarcerated prisoners. 265 Would you believe, we pay Muslim chaplains, unwittingly, to recruit jihadists.

While prison life for men can be "death by a thousand cuts," in contrast women's prisons are more akin to college campuses with TV-equipped, furnished cottages. No male guards are present to observe showering. Imagine the outcry if women prisoners were humiliated as are males. It caused widespread shock when an Ohio woman was forcibly strip-searched as men routinely are. 266 In its 30 years of operation the Minnesota State Women's prison at Shakopee has never had even a fence. Word is that one will be built (It may have been by now).

The Grand Valley Institution for Women, a prison housing medium- and minimum-security inmates in Canada, held a "Women's Spa Day" with pedicures, aromatherapy, and harp serenade on Aug. 21, 2004. Among the almost two dozen inmates at the Spa Day were a woman who killed a child, and a female sex offender. The Correctional Service of Canada defended the activities as a way to teach inmates how to cope with stress and other life lessons. "It's an attempt to make them feel better about themselves," an official said. 267

Laura Pittman, Oklahoma's Deputy Director of female operations has an idea how to save the state money — reduce the number of female inmates. And it's not just her; apparently it is also Michigan's policy to reduce the number of female inmates. As I was writing this, California was considering a program to release more than 4,000 female inmates. 268 Reportedly, La Crosse County Wisconsin intends to let all its female prisoners out of jail. The County Board unanimously approved an alternative jail program whereby the women would go on "electronic home monitoring through 'Justice Sanctions,' and into job counseling, literacy training and other programs," under a $250,000 contract to the YWCA. Later the county will lease or buy a "halfway house" facility in La Crosse where up to 10 women will live "not supervised around the clock."

The Howard League for Penal Reform in the UK gave serious consideration to a proposal to close women's prisons and replace them with small open community custodial units. [269]

Chapter 3. Causes of the War on Men

Women get the best of both worlds; men get the worst. Scientists have created a database called the *Basic Index of Gender Inequality* (BIGI) which deciphers a nation's discrimination. Carried out by the University of Essex and the University of Missouri-Columbia and published in the journal Plos One, the study shows women are better off in more countries than are men. The study, assessing the forms of hardship and discrimination facing men and women, and looking at 6.8 billion people around the world, revealed males have it harder in 91 countries out of 134; women were disadvantaged in only 43. The UK, the US and Australia all discriminate against men more, whereas Italy, Israel and China are harder environments for women. Researchers say this is due to men receiving harsher punishments for the same crime, compulsory military service and more occupational deaths than women.

Law

The famous writer and thinker Dr. Samuel Johnson in the 18th century observed, "Nature has given women so much power that the law has very wisely given them little." That was before the pendulum swung in their favor. Currently, as Blackstone said, "Woman is the favorite of the law." The United States Constitution is the main basis of U.S. law. Article XIV of its amendments provides: "nor shall any state deprive any person of life, liberty, or property without due process of law; nor deny to any person within its jurisdiction the equal protection of the laws." That quaint passage is more honored in the breach than the observance. In a manner that I suspect would astonish the Founders, this basic right has been airbrushed out of the Constitution. There is very little equal treatment or due process for men. Bar associations have sponsored seminars instructing women how to fabricate accusations against men.

A government that would defy the Constitution in so many other ways will defy it also by permitting the denial of equal rights to male citizens. In Turner v. Rogers, 10-10, the U.S. Supreme Court ruled, "the Due Process Clause does not always require the provision of counsel in civil proceedings where incarceration is threatened." New Jersey Family Court Judge Donald Venezia bragged about suspending the Constitution for a male defendant. See the video. [270] He admits he makes up his own rules.

Courts often conjure new rights out of the Constitution. The Equal Rights Amendment sounded like a good concept, and it was; but bad law. It would apply, ratchet-like, in one direction only — to favor women. Most people think it means equal rights for women; in reality, it means special rights for women. In states that previously implemented it, the effect was to eliminate all reasonable distinction between the sexes unless they favored women. Under its rationale, a proposal was made to ban father-son banquets as sexist. Requiring universities to provide athletic budgets for women equivalent to those for men is almost akin to requiring hospitals to provide paternity wards for men (OK, I exaggerate).

A tag-team of liberal extremists and feminists, commencing in Virginia, are joining forces to bring the Equal Rights Amendment (re-titled the "Women's Equality Amendment") back from the grave, making it quite clear that the campaign has more to do with abortion than anything else. Virginia officially became the critical 38th state to ratify the ERA/WEA, clearing the way for likely court fights over whether the measure can be added to the U.S. Constitution. In a bid to revive the ERA/WEA the House approved a measure removing a 1982 deadline for state ratification and reopening the process to amend the Constitution. [271] In opposition, the Justice Department maintains this effort is too late. The Office of Legal Counsel in the Dept. of Justice declared the ERA to be officially dead, saying, "Congress may not revive a proposed Amendment after a deadline for its ratification has expired... This should save girls' sports from ruination by testosterone-advantaged boys, and prevent implementation of co-ed prisons. [272] Should Congress wish to propose the amendment anew it may do so through the same procedures required to propose an amendment in the first instance."

The Spanish Senate was expected to pass a reform to the nation's divorce laws that would require men to contribute as much as their wives to housework and dependent care; nothing included about requiring housewives to have outside jobs.

A federal judge has ruled that a men-only military draft is unconstitutional, but he stopped short of ordering the Selective Service System to register women. That Houston judge sided with a San Diego men's advocacy group that challenged the government's practice of having only men sign up for the draft, citing sex discrimination in violation of the Fifth Amendment's equal protection clause. "This case balances on the tension between the constitutionally enshrined power of Congress to raise armies and the Constitutional mandate that no person be denied the equal protection of the law," wrote U.S. District Judge Gray Miller. Relying on commonsense, this author disagrees with Judge Miller.

Politics

I dislike dragging politics into these matters, but politics have dragged us into them. Politics are easy to criticize, and there is a lot to be critical of. Admittedly, this sub section may seem somewhat irrelevant to the book's title, but politics are relevant because politics often have unfortunate consequences for men and families. John Kenneth Galbraith appraised politics as a choice between "the disastrous and the unpalatable." While conservatism may be the latter to some, liberalism may be the former to all. Grove City philosophy prof. Paul Kengor refers to the left as "Cultural Marxists" preaching on behalf of women, homosexuals, minorities, trans genders and any number of alleged victims of patriarchal white males. Writer Fred Reed criticizes radical conservatives as "Bow wow, bark, woofers." Some of his advice to the U.S. follows: "Impose a literacy test for voting. People too dim to find their way home should not be permitted to influence policies they have never heard of and can't spell. No curriculum containing the word "Studies" should be permitted. Though sometimes over-opinionated, Fred usually make sense, such as, "If we actually wanted to essay democracy in America, which we don't, we would mandate a voting age of twenty-five and require a literacy test — Fifty questions, published in advance. As lagniappe we might demand some minor evidence of good character..."

A major goal of leftists is redistribution of wealth — Robin Hoods taking from those who have, to give to those who have not — i.e. from men to women, from the ambitious to the unambitious — individually and publically. Admiration of mothers, especially single ones, is a new narrative, while our generous welfare state generates, if not mandates, father-deprivation. Income redistribution, in areas even beyond divorce, is inimical to men. In addition to a culture of political correctness, the zeitgeist is seminally opposed to that essence of manhood — rugged individualism. Even the Pope has become a naïve leftist.

It is a cliché of punditry that Republicans are the Daddy Party and Democrats are the collectivist Mommy Party. In his 2005 book It Takes a Family, Republican Presidential candidate Rick Santorum blamed radical feminists for undermining families and for trying to persuade women that they could find fulfillment only in the workplace, saying "The radical feminists succeeded in undermining the traditional family and convincing women that professional accomplishments are the key to happiness." Former Republican presidential candidate Fred Thompson seemed to understand family values better than others. Before the 2008 election, writers Mike McCormick and Glenn Sacks said,

The Democratic National Committee's 'Renewing America's Promise' is bad news for American fathers. The platform's 'Fatherhood' plank put all blame for father absence squarely on men, and promised to 'crack down' on fathers who are behind on their child support. It also promised to ratchet up draconian domestic violence laws.

It is quite evident that rightist politics and politicians are nominally pro-family; therefore, the men's movement has good reason to tend conservative, although some conservatives suffer from the same misandrist instincts as libs. Hoping to garner female votes, even Donald Trump proposed EITC benefits for "stay-at-home mothers," potentially increasing the federal debt hugely.

Women, especially, tend to vote Democrat largely because they prefer to rely on government for support if necessary rather than on a man. This allows throwing husbands out and making them — or government, in the alternative — financially support estranged families. The Republican-led House narrowly passed a sweeping farm bill that would toughen work requirements for food stamp recipients. Democrats unanimously opposed the measure. [273]

Government paid babysitting is high on the left's agenda, as is paid maternity leave. The Center for the American Experiment claims that in 33 states and D.C. infant care is more expensive than college. [274] The St. Paul Minnesota 'Children's Collaborative' recently asked the City Council to make all-day babysitting, disguised as education, available to all 9,000 of the city's 3- and 4-year-olds. Democrat Mayor Melvin Carter is supportive. [275] Recently, Democrats in control of the Minnesota House advocated spending $500 million on public prekindergarten programs, preschool scholarships and the Child Care Assistance Program. [276] I submit that such taxpayer-supported schemes are foolish and that childcare is parents' responsibility, not government's.

In the 2012 elections, President Obama won the votes of 2 out of every 3 unmarried women and 98% of black women age 18-29. Accordingly, that administration was not particularly friendly to men. My guess is that "progressive" voters also chose him to convince themselves and others how open-minded, diversity-tolerant, woke and big-hearted they are. No doubt the same instincts would have worked in favor of Hillary, who played the "woman card" before she ran out of airspeed and altitude. President Trump strongly opposes diversity training in schools and the military.

The British fathers' rights magazine, *Mankind*, informed us that the British Conservative party favored fathers' rights, and the Labour and Liberal parties opposed same. Men of both liberal and conservative parties in the British government planned legislation to grant anonymity to men accused of rape. This commonsense move would protect the huge number of men falsely accused. Women of both parties were outraged, calling the move "deeply disturbing."

False accusations occur in politics as well. The much-publicized witch-hunt connected to Supreme Court nominee Judge Kavanagh was even worse than those befalling Clarence Thomas and Robert Bork. Political motivation behind the farce was preservation of the feminist (therefore anti-male and liberal) 'sacrament' of abortion. The complainant, Christina B. Ford, gave an award-winning act as victim. Fawning praise of her from grandstanding Democrat Senate committee members bordered on sanctification. Later other even less credible women chimed in with Ford. Shortly thereafter, President Trump warned men that they must beware of such false allegations.

Certainly, the U.S. is superior to Cuba in most ways, but not in domestic relations. The Elián Gonzales matter illustrates a colossal blunder conservatives made on sex issues. Poor Elián was nearly drowned when his mother and her boyfriend carelessly put him on a flimsy raft, crossing dangerous waters to spirit him away from a relationship with his father in Cuba (Imagine the posturing in both of our political camps if Elián's father had kidnapped him!). Arguing in favor of keeping Elián in Florida, jingoistic Republican politicians demagogued for the Cuban-American votes, while former President Clinton and his Attorney General Janet Reno, normally not friends of fathers, made more sense. Reno even called the father/child bond "sacred." Her courageous position saved Elián from the jurisdiction of the notoriously anti-father Florida domestic relations courts — which have no business in immigration matters anyway. I shudder to admit that Reno was right for once; children belong with their fathers — even in Cuba. The masses also got it right: Dateline NBC (MSNBC) conducted an online poll on 1/17/99, asking viewers whether Elián should be sent home to Cuba. 86% said "Yes." Fourteen percent said "No."

Some years ago, admitting half his brain was tied behind his back, Rush Limbaugh favored keeping Elián in Florida at the time he was calling himself a "defender of fatherhood." I e-mailed him asking him to drop the pretense. He read the e-mail on his radio show, grumbled a bit, but complied (then resumed his nearly wall-to-wall commercials).

Had Elián remained in Florida with relatives instead of returning with his father, no doubt he would have been a spoiled brat by now. He would have faced the sorry future of father-deprived children that his mother aspired for him had she not drowned. If he married here, he would be reduced to the status of all married men; and in the event of divorce would likely lose custody of *his* son. In Cuba, Elián's future fatherhood (if not his political freedom) is much more likely to be honored. Pictures of him show a well-adjusted person. Now 24-years-old, Elián says he'd like to come back to the United States, but only as a tourist. He is studying engineering and has a fiancée. [277]

The state of Florida seems not to have learned much from Elián's case. In near identical circumstances, the Florida Department of Children & Families gave Rafael Izqierdo's 4-year-old daughter to wealthy foster parents instead of to Rafael after the mother was declared unfit. The Department spent over a quarter of a million dollars in an unsuccessful attempt to keep the child from her father. Judge Jeri B. Cohen wisely ruled against the Department. [278]

During the Covid-19 pandemic, Democrat New York governor Cuomo demanded the federal government assume the financial responsibilities that state and local governments have for their people, while president Trump opted to financially support small businesses that create *jobs* for the people. Now Socialism is coming on strong among Democrat presidential contenders. In proposing funding legislation to attack the Corvid-19 disease, Congressional Democrats have included unrelated and foolish diversity, climate and abortion rights provisions. Democrats' significant leftward movement of late is of a piece with the jihadist camel's nose under the tent.

Grove City philosophy prof. Paul Kengor refers to the left as "Cultural Marxists" preaching on behalf of women, homosexuals, minorities, trans-genders and any number of alleged victims of patriarchal white males. Venezuela has 35,000% inflation, yet Michael Moore, Sean Penn and others maintain it is "the perfect social society."

Donald Trump, that conservative alpha male, is the target of much criticism, some of it deserved. His salty language in private is commonly heard in locker rooms and saloons (including from many women). He doesn't give his guards a proper salute. His egoism, facial expressions and overused superlatives remind me somewhat of Mussolini, but we mustn't forget — Mussolini made the trains run on time. Yes, I know how Mussolini ended; so be wary of ALL politicians.

The English P.M. Benjamin Disraeli said the first thing a conservative must ask himself is what he seeks to conserve; and I would add what progressives seek to progress from and toward. A United Nations-sponsored debate between spokesmen for Communism and for free enterprise might not settle matters but would be highly interesting. Ultimately, neither right nor left favor men in the struggle for fairness. The party most philosophically aligned, theoretically, with sexual equality may be the Libertarian. That sector wants government out of our lives, but until several years ago have been curiously silent when it comes to divorce. Libertarianism has been called conservatism without a soul. Former Libertarian presidential candidate Ron Paul made more economic sense than many other candidates; he acknowledged that VAWA and Title IX are out-of-control federal funding that should be eliminated.

More on politicians in Chapter 5.

Atmosphere

Anti-male mindsets are ubiquitous, with examples appearing throughout this book. Those few mentioned below merely illustrate the atmosphere. It is universal in Western society; Nottinghamshire England has officially recognized misogyny as a hate crime, but not misandry.

In a scheme to sell more products to women, Avon cosmetics hired actress Reese Witherspoon to spout the feminist line for 3 years, claiming that a woman is beaten in her house every 9 seconds and that one in three women are victimized by this "worldwide pandemic." I received a slick, taxpayer supported brochure from an obviously large outfit, *futurewithoutviolence.org*, decrying violence against women only, and pointing the finger at men.

Another political boondoggle is the nationwide craze for "battered women's shelters." At my last count there were 1,800 to 2,000 of these providing "services" to women and their children — rationalized by the false claim that most domestic violence is instigated by men against women. There were fewer than 10 that were accommodating abused men and their children. Male victims are sometimes redirected to charity-funded homeless shelters. Researcher Sara Epstein described the shelter movement as an instrument of a radical feminist crusade to "change societal patterns of violence against women." The purpose of these facades is ostensibly to help alleged victims of domestic violence. But like Potemkin villages, they primarily serve as headquarters to pursue feminist agendas, all to the tune of $100 million in federal taxpayer money each year, a huge cash cow funding feminist schemes and officials.

These outfits are rife with mismanagement and fraud. The Southern Christian Leadership Conference (SCLC) "battered women safe house" in Dayton, Ohio closed its doors in 2004 but continued accepting federal grants to operate, collecting $134,033 from the Federal Emergency Management Agency since closing. In some states, they get kickbacks from marriage licenses.

Some women pose as DV victims to receive free or subsidized public housing, making shelters the sex war equivalents of ACORN. Writer Carey Roberts agrees: "The great majority of shelter residents are there for reasons that have nothing to do with domestic violence." See *Feminist DV service providers fight for cash and control, not equality.* [279]

Arelisha Bridges, a lobbyist for an organization called the National Declaration for Domestic Violence Order, a group supposedly fighting domestic violence, shot and killed her husband of five days during a sidewalk argument. A domestic violence shelter, ironically enough, sponsored a publicly funded "art exhibit" at a public library in Boulder, Colorado which featured 21 ceramic severed penises hanging on a clothesline.

A bill was introduced in Congress by politicians pandering to the women's vote to restore shelter funding for five more years. Known as the Family Violence Prevention and Services Act, the bill carried a nearly $300 million price tag to pay for a program the federal Office of Management and Budget has judged to be "Not Performing — Results Not Demonstrated." They perform and get results all right, but not as purported.

Erin Pizzey, who began the shelter-for-battered-women movement in England in 1971, is among the most vocal of its critics. Bonnie Tinker, founder of the Bradley-Angle shelter in Portland Oregon, admitted, "We knew that foundations were not going to fund a house for a bunch of homeless bar dykes. We realized the language that would be understood was the language of battered women." Reportedly she now operates out of Denver.

A fathers' rights group in Minnesota, r-kids.org, mounted lawsuits to limit "shelter" funding, but the gospel of political correctness prevailed; the suits were defeated at national and state levels by a cabal of leftists in state government and the judiciary.

Chapter 4 Effects of the War on Men

Les Miserables

This war has far-reaching effects on men in such areas as employment and crime punishment that are covered elsewhere in this book, so this chapter will not revisit those.

Effects of Divorce on men

There seems to be a connection between the price of procreation in human males and in males of some lower species. Female Praying Mantis and Black Widow spiders discard the male after he has served his fertilization purpose — or kill him. This trait is not unknown in humanoids, figuratively and even literally.

Suffering children are pitiful, but adult males arguably are more direct casualties, financially and emotionally, of the war on men. Researchers at Binghamton University found that men suffer more than women in the long term after a break-up and may never get over it. [280] His children are a man's raison d' être. Loss and probable estrangement of them are among the greatest injustices that can be visited upon a human being. It has been said that divorced men are "road kill" on the highway of life. Actor Alec Baldwin, whatever you think of his politics, knows whereof he speaks regarding divorce: "[It] is like being tied to the back of a pickup truck and dragged down a gravel road at night." Musician Bob Geldof put losing children well, saying "I was plunged into an ocean of grief."

Lack of a family to come home to has induced many a man to wallow in self-pity. Liquor lounge operators, probably the only non-judicial segment of society that does not despise alimony junkies, reap a windfall from both divorced men and women, but the latter are seldom there to cry in their beer. Sad ex-husbands are holding down bar stools all across the country — and the world. Various forms of drugs become their hemlock, gradually dulling existence.

According to Dr. John C. Cassel, department head at the University of North Carolina's School of Public Health, divorced men have a death rate three to five times higher than married men of the same age. Men without families who manage to survive are highly prone to various illnesses. They tend to suffer severe and chronic physical, emotional illnesses and inefficiency at work. According to a Danish study, divorced men contract tuberculosis more often than married men, ten times more often than married country-dwelling men, and five times more often than married city-dwelling men.

The death of John Fornica, while I worked at Charlie Metz's America's $ociety of Divorced Men, is a case in point. The DuPage County, Illinois, domestic court bears a great responsibility for it. This anti-male redoubt refused, except in token gestures, to enforce visitation provisions of his divorce decree. The daughter he loved too much became so brainwashed as a result that she screamed her hatred at this gentle man. He died of a broken heart, too young, removing items from the room she had occupied in happier days.

Driven Over the Edge

Loss of motivation accompanies the loss of love; and people are just no good without motivation, the sparkplug of life. Life becomes meaningless; frustration and bitterness appear. The loss, the pain corrodes the spirit and paralyzes the will. The shock of aborted love is difficult to measure, and to predict its results is impossible. When you have been seriously wronged, you don't easily get over it. Serene acceptance, if it can be achieved, is a blessing. However, a loved one's defection cannot be simply shrugged off by anyone really in love.

The unforgivable theft of relationships to a man's children and grandchildren, the loss of those irrecoverable joys of sharing their youth is difficult to accept, and engender a wide range of responsive social pathologies with disastrous consequences including familial violence. These situations can cause otherwise intelligent persons to become irrational and behave out of character. They have driven men to extreme measures. Good and evil become indistinguishable in despair.

Crime and behavioral aberrations consequently plague this vale of tears.

Many of the unloved would rather be dead than alive in this world. If you hear about a man committing suicide, the odds are better than 2:1 that he is either divorced or in the process. The study *Marital Status and Suicide* in the *National Longitudinal Mortality Study* by Augustine J. Kposowa, Ph.D., at the University of California at Riverside showed divorced/separated men's suicides to be 14,850 per year (including two of this writer's relatives by marriage). CBS News covered the report in detail. Between 1999 and 2010, the suicide rate for men rose dramatically, attributed largely to loneliness.

Dr. Robert Litman, a U.S.C. psychiatrist with the Los Angeles Suicide Prevention Center, maintains that a divorced man is twice as likely to commit suicide — some say 10 times more likely for divorced fathers — as is a divorced woman, because he suffers more than she does; he is three times more likely to commit suicide than is a married father.

Imposition of exorbitant money demands, on top of the loss of family, compounds the intolerability. An especially poignant case is related below:

Last Will and Testament of A.T. Renouf of Canada 10/16/95):

"Last Friday my bank account was garnished. I was left with a total of $00.43 in the bank. At this time I have rent and bills to pay which would come to somewhere approaching $1,500 to $1,800. Since my last pay was direct deposited on Friday I now have no way of supporting myself. I have no money for food or for gas for my car to enable me to work...

"I have tried talking to the Family Support people... Their answer was: 'we have a court order.' I have tried talking to the welfare people in Markham, since I earned over $520 in the last month I am not eligible for assistance.

"I have had no contact with my daughter in approx. 4 years. I do not even know if she is alive and well... I have no family and no friends, very little food, no viable job and very poor future prospects. I have therefore decided that there is no further point in continuing my life. It is my intention to... feed the car exhaust into the car, take some sleeping pills... "I would have preferred to die with more dignity.

"It is my last will and testament that this letter be published for all to see and read."

A.T. Renouf signed his will on the day he committed suicide.

News of murder/suicide involving married couples is common. Infidelity is often suspected but seldom mentioned. Gulf war suicides were at high level, probably many due to infidelity of wives/ girlfriends. Suicides in the U.S. military surged to a record 349 during one year in

Afghanistan, far exceeding American combat deaths there. 2,700 service members, not including National Guard and Reserve troops, have committed suicide after 2001. [281] According to Col. Elspeth Ritchie of the Army Surgeon General's office, failed relationships are the cause of 70-80 percent of military suicides.

Unstable minds are like unstable air; overheated elements expand adiabatically, feeding upon themselves until they can no longer contain their own frictional energy and must violently discharge like lightening. It is not safe to be in the vicinity. On the razor's edge of existence, "estranged husbands" (as the newspapers describe them) are human time bombs. Cornered animals naturally attack their attackers; but some of these poor devils make headlines by shooting up the town.

If a court took your car from you and gave it to someone else, then required you to make the payments, the insurance, and the gasoline and maintenance costs of the car. What would you do? What is the proper response to a court that takes your children and makes you pay money to the very person who destroyed your family? You would probably be out in the streets rioting. Some do much worse. Reaction to any form of brutality can be passive submission or active retaliation. Because individuals vary, there is no telling who has been driven to the edge of, or beyond, his limits.

Too many men to even begin to list them all have been driven beyond bitterness and suicide, to violence and murder by the unfairness of divorce. Many calculated murders, hard to condemn, have been committed by men wanting only a fair divorce, but cognizant of the impossibility. These have included doctors, lawyers, and others in full control of their senses. Some have never been discovered. Several divorcing men have even irrationally murdered their own children.

Mr. Ray Oehler was a prospective Men's Rights Association member whom Minneapolis Judge Barbeau impoverished in a divorce by giving his ex-wife title to property he had spent a lifetime building. Rough and limited in understanding, he knew only that he had been done wrong, and was livid about it. Ray dispatched his wife with four shotgun blasts at close range. As Judge Barbeau later admitted to a newspaper reporter, this writer warned him three times about possible violence, but to no avail. So it is obvious that even women can be ultimate victims of divorce, especially when courts go too far in their behalf.

While media commentators piously breast-beat about such men without understanding the cause, one can only speculate how many lives could have been saved if fairness existed in divorce court. Many are only an accident of chance away from these ignominious ends. It has been this author's impression that most of the books for both men and children on how to live with divorce are written by dreamers who would expect a lobster to be content with being boiled alive.

Some men take it better than others. A divorced friend of mine rented rooms in his house to divorced friends. It was only half-jokingly dubbed "The Home for Unwed Fathers."

Homelessness

Seventy-five percent of homeless people are men, most being divorce casualties. Veterans are well represented — about 30 percent of the homeless, according to The Philadelphia Veterans Multi-Service Education Center Inc. A report from the National Alliance to End Homelessness maintained that veterans make up a quarter of the United States' homeless population, and as many as 195,800 military veterans are homeless on any given night.[282] There are 22 veteran suicides per day. [283]

When they are not forlornly moving from place to place, the bitter, defeated flotsam and jetsam crowd jails and homeless shelters. Former New Jersey Governor Richard Codey disguised himself and went to homeless shelters in Newark, New Jersey on a frigid night. One rescue mission turned him away because he wasn't on SSI, welfare or disability. No room at the inn. The Goodwill took him in, offering a thin bedroll, blanket and a spot on a floor with 20 other men.

Skid row, that boulevard of broken dreams, is a whole 'nother world. The shroud of despair is apparent. One can cut it with a knife. A grim scene is widespread behind rooming house walls: a cubicle furnished in early Salvation Army, an unmade bed, a bare bulb, a soup pan on the

Skid row Philadelphia, 1976
There but for the grace of God

burner, a lonely man choking down meals of crackers and cheese, and a communal toilet down the hall. It's dreary. Others are just barely better off. Despite appearances, some of these so-called bums are intelligent and philosophical. Interviewing them was enlightening in a depressing way. Marie-Antoinette said, "Let them eat cake," but with these fellas there is no cake.

Effects on Children

'When the bough breaks the cradle will fall,
and down will come baby, cradle and all'[fn21]

The disasters befalling children of divorce do not compare in horror to children gassed to death in Syria, but they are more relevant to OUR society. "Children's rights" and doing things "for the children" are popular themes. However, often lost in those benedictions is the primary right they should have — to a complete family. That happy state is fast disappearing; fatherlessness is widespread, a damn epidemic! The *Washington Post* reported fewer than half of kids are in traditional families. [284] Social observer Herbert London commented that the percentage of children living at home with two married parents in their first marriage went from seventy three in 1960 to forty six in 2014. Mark I. Klein, an Oakland California psychiatrist, says, "Soon, less than 20 % of American children will be raised in two parent households." Raising children without their fathers is simply another, unfortunately accepted, form of child neglect.

That most children are harmed by parental conflict is not in doubt, nor is the fact that very few children benefit from parental separation under the rationale that it lessens their exposure to conflict. Feminist Peggy Drexler's book <u>Raising Boys Without Men: How Maverick Moms Are Creating the Next Generation of Exceptional Men</u> contends that father-absent homes — particularly "single mother by choice" and lesbian homes — are the best environments for boys. Drexler told *Good Morning America* that boys do just fine without dads, and that her "maverick moms" have a better way of handling their sons than dad would. While <u>Raising Boys...</u> may seem like a harmless, feel-good affirmation for these mothers, it could have a damaging impact on children by influencing both family law and the choices women make.

Psychobabble telling us children are better off in single parent households than with bickering parents should not be taken as gospel, as many mothers influenced by supposed intellectuals such as feminist Lynette Triere do. According to her, "It's better for the kids to go through a divorce than to live in a home where parents fight all the time." [285]

Au contraire; Dr. Rex Forehand of the University of Georgia says "Children in high-conflict divorced families did the worst, considerably worse than children who remained in homes where their mother and father fought constantly." [286] "Children," say Psychologists Wallerstein and Blakeslee, "can be quite content even when their parents' marriage is profoundly unhappy for one or both partners. Only one in ten

---

21 That metaphoric passage is figuratively true, marriage being the bough.

children in our study experienced relief when their parents divorced." Others suggest that at most a third of divorces involving children are so distressed that the children are likely to benefit therefrom. The remainder, about 70%, involve low-conflict marriages that apparently harm children much less than do the realities of divorce. As the threshold of dissatisfaction at which divorce occurs becomes ever lower, an even higher proportion of future divorces will involve low-conflict situations in which divorce will be worse for children than continuation of the marriage.

It is better for kids that their parents die than that they divorce. That is the implication of a study by Jay D. Teachman of Western Washington University, who studied the impact of childhood living arrangements on factors related to the likelihood of women having a successful marriage. Starting with data from the 1995 round of the National Survey of Family Growth, Teachman focused his attention on 4,947 women who married between 1970 and 1989. He found that women who grew up with two biological parents were far less likely than women who grew up in alternative family arrangements to form 'high-risk' marriages; they married later, had higher levels of education, married men with more education, were less likely to have experienced premarital conception or birth, and were less likely to cohabit.

Children are routinely deprived of their right to even see fathers unable or unwilling to make alimony/support payments. Judith Wallerstein is a psychologist and researcher who devoted 25 years to the study of long-term effects of divorce. According to her, when it comes to forming relationships in adult life, "it helps enormously to have imprinted on one's emotional circuitry the patterning of a successful, enduring relationship between a man and a woman." Committed loving fathers are needed to model proper behavior for their sons and demonstrate to their daughters the example of a loving and decent man. This is what most children of divorce lack. It is evident that children are best behaved when raised by 2-parent families.

> *The child's sob in the silence curses deeper than*
> *the strong man in his wrath.*
> Elizabeth Barrett Browning.

The destruction, theft actually, of children's families is a terrible thing — unforgivable. The poor kids! The suffering of kids — for their parents' stupidity, and that of divorce court judges — is especially disheartening. Men are in prison for lesser crimes.

Children have a primitive, very real fear of being left on their own. The sense of sadness and loss is profound. When their family breaks up, they become psychologically crumpled; they feel vulnerable, for they fear that their lifeline is in danger of being cut. Besides poverty, paternal deprivation often results, unnecessarily, in loss of kindred, of ancestral, cultural heritage. Children can find themselves cut off from contact with, and memories of, father and grandparents — or placed in foster care, or worse. In his book <u>Twice Adopted</u> (Broadman & Holman), Michael Reagan tells how, as the child of divorced parents, he could see his father, former President Ronald Reagan, only on alternating Saturdays. He wrote, "To an adult, two weeks is just two weeks. But to a child, having to wait two weeks to see your father is like waiting forever." His book <u>Lessons my Father taught me</u> wonderfully depicts the need children have for fathers, among its other gems of wisdom.

Divorce is the number one reason for father-deprivation. [287] Parents breeding children out of wedlock is the number two reason. Children of divorce should be asked this question: "Do you think your mother (or father) had a right to spuriously deprive you of a father (or mother) and normal family in favor of an unfettered life or to search for a new partner?"

Divorce can also spoil children; often they become selfish little monsters playing one affection-competing parent off against the other — being bought off with trips to Disneyland or the like. Improperly raised children may often think that banished fathers owe them something, other than life itself. Those old enough to choose which parent will have custody are in the driver's seat. Many sell out to the highest bidder, which is usually Mom. Dad is forced to become a "Saturday Santa." I call this seeming heyday of a kid's life "Kawasaki time." Later, it can morph into new car time, college education time, etc. It may never end. Urchins are so spoiled nowadays, it's probably foolish to even try pleasing them.

Case in point: Ethan Couch's divorced parents were very wealthy. The boy lived with his mother and was coddled rotten. In 2013 while driving drunk at 16 he struck and killed four pedestrians near Fort Worth Texas. Prosecutors wanted him to serve 20 years in prison. Instead, in December 2013 he got off with rehab and probation after a defense expert argued that the remorseless boy suffered from "affluenza" — an inability to tell right from wrong because he was never punished for bad behavior. Unwilling to endure even probation, he and his mother, Tonya, went on the lam for a month, but were caught in Mexico.

Former President Nixon blamed drug addiction [fn22] among the young on defeatism. He was partly correct; the young men *are* defeated — by the 'rape of the male.' The girls are naturally playing follow the leader; if the boys are defeated, so are they.

---

22 The U.S. consumes 2/3ds of the world's illicit drugs.

Father Deprivation: Delinquency, Other Aberrations.

Wrong couplings can create cascading strings of tragedies, and often do. When children are involved in divorce, tragedy often follows. The collateral damage to children is catastrophic. A 1990 survey from the National Center for Health Statistics found an 'alarmingly high' prevalence of emotional and behavioral problems among all children, with rates two to three times higher for single parent and stepparent families than for intact families. Every relevant study indicates that children raised in single parent homes are more likely to exhibit pathological behavior than those who are not. More than one in three children of broken families drop out of school. The police spend a good deal of time with adolescents who do not live with both of their biological parents. More than two-thirds of the criminal minors handled by the Florida Division of Youth Services are from broken homes. Baltimore, Maryland authorities found 60 percent of their juvenile criminals are from broken homes, a factor which undoubtedly contributed to the riots there. Seventy-five percent of delinquents and most adult criminals are from broken homes. [288] A study by the Bureau of Justice Statistics showed that 72 percent of incarcerated juvenile delinquents grew up in broken homes, mostly female headed; yet such single parent homes are only 24 percent of all homes.

Many social aberrations — namely higher levels of youth suicide, low intellectual and educational performance, greater mental illness, juvenile delinquency, violence and drug abuse — are associated with father-deprived children. In *Social Problems* magazine, James Skipper, Jr. and Charles McCaghy reported that almost 60 percent of strip teasers they interviewed had no father in the home. Media-darling sexpots Marilyn Monroe and Anna Nicole Smith had no fathers. Prostitution is rampant in this set. Aware of the situation, auto insurance companies in some states charge higher premiums for boys living with mothers than for those living with their fathers.

Bad behavior ranges from mischief to murder, and includes a growing contempt for authority. Juvenile violence is out of hand. As most teachers will testify, we have a nationwide spate of disruptive students, punks fighting in schools. The direct, irrefutable correlation between mother-custody and personal problems is presented in a policy brief released in September 2005 by the Washington-based Institute for Marriage and Public Policy, and massively documented in The Garbage Generation, [289] especially in the Annex to Chapter 1. Of course, the modern abundance of self-centered kids is not restricted to products of divorce.

Charles Manson, who masterminded one of the most heinous murder sprees in American history, was given nine consecutive life sentences (and craved brainless "music" by the way), was fatherless. Saddam Hussein and Dean Corn, the Houston mass-murderer, were fatherless. So too, according to Dr. Fred B. Charatan, all seven presidential assassins, including those who attempted assassinations, and the killers of Reverend Martin Luther King and Senator Robert Kennedy, were "lacking fathers through death, divorce, work schedule, or a very poor paternal relationship":

Richard Lawrence—would-be assassin of Andrew Jackson,
John Wilkes Booth—assassin of Abraham Lincoln,
Charles J. Guiteau—assassin of James Garfield,
Leon F. Czolgosz—assassin of William McKinley,
John N. Schrank—would-be assassin of Theodore Roosevelt,
Giuseppe Zangara—would-be assassin of Franklin Roosevelt,
Lee Harvey Oswald—assassin of John F. Kennedy
James Earl Ray—killer of Martin Luther King,
Sirhan Sirhan—killer of Robert F. Kennedy,
Lynette Fromme—would-be assassin of Gerald Ford.

Adam Lanza gunned down 20 children and six educators before killing his custodial mother on Dec. 14, 2012. Steven Paddock, the 2017 Las Vegas character who killed 58 and wounded 500, was fatherless from the age of seven. Granted his absent father was less than ideal, but the fact remains that he had no favorable paternal guidance. In February of 2018 the fatherless, depressed and academically troubled, Nikolas Cruz killed seventeen adults and children with an AR-15 type rifle at the Marjory Stoneman Douglas high school in Parkland, Florida. The baby-faced traitor Julian Paul Assange is the product of a single mother. There have been many other such examples.

We are witnessing the advent of a chaotic reign of youth because evisceration of his authority has left the married father with little control, and the divorced father with practically none. It might appear that a parental (read paternal) responsibility law, such as enacted in several Michigan cities, is the answer to delinquency and crime. Sixty five years ago, it might have been; today it is so overdue that it may be too late, because it is based on the now false premise that parents (read fathers) still have authority. Welfare as a cause of divorce was cited earlier here; it is also a cause of crime, directly or indirectly. It is no secret that gun violence among adults is widespread. One would have to be comatose to ignore the danger.

Other cultures and countries. The consequences of father-deprivation in the trend-setting U.S. are mirrored in other countries. Modern western attitudes toward fathers have contaminated even Asian-American communities, traditional abodes of unquestioned parental respect and one of the last vestiges of realistically-structured families. Consequently, these children also are joining the ranks of delinquents, a trend formerly unheard of in these or any male-dominated communities. A Canadian publication, *Everyman: A Men's Journal,* [290] (now out of print) gave the following information:

Children and Single Moms—What we know about children from single-mother families. [291]

A research team from the Toronto Wellesley Hospital found in a study of glue-sniffers, that only one in twenty-four had a meaningful relationship with his father, while all in the control group had a normal family life. According to a study conducted at Exeter University in the U. K., children from broken homes, as well as children with stepparents, were "twice as likely as children from intact families to have problems in all areas. Where the child experienced two or more divorces, the rate of problems rose exponentially." [292] A study in England, concluded that fatherlessness is directly connected with behavioral problems. [293]

As the idiom goes, it is the exception that proves the rule; or more accurately, that proves the necessity for the rule. There are notable exceptions to the general rule of crime association, Dr. Ben Carson being an extraordinary one. I knew well one Vietnamese mother who arrived in the U.S. penniless on the last flight out of Saigon as the war there ended (her husband had been put in into a re-education camp). All alone, she raised four of the best adjusted, most successful children — now adults managing corporations — I have ever encountered. Actually, it is not so exceptional; she was raised in a strongly patriarchal family.

Obviously, children of intact families have problems also. Perhaps their parents didn't instill decent values in them, nor possibly did *their* parents in them. That parental duty is even more important than providing food and shelter beyond the bare necessities.

Testimony from Experts:

Dr. Shervert H Frazier, in a study of convicted murderers in Texas prisons and mental institutions, has this to say, "...They are males with an absence of a father symbol."

Dr. Wade Horn said:

Boys from a female-headed household had a 60 per cent greater chance of committing rape and a 75 per cent greater chance of committing murder. Most of the inmates in prison come from single parent families. Children from such homes tended to under-perform in education, and many of them lived in poverty, and were themselves likely to end up in poverty.

Sociologist Henry Biller:

Males who were father-deprived early in life are likely to engage later in rigidly over-compensatory masculine behaviors. The incidence of crimes against property and people, including child abuse and family violence, is relatively high in societies where the rearing of young children is considered to be an exclusively female endeavor. [294]

David Popenoe:

Juvenile delinquency and violence are clearly generated disproportionately by youths in mother-only households and in other households where the biological father is not present...[295]

Fatherlessness is probably the single most important factor in the rising juvenile delinquency rate... The negative consequences of fatherlessness are all around us. They affect children, women, and men. Evidence indicating damage to children has accumulated in near tidal-wave proportions. Fatherless children experience significantly more physical, emotional, and behavioral problems than do children growing up in intact families....[T]o reduce delinquency and violence, the child must be reared by a biological father. [296]

Maggie Gallagher cites George Rekers, professor of neuropsychiatry and behavioral science at the University Of South Carolina School Of Medicine, as follows on father absence:

Both developmental and clinical studies have clearly established the general rule that the father's positive presence in the home is, in the vast majority of cases, normally essential for the existence of family strength and child adjustment.

Research shows that children without fathers have lower academic performance, more cognitive and intellectual deficits, increased adjustment problems, and higher risks for psychosexual development problems. And children from homes in which one or both parents are missing or frequently absent have higher rates of delinquent behavior, suicide, and homicide, along with poor academic performance. Among boys, father absence has been linked to greater effeminacy, [fn23] and exaggerated aggressiveness. Girls, on the other hand, who lose their father to divorce tended to be overly responsive to men and become sexually active earlier. They married younger, got pregnant out of wedlock more frequently and divorced or separated from their eventual husbands more frequently, perpetuating the cycle. [297]

Robert Rector:

Children raised in single-parent families, when compared with those in intact families, are one-third more likely to exhibit behavioral problems such as hyperactivity, antisocial behavior, and anxiety. Children deprived of a two-parent home are two to three times more likely to need psychiatric care than those in two-parent families, and as teenagers they are more likely to commit suicide. Absence of a father increases the probability that a child will use drugs and engage in criminal activity. [298]

Several other studies bear on the absence or inaccessibility of the father, and all point to the same conclusions — a father absent for long periods contributes to (a) low motivation for achievement; (b) inability

---

[23] Witness Julian Assange and Bradly Manning.

to defer immediate gratification for later rewards; (c) low self-esteem; and (d) susceptibility to group influence and to juvenile delinquency. The absent father tends to have passive, dependent sons, lacking in achievement, motivation, and independence... When we consult the scientific and medical literature, we find an impressive body of data based on carefully controlled experiments that corroborate the impression that a parent's absence, whether through death, divorce, or time-demanding job, can exert a profound influence on a child's emotional health. The magnitude of this research paints an unmistakably clear picture of the adverse effects of parental absence and emotional inaccessibility. Why has our society almost totally ignored this research? Why have even the professionals tended to ignore it? The answer is the same reason society ignored for scores of years sound data on the adverse effects of cigarette smoke. The data are simply unacceptable. We just don't want to hear the facts because they demand a change in our lifestyle.[299]

> Samuel Osherson:
> The interviews I have had with men in their 30s and 40s convince me that the psychological or physical absence of fathers from their families is one of the great underestimated tragedies of our times.[300]

> Richard T. Sollenberger of Mt. Holyoke College, writing in the *Journal of Social Psychology*, agrees with the foregoing experts, as does Armand M. Nicholi, Jr., M.D. Philosopher James Q. Wilson recognizes fatherlessness as the proximate cause of social problems, but fails to understand that ultimate causes, beyond drugs etc., is misandry and perverted chivalry. The problems need to be reframed.

Parental Alienation Syndrome (PAS)

> *How sharper than a serpent's tooth it is to have
> a thankless child.* [301]

Dr. Richard Gardner, of Cresskill, NJ, a child psychologist and one of the leading authorities on children of dysfunctional families, describes PAS as "a disturbance in which children are obsessively preoccupied with deprecation and/or criticism of a parent. In other words, denigration that is unjustified and/or exaggerated." According to several Spanish educators, one out of four children involved in a divorce and custody litigation is victimized by the Parental Alienation Syndrome. [302] A 12-year study by the American Bar Association found it in sixty percent of custody cases.

The attitudes of custodial parents become imprinted on children, including hostile attitudes toward non-custodial parents. Such children are taught to hate the "targeted parent" to the point of wanting to eliminate them from their lives. They are conditioned to misinterpret negatively things that the target parent does, however innocent.

Many men have been unduly vilified by the estranged mothers of their children seeking to enhance their own standing with the children. Toronto lawyer Gene Colman told a Toronto symposium that of 74 court rulings that found parental alienation since 1987, the mother was the alienator in 50 cases. The father was the alienating parent in 24 of them. With Mom's self-absolving encouragement, Dad is blamed even for his involuntary absence. They see their father through the distorting prism of their mother's hostility. The subconscious minds of these unwitting dupes wait for the least excuse, such as a spanking, or less, with which to confirm what they have been conditioned to believe — Dad is bad.

It takes lengthy brainwashing by evil people to misdirect children's understandable anger, to bring them to the point they throw rocks at Dad's car when he drives up to visit. An example occurred when the 10-year-old son of Dr. Rick Lohstroh, a Houston, Texas surgeon, was so alienated by his mother after a contentious divorce, he shot and killed his father. [303] In real life, a vindictive parent may merely alienate children from their father (or mother). The fable of Medea, the unfaithful wife in Greek mythology who wreaked vengeance on her husband by murdering their children is exemplary. The Oedipus fable can also be illustrative.

Most mental health professionals regard PAS as a form of child abuse. Psychologist Dr. Amy Baker says "to turn a child against a parent (half of his ancestry) is to turn the child against him/herself, since the child's wellbeing requires both parents." Parents teaching their children to hate the other parent are akin to Palestinians teaching children that Jews are pigs and monkeys. Sometimes children begin to resent the entire male sex and/or pass this sickness on to *their* children.

Because the results of brainwashing are so catastrophic, one might consider it more unforgivable even than infidelity. To take beautiful little children, and warp their minds against the other parent should be a criminal offense. Sadly, many of these children will never know how much their father (or mother) may have loved them, and how devastating it was to have them cruelly taken and taught to hate. Some politicians get it. Maine Gov. John E. Baldacci proclaimed April 25, 2006 to be "Parental Alienation Awareness Day." When children are brainwashed, the support money goes grudgingly — if at all.

Inclusion of Parental Alienation Disorder in DSM-5 by the American Psychiatric Association could help 200,000 children in America every year who suffer from this condition. It could also help abate this form of child abuse and bring families better treatment solutions along the way. NOW vehemently objected both to inclusion and to recognition of PAS in court. Their Tracy Simmons whined that inclusion "benefits the abuser, and discriminates against the victims of abuse, which are overwhelmingly women."

Evidently, their efforts have been successful; the American Psychiatric Association considered but rejected inclusion. They indicated that PAS might be considered an example of other diagnoses that are included. This is stunning regarding a manual in which so many diagnostic categories have been included despite there being no solid scientific evidence supporting their existence or characteristics. Based on other kinds of decisions the DSM-5 people have been making, it seems unlikely that concern about the lack of scientific evidence is the real reason they have chosen to exclude it.

Hardly to blame of course, children are on the horns of a dilemma: a conflict between their conditioning telling them Dad is a big ass, and their eyeballs telling them he is not. Intelligent ones, when they become adults will come to realize they have been duped, and how much they and their children have been cheated out of. The biggest problem for them is separating truth from lies. As in so many situations the truth hurts. No kid wants to acknowledge unfavorable features of a parent however true. Thoroughly brainwashed children can actually believe lies about their absent fathers (or mothers). An insidious aspect is that the carriers are unaware of their infection, and may vigorously deny its existence.

If PAS persists into adulthood, it can become irreversible, Humpty Dumpty time (All the king's horses, etc.). Imagine being the targeted parent. It must be living hell. There may come a time when he (or she) must recognize that it's irreversible, and salvage what they can of their life and that of others. It's like airlines advising passengers to put on oxygen masks first; the kids can wait. If this condition applies to your children, try getting them to a hypnotist if possible to clarify their memories. Joe Goldberg, Esq. is a Parental Alienation consultant in California. Excellent factual information on PAS is available on the internet. [304] Parent victims have helpful websites:

    http://www.erosenberg-associates.com/content/important-issues-0
    parental-alienation-awareness.com; mnhypnosis.com
    www.Parentalalienationeducation.com
    www.youtube.com/watch?v=aZeuDXE8OBg&feature=youtu.be.

Michigan's Oakland County Family Court Judge Lisa Gorcyca should be a hero in the men's/fathers' movement for recognizing severe brainwashing of children by their mother. Gorcyca, sentenced 3 children to a juvenile detention center for refusal to visit with their father. [305]

Effects on the Family

A Michigan University study, among others, reveals that divorce adversely affects both men and women financially (see graph at right). About 70 percent of poor households with children are headed by those totems of virtue, single mothers. [306] "Divorce almost always guarantees a woman severe financial hardship," bemoans the *National NOW Times* of Feb/Mar 1989. It is good that it does; *it would be better if it guaranteed more hardship.* To say that divorce hurts women is to say that marriage benefits women (as it also does with men). A primary purpose of marriage is that it benefits all concerned. Robert I. Lerman supports these analyses in an excellent paper entitled *Impacts of Marital Status and Parental Presence on the Material Hardship of Families with Children* [307]

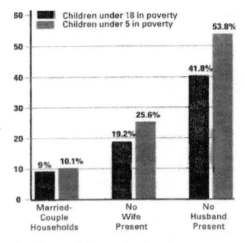

Dan Quayle said, "And for those concerned about children growing up in poverty, we should know this: Marriage is probably the best anti-poverty program of all. Among families headed by married couples today, there is a poverty rate of 5.7 percent. But 33.4 percent of families headed by a single mother are in poverty today." [308] He was roundly criticized for that by leftists. Former DNC Chairman Howard Dean said, "We don't think children ought to go to bed hungry at night." He is right, but tangentially so. KIDS WITH FATHERS DON'T GO TO BED HUNGRY AT NIGHT.

Effects on Society

We are living in a Twilight Zone. Indeed, these are the times that try men's souls. Cops are obviously needed to maintain law and order. Some have been murdered for doing their jobs. Taking his own revenge, five days ago, a rogue cop brutally murdered George Floyd, a drug-impaired black counterfeiter, in Minneapolis 25 miles from here. Rioting, looting and partying broke out in big cities across the nation — indeed the world — in protest. An enormous percentage of the participants were anarchists with no stake in society who violently attacked police and people attempting to defend their property. The devastation was worse than what occurred in Baltimore, Los Angeles, Ferguson and St. Louis, Missouri decades ago. Feral mobs toppled statues of genuine national heroes, and made demands, which were positively obscene from the perspective of history; demands such as abolishment of Independence Day celebrations and the destruction of Mount Rushmore. Normal murder rates increased 51% this year. Over the weekend of July 4th, 2020 roughly 70 persons were shot and 16 killed in Chicago. In New York City the numbers were 44 and 12. Inmates were in charge of the asylum. [24] At least one group of mostly young adults organized in opposition to the mobs, the Proud Boys, but even many moderates and conservatives were ashamed to side with them. The situation remains reminiscent of that in Germany that Wm. Shrier writes of in The Nightmare Years of 1930—1940.

Other large cities suffered as well, largely controlled at every level by democrats, who, eying the voting traditions, sympathized with the mobs. Some even ordered police to "stand down." They are equally guilty. Even some republican senators caved to mob demands.

Some protests may have been legitimate, but lack of discipline among rioters and looters (probably living on welfare benefits) could obviously be attributed to absence of paternal influence. Prof. Stephen Baskerville says, "... fatherless children are tearing down our civilization."

Chapter 5. J 'accuse
Politicians, Legalists

Few of today's politicians are the caliber of our Founding Fathers. Many are by nature prevaricators. Pompous ideologues do what politicians often do — play to the loudest, most active and most emotional group of supporters. Pontificating with moral righteousness, "progressives" swallow feminist notions and economic theories. Equating real reform with anti-womanhood, they must appear engaged in upholding motherhood and apple pie. Many genuflect to sainted 'single moms' blithely unaware that this grouping is largely at fault for social problems. Writer Marc H. Rudov calls them "gynocrats."

Guilty politicians include Bill Clinton, Barak Obama, Senators Bill Bradley, Nancy Pelosi and Harry Reid. Former Democrat presidential candidate Bill Richardson spoke about cracking down on "deadbeat dads." Another Democrat presidential candidate, John Edwards, bemoaned an imagined lack of opportunity for women. Fearing feminists, they outrun each other almost lactating for that vote.

Eager to demonstrate how "woke" they are, sycophants have made the feminist agenda a federal matter. California Governor Jerry Brown signed a law requiring publicly traded companies to include women on their boards of directors. The measure requires at least one female director on the board of each California-based public corporation by the

---

24 An observation: America-haters are, at bottom, self-haters (probably with good cause).

end of 2019. Companies would need up to three female directors by the end of 2021, depending on the number of board seats. Witness also: sponsorship of the abominable VAWA legislation by Democrat presidential candidate Joe Biden. Any male voting for him is a traitor to his sex.

With all the goodwill of Hezbollah, these enablers have facilitated the destruction of the father-headed family and its replacement with the mother-headed matriarchy, often ingratiating themselves with voters by providing modern equivalents of ancient Roman bread and circuses. These bribes are especially attractive to women. Remember Julia? One such monument to invincible ignorance, Pennsylvania Democrat Representative Martin P. Mullen, while honking and blowing against a divorce reform bill decades ago, unburdened himself of this observation, "A woman is born clean and decent; if she is bad, it is because a man made her go wrong." Shit of the bull!! Another, of the same sanctimonious mold, mouthed identical platitudes in the Alabama legislature much later.

A 2015 California law forced pro-life pregnancy centers to advertise availability of abortions. This is like forcing synagogues to distribute Islamic propaganda. The law was struck down in 2018. California's Senate Bill 320 requires that universities provide chemical abortion as the most accessible response to a student pregnancy. The bill is supported by women's and pro-abortion organizations.

While running for president, Barak Obama blamed black fathers for their absence. Many politicians have been bamboozled into thinking that that absence is voluntary. It seldom is. The confirmation of federal appeals court nominee Leslie Southwick was long delayed by Senate Democrats objecting, inter alia, to his joining a decision granting custody to a father instead of to a lesbian mother.

Lilly Ledbetter worked at the Goodyear Tire and Rubber plant in Gadsden, Alabama, and evidently was not performing up to the level of men at the plant. In November 1998, after early retirement, Ledbetter sued the company under Title VII of the Civil Rights Act of 1964 and the Equal Pay Act of 1963 claiming pay discrimination. The jury found for Ledbetter and awarded back pay and damages. Goodyear appealed, arguing that all claims to damages before September 26, 1997 were void due to the statute of limitations placed on discrimination claims. Applicable law mandates that such charges must be filed within one hundred and eighty days after the alleged unlawful employment practice occurred. The Supreme Court agreed with Goodyear's claim, and found no evidence of discriminatory intent.

That didn't end it. In 2007, several Democrat members of Congress introduced the Lilly Ledbetter Fair Pay Act, which revised the law to state that if a present act of discrimination pertains, prior acts outside of the 180-day statute of limitations for pay discrimination can be incorporated into the claim. The bill was an issue in the 2008 Presidential election campaign, with Barack Obama supporting the bill, and John McCain opposed to it. In January 2009, President Obama signed the Act into law. [309]

Betty Dick and her late husband, Fred, owned land in Rocky Mountain National Park, and signed a 25-year agreement with the Interior Department that allowed them to stay on it. After the agreement expired, Rep. Mark Udall, (D-CO) and Sen. Ken Salazar, (D-CO) submitted bills that allowed the widow to remain on the land indefinitely. [310]

Sex prejudice crosses party lines and varies within the parties. The feminist agenda is not restricted to Democrats; conservatives can out-demagogue Louis Farrakhan on the subject of child abuse. Whatever their political persuasion, the overall difference between politicians on gender/sex issues is like that between Tweedle Dum and Tweedle Dee. Most in both camps have erroneous understandings of the problem of fatherlessness and its solution. Neither "progressives" nor conservatives have been friends of the male sex; cross-pollination occurs. Both persuasions are equally adept at posturing and pontificating. Political correctness and gender/sex issues can make strange bedfellows, with huge philosophic blind spots on the left and the right.

Conservatives often go along with liberal nonsense because they don't want to appear unchivalrous. They can be obtuse and, on balance, may be only marginally superior. Many fail to realize that their support of mother custody and wealth redistribution in divorce is an incentive to divorce, more blameworthy than redistribution in welfare. Men's rights are a touchy subject for them, too naïve to grasp that misandry is antithetical to their principles. Right wing anti-male grandstanders include Republicans Sam Brownback, Alan Keys and Robert Bork. Mike Huckabee was on the domestic violence bandwagon. Republican Senators Orrin Hatch and John Heinz swooned over Elizabeth Morgan, joining Democrats in defending her actions. They were accompanied by Chuck Colson, Dr. James Dobson and Oliver North — normally sensible persons. [fn25] Lesser known others too numerous to mention tagged along.

Former Republican presidential candidate John McCain contemptuously dismissed fathers' concerns over family law at a town

---

[25] In the 1980s, Morgan abandoned her husband and falsely accused him of child molestation. She absconded with their daughter to New Zealand after the court, aware it was she who had abused the child, awarded custody of their daughter to the father. The chivalrous New York legislature passed special legislation absolving Morgan of defying the court.

hall meeting in Cedar Falls, Iowa on March 16, 2007, when shared parenting activist Tony Taylor asked McCain if he "would be bold enough to address the issue of equal access to children for fathers that have gone through divorce." Flat Earther McCain testily mimicked Pontius Pilate as he washed his hands of responsibility for crucifying Christ:

> I'm sorry to disappoint you; I am not going to overturn divorce court decisions. That's why we have courts and that's why people go to court and get a divorce. If I as President of the United States said this decision has to be overturned without the proper appeals process, then I would be disturbing our entire system of government... But for me to stand here before all these people and say that I'm going declare divorces invalid because someone feels that they weren't treated fairly in court, we are getting into a, uh, uh, tar baby of enormous proportions.

The foregoing examples are put forth not to criticize good intentions, but to demonstrate the lengths to which politicians will go on behalf of women. Wanna bet politicians, regardless of political affiliation, would engage in such acrobatics for a man?

Tangentially, I am utterly embarrassed to be represented in Congress by the Muslim woman Ilhan Omar who described the tragedy of 9/11 thusly, "Some people did something." Another such flake, Alexandria Ocasio-Cortez, was also elected to congress.

Judges and Lawyers

It has been demonstrated in research projects that the compulsion to favor female litigants is especially noticeable if the woman is attractive. Male judges apparently get an 'ego-blast' satisfying a primitive, self-aggrandizing sex urge or rooster instinct, which they have opportunity to exploit. Eduard Bakalar, Ph.D., a scholar from the Czech Republic, attributes anti-male behavior in government officials to an underlying subconscious mechanism desirous of women's sexual favors. There seem to be other motivations or psychological compulsions difficult to fathom. One is that male litigants are arbitrary scapegoats in an orgy of catharsis or over-compensation for past bias against and imagined suppression of women. Others are barely concealed sadism, masochism, or envy of younger men still possessed of their virility.

Women's tears influence male judges more than does the law of the land. Their falling for female sob stories can likewise affect clergy who are counseling divorce aspirants. I've heard of it often. Charlie Metz got one priest defrocked for consorting with a divorce aspirant.

Presumably, most judges have led a sheltered life and had decent mothers or they would not have achieved such high office. A big cause of their prejudice may be that they equate all women appearing before them with their mothers, and are convinced they are doing something for poor, defenseless women. Big mistake! Many of these women are about as defenseless and cunningly aggressive as healthy lionesses. In their defense, it is just a crapshoot trying to prognosticate which will be the better, or more likely the worse, custodian — between two childishly stupid parents. Of course judges can be crooked; one Hennepin County domestic court referee, at an annual Norwegian aquavit party with several legal types, offered me a proposition — he would give my Men's Defense Assoc. members custody of their kids if I'd steer members to a certain attorney.

Because women are not as chivalrous as men, at first thought one might consider it advisable to have more women judges. At one time, yes — but not now. While male judges can be Jurassic, their distaff counterparts have become even worse since feminists showed them the monetary and career advantages of going along with the program.

The United States has 5% of the world's population and 66% of the world's lawyers! [26] It is said that a lawyer with a briefcase can steal more than a thousand men with guns. Know something about lawyers: most will do whatever is in their interests before whatever is in clients' interests.

Divorce Lawyers

Domestic relations is an especially sordid field, wherein profiteers are paid to orchestrate carnage. The divorce industry is a cash cow, comprising some 35% of civil litigation. [311] Easy fees draw lawyers to divorce like sharks to blood. It's the same reason Willie Sutton said he robbed banks: "That's where the money is." These bottom feeders share with wives the legalized plunder; it is one of their biggest sources of income ("Thar's gold in them thar hills"). In No-fault Divorce and the Divorce Conundrum, Lynn D. Wardle states that "a divorce industry...of professional meddlers...makes millions of dollars every year off marital turmoil, much of which they have a hand in creating themselves." Chicago Judge Nathan M. Cohen says, "Lawyers' fees lie in divorce, not reconciliation." In 1988, Nolo Press estimated that lawyers generate about one billion, three hundred sixty-four million

---

26 Every Democrat vice presidential nominee since 1976, except for Lloyd Bentsen, went to law school.

annually in *unnecessary* fees, almost five hundred million in divorce alone. This is over and above their legitimate charges. [312] Of course, inflation will cause the figures to be higher now; they have been estimated as high as $5 billion or more. The California Assembly Judiciary Committee documents the lack of ethics or morals of the divorce lawyers in its 1965 report: "For them divorce is their rent, their steno's salary, their baby's shoes, sometimes their solid-gold Cadillac... How unrealistic to expect them to forego anything like that for mere considerations of ethics or morals."

Divorce promotion ads can be downright disgusting. In May 2007, a Chicago all-female law firm specializing in divorce, Fetman, Garland & Associates, Ltd., commissioned a large billboard advertisement in that city with the following message emblazoned on it: "Life's Short, Get a Divorce." It was no joke; a spokeswoman for the firm defended the message. An internet ad. was, "Don't waste another day in a loveless marriage.

Wealthy clients especially can expect interminable litigation. L. S. Rosenstiel, former president of Schenley Distillers, and his wife spent well over $1.5 million during a twenty-year divorce. Over half a century ago, John Jacob Astor paid lawyer fees of $105,000 in only one year of a four-year divorce. In September 2006, Los Angeles County Superior Court Judge Robert A. Schnider ordered the late pop singer Michael Jackson to pay $60,000 in attorney fees for his ex-wife in a custody case (She had sought $195,000, and had already received an $8 million divorce settlement). The 80-year-old widow of real estate magnate Sylvan Lawrence sued the Graubard, Miller law firm in New York for $50 million in excess fees and gifts. The firm reportedly attempted to soak her further by getting her to sign a retainer agreement worth in excess of $67 million. [313] Others of similar high cost and duration are on record. In Muskegon, Michigan, Helen Below bequeathed $50,000 to two cats. Lawyers took $40,000 of it. A Fort Lauderdale heir to the Quaker Oats fortune, Mrs. Eleanor Ritchey, left $14 million to her 81 dogs. Lawyers argued about that for years, to the tune of $700,000. Talk about milking situations! Lord knows what lawyers got in the Jeff Bezos and wife McKenzie divorce.

Protracted cases can go into many thousands of dollars for a few more hours of sham. Like surgeons who operate unnecessarily, lawyers can be greater make-work artists than railroad firemen. In a featherbedding scheme to introduce yet another lawyer into divorces to represent children in contested custody situations (at papa's expense, naturally), they demand "Guardians ad litem" in most states. Obviously, this would compound an already bad situation. We have a glut of lawyers now; further groupings are unneeded.

Every lawsuit is fundamentally the same: pleadings, proof, and procedures. Even non-contested actions (also called defaults), which most eleventh graders could handle in an hour or two, are ridiculously expensive. In simple, agreed-upon divorce situations, attorney fees should normally be fixed at not much over $700. If the defendant/respondent hires an attorney in these situations, it should be at clock rate, normally requiring not over a couple hours.

Aspiring divorcees usually blow assets by running to attorneys, forcing partners to follow suit, instead of first attempting to reach mutually agreeable settlements. A wife can hire the most expensive lawyer in town to attack her husband, and, adding insult to injury, make hubby pay for it. Unlike husbands, wives can get help from quasi-governmental sources: the federal Legal Services Corporation and the Legal Aid Society. While indigent males sometimes obtain free counsel if the opponent is not a woman, it is almost unheard of where the opponent *is* a woman. Legal Services Corporation's free lawyers represented women (no men, to my knowledge) in 225,000 divorces in 1985 alone. [314] Meanwhile, men's rights must be pleaded for by hiring mercenaries.

Most divorce lawyers would much rather be on the woman's side of course. When unfortunate enough to represent the man, they find it economically most practical to take his money, pick up the phone and sell him out to their counterpart representing the woman; and many do just that; it takes very little time. Really working for a man's rights produces only a little more income, and involves considerable time (better spent milking some other mark), effort, and antagonizing of judges, before whom they must practice again and again. I have even less regard for such lawyers than for African poachers killing elephants for their tusks. The Men's Defense (formerly "Rights") Association's successful fight against this racket appears in Part IV.

Courts act as collection agencies for lawyers. They do this through the subterfuge of writing the fees into court orders, thus giving them the force and dignity of law. An Illinois appellate court declared "Attorneys' fees awarded in a divorce decree are in the nature of alimony and not dischargeable in bankruptcy... Spouses' award in attorney fees should be treated with some legal significance as an allowance for money to buy food and groceries." [315] Failure to pay can be, and often is, construed as contempt of court — a jailable offense. In good conscience, one *should* be in contempt of a contemptible court.

Often courts order claims against citizens' property or they withhold official records, or do both, until lawyers' claims are satisfied. Provisos have been written into court orders making visitation contingent upon payment of lawyers. Marvin Singer, 71, spent 3 months in a New York jail for failure to pay his ex-wife's lawyer $100,000 for her legal representation during their six-year tug-of-war over marital assets. [316] In Chicago, a reconciled couple tried to have the wife's action for separate maintenance terminated. Her lawyer jacked the fee up far beyond the original quotation, refused to drop the action until paid, and snared them into reappearance in divorce court. There the judge refused to dismiss the action until the alleged debt was paid. [317] Donald Cash was thrown into York County jail in Alfred, Maine, for not paying his wife's lawyer. His salary was $60 a week, from which he paid $36 in support for three children and $25 for room and board. MDA member Lloyd Tourville, a 100 percent disabled veteran, now-deceased, languished in the Ramsey County, Minnesota, workhouse for refusal to sign over his veteran's pension to his wife's lawyers. [318] Paul Hargrove was sentenced in a Nassau, NY civil proceeding to 30 days in prison for not paying $45,000 to his lawyer, a Mr. Gross. [319]

This free, efficient collection service is run by judges for legal professional bedfellows at taxpayers' expense. One law for us yokels, another for the legal profession. Any other businessmen having such privilege would warrant congressional investigation. The Mafia must be envious.

Men representing themselves in court nearly always fight a losing battle. Edward Dufresne, Chief Judge of the Fifth Circuit Court of Appeals in Louisiana directed his clerk to summarily deny all appeals from pro-se petitioners. Guilt-ridden, the clerk committed suicide leaving a note confessing everything.

Even non-avaricious motives are questionable. Like social workers and some judges, the more unscrupulous have a virtual harem of pre- and post-decree divorcees, who are usually sex-starved and willing to do anything for favoritism and best efforts. See an example. [320] Through half-closed eyes, the aspiring divorcee sees only an intrepid champion desirous and capable of tremendously improving her lot in life. An Eagan Minnesota lawyer was suspended for having an affair with a client, then billing her — or more likely her abandoned husband — for time they spent having sex. [321] An old friend of mine, the crop duster Bernie Menier (RIP), a WWII P47 pilot who saw aerial combat in Germany, often railed against these "whoremongers," as he called them. My old roll top desk is a gift from him in return for working on his airplanes briefly. His divorce story was both tragic and comic.

This is not an indictment against all lawyers; many are fine and honest men. However, a man — especially a divorcing man wanting adequate representation — should join a reform organization to find one. See Existing U.S. Organizations in Part IV.

The welfare bureaucracy

When the proper, natural breadwinner is eliminated, the welfare empire eagerly usurps traditional male roles and functions. To maintain their jobs and perquisites, social "workers" assume the male function, replace the man in the family and become surrogate husbands and fathers. They encourage wives to kick husbands out, providing courts with supporting rationale for awarding maternal custody, so as to control the affected lives.

Administrators, while striving to appear virtuous, invariably oppose realistic social reforms, such as father custody and tightening of welfare eligibility, because their careers depend on existence of the support problem. They undermine a society of morally and financially healthy families because they have so much to lose from them. Like other poverty pimps, their interests lie in creating and perpetuating situations to "work with," so it is financially advantageous for governments to discriminate against fathers and stable, two-parent families. This is nothing less than state-sponsored family abuse. Vast sums are expended in this effort.

It is universally customary for welfare officials and prosecutors to transfer their own guilt for the welfare/fatherless mess to ex-father scapegoats by conjuring up an image of children left to starve, while they and legislator allies spout meaningless drivel about supporting families, and maintaining a Florence Nightingale do-gooder image. Assumption of responsibility for the needs of fatherless families builds caseloads and ultimately their empire.

Surely many social 'workers' began with high, altruistic ideals, but soon lose them in the crunch between the managers above and a multitude of demanding clients below — and end up doing more harm than good. Reportedly, recruiters in Florida had a quota of 150 new enrollees per month. Decades ago, one California welfare worker, Mrs. Belva Deltof, was threatened with dismissal for "conduct unbecoming a county employee" because she exposed hundreds of cases of welfare fraud.

Occasionally one reads about social workers cooperating in the removal of kids from single mothers, but only in cases where they had no choice, where mothers were caught doing something like prostituting their daughters — and that is not necessarily sufficient cause.

Looking after and rehabilitating 'helpless' mothers is a major excuse for their existence. Along with recipients, these 'public servants' are equal beneficiaries of the system. Without the empire built on these gals, most of them would be out of work. Years ago speaking to a group of social workers with their cold stares, I felt as if — to steal Bill Buckley's words — I had passed through the Berlin Wall.

Widespread taxpayer-funded babysitting is another area of great concern. For one tiny, localized example, St. Paul Minn. City Council member Democrat Rebecca Noecker submitted a plan to the school board that would subsidize year-round care for every 3- and 4-year-old in the city. [322]

It is amusing to see officials being questioned by the news media in an attempt to determine what is wrong with the system. This is like asking lawyers what is wrong with divorce. Neither will expose the causes of problems nor advocate an effective cleanup beyond the usual platitudes. Like arsonists posing as firemen, they lobby for ever-harsher anti-male legislation, which only creates more need for them. To give the illusion of concern about fraud, welfare departments have periodic or continuing programs of investigating themselves. To no one's surprise, they always come up clean, much as did the U.S. Justice Department whitewashing the Attorney General in the "Fast and Furious" matter and the IRS investigating itself over targeting conservatives.

Office-holding Offenders:

Woe to you,
scribes Pharisees,
hypocrites

Domestic law and practice could not have reached the depths it has without short-comings in the entire legal environment. In addition to judges, legislators and unelected bureaucrats, a square dance of grey mice — "deep state, swamp" apparatchiks sharing a near-identical genetic code — comprise local and national government offices. Anti-male instinct, coupled with incompetence, is the cement of this entire cabal, marinating in the same misandry as high and low level officialdom. The entire 'divorce industry' is a profitable interdependent cabal of those mentioned above and below, working to keep the profits rolling in. A big inventory of psychologists, custody evaluators, domestic-violence agitators and assorted sycophants make a living in this unsavory manner. Former *Liberator* editor John McGuire called it a "Dickensian underworld you avert your eyes from." La Crosse County Wisconsin Supervisor Keith Belzer blamed men for women's incarceration, saying women are almost always in the system "because of some kind of relationship with a man." [323]

David Schorr, a corporate attorney turned consultant with degrees from NYU and Oxford University, was in a custody battle over his son. During Schorr's weekly visitation his son demanded to be taken to McDonald's for dinner — against Schorr's wishes. Schorr offered any other place. The son threw a temper tantrum, causing psychiatrist Marilyn Schiller to file a report saying Schorr was "wholly incapable of taking care of his son" and should be denied his weekend visitation. "Schorr slapped Schiller with a defamation lawsuit. Though I can easily empathize with member/clients who wanted to kill certain officials, I have counseled against it several times.

Government has little concern about solving men's problems. It helps *cause* them. Existence of problems is in government's interest; it provides rationale for expanded agencies to deal with them. Their priority is to justify existence and paychecks. The US criminal justice system largely serves the ambitions of prosecutors — acting with a veneer of virtue while jumping rope to an anti-male beat. Prosecutors in a hurry need high conviction rates to justify their budgets and build their careers. In 1981, there were about 1,500 U.S. attorneys (prosecutors). How many state and local prosecutors exist now is anyone's guess, all trying to get ahead via their conviction records.

After Gerald Amirault was proven innocent of molesting children in the infamous Fells Acres Day Care case, District Attorney of Middlesex County Massachusetts, Martha Coakley, did everything in her power to see that he stayed in prison. Coakley also went on talk shows to spout her views about his guilt. Coakley's actions strengthened Governor Jane Swift's resolve to deny Gerald Amirault's release from prison for an additional 3 years. Gerald served 18 years. Sister Cheryl and mother Violet served eight years. Similarly, a feminist on the Michigan Parole Board stretched out Will Hetherington's sentence — mentioned in the Crime and Punishment section — by almost a decade.

In a trial of the late Alaska Senator Ted Stevens for misconduct, prosecutors withheld information vital to his defense. [324] Catering to the black community's demands in the Trayvon Martin killing, Florida Chief Prosecutor Angela Corey overcharged defendant Zimmerman with 'murder,' and withheld evidence in order to enhance her case.

A move is afoot by ambitious prosecutors to greatly restrict accused men's access to DNA testing. [325] Their goal should be to see justice done, not to win a case by any means. In 2003, WSJ reporter Dorothy Rabinowitz wrote a fine book, No Crueler Tyrannies, exposing such thinking and injustices.

Some time ago, father activists filed a Federal class action suit charging New York State with prejudice against fathers due to its poor record in awarding custody to fathers. While he was Attorney General of New York, Eliot Spitzer argued for dismissal of the suit as being "frivolous." This prompted the New York chapter of NOW to endorse Democrat Spitzer for Governor with the following language:

> On behalf of over 40,000 supporters, NOW—NYS PAC is proud to endorse Eliot Spitzer as the candidate best suited to become New York's Governor. Mr. Spitzer is rock solid on women's rights and has proven he will make decisions that better the lives of women and girls. With Spitzer in office, NOW (the largest women's rights organization in the US) will be most effective in our ongoing work to eliminate discrimination against women and girls.
>
> In today's context of a conservative United States Supreme Court, it is imperative that our state steps forward, stronger than ever, to protect women's civil rights and reproductive autonomy. Spitzer is solidly pro-choice and, in addition, he is a strong proponent of lesbian/gay civil rights and same-sex marriage. Furthermore, Spitzer fully understands the complicated issues surrounding matrimonial law and child custody, and can help balance these areas toward more equity for women and children.

As Attorney General, Spitzer vigorously prosecuted men for patronizing prostitutes, and signed a law increasing the jail term for men who visit prostitutes from 3 months to 12 months. What makes all this ironic is that the hypocrite Spitzer, reputed to be "Mr. Integrity," was caught in a prostitution sting himself, and forced to resign as Governor. As I recall, prostitution is illegal, but selective prosecution is widespread. The extremely high-paid whores involved with Spitzer came out smelling like roses. One was a celebrity that *Hustler* magazine offered a cool $million to pose.

Anti-male bureaucrats stick their noses even into the business of other countries. USAID has a budget of about $100 million for India. USAID openly brags on its website: "USAID's program was instrumental in the formation of Women Power Connect, a national coalition that advocates for women at all levels of the government. WPC's priority issues include: the implementation of the Domestic Violence Act; [and] the 33% reservation for women in Parliament." [326]

Government incompetence, petty, politically correct nonsense, etc.

The field is a clerisy of social administrators, a playground for community organizers, self-appointed elitists. Especially egregious are nanny 'child protective' agencies. Consider the following newspaper article by attorney Jeffery M. Leving and blogger Glenn Sacks: *Choosing Foster Parents over Fathers*.

In the heartbreaking Melinda Smith case, a father and daughter were needlessly separated by the foster care system for over a decade. Last week, Los Angeles County settled a lawsuit over the case for an undisclosed sum. Yet a recent Urban Institute study found that the Smith case typifies the way the foster care system harms children by disregarding the loving bonds they share with their fathers.

Thomas — whose fitness as a father was never impugned nor legally questioned — continued to receive and pay his child support bills. Authorities refused to disclose his daughter's whereabouts, and didn't even inform him that his daughter had been taken by the County. Smith employed private investigators and attorneys to try to find Melinda and secure visitation rights, but he eventually ran out of money.

Rather than allowing Smith to raise his own daughter, the system shuttled Melinda through seven different foster care placements. An understandably angry child, her outbursts led authorities to house her in a residential treatment center alongside older children convicted of criminal activity—when she was only seven years old.

Melinda says that during this period she was told that her father was a "deadbeat dad" who had abandoned her. When Melinda was 16, she told an investigating social worker that the "most important thing" for her was to find her dad. Moved by her story, the unusual social worker began searching for Melinda's father — and found him in one day. In 2005, Thomas and Melinda were finally reunited.

See Truth or Fiction? by Doug Henson, from *The Liberator*:

The following is a fictional Television Public Service announcement from Child Protective Services (CPS).

The scene: A middle class home in suburbia, a Father and Mother are having a heart to heart talk with their 12 year old son, who got sent home from school for taking lunch money from the younger kids.

Dad (with raised voice): Billy, I don't know what we're going to do with you. We've tried talking, we've tried time outs, we've even tried grounding you, and it just doesn't seem to work. Your Mother and I have discussed this and we've decided that you are going to be grounded indefinitely until you pay back every dime you took from those kids. You will come home from school every day and perform a list of chores your Mother and I will draw up. Is that understood?

Billy: You can't do that to me, I'll call CPS and tell them you're abusing me. I know my rights and you can't do anything to me.

Dad to Mom: I told you we should have spanked him when he was younger. My Dad spanked me and I came out all right.

Mom to Dad: Now Bill, we discussed this before the kids were born, we swore we'd never spank them.

Dad to Billy: That's it, go to your room right now, No supper for you tonight! And don't think you can scare me with this CPS talk. I'm your Father and I can most definitely punish you and there's nothing CPS can do.

Billy runs out of the room. Three days later: There's a knock on the door.

Dad (Opens door, to see a young woman; and three police officers standing on his front porch, with hands on their guns): Can I help you?

Young Woman: Mr. Johnson? I'm Liz Feminazi from Child Protective Services. We've had a complaint that you're abusing your child.

Dad: What? That's ridiculous, I've never laid a hand on my son! Who told you such a lie?

Liz Feminazi: That's none of your business, now step aside and let us in, we're here to interview your abused son, Billy.

Dad: No! I will not allow you into my home to interview my son about this. I have my Rights!

Policeman 1 (still with hand on gun): Sir, Step out of the way, immediately, or you'll be placed under arrest for interfering with a government agent, in the performance of her job.

Dad: This is absurd, I'm calling my lawyer.

Dad starts to turn and close the door when the policeman pulls his weapon and yells: (Policeman 1) FREEZE! Raise your hands and step out of the house, NOW! Turn around and lace your fingers behind your neck!

Liz Feminazi: You're obviously a violent man Mr. Johnson. You have no business raising a child. We're taking you in and we're taking your children, Billy and Suzy, into protective custody. I'll make sure you never see them again. We've got a lot of foster families looking for more income, who would just love to have another child to take care of.

This happens more often than people realize. It could very easily happen to you. That scenario materialized when Shawn Moore of Carney's Point New Jersey posted a picture on the internet of his 10-year-old son holding a .22 caliber rifle birthday present. Welfare caseworkers and a SWAT team came to their house. [327]

And it evidently happened again when divorced and retired Army Sergeant Tom Ball was accused by his ex-wife of domestic violence against his 4-year-old daughter, causing him to lose his job and making him unable to continue making child support payments. Monadnock Family Services and numerous agencies got involved. As a result, Ball lost his job and was unable to continue making child support payments. Finally tired of the vicious run-around by the agencies, Ball chose to end his life in the hopes that someone would pay attention to the plight of families destroyed by this horrible system. He immolated himself in front of the Cheshire county New Hampshire county courthouse. The whole story appears on the internet. [328]

There is legitimate concern over the troubling conflict between parental rights and government authority; however, it is important that the rights of citizens be respected. Thomas Jefferson quoted William Pitt the Elder thusly: "The poorest man in his cottage bid defiance to all the forces of the crown. It may be frail, its roof may shake, the wind may blow through it, the storm may enter, the rain may enter, but the King of England cannot enter. All of his forces dare not cross the threshold of the ruined cottage." (Ha).

Baton Rouge, Louisiana mother Schaquana Evita Spears spanked her 10 and 13 year-old boys after they broke into a neighbor's house and stole property. Spears was taken to jail and her other children removed from her home. The kids father was in prison; Spears didn't want the boys following in his footsteps. [329]

It's ubiquitous; in February 2014, the Scottish Parliament passed a "Children and Young People Bill" by a vote of 103-0. It is specifically intended to fulfill Scotland's perceived obligations under the United Nations' Convention on the Rights of the Child (CRC), includes a provision to assign a specific government worker to every child at birth. These "named persons" will be charged with safeguarding each child's welfare and with representing the state to the family.

Besides money and empire, what motivates such officials and citizens? Reasons range from indiscriminate chivalry — the Galahad fantasy — to self-aggrandizement, to fad and political correctness. While many office holders favor women in order that they might receive pats on the head from feminists, others quake in fear of feminist power, genuflecting before it. Lower level mice shine the shoes of their female-pandering superiors.

According to the Election Assistance Commission, voter suppression is occurring within the normally conservative and mostly male military. In 2010 only 4.6 percent of military voters were able to cast absentee ballots that counted. [330] Jan R. Frye, Deputy Assistant Secretary for Acquisition and Logistics claims the Department of Veterans Affairs has been spending at least $6 billion a year on fraud, waste and abuse in violation of federal contracting rules. [331] The *Federal Fumbles* Report documents $250 billion in dubious federal spending.

The Minnesota Assistance Council for Veterans seeking to solve homeless among veterans commenced with 17 homeless women veterans and is currently at six. The year this was written they housed 35 women veterans. Compare this to the number of male veterans seeking housing.

While on the subject of officials, we must not overlook the police. Granted, a few cops are no better than thugs. A sadistic, cowboy minority — reminiscent of the night shift at Abu Ghraib—salivate for the opportunity to rescue damsels in distress and impress the gals. Read A Government of Wolves: The Emerging American Police State by John Whitehead. I had a nasty encounter with one such horse's ass. Sued him in federal court, and found out how hard it is to beat city hall.

These few defame the respectable great majority, and motivate black rappers and foolish demonstrators who advocate the murder of all cops.

Guardians of the peace are necessary because there are so many dangerous people these days. It is not cops' fault if they must enforce bad laws or stupid interpretations of them; they have to hold their noses and do their duty. Most cops are decent guys trying to do a nasty job, front-line troops in the war against crime. President Trump recognized this on TV. The older one gets, the more one appreciates good cops like my dear friend Gary Weimar a big, tough retiree who worked the rough Minneapolis neighborhoods. He called my wife Ritzy "the Martha Steward of (Gopher Prairie.)"

Feminism

Criticizing feminists nowadays is something akin to a hate crime, but here goes:

Feminism's Origin and Spread
Much ado about nothing.

There are as many answers to Freud's famous question — "What does a woman want?"— as there are women. It is true, some women have sometimes been discriminated against. In 1792, a few frustrated women organized to protest and eliminate ideas, laws, and practices perceived to be averse to women. The platform had many picayunish railings and distortions. They considered homemaking wives "parasites." "Housework is shitwork" was a slogan. Theodore Roosevelt termed most of these complainers "fools." Actually, in view of the advantages women had by virtue of chivalry, any disadvantages were of minor consequence; the sole exceptions being voting rights and losing maiden surnames in marriage. But good arguments to the contrary have been made there.

These early suffragettes had a few male supporters; husbands or inheritances usually provided the leisure and funds to pursue their fantasies. So one might say they were biting the hand that fed them. Pioneer Susan B. Anthony was a racist, truth to tell. In 1906, Sir Arthur Conan Doyle founded the Divorce Law Reform Union in England to protect women (in those days the pendulum of power in domestic relations favored men in many regards). Yet, Doyle opposed women's suffrage and false accusations. [332]

The movement got wind in its sails. Like a tsunami, the feminist ascendancy swept over the western world. Partly due to the forces of modernism, the sex-favoring situation changed drastically. Through a barrage of demonstrations, speeches, and publications, the juggernaut became a veritable religion, widely and blindly accepted, much to the detriment of individuals, society and industry. As with a pendulum, the momentum carried sexual dominance to the opposite extreme, to an almost pathologically anti-male position, largely explaining the social and sexual chaos of present society. Prof. Amneus maintained that feminism is in process of altering the male kinship system.

Contrary to defending motherhood, feminists politicized it, piggybacking on arguments of civil rights activists. Witness: the Million Mom March, Mothers Against Drunk Driving, Moms Rising and Code Pink. Feminism has made many inroads into the Girl Scouts (Betty Friedan was named honorary member to the National Board of Girl Scouts — with voting privileges). Many other public institutions provide facilities for the dissemination of their gibberish and accommodation of their huddlings (similar to UFO conventions). Still in diapers, with no adult supervision, carnival-barking feminists got into all sorts of mischief, throwing giant taxpayer-financed jamborees in domestic and foreign fever swamps. The nonsense has even affected Catholic nuns to the point the Vatican has investigated, citing "a certain secular mentality... and perhaps a certain feminist spirit." [333] It is no coincidence that this freak show came to fruition in the silly 60s (1960's).

The *Encyclopedia of Women's Organizations Worldwide* listed 1027 in the U.S. Here's a listing of the U. S. outfits the Men's Defense Association dug up decades ago: Catholics for a Free Choice, Center for Reproductive Rights, Center for the Advancement of Women, Center For Women's Policy Studies, feminist Majority Foundation, Freedom Socialist Party, Institute for Women's Policy Research, League of Women Voters, Malia—Collective of Italian-American Women, NARAL Pro-Choice America (National Abortion Rights Action League), National Abortion Federation, National Council for Research on Women, National Council of Women's Organizations, National Organization for Women (NOW, the feminist's attack dog), National Women's Law Center, National Women's Political Caucus, Older Women's League, Peace and Freedom Party, Planned Parenthood Federation of America, Radical Women, Veteran feminists of America, Women's Policy Inc., Young Women's Christian Association (YWCA). By now, there are certainly more here and many more in other countries.

In July of 2020 I've noticed several strange new offshoots perhaps in the U. S. : Girlboss, Refinery 29 and Women's Strike. Don't know anything about them. May they go the way of the others.

Feminist Philosophy, Positions, Demands
Therein lay dragons.

Since its somewhat rational founding, mission creep has taken hold. Feminism is now a spectrum, ranging from the delusional, pursuing various schemes and fantasies, to the rational if misguided — all advocating under the veil of rights for women. There is also a difference in degree; as with Muslims, a few are stark raving mad, dangerously so. Too many of the gentler persuasions in both of these groupings fail to denounce their radicals' excesses. Strange theories, empirically falsifiable claims, Oprah-land pity-parties and tempests in teapots percolated in a narrow culture where they were reinforced through repetition by like-minded persons, with all the thoughtfulness of a rap message and tampon throwing riot squads.

A basic premise of modern feminism, its Strum und Drang, its diktat, consists of several delusional notions:

— that gender/sex is "socially constructed" by the patriarchy,

— that logic is a male construct,

— that discrimination against women is greater than that against men (Erica Jong declared mothers and children are "the most oppressed groups in society.")

Brilliant Australian Babette Francis ridicules feminist Luce Srigaary who argues that the relativity equation $E=mc^2$ is an unfair masculinism because it "privileges" the masculine speed of light over feminine sound waves. Some even believe that Wikipedia is too masculinist. [334]

When it suited their purposes, feminists considered the sexes both identical, e.g., in employment, and different, e.g., in child custody. Denying innate differences between the sexes, they demanded special privileges to compensate for differences that they deny exist. Their little thoughtlets considered women too fragile to be pinched in an office, but tough enough to engage in combat.

Panting to be "empowered" and uninhibited by reality, they demanded advantages men earned without the disadvantages, such as having to earn them. They wanted equal employment with men, and equal pay for not necessarily equal ability or equal work. They wanted workforce rules to be more female-friendly, despite claiming that there is no difference between male and female. They clamored for fifty percent of women in the Senate, but not fifty percent of military casualties or industrial accidents, or of women in prison cells. They demanded equal representation in the boardrooms of industry, but not in the grubby jobs or among the burned out inhabitants of skid row. These demands are like wanting a one sided coin. Writer Jeffrey Jackson tells us that we are now seeing post-feminist "domestic divas" who seek the advantages of both the feminist and traditionalist worlds, as depicted in *Desperate Housewives*, i.e. the total equality that feministas demand without the "drudgery" of housework.

There is a manufactured atmosphere of male dominance and oppression beyond the reach of rational analysis. Jessica Valenti defined feminism thusly: "Feminism is a structural analysis of a world that oppresses women, an ideology based on the notion that patriarchy exists and that it needs to end." Prime purposes of feminism are "to establish a lesbian-socialist republic and to dismantle the family unit." [335] Ponder this from the *Declaration of feminism* (November, 1971): "The end of the institution of marriage is a necessary condition for the liberation of women. Therefore, it is important for us to encourage women to leave their husbands..." Leftist and feminist discussion blogs on the internet are rife with such sentiments.

Maybe you can't fool all the people all the time, but you can fool enough of them with lopsided factoids and twaddle to ruin a country. This is explained by a founder of modern psychology, William James, who noted that, "There is nothing so absurd that, if it is repeated often enough, will not become accepted." Nazi propaganda minister Joseph Goebbels said if you tell a lie big enough and keep repeating it, people will eventually come to believe it. Nikita Khrushchev could have been a feminist. He once said to Richard Nixon, "If people believe there is an imaginary river out there, you don't tell them there is no river. You build an imaginary bridge over the imaginary river." Feminists learned these lessons well. In their own little world, feminists — even more than most people — believe what they want to believe.

Former Senator Daniel Moynihan said, "Everyone is entitled to his own opinion, but not to his own facts." Employing their expertise at manipulating statistics, feminists made up facts to support their demands. They claimed that women earned only 76 cents for every dollar earned by men. This is a bald-faced lie, roundly rebutted later herein. Yet President Obama repeated that falsehood during the State of the Union address on January 20, 2015. Years ago feminists circulated a myth that the expression "Rule of thumb" referred to a prohibition in law that a man could beat his wife with a rod no wider than his thumb. Actually, that rule referred to a carpenters' measure of approximately one inch; it was quicker than going for a ruler.

To paraphrase Ann Coulter, feminists are constantly rushing in with their rulebook about what can and cannot be said. Beating the victim drum, this habitually offended community wallows in hyperbole and weapons-grade rhetoric. Spokeswomen profess to seek equality but these are largely head-fakes, classic "have their cake and eat it too" situations. The movement is not for equality on the issues of child custody, of battered spouses, of military obligations (rank, yes, but not the draft obligation), of family support after divorce, of creating state men's commissions to examine and recommend solutions to men's problems, of sex discrimination in criminal court, of ladies' nights, etc., etc. Hitting the bull in the eye, men's movement expatriate Stu Miller (now living in Mexico) says, "If feminism is really about 'equality and creating a better world for everyone,' why is it called 'feminism' and not 'equalism'? Probably for the same reason the Violence Against Women Act is not called the 'Domestic Violence Prevention Act'."

Then there is the silly claim that marriage is a trap for women. Au contraire! Who sets the tender trap, baits it, and lures men into it? A traditional wife is not a Stepford wife. Those who prefer the old patterns are not brainwashed. Those who prefer the new feminist patterns are so. Those who tend to their "kinder, kuche, and kirche" are usually happier than bra burners. Any woman who loves her family does not consider taking care of its needs to be demeaning or arduous. Beware the woman who does. A feminist inebriation is that divorce should benefit the woman equally as does marriage. This makes divorce attractive for women. The incidence-of-divorce curve follows the sexual-liberation-of-women curve. In 1953 Israel, Denmark, Sweden, and West Germany had the next-highest divorce rates behind the United States. Contrast divorce rates in these countries of liberated women with the low rates of countries like Japan and India.

Feminists want what it pleases them to call "abortion rights" on demand, divorce on demand, child custody on demand, and Lord knows what other demands. The feminist catechism, while it rewrites and profanes church doctrine, has made abortion a sacrament, helping to convince mothers to slaughter many millions of babies without paternal consent. Murdering babies has more to do with women's convenience than with their 'health.' Feminists sob that it is discrimination if poor women cannot afford abortions. Government agrees. Hear Linda Hirshman in the *Daily Beast*: "support for abortion rights and Obamacare (are) litmus tests for true feminism" (one might wish their mothers had opted to pursue the freedom-to-choose of which they are such hearty advocates). Abortions — 300,000 babies every year — are Planned Parenthoods' primary business. Other services they provide are available at any medical facility. A recent report revealed they received over $1.5 billion in taxpayer funds from 2013 to 2015. [336]

Feminists and sympathizers resent the natural conflict between motherhood and work, demanding paid maternal leave for childbirth. The underlying assumption is that mothers belong in the workforce. NOW filed a lawsuit in federal court against fatherhood programs in Alaska, Idaho and Oregon that provide career counseling to fathers who are incarcerated, in the military or those with disabled children so that the fathers can pay support; the objection being that women aren't included. One can only hope that this suit, if successful, could turn out to be a Pyrrhic victory, in view of the danger to the plethora of government-funded programs that benefit only women.

These noise machines want access to men's clubs, organizations and schools without invitation. Men-only clubs and lounges are considered sexist, but women-only clubs and lounges like the one at University of

California-Berkeley's Boalt Hall are "empowering." Those shrews aspiring to invade male sanctuaries are trading on the false premise (curiously supported by the courts) that a place is public simply because it must meet certain public standards, like obtaining a liquor license. This mania for forced integration of the sexes in pursuit of some questionable right violates a prior right of free association. What would be said if men forced their way into women's beauty salons, private clubs and bathhouses? It would be interesting if some young Lotharios filed suit, under the rationale of Vorchneimer v. Philadelphia School District, to integrate women's schools.

A favorite feminist gripe concerns past reluctance of the business community to extend credit to women without a husband's signature. Sure, it was discriminatory, but no more unreasonable or unjustified than reluctance of insurance companies to provide fire protection in ghetto areas. In both cases, the risk involved is demonstrably high.

Frivolous complaints include fewer Nobel Prizes and less subsidization for women's athletic teams. Denial of free contraceptives constitutes a "war on women." [fn27] Some demands sound reasonable, but closer examination reveals that they want privilege upon privilege. Imaginary grievances are fodder for lucrative lawsuits. Feminists demanded the heads of ESPN's Stephen Smith and NFL Commissioner Goodell for paying insufficient attention to the imbroglio surrounding footballer Ray Rice. Goodell abjectly apologized. In 2016 feminists sued the city of Ft. Collins Colorado in federal court challenging anti-topless laws as "sexist." Barbara Mapes, former student senate vice president, and Sally Hughes, former student senator, and other radicals at the Minneapolis Metropolitan Community College demanded access to men's toilets. Does this support Freud's theory about penis envy?

Feminist Martha Sawyer proposed the subsidization of women by "the most advantaged class in society — white males." Feminist Carolyn Shaw Bell actually proposed taxing all men to subsidize all women. Yet, NOW President Terry O'Neill inveigled against proposals to tax cosmetic surgery because it would unduly impact women. After the Haiti earthquake, women's groups insisted women were more deserving of relief help than men.

During their long march, feminists equated their cause onto that of the much more legitimate civil rights movement, as subsequently and equally illogically did the homosexual element. Their propagandists

---

[27] See a video by Ben Shapiro that absolutely destroys that claim: http://www.westernjournalism.com/ben-shapiro-destroys-lefts-war-women-argument/#l56WYeZ1btmoaZzm.03. May Boko Haram show them what a war on women really is.

employed clever reversals of reality. They cruised in with claims of comparable grievance.

The Cleveland Chapter of NOW "girlcotted" Cleveland Indian baseball games because there were no "bat girls." Connecticut libbers threw fits when the state canine license carried the shape of a miniature fire hydrant. They felt it discriminated against female dogs. One rant is against men sitting with legs spread, called "manspreading." Has anyone else noticed that many women drivers seem obliged to pass every male driver on the road? That directive must appear somewhere in the N.O.W. Assertiveness Manual. One element hallucinates that all men and women who are happy in their sexuality and functional roles suffer from lowered consciousness or sensitivity.

Some object even to the term, "ladies," as does Microsoft Word's spell check. Those who would sacrifice the pedestals of their sisters for their own imagined advantage have suspect motives. Complaints about the idea of pedestals for ladies stem from those not deserving to be placed thereon. Feminists hate beauty contests. Little wonder — few of them are attractive enough to jump out of a cake. They are often shocked — shocked! — about the "exploitation" of women in nudie magazines. Such complaints are misdirected at men; voyeurism is caused at least as much by the exhibitionists as by the opportunists.

Feminists preach that women's accomplishments lie in rivaling males in creativity and external accomplishments. One gimmick is to pick out faults characteristic of a few males, distort and proclaim them to be characteristic of all males. Railing against their feminine nature as if it were a congenital defect, the sisterhood has a running argument with life itself. They must consider men to be superior to women or they would not so desperately emulate men, often our worst qualities at that — brashness and garrulousness among others. Bitchiness seldom equates to manhood. Activists evidently aspire to be second-class males. If successful, they will indeed be female eunuchs, victims of their own destruction.

Before the advent of this aberration, women were on pedestals. May the descent they clamor for occur. However, the price must be paid. Further demands must topple existing favoritism. Feminists are right about one thing — the general unhappiness of women. But they misjudged the cause. It is not oppression by men. It is the desperate, losing attempt to emulate males. Since 1960, paralleling the influence of women's lib., the suicide rate among women has almost doubled. Nancy H. Allen, president of the American Association of Suicideology, cites as a cause "the pressure of the woman going out in the man's working world." Hoist with their own petard!

Maureen Dowd, the professional spinster columnist of the New York Times wrote a book called <u>Are Men Necessary?</u> claiming that men are intimidated by powerful women, a category in which she places herself. Wrong! Men prefer feminine women, fewer of whom are "powerful" in the business sense. Apparently, men have not found her necessary. With some exceptions mentioned herein, I dispute the claim that 'male chauvinists' are actually uncomfortable with their masculinity. If that were true, they would be rejecting it, as those nominally male camp followers of feminism do. Most are obviously more comfortable with their masculinity than libbers are with their femininity. A good article on the silliness of feminists' attempts to de-sex the language appeared in the 6/20/2011 *Human Events* magazine.

Feminists begrudge veterans' benefits, conveniently ignoring the sacrifices of veterans, including the thousands of acres of graves of men killed defending the very existence of this country. [fn28] These women are alive while many of their contemporary men are dead — killed in wars defending them. Their wild demands would not be possible without these sacrifices. Too many of our fighting men have been killed and injured in battle protecting our way of life to lose it to outlandish, misandric ideas.

I tend to reject the artificial distinction between "gender feminists," "equity feminists" (an oxymoron if I ever heard one) and "victim feminists" which insists that women are by definition victims. It appears that accomplished women created a schism between radical feminists, (Radfemlibs — if I may coin the term) the main object of criticism here, and more moderate/rational ones.

Strident feminists, still in puberty, are marching across campus wearing 'pussy hats,' chanting obscene words and selling penis-shaped lollipops to students. Feminist Students United (FSU) of the University of North Carolina — Chapel Hill scheduled a sex party for November 10th, 2005 to include "pin the finger on the clitoris" and "locate the g-spot" games followed by contests to see how quickly and properly people of both sexes can put condoms on bananas, with "lots of information on masturbation, orgasm and contraception, orgasm — how to have better ones, or how to help your girlfriend." Feminist "educators" present a workshop entitled 'The Female Orgasm' at colleges across the nation. The cost of $3,650 is doubtless picked up by taxpayers as with so many other feminist programs. Allegheny College hired professional sex educators to teach students how to reach orgasm in what was billed as an educational seminar. A Twin Cities faux men's group instructor did the same for men (See Internal Problems in the Part V Men's Movement chapter). There is a feminist professor at

---

[28] Someday, with tribute to Thomas Gray, I hope to write an Elegy in a Veterans' Cemetery.

UNC-Chapel Hill who thinks women can form lifelong domestic partnerships with dogs (male dogs, no doubt. You can guess why) and that those relationships will actually be fulfilling enough to replace marital relationships with men.

Often, libbers decry pornography, though their own literature is largely foul and pornographic. Their idea of high art/drama is "The Vagina Monologues" (maybe better titled "The Tender Trap.") V-Day has replaced Valentine's Day on more than 500 college campuses (including Catholic ones); while some of these same institutions ban the Bible. When College Republicans at Roger Williams University in Rhode Island rained on the celebrations of V-Day with a reductio ad absurdum by inaugurating Penis Day and staging a satire called The Penis Monologues, the official reaction was horror. Participants were ordered to cease and desist. You can't make this stuff up. The Eagle Forum proclaimed "One of their most desired results is the smashing of every taboo in Western culture." Whatever happened to propriety? My God! Pray for us.

Political leanings

Feminist-inspired politics are not only nonsensical; they can be positively dangerous. Jeannette Rankin, the first Congresswoman and the "outstanding living feminist" according to N.O.W., cast the only vote against America's declaration of war on Japan. In view of the current dangers to the country, today's peaceniks, largely of the female persuasion, are equally naive. Writer Dennis Prager remarked, "Virtually every car I ever have seen display the bumper sticker 'War is not the answer' was driven by a woman."

Although feminist academics seem to have a certain ersatz intellectual aura, their intellectual seat is portside, a 'ladies' auxiliary of the anti-American left. Those who admitted to no more than being secular socialists include Gloria Steinem, Simone de Beauvoir, Kate Millett (RIP), Eli Zaretsky, Evelyn Reed, Barbara Erenreich, Vivian Howe, Rayna Rapp, Margaret Bentson, Firestone, Bleier, Mitchell, Chodorow, MacKinnon, Sheila, and Rowbotham. At least one modern day presidential candidate is following suit. The harder core with no tether to reality embraced actual Marxism. A card-carrying communist, Betty Friedan (AKA Betty Goldstein) was a political activist and professional propagandist for that party for 25 years. [337] Much of their philosophy is derived from Engels' <u>Origin of the Family</u>. James Bowman said, "Ideological feminism... adapted Marxist class analysis to the domestic sphere and so interpreted love and loyalty in terms of power relationships." Angela Davis, onetime leader of the Black Panther Party, ran twice on the Communist Party USA presidential ticket. Not hard to guess which are the 'useful idiots.' [338]

Despite belief differences between Islamic activists and American feminists, Australia's Babette Francis claims the former have co-opted the latter due to their common enemy, Donald Trump.

Some quotes follow:

"Feminism, Socialism, and Communism are one in the same, and Socialist/Communist government is the goal of feminism." — MacKinnon, *Toward a Feminist Theory of the State.*

"A world where men and women would be equal is easy to visualize, for that is what the Soviet Revolution promised." — Simone de Beauvoir, *The Second Sex.*

"The Women's Caucus [endorses] Marxist-Leninist thought." — Robin Morgan, *Sisterhood is Powerful.*

"...Women's liberation, if not the most extreme then certainly the most influential neo-Marxist movement in America, has done to the American home what communism did to the Russian economy, and most of the ruin is irreversible." — Prof. Ruth Wisse of Harvard in 1998.

Hear Robert H. Dierker, Jr., Chief Judge of Missouri Circuit Court:

If Social Security is the "third rail" of American politics, then sex is the third rail of American law. Anyone who touches it, except in the manner approved by the tyrants of tolerance, is fried. In this realm, the tyranny of tolerance is best described as rule by the radical feminist cadre of liberalism. ...femifascists display single-minded devotion to imposing their tyranny on the American people—and will viciously punish those who resist.

Hear Paul Craig Roberts:

Feminism is the intellectual organization of gender hatred, just as Marxism was the intellectual organization of class hatred. The feminist aim is to overthrow 'patriarchal tyranny.' In this undertaking, males' civil rights count for no more than those of the bourgeoisie in Soviet Russia or the Jews in National Socialist Germany. [339]

Hear David D. Gilmore, Dept. of Anthropology, SUNY/Stony Brook:

Unhappily, feminism is leading to the destruction of the human project — that is, the herculean effort of humankind since the Neanderthals to reproduce its social structures and its children. It will take a few more generations, but civilization is probably doomed as a result of the feminist demonization of masculinity, of motherhood, and of the family. Europe will be finished in 50 years, and America in a little more."

"Radical feminism is the emost dstructive and fanatical movement to come down to us from the Sixties," wrote Robert Bork, "Feminism as we know it is the direct ideological and political descendant of the

Women's Ku Klux Klan (WKKK)." [340]

Political Influence

Powerful mojo, indeed.

These gender/sex warriors have enormous political power. Fevered activists learn tactics from the likes of Saul Alinsky. Akin to the tail wagging the dog, their inordinate influence is out of proportion to their numbers (Don't forget women in general have 54 percent of the vote). Their lobbyists, amateur and professional, are literally swarming in state capitols across this nation, snout to snout with welfare recipients, seeking legislative corrections for problems that don't exist, influencing government policy, spewing anti-male messages before Congressional committees and demanding funding.

Many segments of society clamor for a piece of the government largess pie, usually wanting more than their share, but few as effectively as feminists. Government and philanthropic organizations throw vast sums of money at their crock-pot of programs and office holders. Feminists receive generous funding from the Ford foundation (known for also supporting communist and radical Islamic groups). [341] A secretary at a FAA facility I worked at in Minneapolis was authorized to spend a great deal of time working on feminist and union issues, on the taxpayers' dime. Arguments for spending public funds for feminist schemes lack any coherent rationale.

In times of shortage, government budget cuts are imposed, but funding for feminist programs are sacrosanct; no one dares challenge them. Even though the current levels of funding provide women's advocacy programs nearly a billion dollars per year, NOW instructs their members to ask for still more programs. At the National Council of Women's Organizations' briefing on "Challenges and Opportunities in the 112th Congress: Women's Economic Security" held at the nation's capital, Terry O'Neill, president of the National Organization for Women, and Heidi Hartmann, president of the Institute for Women's Policy Research, urged the federal government not to cut funding for social (women's) programs even at the expense of going further into debt. [342]

Femagogues are turning to the United Nations Development Fund for Women (UNIFEM) to "promote political, economic and social empowerment of women," and are promoting the Millennium Declaration goals as a means of slipping in their pet causes. They are pinning their hope on forcing the U.S. to sign the Convention on the Elimination of All Forms of Discrimination Against Women (CEDAW) treaty. With CEDAW-supporting Democrats holding power in Washington, and Sen. Barbara Boxer well placed as Foreign Relations committee chairwoman, we can expect a concerted effort to seek ratification. The Obama administration supported the CEDAW treaty.

Paying off feminists for their support in his election, Barack Obama proposed a $3.8 trillion budget that would exempt programs for women and girls from the spending restrictions he proposed for other programs. This included one $billion a year to fund VAWA. The payoffs are detailed in a budget document entitled Opportunity and Progress for Women and Girls. "We're looking at a lot of significant funding increases for women's programs in a year when the president has ordered a three-year, non-security, discretionary spending freeze," said White House spokesperson Kate Bedingfield. Expenditure-wise, one woman is worth three men.

Dig this press release from NOW:

Contact: Mai Shiozaki, 202-628-8669, ext. 116; cell 202-641-1906.

NOW Cheers White House Council on Women and Girls: "We Got the Entire Cabinet!" Statement of NOW President Kim Gandy. March 11, 2009:

NOW cheers the formation of the White Council on Women and Girls, which was created by executive order of President Barack Obama today. It was a pleasure for me to be at the White House to hear the president make this commitment to supporting women and girls in such strong and unequivocal terms. It was a heartening moment for those of us who have worked so hard for this day.

There can be no question that the needs of women and girls require the attention of the White House itself. As President Obama pointed out in today's speech, women still earn 78 cents for every dollar earned by men fn29. One out of every four women will experience some form of domestic violence during her lifetime. Women make up more than half the population, yet are only 17 percent of the U.S. Congress. And while women are 49 percent of the nation's workforce, only three percent of the Fortune 500 companies are headed by women.

The make-up of the White House Council is extraordinary. It will be headed by Valerie Jarrett, assistant to the president and one of his closest friends and advisors, and will include every Cabinet secretary and the head of every Cabinet-level agency. The Executive Director of the Council will be Tina Tchen, deputy assistant to the president and a long-time advocate of women's rights.

We asked for a Cabinet-level office to work on women's issues, and we got the entire Cabinet. NOW looks forward to supporting the work of the White House Council on Women and Girls in the months ahead. There is much work to be done.

NOW president Terry O'Neill, in an interview with *The Daily Caller*, explained that she would like to see complete gender/sex parity in Obama's second-term cabinet. "I think that if half of the cabinet were women and half of the Supreme Court and half of Congress were

---

[29] This oft-repeated feminist canard is a blatant lie. As they say, a lie gets half way around the world before the truth gets its pants on.

women, we would see a lot more policies for expanding education and health care and social services that allow communities to thrive," O'Neill explained. [343] Ann Coulter said, "This is what happens when you allow women to think about public policy."

Consider this from the *Phyllis Schlafly Report* of September 2010:

> Congress is now trying to give (President Obama) a Czar with global powers. It would be a Czar over women's issues, worldwide.
>
> Based in the State Department, her statutory title will be "Ambassador-at-Large for Global Women's Issues." Her task will be to assure a "gender integration" perspective in all State Department policies and programs.
>
> The breath-taking reach of her powers is openly stated in the bill's first section: "The Ambassador shall coordinate and advise, and where relevant lead — (1) State Department activities and policies, including as they affect programs and funding relating to prevention and response, including gender integration and women's development internationally as relates to prevention and response." ...
>
> Reinforcing her ukases will be a "Women's Development Advisor" with a desk in the U.S. Agency for International Development (USAID). This is the same federal agency that sent millions to a radical feminist group in India called Women Power Connect, which used U.S. taxpayers' money to lobby for a 33 percent female quota in the Indian Parliament.

The vehicle for this latest pandering to the feminist left is the International Violence Against Women Act called I - VAWA (S.2982 andH.R.4594). The lead sponsors are (Dem.) Senators John Kerry and Barbara Boxer.

The bill broadly defines violence against women to include non-violent "psychological harm," "intimidation at work," and "psychological violence perpetrated or condoned by the government of the country in which the victim is a resident." Naturally, lots of taxpayers' money will be needed for so awesome a task, so the bill authorizes $1billion over five years.

Feminist activists who marched in protest against the election of President Trump and other conservatives called themselves "Nasty women." I couldn't agree more. Their incoherent rants are being echoed by leftist politicians like the weird Elizabeth Warren.

Canadian Premier Justin Trudeau, proclaimed himself a feminist. The governments of Iceland and Suriname hosted a conference in January 2015 to address violence against women. [344] "Sweden's new government is a feminist government," said Sweden's new Social Democrat Prime Minister Stefan Loefven; half his cabinet is female. [345] Norway is also aboard.

Ultra Radical Fringe,
Über-feminist Voices

As Forrest Gump put it,
'Stupid Is as Stupid Does.'
Raging nonsense on stilts.

The political left seems to have lost its grip on reality. [fn30] The "lunatic fringe" (Teddy Roosevelt's description) is composed of wound-too-tight, perpetually indignant misanthropes, and female chauvinist pigs — to hurl a horribly-overworked epithet back across the fence. Regarding radical feminists in general, one of their most desired results is the smashing of every taboo in Western culture. Moving in these circles must have sent them barking mad. They believe all men are guilty of being men, an original sin no amount of virtue can erase, that men are good for three things: donating sperm, changing the oil, and paying alimony/support. In their bottomless ignorance, radicals consider all men to be white-slavers and rapists, those under 13 only potentially so. Banging their spoons on their highchairs, and seemingly infected with Mad Cow disease or permanent PMS, the pouting, screaming and snarls of these Pavlovian types amount to little more than a witches' brew of victimization, insecurity, resentment and hysterics.

On page 19 of his book, <u>The Tyranny of Tolerance</u>, Missouri Circuit Court Judge Robert H. Dierker, Jr. makes it clear: "At its core, the femi-fascist agenda is based on its hatred for men." The passion of radicals overwhelms reason to the point they cannot be taken seriously. Like aliens from a parallel universe, they hide in a Twilight Zone where logic and common sense cannot penetrate. Their mentality is best summed up with the bellow: "I am woman, hear me whine." Methinks they doth whine too much. Verbal grenades sum up their attitude toward men and traditional standards of decency — to borrow Whitman's term, "one long barbaric yawp."

Exaggerated descriptions, you think? Now hear this!:

Robin Morgan, MS. Magazine editor: "I feel that 'man-hating' is an honorable and viable political act, that the oppressed have a right to class-hatred against the class that is oppressing them." In *Theory and Practice: Pornography and Rape*, Morgan claims that "rape exists any time sexual intercourse occurs when it has not been initiated by the woman, out of her own genuine affection and desire." "We can't destroy

---

30   Whistleblower magazine quotes several well-reputed politically neutral surveys that reveal more of this demographic have mental problems than does the conservative demographic. February 2020, pgs 39–41.

the inequities between men and women until we destroy marriage," Morgan wrote in her 1970 book, <u>Sisterhood is Powerful</u>.

Feminist Lynette Triere provides rationale for divorcing women: "There is no reason that a woman should be bound for life to a mistaken choice she made at age eighteen, twenty-four, thirty-three or forty-one. It is an unreasonable demand.... [T]he issue of freedom is important for women. There is joy in freedom.... Perhaps a woman should take seriously the philosophic truism that she is endowed with certain inalienable rights, that among these are life, liberty, and the pursuit of happiness. For many women, the act of leaving is truly a declaration of independence." [346]

"The nuclear family must be destroyed," Linda Gordon declared in a famous 1969 article in *Women: A Journal of Liberation*.

In <u>Professing Feminism: Cautionary Tales from the Strange World of Women's Studies</u> p. 129, Catherine MacKinnon, a professor at the University of Michigan Law School, informs us "In a patriarchal society all heterosexual intercourse is rape because women, as a group, are not strong enough to give meaningful consent."

In a speech at the Stanford University Law School on April 14, 2005, MacKinnon delivered herself of the opinion that all men are in a millennia-long war against all women.

Marilyn French, Author of <u>The Women's Room</u> honks, "All men are rapists and that's all they are."

Susan Griffin, author of <u>Rape: The All-American Crime</u>: "And if the professional rapist is to be separated from the average dominant heterosexual, it may be mainly a quantitative difference."

Typical feminist author, Susan Brownmiller, informs us that ALL men will rape at least one woman during their lives. Lena Dunham posted a video celebrating the extinction of white men. Glory Hole Steinem (a penname): "Every male should spend the ages of 15 through 30 in prison on a conviction of 'Potential Rapist.'" Mary Daly: "Marriage is a male institution and serves male interests... Sisterhood means revolution." [347]

Gloria Steinem (the dashboard saint of feminism. President Obama gave her the Presidential Medal of Freedom.): "A woman needs a man like a fish needs a bicycle." "The patriarchy requires violence or the subliminal threat of violence in order to maintain itself." And "We just need to be whoever the fuck we are and just do it" said in Paris recently at 84-years-old.

Ingrid Bengis, with her hair on fire and hearing little voices: "I thought again of my castration fantasy, of the slaughtered masses that my imagination had laid out on Fifth Avenue as sacrifices to my fury." Ti-Grace Atkinson adds to Dworkin's nonsense in <u>Amazon Odyssey</u> (p. 86): "The institution of sexual intercourse is anti-feminist."

Andrea Dworkin (Known as a "fat dyke." Her main connection to sanity was her anti-porn campaign. She assumed room temperature in April of '05): "Heterosexual intercourse is the pure, formalized expression of contempt for women's bodies." And "Under patriarchy, every woman's son is her betrayer and also the inevitable rapist or exploiter of another woman."

Betty Friedan: "The right of every woman to control her own reproductive life....The right, the inalienable right, to control our own body....To create new social institutions that are needed to free women, not from childbearing or love or sex or even marriage, but from the intolerable agony and burden those become when women are chained to them." [348] (In a late 1950s magazine article, this pseudo-scientific genius warned of "The Coming Ice Age.") Before the global warming fright, she predicted a glacier would cover the northern hemisphere.

Elizabeth Cady Stanton: "The true enemy of woman skulks behind the altar. The Bible is not the word of God. The Bible is the act of men written to keep women subordinate, [and] written out of his love of domination." [349]

Suzie Leather (U.K.): "The view that a child needs a father is a social anachronism."

Unknown feminist Leader: "A woman's right to have a baby without having the father around is what feminism is all about." [350]

Shere Hite: "If the mother-child family was prevalent in pre-history, and indeed is a flourishing form of family in our own societies today, this is something of which we can be proud, not terrified."

Marie Enckendorff: "If ever there was a first and individual woman who...went voluntarily to the man and said: 'Protect me from the enemy and from hunger and let me believe in your gods, and I will serve you, bear your children, and you shall be my master' — If that woman ever existed, who, out of fear of life and its inward and outward experiences, was glad to give herself, body and soul, to a fellow-creature, and bequeathed this position to her sex—she was in truth the mother of sin... [351]

Phyllis Chesler: "Any father who puts a child and his mother through the pain of a custody battle or who attempts to separate them from each other is by definition an unfit father." [352]

Karen DeCrow, a Susan B. Anthony on steroids, lesbian and former president of NOW (died June 2014), in Moscow, Russia: "We are trying to get rid of all distinctions between men and women."

Former Congresswoman Barbara Jordan: "I believe that women have a capacity for understanding and compassion which a man structurally does not have, does not have it because he cannot have it. He's just incapable of it." Another of her ilk, Rep. Rashida Tlaib (D-MI) speaking to MoveOn, December 3rd, 2019, said about President Trump: "we're gonna go in there, we're gonna impeach the motherfucker."

The would-be ball-breaking Feminist Action League (FAL) at the University of New Hampshire (UNH) is out front. In March 2005, they organized an on-campus event to share experiences of oppression in a "comfortable setting." It featured poetry readings, skits, monologues and an open microphone. One member was quoted as saying that "Ninety-nine percent of sexual perpetrators are men. They are the root cause of the rape and oppression against women." Another member's monologue follows: "Hello, my name is 'Mary-Man-Hating-Is-Fun...' I hate men because they are men, because I see them for what they are: misogynistic, sexist, oppressive and absurdly pathetic beings who only serve to pollute and contaminate this world with war, abuse, oppression and rape." Members of the FAL wore scissors around their necks and sang a song about castration. A vindictive, twice-divorced woman, who writes under the pen name "Nomo Wenie," has written a book published in Britain entitled 101 Ways to Castrate a Man: A 'Joke Book.' Some joke! She needs a laxative. The mainstream media, instead of criticizing such obscenities, can promote it; on June 4, 2013, the Huffington Post, featured an illustrated article detailing 8 ways a woman can destroy her man's penis. [353]

Hear the vulgarity of Canadian feminists protesting outside an appearance by the mildly masculinist writer Warren Farrell: [354] Imagine what that twot would shout if it were me speaking instead of the gentle Warren. My advice to Warren: Don't get in a pissing match with a skunk.

Almost as bad as radical feminists was that vulgar bitch headlining the 2018 White House correspondence dinner, masquerading as a comedian. The applause received demonstrates the depths to which the "news" media has sunk. Sara Huckabee Sanders faced terrible personal insults from her with grace and class.

The chants of pro-abortionists in the Texas Legislature exceeded even these obscenities. [355] When Mother Teresa died, Germaine Greer whose spacemobile remains in high orbit, wrote a snippy, catty critique of Mother T. because she opposed abortion. Eleanor Smeal and Kate Michelman, with about as much credibility as littermate Rosie O'Donnell added similar comment later. Similar hatreds against whites are surfacing in today's race riots.

Kate Millet confessed to be a "queer" (that feminists are largely lesbian can be verified by identifying the targets of classified ads in Ms. Magazine); her own mother and cousins tried to have her committed for psychiatric care. Her sister Mallory said "Kate was mentally ill for as long as I remember. Missouri lesbian feminist Senator Jolie L. Justus posted this message to President Bush (granted, some of his policies did defy logic) on her MySpace page: "With all due respect, Mr. President, Kiss my fucking ass."

Stop laughing; they're serious! This is the fruit of feminism!

Rudyard Kipling's instructive poem The Female of the Species warns they are "more deadly than the male" (By the way, only female mosquitos bite). Writer Carey Roberts' remarked "Can you imagine some sweaty working stiff taking a smoke break, and suddenly becoming inspired to enlighten his buddies with that kind of narcissistic drivel?"

Internet blogger Fred Reed asked and answered:

"Why do these sorry twits behave as they do? In part because the American zeitgeist encourages them. Many American women carry The Chip, an anger that so many have. They are 'not going to take it,' whatever 'it' is. They seem to be looking too hard for some of 'it' not to take. So far as I know, only North American women are forever coiled to strike." …"North American women have been so corrupted by angry feminism that they have the appeal of a menopausing crocodile with the hives.

Dirty tactics. There are or were at least 90 pro-male and pro-family websites throughout the world under virus or other attack by feminists at a British entity called O2 and evidently at Symantec (makers and vendors of Norton Antivirus). Target sites include Colorado's Equal Justice Foundation and the Men's Defense Association. Ironically, mysterious attackers have succeeded in getting *our* web pages labeled "hate sites."

Male radicals. Some men, maybe with cause, holler at women indiscriminately (Schopenhauer, despite other insight, may belong in this category), but it is evident that far more feminists are doing the hollering, and much more of it. Some with severely wounded egos or who were driven nearly insane by the system may have gravitated into the men's/fathers' movement, and used it as a platform from which to denigrate all women. Yes, there may be good reason some guys' wives divorced them. Our cause is not well served by our own irrationals. Like men who kick dogs, they are an embarrassment. Very few belong in this category; however, critics found one or two and painted us all with the same brush.

It is irritating to be drawn into the victimization game, but feminists must not be permitted to claim the high (low?) ground by default. Trying to argue rationally with radical gender/sex feminists is like giving a bobcat a prostate exam. You can't do it. Because of their utter lack of logic, they usually refuse debate. It's not that they would lose an argument; they have none. Disagree libbers? I will put up a team of three masculinists against any three of yours. En guarde. Make my day! Twenty-eight years or so ago, masculinist attorney Maurice Franks completely destroyed Gloria Allred on the Merv. Griffin Show. Gad, it was beautiful!

More recently, the Black Power Movement is becoming even more treacherous than feminism. It threatens not just males, but all of decent society.

Women's Lib — Rebuttal
You've come a Long Way Baby

It has been demonstrated that the feminist movement, especially the radical element, is intellectually and morally bankrupt, largely a façade; pull back the rhetorical curtain and there is little behind it. For an extensive internet compilation of anti-feminist arguments, check out this website: https://www.facebook.com/notes/i-dont-need-feminism/anti-feminist-sources/633457830055540

As to the claim that women are "the most oppressed group in our society," any sentient being knows this to be false. Indeed, a good case can be made that western women are actually the most pampered creatures on earth — sacred cows. Women have come to positions of high power politically throughout the non-communist world, and to some extent beyond that. U.S. Supreme Court Justice Sonia Sotomayor, actress Jane Fonda and attorney Gloria Allred were among the inductees at the National Women's Hall of Fame. The Class of 2019 inducted into the hall in upstate New York also included activist Angela Davis, attorney Sarah Deer, fashion designer Diane von Furstenberg , retired Air Force fighter pilot Nicole Malachowski, the late artist and suffragist Rose O'Neill and the late U.S. Rep. Louise Slaughter of New York. Most Chinese and Russian women would gladly exchange places with their American sisters.

In 1831, Alexis de Tocqueville prophetically warned Americans that the new feminist movement would result in the manufacture of "weak men and disorderly women." Vatican officials are beginning to realize feminism is responsible for the erosion of manhood. [356]

The Woman Racket, by British resident Steve Moxon, is a serious scientific investigation into one of the key myths of our age — that women are oppressed by the 'patriarchal' traditions of Western societies. Drawing on the latest developments in evolutionary psychology, Moxon finds that the opposite is true — men, or at least the majority of low-status males, have always been the victims of deep-rooted prejudice. As the prejudice is biologically derived, it is unconscious and can only be uncovered with the tools of scientific psychology. Moxon reveals this prejudice exists in fields as diverse as healthcare, employment, family policy and politics.

Feminists cannot answer the following questions: Why the selective umbrage about alleged mistreatment of women in the U.S. contrasted with blindness toward the brutal treatment of women in Mid-Eastern countries? If sex roles are stereotypes, how and when did they begin?

Employment, wage "differentials"
Women continue to make headway in arenas traditionally associated with men. The male labor force has been in decline for

generations, but not the female force. A report by the World Future Society finds that Generation Xers and their younger counterparts in the Millennial Generation toil in a workplace that is all but sex-blind. According to Suzanne Fields, women now hold half of all the management jobs in America. Writer Tim Goldish calls it the "Glass escalator." They may be a small minority in corporate boardrooms, but women directors typically earn more than men do, a U.S. study has found. [356] Though outnumbered, female CEOs earn more than male chiefs. [357] Female directors in corporate America earned median compensation of $120,000, based on old pay data, compared with $104,375 for male board members. [358] Alexis Leondis of Bloomberg.com said women CEOs earned 40 percent more than men CEOs in 2009. [359] The Bureau of Labor Statistics provides pay comparisons for many jobs; these show that in some areas (for instance, teachers of law, medicine and economics) women earn considerably more than equally qualified male counterparts. [360]

Economist June O'Neill, the former director of the Congressional Budget Office, wrote an article titled *The gender gap in wages, circa 2000* in the May 2003 issue of the *American Economic Review.* By factoring in some of the many work-related differences between men and women such as hours worked per week, danger, travel requirements of the job, years of education, years in the field, and many other characteristics, she found the purported pay gap virtually vanished. By the way, women flooding the workforce drives wages down.

In 2007, the Census Department released its annual survey of income, poverty and healthcare, showing the smallest gap ever between men's and women's pay. [361] An 8/3/07 *New York Times* front page article titled *For Young Earners in Big City, Gap Shifts in Women's Favor*, portends a pay gap favoring women immediately following educational completion." [362] In 1969, data from the American Council on Education showed that female professors who had never been married and had never published earned 145 percent of their male counterparts' pay. The *Times* article goes on to say that New York City women between 21 and 30 working full-time made 117% of men's wages. This point has also been made numerous times by scholars at the American Enterprise Institute. [363] A study of single, childless urban workers between the ages of 22 and 30 found that women earned 8% more than men did. [364] A July 2016 *Newsmax* article essentially supported the above facts. Women who have never had a child earn about 98 cents per man's dollar. One third of wives out-earn their husbands. [365]

Harvard economics professor Claudia Goldin expounded on her extensive gender wage gap research in a Freakonomics podcast, declaring that the difference in earnings between men and women is the result of a difference in priorities rather than blatant sex discrimination. [366]

Dr. Warren Farrell, a recovering feminist (no longer in front of that parade or licensed by them) and friend of mine, is threatened — if not yet wholly mugged — by reality. His book, <u>Why Men Earn More: The Startling Truth Behind the Pay Gap — and What Women Can Do About It</u>, supports the foregoing. Even during the 1950s, Farrell says, the sex pay gap for all never-married workers was less than 2 percent while never-married white women between 45 and 54 earned 106 percent of what their white male counterparts made. Farrell says that apparent pay inequalities disappear as dissimilar factors between men and women are accounted for, and that one way to raise earning power as a woman is to work in a hazardous region. Typically, she will not be in danger; her male colleagues will protect her.

Higher paying jobs are usually more arduous, or require more training and dedication. Men's natural characteristics — especially greater motivation and aggression — as well as social expectations, cause them to seek and excel in these type jobs. Men work harder and longer at jobs that are more dangerous, and prepare themselves better educationally. A London School of Economics study tracking 10,000 post — 1993 United Kingdom graduates from 30 universities found that men tended to stress salary and were more likely to take up engineering, math, and computing. The women were more apt to seek socially oriented jobs, and as undergraduates had tended to major in education and the arts.

In view of actual numbers of qualified women seeking work, there aren't that many available to fill required quotas. By their own preference, most women have not pursued full time careers or obtained the training men have. Men are practically required to work (ask those in alimony jail), while women have greater choices in the matter. The pressure to earn is off most women, who know they can depend on men for a living. While three-fourths of American women between 25 and 34 are in the paid workforce (up from half in 1975), four out of 10 women are the breadwinner in U.S. households. [367]

Low seniority employees are traditionally sent on errands such as to get coffee. When it happens to women, the libbers cry "discrimination." They're strangely silent about men being sent to shovel snow, unload trucks and do other heavy or dirty work, work more undesirable than making coffee. Non-distinction — what feminists consider to be equality — is a mixed blessing, as women are discovering. Arils Flickinger and Mary Patrick, employees of a state liquor store in Sioux City, Iowa, discovered that when they petitioned the state merit employment commission for dispensation from lifting heavy cases and lost. Feminist spokes-woman Edyth Cudlipp admits that there are

certain functions to which women are not fitted; therefore, she maintains, special consideration should be given them. [368] Sorry, no special consideration; there can be no have-your-cake-and-eat-it-too arrangements.

It is nonsense to lower employment standards simply to qualify women for traditionally male jobs. Propelling women into positions for which they are ill equipped is as unfair to them as it is to the rest of the world. Besides being a threat to public safety, it demoralizes the men who must accept the increased risks and responsibilities imposed by working alongside incompetent females.

Employment quotas — otherwise known as Affirmative Action — arguably based on law, are inefficient, dangerous and unfair; they hinder the functions of government and business, [369] and negate equal opportunity. Affirmative action is based on three false premises: that the successes of males is due to discrimination, sociological conditioning or conspiracy; that normal women can do anything that normal men can — and do it as well; and that overall women's pay should equal men's. The underlying intent is to redistribute income and power.

"Comparable Worth" schemes to pay women who opt into plush or comfortable jobs the same as men who do hard or dangerous work are popular with leftist state governments. Justice John Roberts aptly called them "central planning of the economy by judges." All that is needed to implement them is a feminist-oriented bureaucracy willing to declare hard work easy and easy work hard. Like "No-fault divorce," which sent the divorce rate skyrocketing, imposition of them can be a Pyrrhic victory with unintended consequences that could financially break these states.

The laws and clamor to raise women's salaries ignore the fact that the 1963 Pay Equity Act requires equal pay for equal work. It is a feminist lie that that women earn 23 cents (or whatever) less on the dollar than men. Obama repeated that lie on my TV screen on April 12, 2016 (Though it has been demonstrated that his administration paid female White House staff less than male staff). For well over a decade, I and other masculinists have been proclaiming the actual statistics to anyone who would listen. If women actually did do work equal to men for less money, why would anyone hire men?

Wage comparisons should compare apples to apples. The broad wage differential compares the average wage paid to all women with the average wage paid to all men without any reference to the work they do. The wage differential canard deceptively equates women who polish fingernails in plush offices with men who labor deep beneath the earth's surface in coal mines year after year. That figure also includes women who spent over 20 years raising children without any personal income.

On average, men receive better pay because overall they are better, more reliable workers. According to a Rand Corporation study, "The typical male worker has more job skills than the typical female worker, so it's not surprising there's a wage gap." Besides, women quit jobs eleven times oftener than men do. A 2007 report by CONSAD Research Corporation of Pittsburg, PA, commissioned by the United States Department of Labor, finally puts to rest any claims that the pay gap between men and women in this country is the result solely or mostly of sex discrimination. The report is an analysis of some 50 studies of the earnings differential between men and women in the U.S. [370]

Does today's average income differential evidence discrimination? Of course not! In a free enterprise labor market, abilities are not subsidized; that is, they are bought and sold for what they are worth. The market of supply and demand sets wages. All commodities, including labor, reach a price level consistent with their worth, unless interfered with by outside forces such as union or government dictates.

The insightful Cardinal Raymond Burke has claimed that the "radical feminism which has assaulted the Church and society since the 1960s has left men very marginalized." [371] Men have lost most of the jobs in downturns before the coronavirus hit. Andrew M. Sum, professor of labor economics at Northeastern University said, "Men have borne more than 80 percent of the over 4 million job losses since the end of 2007. The biggest losses are in traditionally very male sectors: construction, manufacturing, warehousing and transportation. Construction was the hardest hit, with a 17 percent unemployment rate." According to the Bureau of Labor Statistics, the jobless rate among women was 5.9 percent, while the overall unemployment rate was 9.1 percent, and higher if one considers those who gave up seeking work. According to Gallup, under-employment is almost 20 percent. Despite the fact that most of the jobs lost were male-oriented [372], feminists horned in on the President's 'stimulus' package by demanding half of the new jobs. [373]

True, pay scales several generations ago did provide for more money to men, for good reason — to provide a "family wage" to support the man and his homemaking wife and children, [374] and to assure enough income for every family by having only one breadwinner per family. Scholar David Deming rightly calls that "honestly held cultural values."

This is not to imply that women should never be hired into traditionally male positions, but that individuals, men or women, should not be hired by quota or placed in positions for which they are unqualified. It is absurd to demand or grant unearned reward. The more responsibilities women reject the more unequal they make themselves. Compensation should be commensurate with actual effort and abilities. "As ye sow, so shall ye reap," and only so. One ought to be able to develop his or her capabilities; and ought to be employed or accepted wherever qualified, but not in preference to better qualified persons, in pursuit of egalitarian pipe dreams. Not surprisingly, the unwarranted promotion of women into top-level executive business positions has met with less than rousing success. This is documented in Hise's The War Against Men on pages 63, 64, 67, 69 and139 to 143.

In Academics

Three decades ago, the ratio of males to females on college campuses was 60-40; now it is about 40 to 60; according to the Department of Education's National Center for Education Statistics, 57.2 percent of college enrollees are women. By the 1980s women outnumbered men in bachelors' degrees. A Maryland Higher Education Commission report confirmed this. Women now earn more associates, bachelor's and master's degrees than their male counterparts. In the academic year 2001-02, 57 percent of bachelor's degrees and 59 percent of master's degrees were awarded to women, according to data from the National Center for Education Statistics. Women also earned nearly half of the Ph.Ds. (46.3 percent) as well as first professional degrees (47.3 percent), which include medical, law and dental degrees.

Hear Jeanne Sahadi, *CNN/Money* senior writer, April 27, 2004: "This year, for the first time in the history of Harvard University, the number of women offered admission to the incoming undergraduate freshman class outpaced the number of men. That's just one indication of how far women have come in their quest to achieve educational and professional parity with men."

One hundred thirty-three women will graduate from college for every 100 men. The proportion of Australian women age 25-29 that have a Bachelor degree or higher is 25 percent; of men —just 18 percent. [375]

In General

Capability will out; Margaret Mead, Madame Curie, Ayn Rand, Condoleezza Rice and many others have accomplished great things—

through effort, not shrill demand. [fn31] Lately, more and more brilliant women are coming to the fore. As men abdicate their trousers, women are having to step into them; some doing so quite well.

While pockets of bias against women may remain, the feminist clamor for equality comes from an already overall superior position, even if artificially so. K.T. McFarland, an official in the Ford, Nixon and Reagan administrations, made a quite obvious observation: "This is the greatest time in history to be a woman." Canadian psychologist Susan Pinker says, "in the only two biologically meaningful measures of welfare — longevity and reproductive success — women are and have always been slightly better off than men. [376] That thesis which helped inspire the early feminist movement, John Stuart Mill's 1869 book The Subjugation of Women, despite its fallacies, could be reprinted today with little more than interchanging the words "men" and "women," certainly that portion of it concerning domestic relations; and it would be almost as accurate and contemporary as when published.

"Equality," said Voltaire, "is at once the most natural and most chimerical thing in the world — natural when it is limited to rights, unnatural when it attempts to level goods and powers." The term equality is a two-edged sword; it cuts both ways. Otherwise, the term is meaningless. Equal rights imply equal responsibilities: self-support, family maintenance, military service, arduous labor, guilt and punishment, and equal opportunity to be discriminated against. By defining between men and women in terms of power and competition instead of reciprocity and cooperation, the feminist movement tore apart the most basic and fragile contract in human society. This distorts the true perspective of male/female relationships and upsets the laws of nature with undesirable consequences.

What if affirmative action/quotas were applied in the other direction? What if it were decreed that professional basketball teams must be composed of 70 percent Caucasians, or that henceforth all children of divorce be placed with fathers until their numbers equal those placed with mothers, etc?

Pew Research queried twenty two hundred and fifty adult American couples on decision-making. The survey, released in 2008, revealed that women make more decisions about finances, home purchases, choice of television programs and weekend activities forty percent of the time; husbands make the decisions in twenty five percent, and it splits evenly in thirty one percent. A West Coast men's group reported that, "Women make eighty eight percent of all U.S. retail purchases and handle seventy five percent of family finances." Women influence

---

31 Curie's success was partially attributable to her equally brilliant husband.

two out of every three of the three trillion dollars spent in the U.S. each year!

Insurance company statistics reveal that women already own nearly eighty percent of all wealth in the U.S. The U.S. Consumer Products Safety Commission in Bethesda, Md. claims that women own seventy five percent of the stocks and bonds and sixty five percent of the savings accounts in the country. Forty-three percent of those with assets over $500,000 are women. One out of every 11 women in America owns a business. Some experts predicted that, by 2020, women would control most of the money in America. Such a high return for so little work shows that men, relatively unable to bargain in sex, have paid a staggering price for it. The ten richest women in the U.S. inherited money earned by men. [377] Does anyone believe that all those female donors to PBS documentaries earned their fortunes by their own work? In view of their wealth, contrasted with their efforts, monetary complaints have little basis in fact.

R. Emmett Tyrell criticized radfems thusly: They don't know what they want, but they want it very badly." Simone-Gabrielle Colette said "The woman who thinks she is intelligent demands equal rights with men. The woman who *is* intelligent does not. That would be because she knows she already has greater rights."

Perpend Professor Amneus:

"It is remarkable that the social patterns of the ghettos, despite their poverty, crime, violence, ignorance, illegitimacy, drug addiction, educational failure, and demoralization, should be regarded as worthy of imitation by white feminists, but they are. These white feminists might acknowledge that they would prefer living in patriarchal Beverly Hills to living in matriarchal Watts, but they will deny that matriarchy and female sexual promiscuity have anything to do with the squalor of Watts..." [378]

One might think that legitimate religious leaders would disassociate from feminism, after hearing the vulgar language spewed by followers and spokeswomen, and viewing the printed language on their protest signs.

In all fairness, one must admit that many "equity feminists" are motivated by legitimate concern. Sincere ones could be allies and may actually be prepared to give up women's privileges for men's privileges, to make an effort to ensure equal rights for both men and women. A high level dialogue on the subject occurred at the Humphry Institute of Public Affairs on the University of Minnesota campus in February 2016 between Professor Christina Hoff Sommers, a sensible 'equity feminist,' resident scholar at the American Enterprise Institute, and author of The War against Boys, and Milo Yiannopolous. They received a standing ovation from the audience. [379]

Because women may be discriminated against in some areas and men definitely in others, the *rational* elements of men's liberation and women's liberation have more in common than in contention. If this is agreed, the only significant difference lies in the question of degree — who is discriminated against more — men or women, and where? This should not prevent cooperation for mutual assistance. Libbers can prove sincerity by changing their demands from "equal rights for women" to "equal rights for both sexes" (making sensible provision for legitimate differences between the sexes). Sincerity can be determined with a litmus test question I posed over forty years ago to a Minneapolis group in the belly of the feminist beast: Would you advocate fathers actually having equal rights to custody of their children in divorce? Only one woman, a lawyer, answered "yes." One vehemently disagreed. If more would concur and mean it, though it's unlikely and might be like the WWI Christmas truce in 1914, this writer for one will be out in the streets with them — and Sommers.

The best argument against feminism appears here in Part V, at the beginning of Civilization, Evolution, Devolution..., under "The Sexual Contract."

The rise and fall of feminism
A post-mortem

Fortunately, the feminist swamp is slowly draining itself. The tumor is shrinking. Rumor has it that Betty Friedan in her later years may have become disgusted with man-hating upstarts. Maureen Dowd admitted that feminism had "curdled." After one year of mediocre operation, the feminist radio network, GreenStone Media, folded. Obviously, not enough average people are interested in what feminists had to say. Maybe N.O.W. should change its title to T.H.E.N. Dr. Thomas Sowell put it best when he said, in another context, "In reality, the crusade for civil rights ended years ago. The scramble for special privilege, for turf, and for image is what continues today under that banner and with that rhetoric..." They would have done better, certainly less harm, to join the Ladies Aid Society (How many old Catholics remember that?).

It is important to be aware that modern day feminists, especially gender/sex feminists, are only a vociferous minority presumptuously claiming to represent the views and interests of all women. Those who would deny equal rights for men are not as numerous as the noise and influence they generate would indicate. According to a 1999 Gallup poll, seventy four percent of American women did not consider themselves feminists. A 2005 CBS poll showed only twenty four percent of women considered themselves feminists, seventy percent did not; it also showed twenty-two percent of women considered it an insult to be called a feminist. [380]

Hear true feminists, the adult women
Boat rockers in the distaff ocean

Strangely enough, it is often women who see through the adulation of the female. Father's Day was instigated by a woman, Mrs. John Bruce Dodd of Spokane, Washington, after getting her fill of six decades of Mothers' Day litanies. The holiday was proclaimed in 1966 by Congress — reluctantly, due to worries about diminishing the glory of Mothers' Day.

Many of the grand old dames who fought for legitimate women's suffrage over a hundred years ago would almost certainly reject the absurdities of today's libbers, just as the martyred old Irish heroes who resisted the English occupation, plundering and enslavement of their land and people generations ago, and with whom I empathize, would reject the IRA commi-terrorists and drug dealing thugs in recent decades.

The term "feminism" itself is a misnomer because essentially the zeitgeist is to destroy all traces of femininity. Calling them "anti-feminists" would be more accurate. There is a viewpoint in opposition to feminism represented by detoxifiers like Phyllis Schlafly (R.I.P.), Dr. Laura Schlessinger, Beverly LaHaye, Babette Francis , a strongly conservative writer, activist and widow of my old friend Charles Francis Q.C. of Australia, [fn32] and another Australian Bettina Arndt, a pro male journalist. Also columnists Kate O'Beirne, Kathleen Parker, Suzanne Fields, Ann Coulter, Bay Buchanan, Mona Charen, Star Parker, Dorothy L. Sayers, writer Sylvia Thompson, Heather MacDonald, a Thomas W. Smith Fellow at the Manhattan Institute and others. Phyllis Schlafly's book, Who Killed the Family? is also practically a re-run of this book. I'm proud that we think alike.

Like Maggie Gallagher, Schlafly was honest enough to admit women were better off than men, and to doing all in her power to retain that standing, but later began to understand and strongly endorse the rights of fathers. Decades ago she sent my Men's Defense Association several prospective members. She said that feminists who choose to abandon careers in favor of returning to hearth and home are "mugged by reality." Her June 2010 *Report* is father friendly. Anti-feminist Karen Straughan is 99% brilliant and 1 % foul-mouthed flake. Her 'male' counterpart is Milo Yiannopolous. Both find it necessary to appeal to their juvenile audiences by gratuitous interspersions of vulgarity. Like

---

[32] She likened feminism to Oroboros, a snake swallowing its tail. Her husband, and my dear friend, Charles (R.I.P), was a Queen's Counsel down there.

so many others, they have no notion of what went on in the movement decades before they arrived on the scene.

The popular feminist belief of a utopian matriarchal early "civilization" is discredited by Cynthia Eller, Associate Professor of Women's Studies and Religious Studies at Montclair State University in her book Myth of Matriarchal Prehistory. It is refreshing to find a feminist refuting the myth perpetuated by her Women's Studies peers. Rape fright author Susan Brownmiller has also seen the light, to the great consternation of those still in her old mode. [381]

Camille Paglia claims feminism has "become a catch-all vegetable drawer where bunches of clingy sob sisters can store their moldy neuroses." The reformed Doris Lessisng summarily dismissed feminists as "some of the smuggest, most un-self-critical people the world has ever seen. They are horrible." Judge Beatrice Mullaney of Fall River, Mass said, "Women are anxious to exercise freedoms and permissiveness promoted by the women's movement; and the result is dissolution of marriages, homes and families." Swedish researcher Helen Lindberg (Örebro University, Department of Social and Political Sciences) presented a scathing doctoral thesis called *Only Women Bleed?: A Critical Reassessment of Comprehensive Feminist Social Theory*. A more recent literary rebuttal comes in Andrea Tantaros' book Tied Up in Knots.

Karin L. Agness, a student at the University of Virginia, founded the Network of enlightened Women, or NeW, to counter the feminist influence on college campuses. NeW has 15 chapters nationwide. Objecting to Proctor and Gamble's advertising campaign denigrating males, sensible women in India, launched a Stop the War Against Men and Boys movement. Member groups are Women Against Male-bashing (W.A.M.) and All India Forgotten Women's Association (AIFWA). The Independent Women's Forum is perhaps the best U.S. venue for sensible women. Devastatingly accurate criticisms of feminism periodically appear on their website. [382] Their mission statement follows:

The Independent Women's Forum was established to combat the women-as-victim, pro-big-government ideology of radical feminism. We seek to restore, strengthen, and extend that which promotes women's well-being by advancing the principles of self-reliance, political freedom, economic liberty, and personal responsibility.

Educators Propagandizing Children and Youth

As the twig is bent

Education, like talent in entertainment, does not equate to intelligence. Abraham Lincoln observed, "The philosophy of the school room in one generation is the philosophy of government in the next." Orwell's Ministry of Truth is busily engaged in gender and political propagandizing. A massive, insidious campaign to inculcate and marinate the feminist, and to a somewhat lesser extent the leftist, culture in youth has been mounted in schools and public TV systems. The programming begins with very young children and continues through the school years, and even thereafter. In the early 1970's, the Ford Foundation granted the Women's Action Alliance $95,370 to develop a nonsexist curriculum for preschool children in child care centers. School boys in Victoria, Australia attend mandatory classes in feminism in order to combat violence against women. Schoolchildren in the U.S. who may be "not properly socialized" according to leftist teachers' ideas can be considered "at risk" making them eligible for services paid for by Medicaid, thus enriching school coffers. [383]

Phyllis Schlafly said that the Department of Education's Office of Civil Rights has determined that in all sexual controversies or accusations the man is guilty, and will enforce same with dire consequences. [384] Dr. Christina Hoff Sommers says there are over 300 publications by the U.S. Department of Education promoting parity in education, none of which are designed to improve the situation of males. Education institutions have largely discontinued teaching the classics, while secondary schools teach kids how to put condoms on cucumbers, but not how to hold a pencil properly, [fn33] or to refrain from using "like" and "you know" in every other sentence. No wonder the reading skills of U.S. fourth-graders fell from fifth in the world in 2011 to thirteenth in 2017.

Max Freedman, a former Liberator writer from Brooklyn, said, "A fifth-grade test ... had been expunged, under feminist pressure, of such names as Bach, Napoleon and Mozart to make room for the likes of Phyllis Wheatley." Don't be embarrassed; I never heard of her either. Elite private schools are being pressured by Black Lives Matter supporters to include materials on "institutional racism" in curriculum and student life programs. [385]

Mike Poplardo, an economics teacher at Fox Lane High School in Bedford, New York was suspended for showing his students a Fox News documentary as part of a lesson plan to prepare them for college. He said, "All people (male and female) are at risk of being a victim of sexual violence and are at risk of being accused of sexual violence." To demonstrate the dangers, he showed students a Fox News documentary titled *"The Truth about Sex and College."*

Gladwyne Elementary School, one of the richest in the nation, will require fourth and fifth graders to read <u>Not My Idea</u>, a book about

---

33 North Korea's Kim Jong Un grasps his writing stick more properly than our school children and grads.

whiteness which claims that white people who relate to police officers or decline to watch the news are complicit in racism. The curriculum also assigns <u>A Kid's Book about Racism</u> to kindergarten and first graders, reports the *Washington Free Beacon*. Parents complain that, in addition to turning off CNN being a form of racism, the book also turns kids against their parents for their original sin of being born white.

Virginia's Loudon County School District is working with a far-left group called *Teaching Tolerance* to add "anti-racism" classes to the curriculum, where kids will be lectured about how evil America is because of its history of slavery.

Scholarly Politics

The National Education Association legislative program reads like the Communist Manifesto. Democrat professors outnumber Republican ones 12 to 1. [386] Professor Graham Hillard found strong Democrat-to-Republican ratios among college professors (28 to 1 in New England), creating "a generation of drones ... with an ever-evolving pastiche of political orthodoxies." [387] Michigan State University, member of the left leaning professoriate, William Penn informed his students "Republicans raped this country." A University of Nevada-Las Vegas professor told her class that President Trump is to blame for the Las Vegas massacre. [388] On September 24th 2018 at least 30 Yale law professors cancelled classes to allow students to travel to Washington, D.C. to protest the nomination of Brett Kavanagh for Justice of the U.S. Supreme Court. A similar law school closing reportedly occurred at the University of Mississippi law school. Georgetown University's associate professor Christine Fair turned her rage against Republican senators who supported Brett Kavanagh, saying, "All of them deserve miserable deaths while feminists laugh. We should castrate their corpses and feed them to swine." Apropos of this mindset is the professor who said he could vomit when he saw another man give his 1st class airline seat to a uniformed military man. [fn34] Radical professors Bernadine Dohrn and Bill Ayers behaved similarly. The original advocate of intolerance in the modern era was leftist philosopher Herbert Marcuse.

U. of Illinois math prof. Rochelle Gutierrez maintains mathematics, largely developed by Greeks and Europeans, perpetuate white privilege and racism, that they require abstract reasoning and objective knowledge — difficult for women and minorities. It is instructive that nearly 1 in 3 US physicians were born abroad.

---

34   http://insider.foxnews.com/2017/03/29/drexel-professor-tried-not-vomit-veteran-gave-seat-soldier-george-ciccariello-maher

It's even worse in college

Again, Professor Amneus would be appalled.

These criticisms apply especially to government-funded institutions. At this writing, nineteen women's colleges remain single-sex, one source claims well over 100, including Radcliff, Wellsely, Smith and Wheaton, versus only three men's colleges. [389] Mount Holyoke all-girls college in Massachusetts will allow men – but only if they identify as female. [390] Wesleyan University in Connecticut ordered its fraternities to become coeducational within three years. [391] My all male Alma Mater is now co-ed, and from the looks of its mailings is largely run by women, as are so many others. By opening up to women it almost wiped out a neighboring women's college that was equal academically.

Phyllis Schlafly informed us, "College textbooks portray marriage as bleak and dreary for women, preoccupied with domestic violence, battering, abuse, marital rape, and divorce." Pseudo scholars, educated beyond their capacity and basking in their own imagined importance, publish meaningless gibberish to great acclaim from peers, regurgitate feminist agitprop "herstory" and advocate female "empowerment" to vacuous students at institutional sand boxes throughout the country. [392]

The Princeton University HR department has largely wiped the word "man" from its vocabulary. Other guidelines: "Instead of 'man and wife' use spouses or partners. Switch out 'man-made' with artificial, handmade or manufactured. Don't use the verb 'to man,' as in to work something, instead use to operate or to staff. Throw out workmanlike and replace it with skillful." The memo goes on to list a variety of occupations that typically include the word "man" in them and offers replacements: business person instead of businessman, firefighter instead of fireman, ancestors instead of forefathers, and so on. [393] At the University of Florida, History major Martin Poirier wrote, "Water is a thing prior to man" on a paper for a history class called "History of Water." He was penalized by Professor Jack Davis for writing "man" instead of "humankind" in a class paper. [394] Cailin Jeffers, an English major student at Northern Arizona University lost credit on an English paper for using the word "mankind" instead of a gender-neutral alternative. One of her professors, Dr. Anne Scott, objected to her use of the word as a synonym for "humanity."

Diversity [fn35] and Feminism reign

At one time, education involved a choice of perspectives. No longer; anti-male orthodoxy is obligatory in these cuckoo's nests. Despite proclamations of diversity, diverse opinion is not countenanced. The

---

35 This concept has become ubiquitous, if not mandatory, in politics and the media also. This author considers diversity to be detrimental to American society.

UCLA Diversity Chancellor's pay and benefits average $414,000 — more than faculty salaries. [395]

Reminiscent of China's Cultural Revolution, ideological purity is a prerequisite to attaining a teaching degree at the University of Minnesota. Prospective teachers there must ferret out their latent racism, classism and "hegemonic masculinity." The Duke Women's Center with the help of anti-male males is launching a new initiative called The Duke Men's Project. Based on a similar curriculum at University of North Carolina at Chapel Hill and Columbia University, the nine-week storytelling-based program is focused on redefining masculinity. It hopes to "create a space of brotherhood fellowship dedicated to interrogating male privilege and patriarchy." The goal is to critique and analyze "toxic masculinities and create healthier ones." Topics include male privilege, masculinity and the language of dominance, sexuality and gender diversity intending to help participants undergo a process of "deconstruction and reconstruction." Actress Meryl Streep defied the zeitgeist by claiming the term 'toxic' is damaging to boys/men, and adding that 'women can be pretty fucking toxic' too. For that she received a tounge-lashing from an otherwise adoring mainstream.

A 'men's manager' at Princeton will launch initiatives to challenge "gender stereotypes," and expand the school's Men's Allied Voices for a Respectful and Inclusive Community, a self-described "violence prevention program" that often bemoans "toxic masculinity" on its Facebook page. Gettysburg College addressed "toxic masculinity by showing students who identify as male a docudrama film about masculinity. The film, titled *The Mask You Live In*, was part of lessons warning students that the notion of masculinity comes with harmful side effects, warning that violent outbursts are prompted by masculinity pressures.

Kirsten Powers' book, <u>The Silencing</u>, describes how the political Left is killing offensive free speech. Conservative speakers are shouted down at colleges across the country. One student was prohibited by his professor from quoting Warren Farrell's book in a University of Massachusetts classroom. The class is titled, *Women in Psychology*, but it actually teaches feminism. The class was told that Farrell's book is a compilation of lies, and his theories do not deserve to be addressed. Furthermore, the student may not cite Farrell's books in any research papers.

In the name of diversity, a group of Penn State English Department students removed a portrait of the most famous person in English literature, William Shakespeare, from the walls of Fisher- Bennett Hall, and replaced it with a photo of Audre Lorde, a black female writer. Columbia University's math library displays four large portraits of mathematicians, two males and two females. This is blatant political correctness inasmuch as females constitute only 2 percent of first-rank mathematicians. These substitute females seem to be of totemic significance. Such obvious differences between the sexes are like an elephant in the room. Nobody dares notice them or their careers are in danger. Fred Reed aptly observed, " We are left with a nation of morons who will not know they are morons."

When Lawrence H. Summers, former president of Harvard University and former U.S. Treasury Secretary who had adjudicated questions of the world's financial system, suggested at an economic conference that innate differences between the sexes could help explain why fewer women succeed in science and math careers [396] feminist bedwetters who did not have fainting spells tantrumed at the blasphemy. MIT biology professor Nancy Hopkins developed a case of the vapors. Upon hearing Summers, she "felt I was going to be sick. My heart was pounding and my breath was shallow." And, "I just couldn't breathe because this kind of bias makes me physically ill." She said that if she had not bolted from the room, "I would've either blacked out or thrown up." Evidently, this feminist was not the typical tough broad most like to portray themselves as. She would have one helluva time in combat!

Writer Amity Shales said it was enough to bring the entire educational establishment down upon Mr. Summers' head. The galvanized Harvard Faculty of Arts and Sciences' Standing Committee on Women sent Summers a letter of censure; alumnae threatened to suspend donations; students mobilized, and Summers was barraged by protests from distraught Harvard co-eds who say they felt betrayed and diminished by his words.

Columnist Suzanne Fields likened the hullabaloo to the abuse that Galileo took in the 17th century when he questioned the notion, politically correct for his day, that the earth was the center of the universe. Christina Hoff Sommers defended Summers thusly, "It could explain why there are more men at the extremes of success and failure, more male CEOs, more males in maximum-security prisons." Nancy Pftotenhauer, president of the Independent Women's Forum, also defended Summers.

Attempting to demonstrate his meaning, Summers said "The data will, I am confident, reveal that Catholics are substantially underrepresented in investment banking...that white men are very substantially underrepresented in the National Basketball Association, and that Jews are very substantially under-represented in farming." [397] But because he sinned against ideological conformity, Summers was forced to drink hemlock, grovel and apologize three times. He later resigned. In 2013 President Obama wanted him as Fed. Chairman, but opposition from a combination of feminists and 'progressives' caused him to withdraw from consideration. [398]

Dr. Melita Garza, a professor from TCU called police on a disabled veteran student over a dissenting blog post, labeling the student's opinion that contradicted the professor's feminist opinions as "bullying," calling the veteran's post "dark, offensive and inappropriate." She asked the department chair to have the student removed from the class and to provide police/security to protect her. The student lost his military education benefits because of her actions, has been barred from the communications department, and cannot talk to any other students in the department or in his class. [399] Mark Harwood, psychology professor at Humboldt State University in California truthfully informed his students that women were as likely as men to engage in partner aggression. Feminists raised hell, taunting the professor as a "privileged, rich, white male." The head of the Women's Studies program demanded Harwood be barred from ever again teaching the course. Harwood resigned in protest. Marquette University has moved to suspend and then fire Professor John McAdams for backing a student who tried to defend man-woman marriage when a leftist teaching assistant shut the student down. [400]

One must be leery of any course ending in the word "studies." Feminist inspired studies especially have about as much credibility as The Da Vinci Code or the '1619 Project.' The Ward Churchill episode at Colorado University is exemplary. Churchill's Ethnic Studies (He was chairman of the department), Women's Studies, Gay and Lesbian Studies, and African-American Studies are not merely studies or departments; stacked with intellectual lightweights, they are university-financed movements of the Left. *U.S. News & World Report* Editor John Leo called these courses "part therapy group, part training grounds for feminist cadres to fight the patriarchy." Herbert London says, "Women's studies superordinate the role of women..." There are over 700 Women's Studies programs on colleges and universities throughout the United States teaching thousands or tens of thousands of classes from the gender feminist perspective, but not one program or class, teaching men's studies from the (real) masculist perspective.

The sexual revolution and subjective morality are promoted in higher education The Women's Gender and Sexuality Studies department at the University of Kansas is offering a course on angry white men and the role of "dominant and subordinate masculinities" as they connect to "rights-based movements of women, people of color, homosexuals and trans individuals." The University of Wisconsin, Madison created a postdoctoral fellowship in "Feminist biology," no doubt worried about psychiatric stress, bulimia and anorexia, hosted by the Department of Gender and Women's Studies, not by the Biology

Department. Blogger Paul Elam called such rabbit holes "The Complete Freak Show." [401] Camille Paglia, Professor of Humanities and Media Studies at the University of the Arts in Philadelphia, concurs. Fred Reed mused that feminists may next launch "departments of Resentment Studies." Female Arizona State University students can receive extra credit for refusing to shave for 10 weeks during the semester." Never explained is how women's' study courses prepare students for the after-college work world.

The Indiana University Health Center's three-day "4th annual sex fest" includes booths showcasing various sex toys and flogging mechanisms, complete with diagrams showing students how to use them. Some of the exhibits include free cupcakes and contraceptives, as well as free HIV testing, according to the Indiana Daily Student. Attendees also receive t-shirts that say "I love sex." Student congressman Matt Ahmann tweeted a video of part of the event, which included a man whipping a woman while she was tied up. Ahmann shared the video with *Campus Reform*.

Collegiate male-denigrating propaganda schemes posing as 'male studies' are Trojan horses teaching nonsense. Legitimate men's issues are verboten on Canadian college campuses. [402] Appalled by the disproportionate number of male suicides, Adam Frost a Durham University student in England proposed forming a society for men who may need support – only to find it rejected by the school's Societies Committee as "too controversial, like starting a society for white people's rights." They told him he could have a men's group, but "only if it was a branch of the Fem Soc." [403]

At Springfield College in Massachusetts, English professor Dennis Gouws became interested in the emerging field of men's studies, helped to found a college men's group and taught an undergraduate course "Men in Literature." This irritated campus feminists. In response to feminist anti-rape posters around the campus, Gouws put on his office door flyers that presented statistics on rape that contradicted the widespread claim that one in five women are raped during their undergraduate years. A college official complained that Gouws' posters created a "hostile environment," and the dean of his college called the organizations that had produced the flyer "a hate group." Gouws' posters were torn down and his door vandalized. Later the "Men in Literature" course was eliminated. [404]

Alexander McPherson, a highly-regarded professor of molecular biology and biochemistry at UC Irvine's school of biological sciences, was fired for refusing to participate in feminist sexual harassment training. [405] There's a principled man! Tim Hunt is a 72-year-old British biochemist and Nobel laureate who made the unforgivable mistake of criticizing women in science. For that observation, he was dismissed from several of his posts, ending his career. Mike Adams, a professor at the University of North Carolina-Wilmington is a refreshing counter-culturalist. Professor Steven Baskerville, and men's movement writer, is another enlightened exception (I helped enlighten him many years ago).

College administrators in these modern times permit unlearned student activists to shut down disliked speakers. Unruly leftist students shouted down the eminent social scientist Charles Murray and injured a female professor escorting him at Middlebury College. They didn't like his theories. That fad infected even Notre Dame University, formerly a bastion of common sense. Such students sucking their thumbs and worried about "trigger warnings" are treated to non-confrontational safe spaces, coloring books and counseling in this extended adolescence day care environment — no kidding. Fred Reed calls them snowflakes, and says, "Those who regard universities as centers for infantilism, inclusiveness and narcissistic political theater cannot live side by side with those who want rigorous schooling for the qualified."

A university that allows students to howl contrary views off campus is no longer an educational institution but a nursery. Students have been demanding "trigger warnings" when a course might present material which any student might find unpleasant, and they're demanding "safe spaces" stocked with cookies, milk, videos of puppies, and soft toys where they can recuperate from experiencing any ideas that they find disturbing. One demanded trauma relief from seeing "Trump 2016" chalked on campus sidewalks, despite a long tradition of students writing whatever they wanted on the sidewalks and an even longer tradition of political parties promoting their candidates similarly. Another college body demanded relief from the upset of a lecture they hadn't even attended — the mere fact that unspeakably disturbing ideas had been presented on their campus, out of both sight and earshot, made them need comfort and a soft blankie (This from the internet).

I wouldn't expose myself to these squealing millennial draft dogers again even if paid to do so. Attorney David French proposed a remedy for them in the October 16th 2017 *National Review*.

The Media
A neoliberal atmosphere prevails
The Hollywood echo chamber eagerly clambered aboard the feminist bandwagon. Our local PBS TV channel had a long-running theme: "Eliminating racism, empowering women." The United Nations appointed Wonder Woman as Honorary Ambassador for the Empowerment of Women and Girls.[406]

Empowerment has gone a long way. Columnist Mona Charen said, "Whole forests have given their lives so that the complaints of middle class young women could be enumerated, analyzed, deplored, and sulked about." It is hard to tell if this worshipful amen chorus, all swimming in the same pool, covers feminist doings or sponsors them. It carries more water than Gunga Din. Acolytes follow the script, promoting and parroting it as if prophetic, functioning practically as its bulletin board. Lickspittle commentariat, both male and female, hump the legs of feminists, whose spokeswomen are on the speed-dial of all TV producers. Media personnel not on the feminist payroll are being gypped.

Lifetime Movie Network is a treadmill of misandric screeds. Showcasing this favorite hobbyhorse, Lifetime TV launched a new "reality" show, *Deadbeat Dads. Sleeping with the Enemy*, a program implying that wife beating is ubiquitous, ran seemingly non-stop on cable TV. A PBS program *Breaking the Silence* in late 2005, howling about the sins of accused men, was filled with incredible distortions blaming men exclusively for domestic violence. One of the mothers portrayed as a victim turned out to be a serial child abuser. Two ombudsmen at the Public Broadcasting Service itself, Ken Bode and Michael Getter, charged that *Breaking the Silence* claims were "slanted" against fathers, "incendiary," and "plain wrong," that "there was no recognition of opposing views," and concluded the show was an "advocacy or point-of-view presentation." Further, that it "has been a launching pad for a very partisan effort to drive public policy and law." Oscar movie awardees are now to be chosen according to diversity standards.

The field is loaded with anti-male leanings. Activists, posing as journalists, barking and pushing all the buttons, hyperventilate on allegations of rape, child abuse, etc. They are eager to believe the worst of, and to sensationalize, any man accused of sexual misconduct, be he politician, actor, priest or athlete, and spill copious ink in that pursuit. Columnist Michael Barone wrote that the *New York Times* and *Durham Herald-Sun* "seemed to have a powerful emotional need to believe." CNN's Wolf Blitzer fawned at length over actress Reese Witherspoon's false claims of widespread domestic violence. From media reporting, one would think that sexual assault and rape are the major violent crimes. The reality is that they are a small percentage of violent crime in America, and often based on false allegations. For example, the *New York Times* March 18, 2007 magazine section cover featured a story about women in the military who said they had been raped in Iraq. The next week they printed a correction after discovering that one of them had not even been to Iraq. That failing rag has been going downhill ever since editor Abe Rosensthal left.

Men are victims of about 80% of the assaults and murders in America; yet consider the media umbrage, fixation and cooing over the murders of such cause célèbres as the pretty young North Dakota co-ed Dru Sjodin in May of 2004, over Natalee Holoway in Aruba in May and June 2005 (That practically became a new TV series). The conservative FOX TV network was a heavy offender. Remember the perpetual novenas on the deaths of JonBenét Ramsey murdered on Christmas1996, and of Princess Diana? In contrast, do not expect to see this headline: "The disappearance of an ordinary-looking, middle-aged black man has riveted the nation's attention." The lingering death of the man impaled in a woman's windshield and intentionally left to die an excruciating death elicited relatively little concern.

Programs such as *First Wives Club* would have us believe that it is funny for women to torture, extort, and economically abuse men who have done nothing evidently wrong. CBS's *The Talk* found Catherine Kieu Becker's slicing off of her husband's penis to be high comedy. In August 2009, Therese Ziemann, Wendy Sewell, Michelle Belliveau together with a 37-year-old man's wife, angry that he had bedded them all, used Krazy Glue to stick his penis to his stomach, took his wallet, cell phone and car and left him tied to a bed. The incident was met with widespread media hilarity. Imagine the umbrage if 4 men sexually mutilated a promiscuous woman.

Convicted women seldom receive such opprobrium as do convicted men. Boston mother Angela Lopez murdered her two children in July 2007. Newspaper stories blamed the tragedy on the men in her life. [407] Khandi Busby threw her two young sons off the I-30 overpass in Dallas in a failed attempt to kill them. A reporter described this would-be murderer as "troubled" — a word generally not applied to men who murder children. [408] A *Milwaukee Journal* writer, Beth Slocum, termed it "progressive" when a woman convicted of killing her husband spent only 12 hours in jail; then returned home to live with her children. A teacher had sex with a 13-year-old boy 300 times. The defense brought in a Freudian psychologist who said that teachers sometimes forget they are adults and assume a childlike peer relationship. CNN sided with the defense.

Remember convicted Texas killer Clara Harris who repeatedly ran over and killed her husband for having an affair? In a shockingly irresponsible *Psychology Today* article "Sweet Revenge," [409] Regina Barreca, Ph.D. praised Harris for her "great moment of revenge." One might think a purportedly intelligent publication would have more objectivity than to publish such tripe. When a drunken Caroline Broad intentionally ran her car over and killed her intimate partner, a U.K. judge sentenced her to three years in prison. Blimey, they almost got that one right! But it prompted an anguished article in *The Guardian*

(8/13/09) moaning that the sentence is too harsh because Broad has children. The infamous Casey Anthony was acquitted in 2011 of her daughter's murder. Though the *New York Post* and Anthony's own lawyer called her a partying "slut," Fox News' flaming feminist newshound Geraldo called her a "good mother."

Crystal Mangum, who falsely accused three Duke Lacrosse players of sexual crimes in 2006, was convicted of 2nd-degree murder in 2013. There were 160 major television news stories in the first five days after the players were arrested, but when Mangum was convicted of *murdering* her boyfriend and sentenced to 14 years in prison, there were only 3 major television news stories, a difference in coverage of 5,233%. [410]

A woman in Dearborn County, Indiana falsely accused a man of raping her at the Aurora Little League Park on July 15, 2009. As usual, media referred to the unnamed woman as "the victim" several times, though no crime was committed. Though filing a false charge of rape is a crime, no arrest was made. Again, police and the press gave a woman a pass. [411] Local media graphically focused on covering the Hancock County Maine accusations mentioned earlier, and at times even implied that the acquitted men had cheated justice. One Bangor television station aired an interview with a local rape crisis center official who stated that even if a woman falsely accuses a man of rape, it is most important for law enforcement to believe the woman, act on her report, and do exactly what she wants them to do regardless of the evidence. CNN's Gen Psaki admits agreeing with ALL such accusers.

In October 2007, magician David Copperfield was falsely accused of raping a woman. The media blared his name far and wide, concealing the name of his accuser. Well, her name is Lacey L. Carroll, a former Miss Washington USA contestant. She was later charged in Washington State with prostitution and providing a false statement to police when she claimed to have been sexually assaulted by another man in Washington. [412]

Legal theory holds that suspects are presumed innocent. However, in connection with domestic assault and rape allegations the presumption of guilt automatically attaches to males, while the status of "victim" automatically applies to female accusers. The media and even the police routinely release names of alleged perpetrators, but never those of alleged victims, presumably because the former are primarily male and the latter primarily female. Men should be entitled to know which women in the community are likely to tag them with a rape claim. Use of such terms and publication of the names of alleged perpetrators before it has been established that a crime has been committed is prejudicial and patently unfair. Due process and reliable conclusions demand more than summary pronouncements of guilt as with the Queen of Hearts in *Alice in Wonderland*.

In Minnesota, a 10-year-old girl accused her teacher of touching her inappropriately. Without any proof or conviction, the Anoka County police and the St. Paul newspaper revealed the accused's name. [413] The U.K. coalition government pledged to change their law so as to extend anonymity in rape cases to cover the accused as well as the accuser, at least until and unless a conviction occurs. Feminists throughout the U.K. were livid.

Former CBS news correspondent Bernard Goldberg calls the media "one of America's most pro-feminist institutions." The *Financial Times* has developed a bot that warns journalists when they're quoting too many men or not including enough women in their stories. In his best-selling book <u>Bias and Arrogance</u>, Goldberg claims the influx of women into the media is what turned it leftward. Michael Scherer of *Time* Magazine penned an article implying that an economic crisis would have been avoided if women ran Wall Street.

Media mogul Ted Turner, Jane Fonda's former husband, said men should be prohibited from elective office worldwide. Alan Alda once called testosterone a male poison. While trying to influence the election against President Bush 41, *Newsweek* called him a wimp. [414] Imagine that; this was a guy who did 58 bombing missions over the Pacific, and was shot down defending our nation.

Inclusion of women as high achievers, very often smarter than husbands and male co-workers way beyond reality, is almost obligatory in movies and TV shows. TV's *Deadliest Catch* features a girl playing captain of a lobster trawler in the north seas. The Mars movie and many more not mentioned here are further examples. Witness the many actresses comically playing tough cops and other male roles. It is voguish to portray women as tough martial arts experts beating up men. A widely ballyhooed TV series. "Supergirl," desperately tried to promote that image. A CW' (whatever that is) stand-alone series — *Batwoman* — features Rose [stage name Kate Kane] as Batwoman, an out lesbian and highly trained street fighter primed to snuff out the failing city's criminal resurgence, armed with a passion for social justice and a flair for speaking her mind. TV Kiddie Comics has "The Powderpuff Girls" as crime fighters. Kick-ass female characters, seem maladapted to ordinary life. Digest this from the Oct 8-14, 2007 TV Guide: "Bionic Woman, Faster! Stronger! Sexier! ... fall's butt-kicking new hit." The otherwise good TV series, Designated Survivor, depicted a tough-as-nails Oriental-American woman. In the Star Wars film, The Force Awakens, to quote *National Review*, the female heroine, Rey, is a fighter who can take down six storm troopers in seconds without breaking a sweat. Now comes the latest, 'Captain Marvel' to "save the world." Probably the looniest of all is a TV series called Valor, featuring a heroic female combat helicopter pilot. A show called 'Agent Carter,' the popular movie 'Hunger Game's,' the 2015 remake of 'Mad Max' and the remake of 'Ghostbusters' are in the same genre. While females are weirdly depicted doing the hard (manly) roles, males are equally weirdly depicted doing the soft (girly) roles.

On a flight from New York City to Dallas Texas, Southwest Airlines Flight 1380 a Boeing 737-700 lost one of two engines while at cruising altitude. Pilot captain Tammie Jo Shults performed the engine-out procedure that every multi-engine flight student has been taught. She landed the aircraft in Philadelphia to great acclaim. An ecstatic media compared her to US Airways Capt. Chesley "Sully" Sullenberger, who lost BOTH engines and landed his plane safely in New York's Hudson River in 2009. Much more difficult piloting would be required to control a multi-engine aircraft while climbing out of an airport, as happened to me while leaving Birmingham, Ala. enroute to Gulfport, Miss. in a Cessna 320. Again, the procedure (props, throttle, flaps, gear, test, feather, trim — I can never forget that) is burned into every non-jet multi-engine flight student's head. [415]

In 'heroic' situations, military or otherwise, the media likes to use the term "men and women" even if there are few if any women involved. I'm surprised they didn't refer to the men "and women" of Seal Team 6 that rendered Osama bin Laden hors de combat (He now sleeps with the fishes). Female officer Kimberly Munley, who was wounded by the Islamist radical Nidal Hassan — murderer of 13 military personnel at Ft. Hood Texas, was widely credited with shooting Hassan. In reality, it was Senior Sgt. Mark Todd who brought the shooter down. [416]

On January 8, 2011, a gunman of undetermined political leanings, Jared Loughner, murdered 6 people, including Federal Judge John Roll and wounded Congresswomen Gabrielle Giffords. The media, across the entire political spectrum, even that media darling — President Obama — fixated exclusively on the congresswoman practically ignoring the murdered people (It took my wife to notice the popular bias). Two men tackled the shooter, and Patrica Maisch picked up the gun magazine after he dropped it, but the media credited her with the tackle. Shades of Jessica Lynch. Two women, one a civilian policeperson the other a military guard pulled guns on the Ft. Hood Army base mass murderer. They didn't fire a shot, but were proclaimed heroes by the media and Army brass.

The treatment of men's rights activists. While taking at face value most anything feminists say, seldom asking for proof, the media echo chamber smears and opposes any who contradict them. Legitimate advocates for men and fathers have genuine arguments and gripes; but — because they go against the narrative — are ignored, censored, denigrated and gobsmacked. (This book will get the same treatment). Men's movement advocates have to affirmatively prove our claims, and are subjected to journalistic cheap shots. Using "gotcha" journalism in adversarial, agenda-driven sessions, interviewers with about as much objectivity as Rolling Stones reporters treat us like fire hydrants at a dog show. Conservative interrogators are every bit as rude as liberal ones.

Some years ago, the best parts of my appearance on Tom Snyder's "Tomorrow Show" were left on the cutting room floor, and a file of evidentiary clippings I loaned the female producers became "lost." I seldom participate any more. CNBC Hardball host Chris Matthews, Sean Hannity and Alan Combs are vicious interrogators. On his "Hardball" show, Matthews savaged masculinist Professor Stephen Baskerville. Matthews and Combs shoot at us from the liberal side. Geraldo and Glen Beck from the conservative or semi-conservative side. CNN's Nancy Grace has brayed right up there with them. Chris Cuomo is bright, but virulent. Few male advocates are loquacious or glib enough to compete with grandstanding pros butting in rudely. In some interviews, I have felt like Daniel in the Lions' Den. Not having Obama's silver tongue or Donald Trump's chutzpah, I don't relish mud-wrestling with media Hulk Hogans or jousting with sharpies. Any further communication will probably be by e-mails or responses to written questions.

Former big time broadcaster, Bill O'Reilly on the Fox network was basically sensible, but tough with disfavored interviewees. He did tell it like it is regarding gender/sex one time. [417] It was nothing this writer hasn't been saying for decades, but millions got to see and hear O'Reilly. No doubt O'Reilly thought it was his own idea. CNN dropped commentator Pat Buchanan for stating similar politically incorrect sentiments.

As many authors have discovered to their chagrin, an unhealthy conspiracy of silence about matters raised here pervades traditional publishers. They seldom publish politically incorrect books, especially those by unknown authors without agents, and agents are almost never interested in pushing books defending real males; I contacted over a hundred re. this book, no real interest — exemplifying the 'woke' leftist bent of the industry. Some principles, subjects and opinions herein, were too much even for some strongly moral conservatives, whom I highly respect. Compounding the difficulty is the reality that agents, publishers and ad. agencies are normally staffed with squadrons of disagreeing or censorious females, if not actual feminists. Getting this manuscript past feminist sympathizers at every step of promotion is extremely difficult. I shopped earlier versions around to various, mostly conservative, organizations and individuals for opinions and review. Response was disappointing. Media balance is feigned by publication of writings from anti-male male authors, arguably on the philosophical fringe of our movement, under the guise of "masculinist" material.

Media bias extends beyond gender issues also. Commentariat representing primarily liberal positions is staffed with "woke" arbiters of 'truth.' News hosts are prone to put their opinions above those of the experts they are interviewing. Opinion and the reading of tea leaves masquerade as news. The watchdog group Accuracy in Media documents the portside tilt. Fixating on negatives of conservatives, nitpickers make mountains out of molehills. Many don't even pretend objectivity. A CBS VP and senior counsel Hayley Geftman-Gold, sent this Facebook comment about the victims of the Las Vegas massacre. "I'm actually not even sympathetic because country music fans are often Republican gun-toters." She was fired for it.

There exists an ankle-biting Trump Derangement Syndrome. A report from Harvard Kennedy School's Shorenstein Center on Media, Politics and Public Policy and the Pew Research Center analyzed news coverage of this president's first 100 days in office concluded it to be eighty percent negative. [418] An analysis of 3,000 stories across 24 different media organizations found that reporting on Trump has been the most negative compared to other presidents over the past 25 years. CNN's Cuomo outdoes the other pecksniffs there. The research showed that only 5 percent of media reporting during the period was positive. Sixty-two percent of the stories were negative, some almost fanatic about it, and 33 percent were neither positive nor negative. Don't forget the gleeful delight when he caught the Coronavirus; one commentator compared them to a pack of hyenas. Though God knows Trump has many flaws, he tells it like it is and calls a spade a spade, ordinary people understand and like that.

On TV I watch CNN for the leftist slant (although it has gotten harder to stomach). Political correctness dictated that the armed, but law abiding defenders of confederate statues in Charlottesville, Virginia be condemned, while their armed and violent attackers not be condemned. For the conservative slant I watch Newsmax and Fox. OK, perhaps somewhat for the female eye candy, mostly leg shows, they exploit so much. Fox often substitutes giddy "entertainment" for the unwashed, while CNN usually sticks to real news (however slanted portside).

Regarding Covid-19, the media in general praised New York Democrat governor Cuomo who had a deplorable record confronting the

Pandemic, while criticizing Florida's Republican governor DeSantis. who had a praiseworthy record there.

The media and its Hollywood echo chamber is rife with dingbats barking at the moon like Joy Behar or masquerading as comedians like that bitch headlining the 2018 White House correspondence dinner. The applause she received demonstrates the depths to which the "news" media has sunk. Sara Huckabee Sanders faced her terrible personal insults with grace and class. Mustn't forget actor Robert DiNero's vulgar expression at the June 2018 Tony Awards. "Comedians" Steven Colbert and Bill Maher are especially crude. Michael Moore is another unmitigated ass. Archie Bunker's "Meathead" still lives up to his nickname. Pat Buchanan described the media as an "effete corps of impudent snobs."

Calling Julian Assange a 'journalist' is like calling Nazi doctor Josef Mengele a scientist. It is almost laughable to hear questionably intelligent media persons refer to each other as "colleagues." While genuflecting to one another at the January 2018 Golden Glove awards, celebrity narcissists suggested Oprah Winfrey for president; can you imagine? What, pray tell, makes celebrities experts on anything beyond their specialties.

This is not a blanket condemnation of the chattering class. There are many competent (and attractive) female TV reporters and commentators these days, professional and brave like CNN's Clarissa Ward. The courageous journalist Marie Colvin was killed in Syria while covering a war few men dared get close to. Lara Logan is another good one. Russian Rulia (Yulia) Latynina defies Putin at risk of her life. There are reporters living in Mexico with the courage to expose drug trade members. About seventy have been killed, gruesomely, in the last decade and over two hundred and forty five have been assaulted; [419] many are women.

Inexplicable entities

What would normally be substantial, direct beneficiaries from a reduction in the divorce rate — like the insurance industry, lending institutions, and taxpayers, and most religions — demonstrate sublime indifference. The ACLU, the Center for Constitutional Rights, Big Brothers Inc., certain philanthropic organizations, and so on — are placidly ignorant of or disinterested in these issues and their effect on men, children and the country. Many members of the clergy seem to feel that reform favors men or facilitates divorce, and that by blocking reform they become instruments of God's will. In effect, they have punted. They are the dogs that don't bark. Their passivity is incomprehensible. Let's just say it is easy to bear injuries — to others.

Men, Ourselves

Beyond a small minority, can male victims be blamed for our plight, for the death march of the western male? Damn right, we can! We let it happen. Our true enemy is often in the mirror. The decline and fall of the male has been far too voluntary and justified — made so by the vast majority of near-normal males who have simply and quietly abdicated their own trousers.

It is easy to say the system has failed us. Not completely, we failed the system. As helpless animals caught in car headlights, we stood by while our rights and responsibilities were taken away. We meekly accepted false accusations and rolled over like submissive dogs. We seldom support one another in confrontations with women, even when in the right. Failure to cooperate with other men amounts to sawing off our own testicles. It is a mystery why most men fail to fight back. It seems to be an inherent biological flaw built into us. To repeat Linda Bowles "...I don't know why they (men) put up with it..."

It seems that male characteristics are also liabilities; the qualities that cause us to excel — ego, rugged individualism — prevent us from defending ourselves. The average man is conditioned to peace, to old school honesty and fair play, as incapable of fighting back as Little Bo Peep. He lies down and takes a screwing just to make people think he's a good boy. He labors under the naiveté that he will avoid injustice simply by virtue of a pure heart. Bunk! A man like that is at a disadvantage more than at an advantage in this practical, everyday world, especially in court. The allegorical significance, if nothing else, of the crucifixion is undeniable. That is what happens to good guys. Leo Durocher's observation that "Nice guys finish last" is appropriate.

Many men, not necessarily stupid ones, create a psychological block against responding to summons for divorce or other domestic relations issues. That is like putting a loaded gun in your mouth and pulling the trigger. I have counseled many of them after they signed whatever papers their divorcing wife's lawyer put in front of them. I could have slapped them, if they had not been hurting so much — almost in shock. Such submission is suicide. Rolling over like a dog will get your belly bitten out by unscrupulous lawyers.

David Blankenhorn at the outset of his otherwise admirable book, <u>Fatherless America</u>, makes an unsubstantiated assertion that lies at the heart of his claim to be an authority on the fatherhood crisis. He writes, "Never before in this country have so many children been voluntarily abandoned by their fathers." In addition, "Today, the principal cause of fatherlessness is paternal choice...the rising rate of paternal abandonment." Blankenhorn cites no source and evinces no evidence for these assertions. Aside from the question of how he can be privy to the volition of other people, this statement represents an odd abdication of the scholar's critical function. Deploring the breakdown of marriage, he and many others in the so-called 'marriage movement' myopically dismiss the primary culprit — misandry in and out of the courts. The normally astute *U.S. News & World Report* editor, Mortimer Zuckerman; in a 10/25/04 editorial bemoaned "fathers abandoning their families." (What can you expect from a former suitor of Gloria Steinem?)

Such opinions have been called into serious question by in-depth investigations. Research published in refereed journals by respected scholars like Stephen Baskerville, Sanford Braver, Margaret Brinig, Douglas Allen, Ilene Wolcott, Jody Hughes, Judith Wallerstein, and Sandra Blakeslee, and corroborated by the professional experience of authors as ideologically diverse as Constance Ahrons, Shere Hite, David Chambers, Robert Seidenberg, and Rosalind Miles indicates that paternal abandonment cannot account for widespread fatherlessness.

Often white-collar men hold themselves above their sometimes more masculine blue-collar brothers. Downright pitiful is a gelded, desperately trendy and confused segment living a de-gendered life. Often called SNAGs [fn36] (sensitive, new age guys), they would surrender their manhood to gain acceptance and equality with women. That is too high a price to pay. Clint Eastwood aptly calls them the "pussy generation." Numbered among feminism's useful idiots, these fops hold manhood cheap. Self-described gay columnist Zach Stafford says the very concept of manhood in modern society should be eliminated. [420]

In 1945 Rev. Martin Niemoller said:

First, they came for Communists, and I didn't speak up, because I wasn't a Communist. Then they came for the Jews, and I didn't speak up, because I wasn't a Jew. Then they came for the Catholics, and I didn't speak up, because I was a Protestant.

Then they came for me, and by that time there was no one left to speak up for anyone.

---

[36] That term may be a bit harsh and dismissive, but conceivably this element could be allies in the struggle to save the males.

Part II. Sex and Gender

Gender/sex issues are myriad, beyond the biological and perhaps more important than "man-caused global warming"— or cooling, whichever is current. Due to similarities and confusion over the terms sex and gender, largely a matter of semantics, I try to use the appropriate term here, sometimes using "sex/gender' where it seems appropriate. Lately the term gender is considered by some to be whatever the person referred to considers himself, herself or itself to be. Such a definition can prove harmful to women and girls as explained herein.

Chapter 1. Sex Differences and outcomes

Albeit anathema to androgyny advocates, there are givens in nature; males and females of most species are vastly different physically and anatomically, and — especially in the human species — emotionally and psychologically. The differences — physical, mental, emotional, etc. — between normal men and normal women are wide, deep and obvious "as any fool kin plainly see" (apologies to Li'l Abner). There is none so blind as he who will not see. Researchers scanning the brains of 118 fetuses in the second half of pregnancy found that differences between men's and women's brains start in the womb and therefore are biological. This, according to a US study, published in the journal *Developmental Cognitive Neuroscience.* [421]

To deny differences is to deny science, behavioral and biological, as well as the evidence of one's own powers of observation. The differences, averages I hasten to add — not all humans exhibit them — are biologically rooted, and for those who believe in the Creator, divinely ordained. Society must recognize that the differences between the sexes are what make the world go around. No amount of shouting, constitutional amendments or suspension of reality can eliminate the difference — thank God! Vive la difference!

An enormous literature on sexual differences has been piling up for more than 30 years. Some excellent works prove the distinctions: As Nature Made Him by John Colapinto (HarperCollins), Taking Sex Differences Seriously by Steven E. Rhoads (Encounter Books), The Biological Basis for Gender-Specific Behavior by Gregg Johnson Professor of Biology at Bethel College in Minnesota, and Recovering Biblical Manhood & Womanhood. [422] A study by researchers at the European College of Neuropsychopharmacology (ECNP) suggests that sex hormones create a "genuine difference" in brain structure between men and women. [423] The journal BMC Biology published a study in its February 2017 issue by Israeli scientists who have uncovered 1,559 genetic differences between males and females that relate not only to sexual organs, but to such other organs such as the brain, skin and heart. [424] Neuroscience maintains that the part of the brain that stimulates anger and aggression is larger in males than in females (for evolutionary — meaning adaptive — reasons), and the part that restrains anger is smaller in males. This clashes with Aristotle's observation that women are more likely "to scold and to strike."

These sexual and functional differences exist in nearly all higher species. One would be hard pressed to find in biological literature an instance of identical behavior of males and females. Sure, lionesses do most of the hunting and killing, but that relates to women shopping for groceries; lions still rule the pride. Despite the five-pound handicap in favor of fillies (female horses) racing against colts (male horses), only three fillies ever won the Kentucky Derby: Regret (1915), Genuine Risk (1980) and Winning Colors (1988). In 2009, Rachel Alexandra won the Preakness, the first filly to win that race in 85 years.

Social scientists have determined that traditional sex distinctive child toy choices exist even in monkeys; but in humans a peculiar effort to defy nature by eliminating differentiated boys' and girls' toys exists. The fact that these universals transcend divergent animal groups and human cultures suggests that there must be more than a cultural basis for these differences. These distinctive, natural characteristics, predominant in each sex, are the result of eons of evolution, not the result of recent adverse sociological discrimination.

Sex differences are "hard-wired" and fundamental to the survival and progress of the human race. Biological polarity between the sexes is essential to life itself. Past civilizations that lost these distinctions have ceased to exist. [425] In a survey of 2,000 different cultures Charles Winick, Professor of Anthropology and Sociology at the City University of New York, found that some fifty-five were characterized by sexual ambiguity. Not one of those cultures has survived. Presumably, street demonstrations against normality and law and order such as we see in cities today also expedited their demise. This is further corroborated by studies of eighty primitive and civilized societies conducted by Oxford Professor J. D. Umuin, and by the studies of Harvard Professor Emeritus Carle Zimmerman. It is only logical that there be separate functions, addressed later, determined by these differences.

Equality does not translate to sameness. The following passage from a forgotten source sums it up nicely:

Not all inequality is based on superiority and subordination, in other words the kind of inequality that exists between king and subject, or master and slave. A saw and a hammer are certainly unequal, but their inequality is not one of worth or status; it is one of type or purpose. This inequality does not reflect adversely on the value of either — indeed, both are necessary to build a house.

The inequality of man and woman is similar. A big and healthy difference between the sexes is essential to the natural scheme of things. To quote Margaret Mead, "If any human society large or small, simple or complex, based on the most rudimentary hunting and fishing, or on the whole elaborate interchange of manufactured products is to survive, it must have a pattern of social life that comes to terms with the differences between the sexes." [426] The sexes are complimentary, or should be. They need not be at odds personally or employment-wise. They must reestablish mutual harmony and respect. Men should be proud of their masculine characteristics and resultant abilities, as women should be of theirs. Human value is not derived from function. The obvious functional superiority of males in some areas is counterbalanced by certain feminine assets and characteristics.

"One of the nice things about reality is that it is what it is, no matter what anybody says it is." — Fred Reed.

The sexes are not interchangeable, feminists and mod/libs to the contrary notwithstanding. The male qualities they abhor are what make males male. And the female qualities they abhor are what make females female. Even Betty Friedan somersaulted, admitting, "Women aren't male clones." Most men need a woman to mature. Most women need a man to mature (From Jordan Peterson's 12 Rules for Life).

The following "Statement of Gender" was penned by philosopher George Silos,

Gender exists throughout the universe, and the universe could not exist without the influence of gender...

The production of things, the movement of life, the relationship of people, and the well-being of society depends upon the principle of gender. In order for electricity to flow in a battery an anode and a cathode are required, and in all else there must be a positive and negative condition for energy to flow, things to grow, and life to move.

Most women want their men to be more dominant, not less. According to the psychologist Karl Menninger, for every woman who complains to her shrink that her man is a brute there are a dozen who complain that he is a wimp — incapable of acting like a father who takes charge, accepts responsibility and gets things done. Surveys have shown that most college women prefer dominant and aggressive men. Someone said, "Men have special duties. They have to be brave, protect women and take responsibility for wrongdoing."

The lessons of The Bell Curve (next page) apply to sex equally as to race. The depiction, on the next page, was contributed to by Eduard Bakalar, Ph.D. of the Czech Republic and Lloyd Selberg of Missouri, who says that generally feminine thinking is more emotional while male thinking is more rational. If we represent the number of men and women on the vertical axis, and traits on a horizontal axis starting with geniuses and saints on the left and moving to the villains and the drop-outs on the right we would get Gaussian distribution shapes with average traits in the center representing the majority of each sex. The flatter the curve, the greater the standard deviation from the average. From the shape of the curves, we conclude that men have a greater standard deviation than women, making the extremes more probable. At both the saints' end and the sinners' or we could call them altruists and psychopaths ends, men appear in reasonable numbers; women, on the other hand, hardly at all.

Gender Population Distribution v. Traits

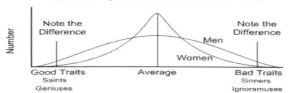

So why is it that maleness and high achievement go so closely hand in hand? Dr. Charles Goodheart at Gonville & Caius College, who has studied the difference in the results between the sexes for 16 years, states quite frankly that it is all a question of testosterone, the male hormone that gives men "forcefulness, aggression, ambition, originality and general push." Women underachieve because they convert the majority of this hormone to estrogens. The same hormone that produces the yobo also produces the genius. The higher male levels of testosterone with its associated mental effects clearly explain the greater deviations from the norm, be it for good or for evil.

Selberg suggests, "The greater diversity in males is explained by male XY chromosome compared to the female XX chromosome. Differences in the XX chromosomes are averaged, but there is no equivalent averaging between the XY male chromosomes." Studies of the brains of psychopaths and altruists demonstrate that brain structure appears to influence those at both ends of the spectrum. [427]

It is true, many males are brutal, villainous or incompetent; even less desirable male behaviors such as rape, violence and arguably warfare are mere extremes or mutations of our very sexual essence; but we mustn't permit feminists, SNAGS and sex melders to use them as straw men to completely denigrate testosterone. Big media, and particularly female writers and women's magazines, consider mostly the right end of the men's line, but concentrate almost exclusively on the left end of the women's line.

Nevertheless, men at the left end of the line have achieved the greatest accomplishments of civilization; they are primarily the thinkers, the inventors, and the saints. Over 300 firemen and 73 cops, not a woman among them to my knowledge, lost their lives running INTO the Twin Towers on 9/11. Anthropologist Joyce Benenson defined men as, "someone you can count on when the enemy comes."

The Creator and Satan are both widely regarded as males. Professor Camille Paglia put it rather well when she said, "There is no female Mozart because there is no female Jack-the-Ripper." Professor Johnson, mentioned earlier, tells us,

> Among most higher social mammals, males are more aggressive than females, and take dominant leadership roles in social groups. Males are territorial. Males tend to build hierarchical social order. Females of most groups studied are not as driven by competitive, territorial or hierarchical urges... [and are] less confrontive and combative and more interested in building and maintaining social bonds. They are peacemakers and conformists to group expectations. Anthropologists find similar kinds of universal sex-specific behaviors among human cultures. Male dominance is universal. Of two hundred fifty cultures studied, males dominate in almost all.

The Accomplishment Difference

Facts are stubborn things. Throughout history, a man or men — few women — accomplished practically every human achievement worth noting and requiring conscious effort. Eighty-two percent of all the saints are men. Almost every top chef is a man. The best orchestra in the world, the Vienna Symphony Orchestra, is composed entirely of men, as are all noted composers of classical music. No woman has ever won the world chess championship despite equal encouragement of the sexes in many countries.

Anthropologist Desmond Morris says the history of humanity is the history of man, not of woman. His book The Naked Man (Amazon.com) takes an unfashionable look at the triumph of the human male, claiming, "For every great woman, there have been 100 — even 1,000 — great men in the same field." Morris attempts not only to explain why this is so, but also to contest that reports of the death of masculinity have been exaggerated. While women are proficient in many fields, men generally pioneered those fields, and instructed women therein.

Internet blogger and raconteur Fred Reed says:

Men hold nearly every Olympic record in sports in which men compete. In professional sports, the sexes compete separately because otherwise there would be no women's sports. On test after test of mental ability, men regularly outscore women: SATs, GREs, National Merit, and so on. In psychometry, it is settled knowledge that at the high end of the scale of intelligence, men outnumber women, and that the higher you go, the more preponderance. The disparity in mathematical talent is stark." Reed added, "Without men, civilization would last until the oil needed changing." [428]

The beginning of wisdom might be to note the utter dependence of the US on white men — men, guys, hombres — who have contributed virtually everything that keeps the affirmative-action classes from living in grass huts.

Camille Paglia observed, "As I drove across the Verrazano Bridge, I thought, 'Men built this.' As I looked towards the New York skyline, I thought, 'Men built that.' If women were in charge of culture, we would still be living in caves, well-decorated caves, but caves." She also said, "It's a man's world, and always will be. The modern economy is a male epic, in which women have found a productive role — but women were not its author." PBS rightfully acknowledges its many female financial contributors; but I can't help thinking that their main contribution to anything is having slept with fortune-building husbands.

Normal Sex Roles

The foregoing observations refer primarily to averages, and the assertions below are generalities, not applicable to all. Emphasis is on the word "normal." Normal male functions, deriving from the well-established gender/sex differences, range from provider to authoritarian, and are often arduous, and under-appreciated. Normal men, as distinguished from wimps and clods, are naturally the 'load bearers' (both physically and psychologically). Though both sexes have gotten softer and lost traditional abilities (few men today can build a birdhouse or women iron clothes or sew buttons on a shirt), male abilities and characteristics are more suited for the arduous functions. Normal female functions range from procreator, tamer of men, nursemaid and housekeeper, through career roles requiring attention to detail — like medical or clerical. [fn37] They are often considered tedious. Women in the days of our ancestors were tougher in many ways than most men are today.

Normal sex attributes dictate that the best football linebackers and surgeons are men, and the best seamstresses are women (Years ago, I had an argument with a feminist at a University of Minnesota panel discussion who maintained that women could eventually play linebacker in professional football). Likewise, if a couple has a flat tire on a rainy night, the man, a normal one, gets out to change it (A man's got to do what a man's got to do). If there is housework to be done, the woman normally does it. Good women have or retain the nursing instinct. Sex melders mistakenly attribute these function distributions solely to 'tradition,' but there is solid reason behind them. That pattern

---

37 George Gilder was tossed off the Oprah show for suggesting these functions for women.

is necessary to sustain a healthy society. A good book on the subject is Raising Boys Feminists Will Hate.

However the liberal American Psychological Association begs to differ. The APA released guidelines concerning men and boys, saying that so-called "traditional masculinity" not only is "harmful" but also could lead to homophobia and sexual harassment. "The main thrust of the subsequent research is that traditional masculinity – marked by stoicism, competitiveness, dominance and aggression – is, on the whole, harmful." But let us consider the hormonal makeup of those nominal males.

James Damore is a former Google engineer known for the truthful memo he circulated within the company arguing that men and women are inherently biologically different, and thus suited to different lines of work and that the lack of 50/50 gender proportionality at Google and other tech firms was largely due to female preferences rather than to gender bias. Damore was fired for that politically incorrect heresy.

This is not to imply that men are better than or superior to women, only different, and just as good. Nor is it to denigrate the many accomplished women out there, but to speculate, or even posit, that they may possess masculine characteristics. Granted, some persons are mentally or hormonally *of* the opposite sex. On the rare occasion when a woman becomes a high achiever, she usually almost reaches masculinity, losing her femininity. It is because of this that men do not feel attracted to such a woman. It has little or nothing to do with the fact that she is successful. I recall a woman — one of my flight students with a dual personality. Sometimes she acted like a second mate and was better at business than most men; but when she wanted to be feminine, she appeared highly attractive.

These observations are not to be construed as threats to the advancement of any single woman. Obviously, some women are competent to handle top-level jobs. My congratulations to those who *have earned* success. There have been outstanding women leaders, Golda Maier, Margaret Thatcher and German Chancellor Angela Merkel for instance. Heather MacDonald — a Thomas W. Smith Fellow at the Manhattan Institute also qualifies. Some women meet the rigid qualifications of an airline pilot. Astronaut Eileen Collins may have been such a woman; yet I will bet my bottom dollar there were better-qualified male candidates available when she was picked for the job. Wisely, she cut short her career to return to hearth and home. Some of the best officers and workers at our local American Legion post are women.

Many more people (38%) would prefer a male boss if given the choice than would prefer a female boss at the workplace (12%). This is truer of women (43% of whom would choose a male boss) than it is of men

(32%). Only 13% of people would actually prefer to work for a woman. [429] A stewardess of my acquaintance told me other stewardesses prefer to work under a steward than under another stewardess.

Although stereotypes are generally based on reality, they are not always valid. Undoubtedly, there is some individual overlap in abilities between the sexes. Not all persons fit into traditional sex roles, nor should they. There are exceptions to every rule that make strict adherence to norms an oversimplified and unfair solution. Some women, with interesting concoctions of hormones perhaps, can lift the front end of a 1960's Volkswagen (I saw a photo of a 'women' muscle builder who had muscles the envy of most male muscle-builders), while some evidently normal men cannot lift 120 pounds. Because some women can match some men in some respects, it is illogical — reasoning from the specific to the general — to claim or imply that all women can do so. Some women can get through military Commando training, but damn few, not enough to change procedures, contrary to feminists' shrill demands.

Traditional family structure and functions have developed over millions of years as the soundest way for men and women to live together and survive. The family functions most smoothly and efficiently in this manner, both positively motivated to work — each in their own natural spheres; it more easily prospers. Polls show that 60% of employed mothers with minor children prefer part-time work, and 19% would like to give up their workforce job altogether. [430] Gilder again: "The fact is that the role of the housewife is arguably more important than any other broad category of work in the society (Some prefer the term 'stay-at-home mother' instead of 'housewife')." *Why Women Still Can't Have it All* by Anne-Marie Slaughter is an excellent article on this subject that appeared as cover story in the July/August 2012 issue of *The Atlantic magazine*.

The estate of woman, as wife and helpmeet, mother and nurturer of children, is no less (and no more) worthy than that of man as husband and breadwinner, paterfamilias, and defender of his native heath. Each complements the other, and both are necessary to create a family. Such families, in turn, are the building blocks of the larger society, and on their strength depends the soundness of the whole edifice. Can we go back to that happy era when girls were girls and boys were boys, when men respected woman, at least most of them did, and women were respectable, at least *most* of them were; when women were willing to be wives and mothers — to perform maternal functions as their grandmothers did, when the resulting family stability made more people better off than they had ever been? A Norwegian study demonstrated the desirability of this division of duties. [431]

Marriage is like a dance; in dancing, one leads while the other follows. This does not imply that both are not contributing equally. It has been my experience that the best women dancers are those used to following men in other regards. They are like feathers in your arms. With others it can be like driving a truck.

Times change; my co-workers at MSP tower were typical old-fashioned men's men. Years later after returning to the FAA in Crystal tower in Minneapolis, most were much different, watching or listening to soap operas and discussing them with other males and females.

Employment: Quotas, Affirmative Action

Plato said (paraphrasing), "No two people are born exactly alike. There are innate differences, which fit them for different occupations." Despite those words of wisdom, vast social engineering schemes and prejudices are working to the detriment of traditional men and families, indeed of society. Quotas in hiring and promoting employees are mandated by social levelers, defying traditional sex roles. Women are parachuted into job slots ahead of men with more ability and seniority. Affirmative Action (A.A.) is sometimes called "reverse" discrimination, but wrongly so because little original discrimination actually existed. Thanks to A. A., males find it difficult to obtain employment and to gain admission to institutions of learning, though it is usually men who must bring home the bacon. If a well-qualified man applies for work or promotion in government or big business, and a woman applicant is even remotely qualified, she will likely get it.

In the early days, C.B.S. Television made Sally Quinn into a major network news broadcaster when, according to her book, We're Going to Make You a Star, she didn't even know until later that the red light on top of a camera meant that it was active. That may be why Rush Limbaugh deplored "the chickification" of the news.

Demonstrating unintended consequences, Affirmative Action sex quotas became official quite by accident. On June 19, 1963, President John F. Kennedy sent the Civil Rights Act (CRA) to Congress to counter racial discrimination in the work place. This Act, intended primarily to help blacks, met stiff political opposition from Southern politicians. On November 22 that year Kennedy was assassinated. His successor Lyndon B. Johnson proclaimed, "No memorial oration or eulogy could more eloquently honor President Kennedy's memory than the earliest passage of the civil rights bill for which he fought so long."

Opposition remained. On February 8, 1964, Congressman Howard W. Smith of Virginia made a colossal miscalculation in the House of Representatives. In an attempt to block the CRA, he suggested inserting the word 'sex' after the word 'religion' whenever it appeared in Title VII, which guaranteed fair employment practices. By tying it to the then controversial women's movement, Smith hoped to kill the

Civil Rights Act, intending it as a poison pill. The bluff backfired. The Civil Rights Act passed; the Equal Employment Opportunity Commission (EEOC) was formed. The EEOC's mission now is largely to move women and minorities (whatever that means) into certain positions, and to force employers to accept them almost regardless of qualifications.

Gender questionable women gravitate to traditionally male-dominated jobs. The Labor Dept. sponsored symposiums designed to condition women to reject traditional patterns and to rely on government. The government threw itself into new areas of human endeavor, gates opened and incredible pressure was put upon government agencies to conform to quotas. The EEOC requested a budget of $310 million for fiscal year 2002. I don't know what it is now, but it should not take a budget like that or a staff of thousands to enforce the already mandatory principle of equal opportunity.

Not enough minorities and females passed the Dayton, Ohio Police Department recruiting exam, so under pressure from the Dept. of Justice, the police department drastically lowered its testing standards. [432] In Detroit, during a reduction in force due to budget shortages and by court order, senior male policemen were laid off, but not newly hired female "police-persons," understandably sparking a riot. Eagle Forum informed us that, goaded by feminists, the Obama administration sued the state of Pennsylvania because not enough women could pass the physical requirements to be state troopers. Twelve female Colorado Springs officers filed a civil suit claiming fitness tests are discriminatory. So the tests were suspended. The suit moved to federal court. [433] The Royal Canadian Mounted Police ceased recruiting male officers until the number of female officers attained a politically correct percentage. [434]

A Minneapolis mayor appointed an affirmative action police chief, lesbian Janee Hearteau. A token white male would be present at her press conference gatherings which has since become commonplace across the country. Minneapolis police captains sued Hearteau who had demoted them in order to make room for her favorites. Continuing the circus, another Democrat mayor fired Hearteau, and appointed an affirmative action replacement (a black man). Seattle's black female police chief sports four stars on her shoulders

In order to recruit a Somali woman, the St. Paul, Minn. police dept. had to permit her to wear a head scarf. Australian contacts say things are completely bonkers down there, with police recruiting standards nearly eliminated in order to recruit mostly women. Next came an uproar over lack of black NFL coaches.

Reality rears its head. This political pandering has done more harm than good. Affirmative Action mandates have created dangerous, inefficient and bizarre results. Putting uniforms on women can't make them cops. Imagine a woman cop trying to just exist in Detroit's mean streets or Chicago's South Side without strong male reinforcement. I had a phone interview on radio station WXYZ Detroit the evening of 10/6/75, during which a policeman called in to relate the following incident: another Detroit policeman and his female partner, answering a domestic call, accosted a shotgun-toting angry man. Drawing his own revolver the policeman forced the man to lower the shotgun. Looking around after this deadly serious confrontation, he found the police-woman, who was supposed to be covering him, hiding behind the squad car. No action was taken against her. A man would have been summarily fired for cowardice.

At his trial, Brian Nichols, an Atlanta rapist and 200-pound former linebacker, disarmed a woman deputy — a 5-foot-tall 52-year-old grandmother, murdered four people, wounded one and made a getaway. On September 19, 2014 Omar J. Gonzales jumped the White House fence, overpowered a female guard who failed to lock the door and made it well into the house before being stopped by male guards. Heads should have rolled on that. A suspected drunk took the stun gun of a female state trooper trying to arrest him, and assaulted her with it. [435] A Washington courtroom contestant snatched a .45-caliber handgun from Deputy Polly Davin and fired twice, hitting her in the shoulder. The *New York Times* proclaimed such situations to be caused by insufficient government spending on courthouse security. It figures!

A female Edina Minn. police officer arrested a drunk driver, put him in handcuffs, and placed him in a squad car. He got out, knocked her out and escaped. [436] In March 2014 aboard a destroyer at the Norfolk Naval Base, Jeffrey Tyrone Savage took a pistol away from a female Navy guard and killed a sailor with it. On March 19, 2017 at France's Orly Airport, Ziyed Ben Belgacem attacked a female guard and took her assault weapon, shouting he wanted to kill and die for Allah.

"IS THIS TRUE?
YOU MADE THIS
OFFICER CRY?"

Instead of "de-escalating force" through their superior listening skills, female officers are more likely than their male counterparts to shoot civilians. Hummelstown, Pennsylvania police officer Lisa Merkle shot (twice) and killed the unarmed David Kassick in the back as he lay face down on the ground. A chivalrous jury found her not guilty of murder and manslaughter. Another female

Santa Ana California police officer shot and killed an unarmed homeless man, Hans Kevin Arellanohttp, on July 30, 2013 when he called her a "bitch." In September 2016 in Tulsa Oklahoma Betty Shelby, a tiny woman cop, tried arresting a big black man who ignored her commands. Fearing he would harm her she shot and killed him. Unable to physically restrain arrestees, many female officers use Taser weapons. Dallas woman cop Amber Guyger shot and killed a man in his own bathroom, allegedly thinking it was her house. Found guilty. Bawled like a baby during her trial.

Female law enforcement officers are more likely to be assaulted than male officers are — as the whole country saw with Brian Nichols. Economist John Lott has looked at the actual data. [437] According to Lott's analysis, each 1 percent increase in the number of white female officers in a police force increases the number of shootings of civilians by 2.7 percent, though another study seems to dispute this. Lott also found that "Increasing the number of female officers by 1 percentage point appears to increase the number of assaults on police by 15 to 19 percent."

Beyond all that, I find it bizarre to see women pretend cops swaggering around with guns, handcuffs, and mace on their belts; it ruins some good TV shows. Needless to say, it's unfeminine, which is of little concern to a certain element. U.S. liberals complain that males dominate top law enforcement jobs (Surprise, surprise!) [438] A while back on TV, I saw a picture of a female California sheriff (didn't catch the county) who has 4 stars on her shoulder, the same as many male wartime generals, and admittedly some male officers. To paraphrase Dr. Samuel Johnson: "A woman in a man's shoes is like a dog walking on his hind legs. It is not done well; but you are surprised to find it done at all." Max Rafferty, former Dean of Troy State U., eloquently shared this view.

Consider the female "firepersons" who are incapable of lifting a ladder or a two-hundred-pound man or climbing a six-foot fence, and who prove their upper body strength by performing push-ups from their knees rather than from their toes as men are required to do? A retired Saint Paul Minnesota firemen complained they can't open fire hydrants or start and handle large chainsaws. Previously, three firemen complained to me that their department hiring policy, and probably those all across the nation, maintains two lists of firefighting applicants — one for men and one for women. They said the top woman applicant might be hired before the top applicant on the men's list, though her qualifying score would be equivalent to the 45th on the men's list. "Diversity (is maintained) at all costs," one official ruefully explained. In New York City Rebecca Wax failed the required Functional Skills Training test, but was accepted as a full-fledged "firefighter." [439]

Thirty-one-year old Wendy Tapia failed the New York City Fire Academy's running test five times despite training. Nevertheless, she was allowed to graduate. After failing the 6th time she resigned. [440] While they can be good paramedics, it is only a matter of time before female firepersons cause tragedies.

Affirmative Action hires are concealed in bureaucratic mazes. I know from personal experience that for years the Federal Aviation Administration (FAA) hired women and minorities who did not know the front end of an airplane from the back; and tried, largely unsuccessfully and at great expense, to train them as air traffic controllers and flight service specialists, while experienced male pilots were passed over. This idiocy was repeated. [441] It was absurd to put Lisa Nowak, that diaper-wearing, alleged would-be-murderer astronaut, and the female United Airlines pilot who went ape ranting about her divorce and other bizarre subjects over the intercom just before a flight (She had to be replaced), in positions to endanger lives and billions of dollars' worth of equipment. The Veterans Affairs Department removed the head of its Phoenix hospital facility Sharon Helman, more than six months after whistleblowers said veterans were dying while on secret wait-lists there.

Amazon scrapped a politically incorrect new AI experimental recruiting tool. The tool used artificial intelligence to give job candidates scores ranging from one to five stars. However, the company soon realized the new system was not rating candidates for software developer jobs and other technical posts in a gender-neutral way by not favoring women. A scathing critique of the rush to prioritize gender and race diversity over talent appears in the April 28th issue of Hillsdale College's scholarly Imprimis newsletter, authored by Heather Mac Donald of the Manhattan Institute. It is obligatory for prospective presidential candidates for the 2020 election to include women and minorities; so say neoliberals and the media. Minnesota Governor Tim Walz's administration signed an executive order creating the "OneMinnesota Council on Diversity, Inclusion and Equity," intending to be more equitable, inclusive and hire people of color and those with disabilities and to contract with firms owned by women and minorities. Minnesota hired a Chief Inclusion Officer at a salary of $147,580 per year.

Pat Buchanan wisely said, "Liberty has been supplanted by diversity, justice by equality." Many government clerical employees, not only minorities, both federal and state, seem astoundingly incompetent. Trying to deal with or even communicate intelligently with them is a nightmare. I've had many holds approaching an hour just trying to contact a human being to comply with provisions of my retirement-connected federal health insurance. Such situations at the

IRS are worsened by incomprehensible regulations and downright hostility toward conservative organizations. Obama's IRS made those and religious ones wait years to obtain tax-exempt status, but an after-school Satan Club got its non-profit status in just ten days. Curiously, harassment ceased after President Trump's election. The TSA can't detect fake bombs.

Incompetence is driving the U.S. Postal Service out of business. This branch of government has wasted beaucoup billions of dollars. Labor costs exceed 80% of revenue. Customers experience long waits and tracking snafus. We can hardly afford to send Christmas cards anymore, but stamp prices increase seemingly every year. Remember when the postal slogan was, "Neither rain nor snow, etc. was the byword? Now that more favored groupings are delivering mail the service shuts down on cold days. Things were better when mail was delivered to the right place on time. Remember when stamps were three cents? If many government departments were private companies, many employees would be fired or the companies would go broke, though these preferences may not be sex-related. Ayn Rand saw it coming.

Phyllis Schlafly said, "Obama ... caved in to the feminist tantrum and give the majority of stimulus jobs to women, not to the men who lost their jobs." [442] Law in the People's Republic of Minnesota provides that women must not be hired at wages below that of similarly situated employees. The same protection does not apply for men. [443] Affirmative action types here rejected a low bid by a superior construction company in favor of a higher bid by an inferior company in order to meet liberal goals to utilize women and minorities in construction of the St. Croix river bridge approach. [444] Our liberal governor and legislature created legislation to build a new football stadium for the Vikings team, with the proviso that minorities make up a third and women make up 6% of the workforce.

The third-rate TV series, *Commander in Chief*, promotes the image of a woman president. One shudders to think of rule by the likes of Rosanne Barr or that circus horse, former N.O.W. president Bella Abzug. [445] The failed nomination of Harriet Miers and the successful nomination of Sonia Sotomayor, Obama's choice for the Supreme Court, are exemplary. Marginally competent — overturned 60 percent of the time — Sotomayor is sexist, prefers women's thinking over men's, and misunderstands the purpose of the court, saying "... a wise Latina woman...would...reach a better conclusion than a white male..." Other female Supreme Court Justices are only marginally better. Minnesota now has a majority of women on the state Supreme Court. Democrat presidential candidate Joe Biden committed himself to choose a woman Vice President if elected!

In 1999 an unprepared Carly Fiorina became CEO of Hewlett-Packard, only to be dumped after incurring financial losses, but was a star in the feminist firmament, until she became a Republican presidential candidate. Julia Pierson, Director of the (misnamed) Secret Service, was forced to resign due to many lapses of security during her tenure, putting the president at risk. I don't begrudge jumped-up women their jobs, but resent them being pushed to the head of the line ahead of more talented applicants. Obama's Attorney General Susan Rice blamed (well-justified) criticism of her on racism and sexism. That's rich; she got her job due to race and sex *favoritism*.

On Sept. 30, 2018 California Governor Jerry Brown signed a law requiring publicly traded companies to include women on their boards of directors. The measure, one of a series of laws boosting women, required at least one female director on the board of each California-based public corporation by the end of 2019. Companies would need up to three female directors by the end of 2021, depending on the number of board seats.

For the first time in NFL history, there were two female coaches on the sideline and a female official on the field when the Browns hosted the Washington Football team in 2020. Sarah Thomas was the first woman to officiate an NFL playoff game. Diversity also dictates that women who never played a day of football now announce games and stand on the sidelines all around the country. ESPN has a woman announcing pro football games. Women sports coaches in Minnesota sued for pay equivalent to men, despite lesser fan interest in their events.

Carolina Panther quarterback Cam Newton sparked outrage when he responded to a question from female reporter Jourdan Rodrique with "It's funny to hear a female talk about routes." (referring to pass receivers' tactics). Rodrique moaned that she felt belittled. Newton apologized, no doubt involuntarily.

As reported at NPR.org, the Phoenix aquatics department noticed a "problem." At the public pools that are used mostly by black and Hispanic kids, the lifeguards were mostly white. Horrors! A quest began to recruit more minorities to be lifeguards. Standards were dropped accordingly, [446] and a push commenced to hire minorities, even if they couldn't swim!

Hear internet raconteur Fred Reed on Affirmative Action (Speaking of a black Mississippi school teacher):

> She clearly is barely literate, and should be in the first grade instead of teaching it. Firemen of my acquaintance tell of women too weak to handle a hose, of female paramedics who can't carry a stretcher. While I was on the police beat at the *Washington Times*, I encountered a tiny policewoman who never had to drive the paddy wagon because her feet didn't reach the pedals. When you regularly pass over the first 135

people, all white, on a test for promotion to sergeant in a police department, so as to get to the blacks and Latinos, what kind of police department do you get? If you hire someone to do a job who can't do it very well, it doesn't get done very well. This doesn't strike me as a profound thought, but it eludes many people.

This passage from the Feb. 8, *2010 National Review* was referenced to race, but it applies equally to gender/sex:

Using the standard of "disparate impact" — under which almost any test, no matter how carefully vetted, can be ruled illegally discriminatory if some group does not score high enough on it — the Department of Justice has filed suit against New Jersey because of its exam for police sergeants. The mere threat of such litigation has made Chicago consider completely abolishing its testing of police applicants.

National Review says the CIA is being required to recruit from "diverse communities:" African, Asian, Hispanic, Middle Eastern, South Asian, Native American, homosexual, bisexual, transgender, disabled. That ought to make us sleep better. In his 11th State of the City address the Democrat St. Paul, MN mayor announced his intention to 'diversify' the city staff, thus creating a conflict between the rights of veterans and of minorities.

The silliness can adversely affect women. In The Feminist Dilemma: When Success is not Enough, Diana Furchtgott-Roth and Christine Stolba cite a lawsuit initiated and ultimately won by the Equal Employment Opportunity Commission (EEOC) against Joe's Stone Crab Restaurant in Miami Beach, Florida. This woman-owned, woman-operated business was compelled to undergo ruinous legal costs and "discrimination" penalties because, in a certain time period, 22 percent of its new hires were women, whereas the available labor pool was supposedly 31.9 percent female. The court's ultimate conclusion: discrimination. The owners had to pay back wages and benefits to four women, two of whom had never even applied for a job but who told the judge they had considered applying. No individual ever lodged a complaint against Joe's. EEOC commissioners are empowered to bring such lawsuits even in the absence of any complainant! [447]

Europeans are currently pushing for mandatory corporate board quotas for women. [448] Germany is preparing a law that would force leading companies to allocate 30 percent of the seats on non-executive boards to women. [449] Norway has said it might close down companies that fail to meet proposed boardroom quotas for women. A coalition government in Oslo has passed a law that requires 40% of boardroom posts be filled by women. A Spanish quota of 40% had to be reached by 2015. In Iceland, firms that employ more than 25 people must obtain a government certificate demonstrating pay equality, under new rules that kicked in on 1 January. Those who fail to show equality would face penalty fines

Italy, France and Belgium are considering similar bills. [450] The National Film Board of Canada, the country's public filmmaker, has promised half the movies it finances will be directed by women, and half of all production financing will go towards helping women tell their own stories. This nonsense extends beyond sex; in the U.K., a government factotum at 'Jobcentre Plus' refused to run an ad. for "reliable" workers because it might discriminate against unreliable workers.

Since the mandates to hire women, and the floodgates of illegal immigration opened, it's hard for men — especially uneducated ones — to find adequate employment to feed their families. When did it all start? Women took on non-traditional roles when men left to fight the Punic Wars, and remained in those roles afterword. Ad. agencies now put tool belts on women actors in ads to pretend they can be carpenters. Admittedly, women remaining in the workforce — together with computerization — contributed to economic growth, but at what cost to society?

In the Military
Political correctness reigns.

Topics relating to war may seem tangential, but wars have to be fought, at least the hard parts of them, by men — those special men who must do the fighting, admittedly with help in some specialties from women. Fourteen and one half percent of active duty military personnel are women.

Pentagon sources told *NewsMax* that political correctness rules over sound military practices. The U.S. military has lowered physical fitness and other standards for women in order to fit them into M.O.S.'s (military occupational specialties) formerly held by men. To pass the physical fitness test, 17-year-old women have to train to only the standards of a 61-year-old man. These lowered standards have admitted many thousands of women into the military. Another concession to women is that recruits do not get the same close-cropped haircuts men get. Might lower their self-esteem. [451]

Like the St. Paul, Minnesota firefighters, women cadets at West Point do not compete with the men, but compete only against each other for designated female quota slots. In a hearing intended to prove that sexual integration was a success, spokesman Col. Patrick Toffler failed miserably. "During five hours of cross-examination under oath," said Mrs. Schlafly, "he revealed a lot of things that West Point has heretofore concealed." Col. Toffler admitted that West Point has a sexual quota system for the admission of women cadets and for their assignment after graduation. "Those quotas have got to be met," he said. Col. Toffler also admitted that West Point does not require the same physical or academic performance of female cadets that it requires of male cadets, [452] and that if they perform the same task the women are given higher grades. Female cadets are allowed to hold leadership positions based on their padded scores.

Combat is difficult for average men, impossible for average women. Women may be able to pull the lanyard on an artillery piece, but may not be able to lift the ammunition. They may be able to drive a five-ton truck, but need help changing its tires. At an American Legion conference I attended, a Command Master Sergeant just back from Iraq related that a female gunner in his outfit needed help from her female driver to mount her 50 caliber machine gun atop their Humvee. It took them two trips, one to carry the barrel and another to carry the receiver group.

Writing in the *Orlando Sentinel*, Kathleen Parker said "A 5-foot-4-inch 100-pound woman has no place in a war zone nor, arguably, in the military." Parker goes further, "The feminist argument that women can do anything men can do is so absurd that it seems unworthy of debate." Phyllis Schlafly spoke of the "mountain of evidence that women are not performing equally with men in military service." An article by her quotes a woman soldier, "We can't carry as much or stand up to the pressures and conditions. Whoever tells you we can, don't believe him. Those who tell you we can are military spokesmen…who are compelled to speak through the preposterous masks assigned by politically correct pols and bureaucrats to proclaim the feminist party line which they know to be untrue. Put it down to a few officers hoping to advance their careers."

Because all soldiers are expected to do the same basic tasks, the Army has devised a new gender-neutral fitness test called the Army Combat Readiness Test that all have to pass. In all probability, men may find it easy, but not so for women.[453] Eighty four percent of women failed it. [454]

More than half of female Marines in boot camp can't do three pull ups, the minimum standard, prompting the Marine Corps to delay the requirement. They have largely integrated the sexes in officer and enlisted ranks by lowering standards, but have been unable to get women to pass the Combat Endurance Test for COMBAT infantry officers at the Marine base in Quantico, Virginia. Twenty-nine tough gals have attempted, but none have passed the test. Only 3 made it past the first day. [455] In 2015 the Marine Corps conducted experiments for nine months in integrating women into simulated combat roles. Even though the women were given advanced training, the results did not favor integration. Numerous negative considerations were cited. [456] Since then eighty-six percent of women failed the marines' combat fitness test. [457] The Marine Corps has promoted at least one woman to the rank of Gunnery Sargent. Reports are that the Corps will integrate female and male platoons during boot camp at Recruit Depot Parris Island in South Carolina.

The military is desperately trying to qualify women for elite units. The only female officer enrolled in the Marine Corps' Infantry Officer's Course (my old outfit) dropped out after failing to complete two conditioning hikes. It was her 2nd second attempt to pass the course. [458] In January 2017 for the first time, the Marine Corps put three enlisted female Marines in a ground combat unit once open only to men. Their outfit, the 1st Battalion 8th Marine Regiment, already has three female officers "to help integrate the enlisted females into the unit." The move is in compliance with former Defense Secretary Ash Carter's directive to open *all* military jobs to women. As of November 2017, the only woman in the Navy SEAL training pipeline has dropped out.

Carrying Affirmative Action and sex-norming to ridiculous lengths, Rep. Loretta Sanchez (D-CA) proposed an amendment to the 2011 National Defense Authorization Act stating, "Female Soldiers Should be Given the Opportunity to Serve in Combat." During a pre-election Democrat party debate, both Sens. Hillary Clinton and Barack Obama indicated that all female U.S. citizens should register for the Selective Service. Neither candidate was as ridiculous as former Alaska Democrat Sen. Mike Gravel, who said, when it comes to men and women being drafted, "What's the difference?" [459] In April 2016 the Republican-led House Rules Committee defeated a female registration attempt. Bills continue to move through Congress which would require all women between 18 and 25 to register. Former U.S. Defense Secretary Ash Carter, keen to expand the number of women and minorities in military leadership, endorsed "Lean In" discussion groups supported by Facebook Chief Operating Officer Sheryl Sandberg. [460]

On February 8th, 2012, the Pentagon proposed rule changes to allow more women to serve in jobs closer to the front lines. [461] Pentagon chief Leon Panetta, ignoring biological reality, removed the military's ban on women serving in combat, opening integration into Rangers, SEALs and Special Forces. [462] Imagine a woman marine facing the horrors of war at Iwo Jima, fouling her lace panties and bawling like Paris Hilton going to jail. Even men have been known to dribble a bit, hence the expression, "Keep a tight asshole."

Allowing women in combat zones has proven a serious blunder. On August 18, 1976, writes Brian Mitchell, a detail of American soldiers was pruning a tree in the Joint Security Area separating North and South Korea when they were suddenly attacked by a truckload of axe-wielding North Korean guards. Two officers were killed. Nine other soldiers were wounded. Major General John Singlaub, chief of staff of U.S. forces in Korea, decided to take limited military action; United Nations forces in the South prepared for the worst. Forces moved into positions and air forces were called in from Alaska and Japan.

As soon as it became clear that the alert was no ordinary training exercise, commanders throughout Korea were flooded with requests from female soldiers for transfers to the rear. War was more than these women had bargained for when they joined the Army. Most fully expected to be evacuated in the event of hostilities, but when the question was raised at higher headquarters, Singlaub nixed the idea immediately and ordered all soldiers to their posts.

Later, when the emergency was over, Singlaub learned that his order had not been strictly obeyed. Many women had abandoned their posts near the border, and headed south on their own. Some turned up later in units well to the rear. Others reported for duty with dependent children in tow, since their arrangements for child-care did not cover the event of war. In some instances, male noncommissioned officers had left their posts temporarily to tend to the safety of wives and girlfriends in other units. [463]

The saga of Jessica Lynch demonstrates the folly of sending women to do men's work. She was the pretty co-ed soldier captured and brutally raped by the enemy in Iraq. Lynch was put into that situation because the Pentagon caved in to feminist pressure. She joined the Army to get the college tuition she needed to become a kindergarten teacher. However, she ended up in a combat situation that nearly cost her life while in captivity, and left her shattered. The media painted her as a hero who went down firing her weapon, which was not the case; actually, she was knocked unconscious when the vehicle she was riding in ran off the road. The Army awarded her the prestigious Silver Star (no doubt, the only one ever awarded a soldier who never fired a shot). She still enjoys celebrity as a motivational speaker. U.S. Senator Martha McSally, whom the media claims to have flown in combat, was raped by a superior officer while in the service. Admittedly, she did not report it. Could that have been to maintain her rank? Feminista Peggy Drexler of Stanford U. actually gloated that single mother Lori Piestwa was the first female soldier to die in Iraq. Why should we permit feminists to so toy with life and death combat situations?"

Elaine Donnelly said there is strong evidence the U.S. lost the opportunity to capture or kill Osama bin Laden, the architect of 9/11, because of politically correct Pentagon policies to have more female warriors. At the end of 2001, a combination of Afghan fighters, American military advisers and U.S. air power was used to attempt to catch the most wanted criminal on the planet — then believed hiding in the remote, mountainous Tora Bora region of Afghanistan. Bin Laden was seen heading out of the Afghan city of Jalalabad toward Tora Bora in a convoy on Nov. 15, 2001. [fn38] At that critical moment, one well-connected military source says the U.S. was unable to commit desperately needed personnel because women had been mixed into units that were at strong risk of seeing combat. A Pakistani official suggested that some 4,000 al-Qaida members also escaped. Had this integrationist policy not been in effect, the Twin Towers probably wouldn't have been demolished on 9/11.

Women with children usually join the military to have steady or extra income, or obtain a free education. When treated like males, i.e., subjected to deployment, some strenuously object. Unmarried Spc. Alexis Hutchinson, who had a 10-month-old son, refused to deploy to Afghanistan. [464] In September 2012, Air Force member Judy Groomes convinced her husband to wound her with a pistol shot in order to avoid her deployment. [465] Ready Reserves member Lisa Pagan refused deployment to Iraq because she had two children and their father's employment required him to travel a great deal. Pagan was given an honorable discharge.

While women may volunteer for combat jobs, men have no such choice. Male-only Selective Service registration remains in place; only men face penalties for failure to register, including five years imprisonment and a $250,000 fine. Some "male advocates" maintain that it would be anti-male discrimination and a double standard to exempt women from the draft and from combat. Nonsense. Denying women access to certain military positions is no more discriminatory than denying induction access to the flat-footed.

Promotions come easier to women. In WWII, a man would have to be in service nearly a lifetime to earn the rank of Master Sergeant. Now, a woman who hangs around a few years can attain that rank (or a man can if he's in the Air Force band). Nearly 500 female drill sergeants have been created, about a third of the total number of drill sergeants. [466] The Navy has a rule that requires discharge of a lieutenant who fails twice to be promoted to Lieutenant Commander. This rule exempts women unless they have had 13 years of commissioned service. The U.S. Supreme Court pronounced this to be justifiable discrimination.

Is anyone surprised at these situations? Is anyone critical? Of course not. Military policy permits no negative comment about the performance of women. [467] Similarly, males are forbidden to laugh at the female wanna-be soldiers at the Citadel and the Virginia Military Institute.

---

38 Bin Laden was caught and killed much later. RIH (Rest in Hell).

In June of 2011, a jumped up Brigadier General (no less) Lori Reynolds was given command of what is arguably the world's toughest military training facility, the Paris Island Marine Recruit Depot. And now the White House has picked her to be the first female and the first non-pilot to head the Air Force in the Pacific. Topping it off, Brig. Gen. Diana Holland, first female general of the U.S. Army Fort Drum & 10th Mountain Division was installed as the 76th Commandant of West Point. Brig. Gen. Laura Yeager became the first woman to command a U.S. Army Infantry Division, the California National Guard's 40th Infantry. Fortunate to be out of the military, I'd shudder to salute an officer I didn't respect.

The climate of political correctness makes it almost impossible to discipline a woman — and risky for a man to attempt it. Eleven soldiers were court marshaled because of the breakdown in discipline among MPs at the Abu Ghraib military prison, but the woman commandant ultimately responsible, Brig. Gen. Janis Karpinski, was wrist-slapped with reduction in rank to Colonel and suspension from duty.

Nightline called the orgies at Karpinski's Abu Ghraib prison "a twisted tribute to gender integration in the U.S. military." Army Pfc. Lynndie England, a female M.P., was photographed smirking at naked Iraqi prisoners' genitals and holding one on a leash. The photos, a worldwide public relations disaster, set off a wave of embarrassment for the U.S. How many of those former prisoners do you suppose blew up our troops with roadside bombs because of that shame? The murderer of 12 cartoonists and 8 employees of a Jewish bakery in Paris, France in January 2015 claimed that as his motivation.

Female guards at the Guantanamo Bay prison filed complaints with the Defense Department's Office of Diversity Management and Equal Opportunity challenging court orders barring them from jobs that require touching detainees while escorting them to hearings and attorney meetings. The women claim the orders amount to sex discrimination. [468]

Now, women are being squeezed into the submarine branch, [fn39] causing even more problems [469] The equipment modifications necessary to pretend that women can be warriors are formidable. Henceforth, the Navy's new aircraft carriers will be built without the traditional urinals in order to accommodate the increased number of female personnel. [470]

According to interviews, documents and surveys, men in U.S. special operations forces, the men actually doing the work as opposed to social experimenters, do not believe women can meet the physical and mental demands of their commando jobs, and they fear the Pentagon will lower

---

[39] One in training there as this was written.

standards to integrate women into their elite units. [471] Though they may find a few freaks of nature to qualify, it is utter stupidity! Even the Navy seals have succumbed to political correctness, having changed the wording in their Creed to gender neutral terms.

The reality is that a military made up of an inordinate number of women soldiers is inefficient. Responsible military officials have maintained that our combat forces are too watered down with women to be effective.[472] Former Defense Department Inspector General Joseph E. Schmitz, who was the Defense Department's top investigator and logged 27 years in the Navy, predicted that allowing women into combat will lead to a "degradation of good order and discipline." Gen. Patrick Brady is absolutely correct in saying that putting females in combat poses "an insane burden on readiness."[473] Their presence erodes that unit cohesion so necessary to fight effectively, and the inherent chivalrous favoritism undermines morale. Medals are awarded for operating computers, not shooting." [474] "It's killing our [combat] readiness...all across the board," says a Navy spokesman. [475] Legendary Viet Nam hero Lt. General Wm. Boykin says, "Women will reduce the readiness of units.

It's not hard for a woman to fly an airplane; I've trained a couple. It *is* hard to engage in aerial combat. More so for women. The Navy's lower standards for women pilots have been especially disastrous. Lt. Kara Hultgreen, one of the first two women trained to fly the U.S. Navy F-14 Tomcat, is just one example. In October 1994, she crashed and died while attempting to land on the carrier U.S.S. Abraham Lincoln. Her colleague, former Lt. Carey Dunai Lohrenz was removed from carrier aviation in May 1995 due to flawed flying techniques that her superiors described as "unsafe, undisciplined, and unpredictable."

In 1995, Elaine Donnelly president of the Center for Military Readiness (CMR) organization published a 20 page CMR Special Report: *Double Standards in Naval Aviation Training*. This report, backed by 104 pages of training records and related documents, exposed a pattern of low scores and major errors in the F-14 training of both women. With the help of attorney Susan Barnes, feminist activist Lohrenz filed a lawsuit in April 1996 blaming Donnelly for causing her to wash out by publishing the report, and claiming that inadequate training of both women contributed to the tragic death of Hultgreen (actually, they usually receive extraordinary training, especially if they're good looking. No doubt many will dispute these statements, but almost everyone knows damn well it's true). On August 16, U.S. District Judge Royce C. Lamberth of the U.S. District Court for the District of Columbia granted CMR's Motion for Summary Judgment, dismissing Lohrenz's action "with prejudice." Air Force Secretary

Deborah Lee James reposts that fifty percent of AF combat forces are "not sufficiently ready" for a "high end fight." [476]

Apropos of that, Capt. Zoe Kotnik, the first female pilot to head the F-16 Viper demonstration team, was relieved from command at Shaw Air Force Base in South Carolina in February 2019 due to a "loss of confidence in her ability to lead and command the Air Combat Command F-16 Viper demonstration team."

Some brave men have addressed the subject of pretend soldiers: some paid the price. In 1979, Virginia Senator and former war hero, Jim Webb, wrote an astute article entitled *Women Can't Fight*. But, as a 'born-again' Democrat running for office, Webb morphed into political correctness, renounced that position and apologized for it. Brian Mitchell's great book, <u>The Weak Link</u>, first addressed this subject.

Boeing's Communications Chief Niel Golightly resigned in July 2020 following an employee complaint over an article in a 1987 issue of the U.S. Naval Institute magazine saying "introducing women into combat would destroy the exclusively male intangibles of war fighting and the feminine images of what men fight for – peace, home, family,"

As a result of all this, we have been treated to the spectacle of girls playing soldier as children do, some parading about trying to prove their 'manhood' with barracks-room vulgarity. Women pretending to be soldiers are like homosexuals pretending to be proud of their condition.

The whorehouse atmosphere in our military can only weaken it. An article in the *Salt Lake Tribune* of Oct. 12, 2005 titled *Sex Runs Wild in U.S. Military* claimed, "Sex is rampant among the men and women in uniform serving in Iraq." It went on to say nearly all military women there have bedded either men or other women). Some units no longer even keep separate sleeping quarters for the sexes. Female Marines posed naked for compromising photos of themselves; Facebook group, Marines United, disseminated them. Sen. Kristen Gillebrand at a committee hearing reamed out Marine Corps Commandant Gen. Robert Neller, who meekly apologized. Chesty Puller, would have replied, I will tell women to "keep their Goddamn clothes on."

A 1991 Navy study revealed that 65 percent of enlisted women in the pay grades E-4 and below became pregnant while on sea duty). During the 1991 Persian Gulf War, the press branded the destroyer tender USS Arcadia the "Love Boat" after 36 sailors, 10 percent of the women aboard, became pregnant while deployed in support of Operation Desert Storm. The pregnancy of the unmarried Pfc. Lynndie England of Abu Ghraib fame is example. [477] One female Marine actually gave birth on a warship.

The Lactation Brigade

To teach sympathy for pregnant military women, the Army is ordering some of its NCOs to wear "pregnancy simulators." [478]

More evidence of political correctness in the military was shown when Lt. Col. Jimmy Keith Brown was relieved of command because he stated the truism that "pregnancy could negatively affect a woman's career." [479] Brown was Squadron commander of the 90th Missile Wing at F.E. Warren Air Force Base, Wyoming that controls 150 of the Air Force's 450 Minuteman 3 nuclear intercontinental ballistic missiles.

The Army surgeon general says military women not only suffer more injuries than men during combat training, but active-duty female soldiers also are stricken with significantly higher rates of mental health disorders. [480] "Women in the Navy are hospitalized with psychiatric problems at more than four times the rate for Navy men and much oftener than civilian women," according to *Military Medicine* magazine. A statistic buried in the study: 23.6 percent of women reported a mental health concern compared with 18.6 percent of men. Though women are almost never near combat, they experience Post Traumatic Stress Syndrome at twice the rate of men. [481]

One out of every five female vets from Iraq or Afghanistan is diagnosed with PTSD. [482] Discharges for 2008, according to the Defense Department: Drugs: 5,627; Serious offenses: 3,817; Weight standards: 4,555; Pregnancy: 2,353; Parenthood: 2,574; Homosexuality: 634. Army surgeons performed 496 breast enlargements and 1,361 liposuctions on military females plus nose jobs, teeth straightening and other cosmetic surgeries between 2000 and 2003. One in five female VA patients says they were sexually assaulted or harassed in service. The V.A. reports that one in four female veterans have screened positive for sexual trauma, as opposed to one in a hundred men; [483] Boo hoo.

There are exceptions to any rule; I will give credit where it is due. A non-combatant Mary Edwards Walker is the only woman ever to receive the Medal of Honor. A Northern feminist, abolitionist, prohibitionist and surgeon in the American Civil War, she crossed enemy lines to treat wounded civilians and was arrested as a spy by Confederate forces. Leigh Ann Hester was awarded the Silver Star for bravery (possibly well deserved) in the battle of Salman Pak in Iraq. The afore-mentioned retired Air Force Colonel Martha McSally was evidently a competent pilot. National Guard officer and former pilot, Tulsi Gabbard may have been a highly competent officer. A female nurse in Afghanistan was awarded the Silver Star for simply doing her duty, albeit with bravery. I knew a couple other sharp female soldiers (who never saw combat). That some women are as able as some men in some circumstances hardly constitutes a defense for 'girling' down our military and putting men at greater risk — so that the Jessica Lynches can become kindergarten teachers.

While I deplore the integration of women in the military in pursuit of a foolish 'diversity,' I applaud their promotion on a basis of ability — only. The military needs women in some jobs, but not in combat. God bless the nurses who patched up the wounded. It is true that the nature of combat has changed; there are very few "front lines" anymore. In this brave new world, we must gird for a new type of non-traditional warfare in which women may be useful. Fortunately, special operations, the newest kind of warfare along with a recently reduced military budget, should lessen the need for women in combat.

Blogger Jim Peterson reports, "the feminist controlled governments of Sweden and the EU have established an organization called "Genderforce," with the purpose to force the armed forces to become more 'feminine.'" Left-leaning Sweden and Norway have instituted military draft for women. Australia has jumped aboard the integration bandwagon too; that country is to remove all barriers to women in combat in the next 5 years.

The inimitable Fred Reed brilliantly opinionates on the subject. [484] History is strewn with the remains of great civilizations that lost the capacity to protect themselves. Woe is us.

Sex Perceptions: Image
Sacred cows and nasty bulls

Female glorification or gynocentrism, [485] not of the fairy godmother type, reigns. Women are practically canonized by simple virtue of being female. Not for nothing is the most powerful chess piece called the queen. Writing in *Huffington Post.com*, California Governor Schwarzenegger's former wife Maria Shriver said, "...Clearly, this country is now what I like to call "A Woman's Nation." One hundred and twenty-three thousand dollars has been earmarked to support an International Mothers' Day Shrine in Grafton, West Virginia. For almost 20 years, liberals have batted around the idea of building a National Women's History Museum in D.C. to honor the likes of Margaret Sanger, Georgetown Law's Sandra Fluke (of all people), Victoria Woodhull, et al. The brilliant writer, philosopher and prophet extraordinaire, Philip Wylie, wrote extensively about the adoration of women.

If women are not being deified, they can be perceived as long-suffering heroines, all but gleaning coal from railroad yards. Females must be condescended to like "special" children whose crayon drawings of flowers everyone must praise (although there is a glaring exception regarding conservative female political figures, e.g., Palin, Bachmann, Fiorina, Rice, De Vos, etc.). And of course, society lionizes "single moms" ad nauseam. The widespread mourning and physical preservation efforts over the brain dead Jahi McMath would never have occurred if she were male. Similar, if lesser, deference and fear of offending applies with certain religious, racial and sexually confused minorities.

There was a joke about an imaginary headline in the *New York Times*: "Tidal Wave Strikes New York; Women and Children Suffer Most." Well, it is no longer a joke; an AP story reported just that: Angie Daze, a program manager with a Canadian group called Reducing Vulnerability to Climate Change, said in a Dec. 6-17, 2004 conference, "Severe weather caused by global warming can pose greater physical danger to women than men." Rep. Barbara Lee (D-CA) and a dozen other Democrats are calling on Congress to recognize that climate change is hurting women more than men, and could even drive poor women to "transactional sex" for survival. [486] Gerd Johnsson-Latham of the Swedish Ministry for Foreign Affairs asserted that men are primarily responsible for global warming. After the Haiti earthquake disaster, women's groups sought to deny relief to men, claiming women deserved and needed relief more.

In warfare, men sacrifice life and limb in defense of women and children. Still, Marylin French in her book The War Against Women absurdly claims most casualties in wars are women and children. "Women have always been the primary victims of war," said Hillary Clinton while at a conference on Domestic Violence in San Salvador;" she said that "because women lose husbands, fathers, and sons in combat."

Orwellian 'doublethink was further demonstrated by the demand for a statue of a "combat woman" to be erected at the Vietnam War Memorial to specially and separately memorialize the eight women nurses who died in Vietnam, only 1 by hostile fire, contrasted with 58,000 men who died there, most by hostile fire. If 58,000 women had been killed in Viet Nam and only 8 men, would Hillary and Marylin French suggest men were the primary victims of that war? The ratio is similar in recent Mid-Eastern wars: 2% women to over 98% men. Yet equality and diversity demands there must be an equal number of women in military presidential Honor Guards

On a flight from New York City to Dallas Texas, Southwest Airlines Flight 1380 a Boeing 737-700 lost one of two engines while at cruising altitude. Pilot captain Tammie Jo Shults performed the engine-out procedure that every multi-engine flight student has been taught. She landed the aircraft in Philadelphia to great acclaim. An ecstatic media compared her to US Airways Capt. Chesley "Sully" Sullenberger, who lost BOTH engines and landed his plane safely in New York's Hudson River in 2009. Much more difficult piloting would be required to control a multi-engine aircraft while climbing out of an airport, as happened to me while leaving Birmingham, Ala. enroute to Gulfport, Miss. in a Cessna 320 (I can never forget the procedure that is burned into every non-jet multi-engine flight student's head: "props, throttle, flaps, gear, test, feather, trim").

Few undeserving men have ever reached the same level of sainthood as have women. In many circles, opprobrium attaches to being pale and male — almost an 'Original Sin.' The sport of male bashing is widespread. The image of men has suffered greatly in the last several generations: woman/good — man/bad.

The American Psychiatric Association (APA) climbed aboard this theme, claiming that traditional masculinity is not only "harmful" but also could lead to homophobia and sexual harassment, and is marked by stoicism, competitiveness, dominance and aggression. A University of Texas course treats Masculinity as a 'Mental Health' Issue.' [487] Duke University sought applicants for its "Men's Project," a nine-week program that helps men examine how their masculinity exists "often in toxic ways." The program meets weekly at the university's Women's Center, an on-campus office for students interested in learning how to "resist patriarchal oppression." [488]

In a misguided attempt to increase sales, the Gillette razor company created a TV ad. showing men and boys engaging in bullying and sexual harassment and encouraging men to "say the right thing" and "act the right way." *Fox Nation* host Tomi Lahren ripped Gillette for the ad., saying women are also capable of bullying and harassment, but claiming feminists pass that off as "female empowerment," not "toxic femininity." In a lonely defense, the Egard watch company prepared a video defending masculinity. Granted, the attitudes of some men and boys can be toxic, as can attitudes of some women and girls. However, surrendering to this 'woke' attitude is avaricious and cowardly.

"Dead white males" are high on the list of fem/lib bogymen. White, heterosexual Christian males are the only group one can safely denounce, because of their alleged racism, sexism, homophobia, patriarchalism and xenophobia. "Angry white males" is supposed to be a pejorative. I don't know why. Some people love to watch bulls being baited and killed. T-shirts sporting "Boys are stupid, throw rocks at them" were popular items with girls.

TV shows, even common gossip, make men out to be all types of bad guys — from litterbugs, through abandoners of pregnant women, to bloodthirsty killers. We are often depicted as knuckle-dragging abusers who beat our wives on Super Bowl Sunday (a disproved contention). Perhaps the most outrageous example of human misandry is the Verizon Foundation's widely distributed video entitled "Monsters," which portrays the average American home as a secret chamber of horrors, in which behind a pleasant façade hides terrified mothers and children, stalked by the shadowy figure of the family monster, the husband and father. It is chilling to watch; any woman or child ignorant of the actual facts around domestic violence would walk away from it convinced that they were in imminent peril, and that at any moment their beloved husband or father might transmogrify before their eyes into a veritable Mr. Hyde. [489]

In June 2012, an Arizona man was ejected from a bookstore simply for being alone in children's section while shopping for grandchildren. [490] Fearful of molesters, Air New Zealand and Qantas have a policy of moving men sitting next to unaccompanied children. When I took my partially paralyzed wife to clinics, nurses were required at times to, however embarrassingly, ask her if she felt safe at home.

If a man cheats on his wife, he is an unfaithful, philandering playboy. If a woman cheats on her husband, she is searching for a meaningful, emotional relationship. It is often claimed that fathers abandon their families. In reality, mothers often leave with the kids and/or kick the father out. On a radio show over 30 years ago I was challenged to fight a woman, a bull dyke no doubt. I declined. It was a no win situation; if I lost it would be embarrassing, and if I won I'd be called a woman beater.

The Negro male is a victim of prejudice in both dimensions: race and sex. The federal government has conscientiously pursued, and rightly so, a course of eradicating discrimination based on race but has studiously ignored that based on sex (except for alleged anti-female discrimination). This has helped make the black family an infrequent, or at best matriarchal, arrangement. Two hundred plus Nigerian girls were kidnapped by Boko Haran to be sold into slavery. The media went nuts, ignoring the fact that many more boys are kidnapped for use as soldiers, barely mentioning the 60 who were burned alive. Al Jazeera America had a special portraying the conditions of female child sex "workers" in India as more pitiful than destitute young boy miners there.

Advertisers have a strange notion of hilarity or a low, if accurate, opinion of the average viewer's intelligence. Popular entertainment argues for the latter. According to Liberty Mutual insurance company TV ads, only men do dumb things to wreck cars. A Sony ad. aired in

April and May of '07 depicted men as "horses' asses." Portrayal of males as Homer Simpson types are common. In the "All in the Family" series, only Archie Bunker was ever heard flushing the toilet, to great laughter. Apparently Edith and Gloria, like Kim Jong Il, never defecated. It is almost de rigueur for movies to show men urinating, but never women doing so. NCIS's Gibbs could slap Tony DiNozzo's head when he commited a faux pas, but not Ziva's. Of course — she couldn't commit a faux pas. In TV ads, it is considered comical to kick men in the testicles; a 2008 Pepsi Super Bowl ad. was an egregious example of that. Both of Pepsi's top executives are or were women, Indra Nooyi and Cie Nicholson; and the ad was designed by BBDO, a prominent advertising agency with a track record of making commercials which denigrate men and fathers.

Men, however rough appearing, are seldom evil, and usually as decent as women are perceived to be. It is generally assumed that men commit the preponderance of big time embezzlement. Au contraire; over 60% of company embezzlements are committed by women, with an average loss of over $1,000,000. [491] Admittedly, we find many males, including fathers, among lowlifes doing unpleasant things. However, I submit, this is usually more due to their lack of proper paternal discipline and influence than to their maleness per se.

Words must conform to political correctness. At Princeton University, the word "man" is considered sexist. Elsewhere, we are not supposed to use the terms "policeman," "fireman," "mailman," "foreman," "congressman" or "chairman," because the connotations are good, or even penmanship and journeyman. However, we can say "gunman," "con man," "garbage man," "bad guy," "manhunt" and "Chairman Mao" because those connotations are bad. We must invent such contortions as "person hole" and "chairperson." Washington State's governor signed into law the rewriting of state laws using sex-neutral vocabulary, replacing terms such as "fisherman" and "freshman" with "fisher" and "first-year student." [492] Mother Nature and Old Man Winter are still OK.

Listen to the experts: Esther Vilar, in her best seller The Manipulated Man, calls the American male "the most exploited, the most suppressed, the most manipulated man on the face of the earth;" Linda Bowles said "It isn't even close, the most abused, vilified, and sexually harassed Americans are white, heterosexual males. I don't know why they put up with it — and I wish they wouldn't." Several Fathers' Days ago Kathleen Parker satirized the image of the "Three-D Dad: dumb, dorky and dispensable." She said, "It is a wonder men still submit to the altar. If we did to motherhood what we have done to fatherhood, we would all be wearing riot gear. That a father revolt is inevitable seems a matter of cultural physics and human nature.

Human beings can withstand only so much contravening pressure
against what is in their interest or necessary to their survival."

The attack on males and manhood may be a rebellion against
authority, with which men are often identified, or were. Ironically,
these sentiments adversely affect women also, because attacks on
manhood are attacks on all humanity — and on creation if you will.
The very term, "men's rights," reeks of political incorrectness. It turns
off neo-liberals [fn40] and conservatives alike.

Manhood, Fatherhood, Womanhood
When knights were bold

Manhood (hombria) means for men what feminism should mean for
women. It is the age at which males come to accept adult
responsibilities. It entails the work ethic and rugged individualism. It
can evoke the much maligned, but arguably admirable, 'cowboy' image.
It threaten the left. Machismo may not be majestic, but preferable to
its opposite — sissyhood. It is more assertion than aggression.
Toughness' is not the thing to strive for; someone is always tougher
than you. The bull's male nature ends him on the matador's sword;
men must be smarter than bulls. Real men don't walk about with
glasses perched atop heads carrying water bottles. To be a man you
don't have to stand up to piss, but that's OK. To term a man's penis his
"manhood" is beyond ignorance. NYC firemen and police, responding to
the sucker punch of 9/11/'01 at the Twin Towers, demonstrated the
essence of manhood, yet white male cops are a huge target of misandry.

Our best and most courageous men die in wars and dangerous
occupations to build and protect society. It was men who fought to
defend Western civilization, from the Barbary War in 1801 to today in
the mid-east — admittedly with some help from women in later years.
George Orwell said, "People sleep peaceably in their beds at night, only
because rough men stand ready to do violence on their behalf." And
this from an anonymous source:

> It is the soldier, not the reporter, who gave us freedom of the press.
> It is the soldier, not the poet, who gave us freedom of speech.
> It is the soldier, not the agitator, who gave us freedom to protest.
> It is the soldier who salutes the flag, serves beneath the flag, whose
> coffin is draped by the flag, who gives that protester the freedom to
> abuse and burn that flag.

As we say at veterans' funerals, "A grateful nation honors them."
Some have criticized male warriors for savagery in battle as
symptomatic of all men. May I point out that war is not volleyball.

---

40 I prefix this word to distinguish modern liberals from the classical definition of
liberal which had an honorable connotation. Henceforth, for brevity, I shall refer to them
merely as liberals.

Circumstances dictate behavior. It was men like General Patton who preserved the very existence of this nation. Yet, contrast his popular appeal and remuneration with the non-masculinist likes of Liberace and Michael Jackson the child groper. Really good people — athletes, scholars, and the like — take a back seat to all sorts of braying, gargling jackasses who make a fortune picking guitars. Their ilk inherits the earth while better men die poor. However, this is more symptomatic of generally low values than it is of sex discrimination.

In days of yore in this country, manliness was considered a virtue. University of Minnesota football teams, under coach Bernie Bierman, represented that image and were among the nation's best. My old scoutmaster, Herb Joesting, was an All-American on one of those teams. More recently, a liberal ("feminizing" if you will) political atmosphere has gradually gained popularity. That phenomenon infected the University, resulting in de-emphasis on men's sports and weakening of its football teams, luxurious locker room with pictures of past legends apparently to the contrary, notwithstanding. Recently ranked 57th in the nation, the school is seldom a contenders even within its league. Pre-season games have been against third rate teams. More recent ideals of men must include such as Brett Farve. On the other hand, Colin Kaepernick is the embodiment of what ails this country.

A shot and a beer cop hangout, Alarys sports bar in downtown St. Paul, Minn., is one of the last redoubts of testosterone-laden masculinity (Google it), complete with serving wenches comely enough to throw feminists into fits of envious anger. I discovered it by accident when taking their shuttle service to the state high school hockey tournament (Played in that tournament in 1949. Got pictures and write-ups to prove it).

Being male is a matter of birth. Being a man is a matter of upbringing. Being a gentleman is a matter of choice. Men must reclaim their roles, and be competent to do so. Inner strength should be the goal. These inherent characteristics are not 'attitudes,' subject to change. A man shouldn't need a big Harley hog, a monster pick-up, big biceps or a semi-automatic weapon to feel important.

Katherine's speech at the end of *The Taming of the Shrew* has this:
> He cares for thee and for thy maintenance, commits his body to painful labor both by sea and land to watch the night in storms, the day in cold, whilst thou liest warm at home, secure and safe, and craves no other tribute at thy hands but love, fair looks, and true obedience, too little payment for so great a debt.

Women in general are considered, wrongly so, to be morally superior, and single mothers have been elevated to the status of sainthood; opinion contrary to that is frowned upon. Well, in truth, women are no more moral than men, even if some appear to be. Women's sexual desires may be less overt, but equally present. Verdi's dark tragedy, *Rigoletto, La Dona e mobile*, put it well. Women are well aware of the attraction they have for men, and many use it to great advantage. The porn industry has no trouble recruiting attractive nude models.

Garson Kanin, the writer and director, put it well: "I don't think the basic separation in the world is male and female, or rich and poor. From my perspective, the basic separation is between the slobs [41] and the non-slobs." Lord, deliver us from low lifes of both sexes!

While masculinity is denounced in the media as "macho" and many male figures are models of neutered masculinity, true femininity is likewise denigrated. This from National Review says it well: "Announcements on London's Tube have always referred to riders as 'ladies and gentlemen.' No more: the phrase is being scrapped because authorities believe that it makes some people feel excluded. When I was young some circuses featured tattooed 'ladies:' many women could join circuses nowadays. The term, "tattooed lady" is an oxymoron (a contradiction in terms, something that can't be). One by one, the graces die — and we salute them as they go."

Non-masculinist thinking, as has been prevalent in government, would seek "common ground for dialogue" with cold-blooded enemies. This approach is suicide. Resurrection of masculine fortitude and qualities can avoid that approach. Saving the males entails saving all of society, ensuring that it not regress to a pre-civilized state. For civilization to survive in a deteriorating international situation and in anticipation of war between cultures, anti-social elements like street gangs, the Black Panthers, neo-Nazis, pathological Islamic State and Khorasan militants, the Taliban, al Qaeda and their ilk aspiring to form a Caliphate or reinstate the Ottoman Empire must be converted or harshly dealt with. It will take strong, fearless men to destroy or utterly isolate such savages.

The Phenomenon of Chivalry

To understand how sex prejudices came about and to confront them, we have to go back to the days of patriarchy ("Once upon a time") when manhood was of higher status than currently and much more was expected of men. Woman-protective ideas, laws, and practices were in vogue, many of which persist to this day. A large reason for this is biologically rooted: perpetuation of the species; it is the same with animal hunting regulations. [42]

These customs, commonly referred to as "chivalry," elicit undeserved deference and postulates the false planted axiom that all women are ladies. That notion is similar to the Congressional declaration that all

41 Such as men wearing baseball caps while eating dinner

42 Though the world is already arguably overpopulated, to the point of endangering several countries

military officers are gentlemen; although the latter is more reasonable in that certain objective standards have to be achieved and maintained. Originating in the 12th and 13th centuries, chivalry was a quaint consideration, not unlike the bowling handicap, extended to ladies — as distinguished from all women — in deference to their feminine charm, their gentle and retiring ways, general physical weakness, as well as to their baby-making capability. Many privileges attached. Men are expected to gift women generously, and wait for women to initiate handshakes.

In pursuit of chivalry, men went to war, gave up their seats in lifeboats ("Women and children first"). At the sinking of the Titanic, 324 women survived [seventy-two percent] 114 died, as opposed to 325 men survivors [only nineteen percent]. Thirteen hundred thirty nine men died. Feminists of the day considered that only natural and as it should be. [493] Men worked physically harder, placed ladies on pedestals, and offered a host of other considerations. Knightly gallantry was presumed. Three female survivors of the Colorado movie-theater massacre escaped with minor wounds, but were left with broken hearts because their heroic boyfriends died saving them. In final acts of valor, Jon Blunk, Matt McQuinn and Alex Teves used their bodies to shield their girlfriends as accused madman James Holmes turned the Aurora Cineplex into a shooting gallery. [494] And a similar occurrence took place On December 17, 2015 when Zaevion Dobson, a 15-year-old football player at Knoxville's Fulton High School jumped on top of three girls to shield them from gang bangers with guns. Dobson was struck and killed, police said.

Though classic chivalry is dead, thanks to feminism, perverted chivalry thrives. Greatly diluting its original intent, chivalry is now generally extended to all females, most offensively by judicial Galahads — few of whom can or do distinguish between ladies and women. Regrettably, indiscriminate chivalry causes most of men's gender/sex problems. Thanks to modern life its reasonable and once-mutually-beneficial tradeoffs have mostly disappeared for men. This, of course, gives all women the best of both ways of thinking. Lip service is paid to equality, but women are considered more equal (*Animal Farm* again). The ancient Greeks idealized the goddess Hera. Many take advantage of their perks, thanklessly and undeservedly expecting or demanding all sorts of considerations, just by virtue of being female. They play the "woman card."

If women are pretty enough they don't need to play that card; men will play it for them. In 1921, the highest ranking female judge of the period, Florence Ellinwood Allen of Cleveland — descendant of American Revolutionary War hero Ethan Allen — speaking before the Women Lawyers' Association, had this to say about chivalry as it relates to law, "This fault should be corrected. It is not born of chivalry, but of what men choose to call chivalry, something totally different."

Chivalry may have peaked when President Obama, as he was leaving office, commuted the 35-year sentence of the traitor Bradley Manning, now a woman named Chelsea.

Chivalry Trade-offs; The Double Standard Boldly and Logically Justified.

Chivalry must not be blind. A double standard is essential to civilized society. With recognition of proper distinctions, chivalry can be mutually beneficial to both sexes, especially ladies and gentlemen. Ideal relationships entail mutual trade-offs. What trade-offs?

From men: ideally, we expect serious sacrifice as mentioned earlier, higher work output, and a duty to fight and die in wars defending country and family, etc. Expectations are great, sometimes too great (That can be said of women as well). *To* men: head of household status, the male kinship system (the tradition of patrilineal surnames, not in Japan however), veterans' preference and lesser expectations in sexual behavior and in language

From women: higher degrees of sexual purity, marital fidelity and — especially from ladies — refined dignity. *To* women: sustenance, protection and deference in numerous and obvious situations — lifeboats, pedestals; i.e., the benefits of chivalry — especially to ladies.

It is entirely reasonable, that women have a higher obligation to chastity than do men. There are practical reasons for this double standard, chief among which is that husbands cannot surreptitiously introduce extra-familial children into their families, but women can. They often do; recent studies show an amazingly large percentage of children (even in white, middle-class families) genetically unrelated to their putative fathers. As documented here in Part 1, *Paternity Fraud*, the figure is at least 10 percent in the U.S.

Hear Amneus eloquently on the Double Standard:

The hated double standard, which feminists see as the core of women's oppression, should rather be seen as the source of their bargaining power. The repudiation of the double standard and consequent de-regulation of female sexuality deprives children of fathers and men of families, and hence of motivation to provide women with the benefit stipulated by Briffault's Law, which says that a woman will not associate with a man who has no benefit to offer her. Women must be made to see that men's loss of the motive to provide them with a benefit deprives women of their bargaining power with men. The double standard demands more of men. A man's virtue is his integrity, his courage, his honesty. Not so with women.

(Girls) should be learning, but nobody will teach the advantages of accepting the double standard and the patriarchal sexual regulation which entitles (them) to the benefits offered by patriarchy to chaste women — including a stable family, higher status and a higher standard of living.

Cheating on spouses is now an equal-opportunity sport. Equal opportunity but unequal damage, since the woman's sexual loyalty to the man is of greater importance to him than is his sexual loyalty to her. Her sexual loyalty is her primary contribution to marriage, comparable only to her husband's economic loyalty.

Male chastity has no importance comparable to female chastity. The female body is the vehicle by which the race is reproduced. The wife's primary contribution to the marriage is her consent to share her reproductive life. She must be rewarded for this commitment and must not be rewarded for refusing it by un-chastity or revoking it by divorce. The husband's primary contribution to the marriage is to supply this reward — to be a provider.

If things were ordered rationally, these tradeoffs would be mutually acceptable. Is it fair that sexual strictures should not apply equally to men? Yes, considering the other expectations attaching to men, the sexual tradeoffs discussed earlier, as well as the paternity issue. The strictures may not seem fair to some; however, the dictates of nature (i.e., female pregnancy and male sexual desire) are not subject to chivalrous notions of fairness. Persons wishing to argue the issue of fairness in nature should take the matter up with The Creator. This book deals with temporal realities.

Is it reasonable to expect ordinary men and women to agree to the trade-offs? Perhaps not, unfortunately. Ladies and gentlemen — yes. To some extent the mutually-beneficial tradeoffs have disappeared for women also. How often do you see men give up their seats on busses these days, or hold doors open for women?

Civility entails recognition of distinction between ordinary women and ladies, and between ordinary men and gentlemen. For men to be gentlemen, women must be ladies. There are separate standards for each, and properly so. According to dictionaries, ladies and gentlemen are (1) "persons who exhibit the traits of kindness, courtesy, courage and self-control," and (2) "persons with high moral qualities." I would add, 'and are well-mannered.' Ladyhood need not necessarily be declared by the peerage. A quote on a Houston Texas school wall gave good advice to kids: "The more you act like a lady, the more he'll act like a gentleman." But that outraged feminists who caused it to be taken down.

This writer is sometimes asked how he distinguishes between ladies and women. That is easier to exemplify than define. Apropos of that, in 1964 Justice Potter Stewart tried to explain "hard-core" pornography, or what is obscene, by saying, "I shall not today attempt further to define the kinds of material I understand to be embraced . . .

but I know it when I see it . . ." The simplest answer seems to be that a lady has dignity, or to use theatrical examples: Grace Kelly [fn43] and Clare Booth Luce were ladies. I knew several others including my late wife. Two of the classiest ladies I have ever seen were present at my seminar in Doha, Qatar, both highly intelligent and beautiful: the wealthy Sheikha Moza bint Nasser who sponsored the seminar and a Professor from the U. of Wisc., Madison. Trump's Covid-19 team member Debora Brix may also qualify. "Lady" Gaga does not. Political commentator Susan Estrich is a woman; Elizabeth Taylor was also one. *Playboy* magazine portrayed women. It is nice to see ladies that know how to dress, however rare.

It offends any sensible person more to hear a woman belch, fart or swear than it does to hear a man do so. Some women use language that would make a G.I. blush. In Britain, a mother having sex with her son wants to have his baby. [495] Definitely NOT a lady.

Gabrielle Reece, the former volleyball star and model has created a media firestorm by writing the book My Foot Is Too Big for the Glass Slipper, in which she advocates: "To truly be feminine means being soft, receptive, and – look out, here it comes – submissive." [496] In Either/Or, Kierkegaard lovingly described the essence of womanhood, real womanhood, not that of feminist lore. True love was illustrated when George Wallace's wife Lurleen threw herself over George to prevent further bullets hitting him, contrasted with Jackie Kennedy scrambling out of the convertible as husband John was being assassinated.

Dorothy Evslin says in The Fortunate Sex, "the housewife has a gift she (too often) neglects to open: the gift of true freedom." Being a true woman is the ultimate liberation.

Apparent Dilemma Resolved

Perceptive persons might ask if there is not an inconsistency in my arguments. They ask how I can defend traditional sex roles in some instances, as in employment and chivalry, and attack them in others, as in custodial preference. Additionally, the dichotomy between those acknowledging sexual distinctions and those minimizing them brings forth a seeming problem for men in our quest for legal and perceptive equality with women. If the claim of big differences is true, the argument for maternal preference in young child custody, male preference in jobs, including combat 'jobs,' and harsher treatment for males in the criminal system seems plausible. If differences do not abound, existing preferences are obviously unjustified prejudices. Either way, men come out short; the conservative, separatist approach would cost us custody, while the liberal, unisex approach would cost us job preference and the traditional masculine image.

---

43 I never forgave Prince Rainier for sticking his tool in her.

Let us consider the possibility that the contradictions are merely paradoxical, and that the problems can be reconciled. Making merit and normalcy the criteria for role assumptions, removes the problem. Normal men and normal women, normally endowed and under normal circumstances, have normal (i.e., traditionally sex-differentiated) roles to play in life. On the other hand, abnormal circumstances discussed later — such as divorce, immorality, hormonal imbalances, strange personal preferences, etc. — require individual considerations based on these unique circumstances.

Making merit and normalcy the criteria for role assumptions, removes the problem.

In abnormal situations, sex roles must be flexible. Because often they are not, exceptional men and women are subjected to gross discrimination. These exceptional men and women are legitimate members of their respective liberation movements, and comprise the rational elements thereof.

As mentioned earlier, as children grow older they need their mother's maternal qualities less, their father's socializing, disciplining, toughening qualities more. However, due to individual circumstances, certain fathers should have custody of very young children and certain mothers should not. Likewise, certain mothers should have custody of older children and certain fathers should not.

If merit and normalcy criteria are used, reasonable tradition will be preserved, pleasing conservatives, while the absence of unreasonable tradition should please "progressives" — intelligent ones. To establish norms based upon exceptions, and to refuse to consider exceptions both defy common sense. Under the normalcy test more men than women will be top executives and foxhole "grunts," certain women could be professional boxers, beef luggers or used in combat, and certain men could not. More men than women would serve "hard time." Certain male prisoners would be incarcerated in sorority-house-like facilities and certain women prisoners in concrete dungeons. However, these decisions and choices will have been made after reasonable scrutiny.

If society, especially judges, continue to prove incapable of reasonable scrutiny, our only salvation may lie in resort to the Amneus prescription of invariable paternal custody, no alimony or child support, men in all arduous jobs, women largely in the bedroom and kitchen.

Patriarchy and Matriarchy.
Meeting Half Way

Patriarchy created civilization;
traditional manhood is the best pattern to save it.

Some say Patriarchy is an outmoded value system. Au contraire!
The Bible, for those who believe, is replete with references to husbands'

authority over wives, "He shall rule over thee" (Genesis 3:16) —
beneficently, of course.

Despite Professor Amneus' persuasive intellectual arguments for
Patriarchy, that ideal is not likely to be restored — not in this day and
age, given the popularity of modern, feminist thought. Nevertheless,
an apologia citing its advantages must be mounted. This was well done
in Professor Amneus' masterpiece, titled Back to Patriarchy. [497] While
there are no easy answers to complicated problems, the attempt to
restore patriarchy will help return the pendulum away from
Matriarchy (or Gynocracy, if you prefer that term), toward the center.

Acknowledging that Patriarchy (Islam, an extreme example) and
Matriarchy (feminism, the other extreme) are philosophical opposites, a
'happy medium' compromise, as advocated by many reformers in the
legitimate men's movement, would appear reasonable. However — and
this emphasizes the importance of Professor Amneus' position — there
is a practical problem with advocating the happy medium up front.
Any marketplace haggler knows that one commences bargaining from a
lower price than the one he is prepared to pay.

It is unwise to subscribe to Hazlitt's commonplace critic who
"believes that truth lies in the middle, between the extremes of right
and wrong." It relates to writer Lawrence Henry's football analogy:
"When you play mid-field ball against a team that plays end zone ball,
you lose." Because Matriarchy (Point A on the illustration below) is
extant, men's activists would be well advised to commence from the
position of advocating Patriarchy (Point D on the illustration, i.e. the
Amneus position) in order that the inevitable compromise comes at the
happy medium or mid-point (Point C on the illustration), and not at an
undesirable compromise (Point B on the illustration) between the mid-
point happy medium and Matriarchy, which would have been the result
had we commenced at the happy medium.

Point A	Point B	Point C	Point D
Matriarchy (feminism)	Undesirable Compromise	Happy-medium	Patriarchy (Masculism)

Patriarchy, involving greater paternal influence, would have
beneficial effect — especially in crime-ridden cities. Crime statistics
show that patriarchal countries like Japan and Switzerland, where
fatherlessness is rare, have a crime rate only a fraction of that in
matriarchal countries such as the United States; and they are
outpacing culturally, educationally — and to a growing extent
economically — countries that have embraced matriarchy. The U.S.
murder rate is 6 times that of Japan. [498] The U.S. was a much better
country in every way in early patriarchal days when kids respected
their fathers and obeyed them (or else!).

The patriarchal advantage may be difficult to comprehend in changing societies, because of institutionalized habit and the generations-long time lag. An economic tailwind (as well as ethnic and demographic advantages) permitted Sweden and Holland to remain relatively civilized after rejecting patriarchy in favor of androgynous matrifocality. Socialized European countries can stay afloat longer than the U.S. because they have fewer criminals and lowlifes than we do, though that has greatly changed. Maybe an idealized society would not be patriarchal or would be a softer, gentler form of it than commonly understood, just as an idealized economy might not be market-oriented. However, this is the real world. These forms have proven themselves.

There is an exception to the general beneficence of patriarchy. In the western world it was benign, and still is so — where it exists; but centuries ago in the mid-east, it took a religion-based divergent path, becoming un-benign practically to the point of lunacy. The desperation of living in Islamist (and communist) countries negatively affects men and boys as much as it does females. It is important that disillusioned young Islamic males be saved from the dangerous clutches of extremists. The fact that these cultures normally do not believe in equal rights for women may contribute to their overall backwardness.

In April of 2014 at a family conference in Doha, Qatar I made the point, to the great appreciation of one Islamic educator from Kuwait and his wife (both with Ph.Ds. from Penn State University), that the deification of men in Eastern cultures may be as harmful as the deification of women in Western cultures, and that the custom of Arab Muslim women hiding their faces is no more extreme than Western women dressing immodestly. [44]

Sexual confusions and sex melding

Mandatory sex melding in sports. A 1972 amendment to Title IX of the 1964 Civil Rights Act has been (wrongly, I submit) interpreted by feminists in the Department of Education and former President Clinton's Office of Civil Rights to enforce a proportionality quota system that blatantly discriminates against male athletic teams. Courts perform legalistic contortions to support such notions — contrary to the statement of Title IX's author, Rep Edith Green, that "...the establishment of quotas would be prohibited." Title IX proponents are attempting to expand its application to achieve sex parity in science, technology, engineering and math education, despite a natural female disinclination to these fields. Doing nothing for

---

44 That presentation appears in the Men's Defense Assoc. Website: mensdefense.org.

women, Title IX nonsense simply feeds the anti-masculine animus of feminists.

The numbers game has resulted in the elimination of hundreds, maybe thousands by now, of male teams: 171 colleges dropped 476 wrestling teams, [499] 37 colleges dropped football, 27 dropped outdoor track, 25 dropped swimming, and 10 abolished ice hockey. In some schools, men's track and field and gymnastics went by the boards. Title IX killed the University of California's Los Angeles swim team that spurred Mark Spitz to his records. Private swim clubs can still train champions, but other sports such as wrestling and track depend entirely on school-based competition. The promising baseball players at Howard University lost their chance to develop their skills and become stars. High schools are next. Our future Jesse Owenses have been replaced by less talented women who took an athletic scholarship to get free college tuition, not necessarily, because they were keen on sports. A legal petition filed in October 2017 by the Pacific Legal Foundation complains that that Title IX limits opportunities for men rather than creating opportunities for women. [500]

Title IX's interpretation — the "proportionality test" — pushes girls into sports in which not many are interested and many get hurt. Nevertheless, female student athletes in California sued their university alleging they have been discriminated against because opportunities for women's athletic participation is not proportional to their numbers in that school. [501] A few years ago, only 200 U.S. high-school girls participated in ice hockey nationwide, [502] however poorly (admittedly many more play now, and better). Justine Blainey and Hayley Wickenheiser fought for and won the right to skate with the boys. In Canada Brigitte LeBlanc, a 14-year-old Moncton girl, wasn't satisfied playing hockey with the boys. She wanted more, so she petitioned the New Brunswick Human Rights Commission to grant her the right to use the boys' locker room. Astonishingly, she won. Coaches have aptly called these schemes "sheer idiocy." This is not meant to be critical of girls and women in sports, merely the undeserved adulation of same.

Of course, the gym doors do not swing both ways; while female athletes continue to have the luxury of maintaining girls' teams and girls' clubs, the privilege to elbow their way into women's schools and clubs has not been available to men. That is discrimination. Surely, a few 14-year-old boys out there would not mind gaining entry to the girls' locker room. Two teenage boys Dmitri Moua and Zachary Greenwald, juniors at high schools in Roseville and Hopkins Minnesota, sued the State High School League alleging it maintains unconstitutional rules that bar boys from joining girls' competitive high school dance teams. They can now do so.

The Democrat-controlled House of Representatives on May 17, 2019 voted 236-173 in favor of the Equality Act, which would require schools to include male athletes who identify as transgender girls on female sports teams. Eight Republicans crossed party lines to vote for the bill, which had unanimous Democrat support. The bill amends the Civil Rights Act of 1964 to make "sexual orientation and gender identity" protected characteristics under federal anti-discrimination law. Among other things, that would force public schools to expand female athletic teams to include biological males who identify as transgender girls.

Then there are the female impersonators. High school transgender wrestler Mack Beggs, after an undefeated 56-0 season, won the state girls wrestling title on February 25th, 2017 at the Texas girls state tournament. Beggs was born a girl, but prefers to be a boy, and has been taking testosterone treatments. The rules permit the use of drugs in athletic events if they are medically prescribed. [503] Nattaphon "Ice" Wangyot, a transgender former male senior at Haines High School, qualified for the finals at Dimond Field in Anchorage during the Alaska girls 100 and 200-meter races on June 3rd, 2016. Terry Miller finished first and Andraya Yarwood finished second in the June 2018 Connecticut track and field girls' championships. Both were born males, but chose to claim girlhood. Gabrielle Ludwig, a 50-year-old 6-foot-6 transsexual Army veteran, father and former college basketball player, returned to Mission College in Santa Clara, Calif. to play on the women's' basketball team. On May 1st 2019 at the Raw Weightlifting Federation competition in Virginia transgender Mary Gregory smashed all women's world weightlifting records. In Australia, former male — now female — Lauren Hubbard won the International women's weight-lifting competition after lifting 591 pounds. She competed for New Zealand in men's weightlifting before her transition to female in her thirties, and won two golds and a silver in three of the women's heavyweight categories at the July 2019 Games in Samoa. Mixed Martial Arts fighter Fallon Fox — formerly a man — now fights with women, and has caused serious injury to opponents, including shattering Tamikka Brents's eye socket and giving her a concussion. Indisputably, female athletes sustain two to three times as many injuries as do males.

A biologically male marathon runner who identifies as a transgender woman is set to make history by competing in the USA Olympic trials. Megan Youngren "is the first openly transgender athlete to compete at the U.S. Olympic marathon trials," *Sports Illustrated* reported. Youngren qualified for the trials after a strong performance on Dec. 8, 2019 in the California International Marathon. [504] In Cromwell Connecticut, biological male Andraya Yearwood — sprinting on the girls track team — consistently takes 1st place. The Big

Sky Conference named University of Montana runner June Eastwood, a biological male who identifies as a transgender woman, the 'cross-country female athlete of the week.' [505]

Such bizarre occurrences as mentioned above will be legally supported by the Equality Act of 2019 (H.R. 5) if it passes. The original Equality Act was developed by U.S. Representatives Bella Abzug (D-NY) and Ed Koch (D-NY) in 1974. It amended the Civil Rights Act of 1964 to include prohibiting discrimination on the basis of sex, sexual orientation, and marital status in federally assisted programs, housing sales, rentals, financing, and brokerage services. It authorized civil actions by the U.S. in cases of discrimination on account of sex, sexual orientation, or marital status in public facilities and public education. The current iteration of the Act was sponsored by 43 Democrats, 2 Independents, and 1 Republican in the House of Representatives, and by 237 Democrats and 3 Republicans in the Senate.

The families of three female high school runners filed a federal lawsuit on February 12th, 2020 seeking to block transgender athletes in Connecticut from participating in girls' sports. Selina Soule, a senior at Glastonbury High School, Chelsea Mitchell, a senior at Canton High School and Alanna Smith, a sophomore at Danbury High School are represented by the conservative nonprofit organization Alliance Defending Freedom. They argue that allowing athletes with male anatomy to compete has deprived them of track titles and scholarship opportunities. [506]

A Minnesota court decision could create serious institutional difficulties for women's sports at the professional and amateur levels; a transgender woman named Christina Ginther was awarded $20,000 in a lawsuit against a women's football team that declined to offer her a place on the team on account of its male biology. Ginther had filed a lawsuit against the owner of the Minnesota Vixen, Laura Brown, and the Independent Women's Football League, which does not allow transgender women (possessing male physiology) to participate. It seems that policy evidently violates the Minnesota Human Rights Act's anti-discrimination provisions,

Critics claim women with female biology cannot compete in many areas, and that political correctness has lowered the standards so much that it will almost certainly mean the end of women's sports. Former Wimbledon champion and homosexual rights campaigner Martina Navratilova complained that allowing transgender "women" (formerly men) to compete in women's sporting tournaments was "insane and cheating," somewhat ironic inasmuch as her homosexual makeup gives her an advantage also, over real women. The prize-winning U.S. women's soccer team evidently included many lesbians, not to mention a publically foul-mouthed co-captain.

What if Bruce/Katlin Jenner decides to compete as a "female" athlete, a la Richard Raskind, former captain of the Yale men's tennis team? Author Steven E. Rhoads says, "Only when we begin to take sex differences seriously enough to see that men are intrinsically more attracted to sports — and need sports competition more than women do — will we be able to design public policies that are just, functional, and sensible." [507] The George W. Bush administration wisely authorized rules allowing schools to use surveys to gage in which sports students want to participate, surveys that can provide evidence in defense of commonsense proportionality in providing sex-based activities.

Though few people other than parents watch them, sports writers maintain the pretext of great importance for girls' sports. I actually approve of girls playing sports (some play well in basketball and softball as well as hockey), but not of the elevated importance attached to it. Of course, there are exceptions to every rule: 13-year-old Mo'ne Davis is an exceptional Little League baseball pitcher. Babe Didrikson Zaharias was a hell of an athlete, but I couldn't imagine being married to her, or anyone like her.

Football, that noble, masculine sport, is being feminized. The camel's nose is under the tent; the Washington D.C. Coolidge High School chose Natalie Randolph as football coach, high-schooler Robyn Waite played quarterback on the Ontario boys' team, and it seems females are kicking the ball in high school and the pros. Becca Longo Longo, a highly accurate high school field goal kicker, is the first woman to receive a college football scholarship. She signed with Adams State University in Alamosa, Colorado, as a kicker. Some will scream to the high heavens if she gets hurt; hell, I might! In Minnesota high school girls wrestle with boys. [508]

The mainstream media would probably ballyhoo the "sport" of women jumping around in sacks — if there were such a curiosity. Even the Olympics have gone soft. The International Olympic Committee tried to abolish wrestling, but retain water dancing and sliding downhill, and are considering inclusion of pole dancing. Expect to see synchronized goat milking next. They don't have the one thing I believe they should: Tug of War.

A woman could play on the men's PGA golf tour, but a man could not play on the women's tour. The LPGA was not good enough for Annika Sorenstam, so she decided to tee off with the men during a 2003 PGA tournament. One bright, shining exception to this nonsense was the success of Hootie Johnson, Chairman of the Augusta National Golf Club — home of the Masters Golf tournament. The National Council of Women's Organizations pressured major advertisers financing the Masters to require sexual integration of the tournament in 2003. They lost that battle when the tournament proceeded without advertising revenue. However, male exclusivity of the Augusta National Golf Club ended in 2012.

Finances play a part. Some years ago, sex-benders concocted a sham boxing match between a professional woman boxer (loaded with male hormones, no doubt) and a little man who had never won a fight. They also swooned over the young Billie Jean King's tennis victory over the old Bobby Riggs. At Wimbledon, women tennis players are paid the same for playing three sets as men are for playing five. Former *Liberator* writer Max Freedman objected to the zeitgeist thusly, "The woman's champion runner in this year's marathon is getting $30,000 more than the male winner! (Not to mention some $130,000 more than those few dozen men who will finish ahead of her, but will be paid zilch.) Men are too intimidated to complain."

Androgyny, Inversions, etc.

Vos ist Los?

Gender/sex confusion and sexual anarchy are infections attacking the masculine and feminine images these days. The male qualities that protected and preserved the race down through the ages are largely shunned as undesirable in modern society. Like a child going through phases, the Western world has in the last several generations experienced innocent-appearing egalitarianism and inter-sex exchange of functions, phenomena considered by many, including this writer, to be unhealthy, neither fish nor fowl.

Seemingly at war with normal life, and aspiring to achieve social integration, the diversity gods have mounted an effort to rid us of all distinctions between men and women. As Pat Buchanan said, "Liberty has been supplanted by diversity, justice by equality."

Sex-melders would create a unisex society by eliminating sexual distinctions and traditional functions based upon them. This element considers normal sexual characteristics restrictive and resent traditionally distinctive members of either sex.

One can hardly distinguish sex by given names anymore. To tell the boys from the girls these days one often has to check the sweaters; and that is not foolproof. Consequently, sex distinctions are fading and unisex is on the rise. How can one distinguish males (or females) if one can't tell the difference? A sex-melder asked me at a seminar why I would want to know the difference. I said 'Because I look at and talk differently to women than to men, as would any normal person. Some others must operate on the pretext that sex doesn't exist.

Girls can wear boys' clothing, but boys can't properly wear girls' togs, not that they should. Women are buying almost as many pants in department stores as are men. Men are buying clothes, cosmetics, earrings and other female accoutrements. [509] According to the latest Paris fashion show, men can dress like women. Gucci's new menswear can't be distinguished from ladies wear. Tasseled loafers anyone? Waitresses wearing neckties look somehow out of place to many people. Long hair and earrings on men are ubiquitous. Torrin Polk, a University of Houston football player, said about his coach, John Jenkins: "He treats us like men; he lets us wear earrings." Athletes sport foolish haircuts (or lack thereof), some with hair or 'dreadlocks' half way down their back. Imagine — hair dryers in the locker room.

A "Gender Identity Procedural Directive" told teachers to eliminate gender in their classrooms. It probably irks a certain element no end to hear Lawrence Welk refer to "boys and girls" (not that they watch the show). A Public middle schools in Lincoln Nebraska discourages use of those terms, suggesting strange alternate ones. KOB-TV in Albuquerque reports a Carlos Rey Elementary School assistant principal sent teachers a letter ordering them to no longer refer to students as boys and girls. [510]

Gender/sex is becoming more and more a spectrum than a binary. Future identity forms may list M, F and O (for other). Democrat lawmakers in California have made that state the first in the union to add a gender option other than male or female on state-issued identification. Vermont's Department of Motor Vehicles' will also allow a third gender option on drivers' licenses. There are fifty-eight options according to ABC News. The shorthand is LGBTQIA (lesbian, gay, bisexual, transsexual, questioning, intersex, asexual). However, it is oxymoronic to be one sex and another gender. My associates in Australia say the same issues arise "down under." Labor and Greens voted to remove gender from birth certificates in Tasmania, Australia. [511] The brilliant Australian pro-life activist Babette Francis writes, "All human beings come in two categories male and female, with XY or XX chromosomes respectively, fixed from the moment of their conception. The very rare exceptions on this are abnormalities, not new genders."

Recognizing many genders is sexual anarchy. However, it is true that degrees of sex does exist within the two primary categories, and can be a matter of concern. It may be more appropriate to describe individuals as mostly male or mostly female and even to use the pronoun "it" instead of "he" or "she." The City University of New York's Graduate Center has banned the words "Mr." and "Ms." from official correspondence in order to comply with Title IX, and because the terms are not sensitive to "transgender" students. [512] The liberal NYC Commission on Human Rights recognizes 31 different genders, and woe betide anyone who misidentifies them; reportedly, there's a $250,000 fine. California law, S.B.219, provides 12 months imprisonment for failing to use the correct gender pronoun, for using terms like "he and "she, when addressing seniors"

The use of associated personal pronouns is bizarre. Several publications including the St. Paul *Pioneer Press* refers to individuals as "they" to avoid specifying a gender. To use such neutral pronouns is awkward and wooden. Facebook acknowledges 57 genders. The British Broadcasting Company (BBC) tells primary schoolchildren that there are over 100 genders as part of its "Teach" video series, which has some concerned parents and observers up in arms. [513]

Canada's Senate passed Bill C-16, which puts "gender identity" and "gender expression" into both the country's Human Rights Code, as well as the hate crime category of its Criminal Code. Justin Trudeau, Canada's liberal prime minister called it "Great news." The New York City Health Dept. form asks parents if the 'woman giving birth' is male or female. [514] The French government is preparing to ban the words "mother" and "father" from all official documents under plans to legalize homosexual marriage. [515] Some U.S. municipalities are attempting to replace gendered terms in their codes, like "manhole" and "manpower," with gender-neutral ones like "maintenance hole" and "human effort."

In the U.S.A. the Boy Scouts and Girl scouts are both struggling to increase membership. The Boy Scouts are officially open to girls ranging from Cub to Eagle Scout level. Now called the Scouts BSA, the Scouts are open to boys and girls between the ages of 11 and 17. Grove City college professor Paul Kengor wrote, "It is another scalp on the cultural-ideological wall." The president of the Girl Scouts is highly critical. The Boy Scouts already include homosexuals and transgenders, and now have female leaders. BSA leaders are making their leftward lurch complete with the announcement that birth control instructions will be provided at their next 12-day jamboree where 12-to 17-year-olds will convene.

Harvard's fraternities may also be succumbing to integration. Several national fraternities and sororities sued Harvard University over a 2016 rule that discourages students from joining single gender social clubs, marking the first legal challenge to the school's policy.

Two fraternities and two sororities filed a lawsuit in Boston's federal court, while another sorority separately sued the school in Massachusetts state court. Both cases argue that the school's policy discriminates against students based on their sex, and spreads negative stereotypes about students who join all-male or all-female organizations.

The Quarante Hommes et Huit Chaveau is an honor society of the American Legion (called the 40 and 8 for short) to which I used to belong. Its name, painted on the sides of the boxcars that transported WWI troops to battle in France, translates to 40 men & (or) eight horses. Its originating charter restricted it to male members, because only males rode those boxcars, two of my uncles and a friend — he as a German prisoner in WWII who had earned the Distinguished Flying Cross for saving his P51 by landing it despite having its hydraulics shot out. Ponder an experience that prisoner — locked in those boxcars for days eating slop — related to our group: One day the train pulled into a German town where the populace was waiting to see them. The guys just dropped their pants and defecated (he used another term) in front of the crowd. He said "We were like animals."

Feminist-inspired modernizing influenced the 40 and 8's national leaders, with shady maneuverings, to admit women members despite the absence of women in those WWII boxcars. For that and other stupidity, I resigned from membership, as many of us did when Toastmasters was integrated and similarly messed up.

Dig this: an "Equality Bill," going through the U.K. Parliament, will make it illegal to imply that women are not as physically strong as men. Apropos to this in France, in 1831 Tocqueville said:

It may readily be conceived that by thus attempting to make one sex equal to the other, both are degraded, and from so preposterous a medley of the works of nature nothing could ever result but weak men and disorderly women." [516]

Incredibly enough, the sexual confusion phenomenon is heavily funded by major corporations. Until reform comes about, freedom of association will continue to be trampled upon to promote less important rights. If some persons choose to live non-traditionally, they should have that right. They should not have the right to expect others to submit to their deviations. 'Brave new world' my ass!

Feminized males

Manhood has been debauched along with the U.S. currency. *Human Events* editor Wesley Pruden insightfully called this "The Gelded Age." Opponents of the concept of manhood have successfully imposed a perverted definition of manliness on American men.. We cannot strengthen the weak by weakening the strong.

C.S. Lewis is quoted:

We make men without chests and expect of them virtue and enterprise. We laugh at honor and are shocked to find traitors in our midst. We castrate and bid the geldings to be fruitful.

When during a boy's formative years, his father is sabotaged and men in general are objects of judicial contempt and social disrespect, can there be any doubt why he would emulate women, especially assertive women?

Even China has recognized a "problem of timid, self-centered and effeminate boys idolizing makeup and earring-wearing male TV, film and pop idols who have gained popularity here." The state-run media condemned these young idols, calling them "sissy pants." Deploring a "masculinity crisis," some educators are working to reinforce traditional gender roles and values in the classroom. In Zhengzhou, schools have asked boys to sign pledges to act like "real men." In Shanghai, principals are trying boys-only classes with courses like martial arts, computer repair and physics. In Hangzhou, educators have started a summer camp called West Point Boys, complete with taekwondo classes and the motto, "We bring out the men in boys." [517] Former schoolteacher Tang Haiyan founded the Real Man Training Club to combat what he and others in China see as a masculinity crisis. "If you are promoting these effeminate figures," Tang said, "it's a calamity for our country."

Transgenderism.

There is a significant psychological phenomenon wherein some children and adults imagine themselves, or their children, to be of a sex other than that into which they are born. Formerly an outlier, "transgenderism" is gaining attention.

Californians David Stocker and wife Kathy Witterick, both from liberal families, give their children "the freedom to choose their sex, unconstrained by social norms about males and females." Extremists in the journal *Pediatrics* claim that encouraging mothers to breastfeed babies is unethical because it reinforces gender roles. Two Minnesota parents evidently want to change their 5-year-old child's gender, and are suing the state for paid counseling to support that scheme. It's a scam. What 5-year-old would even know which gender he belongs in without parental pressure?

One Stockholm, Sweden kindergarten encourages parents to clothe their sons in dresses and give them female first names. In Sweden, he is han, and she is hon; sex melders there have proposed the use of hen to signify either. Some U.S. government agencies have gone a bridge too far in requiring 'newspeak' pronouns adopted by the Swedish kindergarten mentioned above. [518] Also in that country, Mr. Ragnar Bengtsson has been attempting to pump his own breasts for milk. [519]

Children who are distressed about their biological sex are said to exhibit "gender dysphoria." The American Psychiatric Association defines this as "a conflict between a person's physical or assigned gender and the gender with which he/she/they identify." A bill in the U.S. Senate would require insurance providers to cover sex reassignment surgery in such cases. An "affirming" approach for such children is practiced in the Netherlands wherein puberty blockers (cross-sex hormones) are prescribed — estrogen for boys and testosterone for girls. Surgery may follow, including double mastectomies for girls and genital surgery for boys. That "Dutch protocol" carries many medical risks: sterility plus increased risk of cancer, liver disease, diabetes, stroke and heart attack, according to the Transgender Health Program of Vancouver, Canada. Lifelong dependence on the medical system is likely. Dr. Paul McHugh of Johns Hopkins School of Medicine believes gender dysphoria is nonsense.

On September 23rd 2013, the White House celebrated Bisexual Visibility Day with an official closed-door event. The Obama administration attempted to by-pass Congress by writing law to withhold federal funds to states and institutions that drag their feet in de-sexing people (Federal involvement appears because they are served by public roads perhaps). All sorts of federal legislation exist to this effect. Federal courts have declared sexually segregated schools to be unconstitutional, excepting women's schools for all practical purposes. Most high schools, colleges and universities in the U.S., including the military academies, have been forced or persuaded to integrate by sex. The very idea probably qualifies for government grants. Eleven states sued the Obama administration over its directive requiring schools to open bathrooms and locker rooms to either sex.

Two Wisconsin residents who want gender reassignment surgeries paid by Medicaid filed a lawsuit against the state, contending their denials of service are discriminatory and violate the federal health care law. The lawsuit also seeks compensatory damages for emotional distress and plaintiffs' attorneys' fees. The federal lawsuit from Cody Flack, a 30-year-old transgender man, and Sara Ann Makenzie, a 41-year-old transgender woman, challenges a 1997 state regulation that deems "transsexual surgery" as medically unnecessary and therefore not eligible for Medicaid coverage. 18 states and the District of Columbia do provide coverage for those procedures under Medicaid.

The Obama administration decreed that millions of patients should be notified in multiple languages about their rights to such services in insurer "explanation of benefits" forms. The Trump administration says the notice requirement has become a needless burden on health care providers, requiring billions of paper notices to be mailed annually at an estimated five-year cost of $3.2 billion. Fortunately, Judge Reed O'Connor in the Northern District of Texas vacated that regulation.

Experts claim 1.4 million adults are afflicted with the disorder in the U.S., or about 0.6 percent of the adult population. Nearly 2 percent of high school students in the United States identify as transgender, according to data published by the U.S. Centers for Disease Control and Prevention. Minnesota Republican Rep. Mary Franson perfectly described the condition when she tweeted, "A guy who thinks he's a girl is still a guy with a mental health condition." An excellent analysis of the subject appeared in the November 2015 issue of *Whistleblower* magazine.

It's infected even the comics; superhero Thor will become a woman. In Huntington Beach, California, a 'male' transsexual high school senior was chosen homecoming queen. With federal encouragement, girls in California (Where else?) can be elected homecoming king. A New York doll maker intends to sell a transgender doll. In January 2017 the Boy Scouts began allowing transgender youths to join local troops. The Palm Springs, Calif. City Council now has transgender and bisexual members – and is entirely LGBT. Two black transgender persons were elected to the Minneapolis City Council in November 2017.

Laws have proliferated around the country to accommodate the desires of transgender people. According to the Capitol Resource Institute (CRI), legislation sponsored by California lesbian Sen. Sheila James Kuehl "could potentially require sex-neutral bathrooms in our schools, and all references to 'husband' and 'wife' or 'mom' and 'dad' removed from school textbooks as the norm." The law promotes sexually deviant lifestyles in school books, and gives the state Superintendent of Public Instruction power to withhold funds from school districts that do not promote trans-sexuality, bisexuality, and homosexuality. [520] California Democrat Assemblyman Tom Ammiano proposed a law to allow public school children to use bathrooms designated for members of the opposite sex if that student's "sex identity" differed from the student's biological sex, and to "participate in sex-segregated school programs and activities, including athletic teams and competitions, and use facilities consistent with his or her sex identity, irrespective of the sex listed on the pupil's record." [521] Senate Bill 777, now law in California (where else?), removes all references to gender/sex in public schools. California law AB1266 will allow transgender kindergarten-through-12th grade students access to whichever restroom and locker room they want based on their self-perception and regardless of their birth sex. [522] Such absurdities could be expected from a state with a governor nicknamed "Moonbeam").

Bowing to pressure, North Carolina, partially repealed local laws banning restriction of bathrooms and locker rooms to the sex registered at birth. The Charlotte-Mecklenburg Schools system in North Carolina planned to use a picture book for first graders named *Jacob's New Dress* about a young boy who likes to dress in feminine clothing. The North Carolina Values Coalition got wind of the plan, and objected claiming it is meant as a tool of indoctrination to normalize transgender behavior. "The purpose of our elementary schools is to teach writing, reading and arithmetic, not to encourage boys to wear dresses," they said.

We have a similar situation 'right here in River City,' Minnesota; a kid born a boy, acts like a girl, his/its parents are suing his/its school.

In my day, misbehaving little boys would be dressed in women's clothes. Boy, was that embarrassing!

The Michigan State Board of Education quietly — without a press release or parental notification — issued guidelines in its "Statement and Guidance on Safe and Supportive Learning Environments for Lesbian, Gay, Bisexual, Transgender, and Questioning (LGBTQ) [fn45] Students" to public schools that instructed teachers to allow students to choose their own gender and which bathroom to use, all without parental involvement.

New York City Mayor Bill de Blasio signed an executive order 2/7/15 taking all gender restrictions off of city-owned bathrooms — meaning anyone, male or female, can enter any bathroom, for male or female, at city playgrounds, pools, or offices without worry or hesitation, and will never have to show an ID to prove their identity. The Charlotte, NC City Council approved a measure that allows transgender people to use the restroom aligned with their gender identity. In response, Gov. Pat McCrory signed a bill that prevents local governments from setting their own anti-discrimination rules. In response to that, boycotts of states whose commonsense laws disfavor sexual misfits are beginning to cost these states many jobs. Minnesota's liberal former governor Dayton vowed to veto any laws unfavorable to sexual misfits, and wanted to join big businesses in banning official travels to No. Carolina due to their laws hostile to them. I had a notion to test Dayton's resolve by invading women's' rest rooms at the state capitol building. BTW, Dayton also aspired to enable undocumented immigrants to get Minnesota driver's licenses. Now his Democrat successor concurs. In Minnesota (of course) a judge found the state's refusal to fund transgender reversing surgery to be unconstitutional.

Federal education authorities found that an Illinois school district violated anti-discrimination laws when it did not allow a student born male but now identifying as a girl to participate on a girls' sports team and to change and shower in the girls' locker room without restrictions. [523] The Department of Education's Office of Civil Rights determined that a Chicago area school has violated a transgendered student's rights by protecting fellow students from exposure to the transgendered student's nakedness.[524] These objections can also apply to any effort to reinstate the "Equal" Rights Amendment.

"Progressive" Montgomery County, MD passed ordinances permitting men to frequent women's restrooms if they "feel" that they are really women. [525] The Queer Student Union at California Polytechnic University orchestrated a three-day "shit-in" at which

---

[45] The dictionary definition of freak would seem to apply: A thing or occurrence that is markedly unusual or irregular; an abnormally formed organism, especially one regarded as a curiosity; a sudden capricious turn of mind; a whim."

students preached "Gender Diversity" and encouraged students to use solely sex-neutral bathrooms on campus. [526]

Gavin Grimm, 16, a female student at Gloucester High School in Gloucester, Virginia identifies as a male and demanded the school district allow her to use the boys' restroom. Her request was denied. She/he took the case to a federal court, citing federal Title IX sex discrimination rules. Grimm maintained that the federal government can force schools to allow transgender students to choose whatever bathroom they feel like using. In a 2-to-1 ruling the U.S. Fourth Circuit Court of Appeals sided with Grimm, saying the lower court should have agreed with the student's interpretation of discrimination rules. [527] The Trump administration has revoked federal favoritism for the right of transgender students to use either school restrooms they choose, but the entire issue may end up before the Supreme Court.

Get this: Madison, Wisconsin public schools let students be the opposite sex at school, and staff are ordered to not tell parents! Imagine dropping your son (of any age) off at public school, never knowing that he lives a completely different existence as a girl for eight hours a day — and everyone knows it but you. And not only do teachers know it, but they go to great lengths to hide it. That's the reality in Madison, Wisconsin, where moms and dads have been furious to find out that not only is the district keeping their children's gender expression a secret, but there's an elaborate scheme in place to keep parents from ever finding out! Check out the link to Family Research Council; [528] (I've long said, "There's something in the water down there.")

A transgender supportive website is transstudent.org/student. This influence is spreading worldwide. In England, the Brighton and Hove City Council wrote: "We recognize that not all children and young people identify with the gender they were assigned at birth or may identify as a gender other than male or female, however the current systems (set nationally) only record gender as male or female. Please support your child to choose the gender they most identify with." [529] The Australian government made international headlines for officially recognizing 3rd category, "non-specific sex," on a state-issued document.

Using the wrong pronoun could turn into a firing offense at the University of Minnesota. The U is considering a "gender identity" policy that would assure transgender men and women, as well as others, the right to use whatever pronoun they wish on campus — whether it's he, she, "ze" or something else. And everyone from professors to classmates would be expected to call them by the right words or risk potential disciplinary action, up to firing or expulsion. In December 2018 the West Point Virginia School Board voted 5-0 to terminate Peter Vlaming, a courageous French teacher at West Point

High School who resisted administrators' orders to use male pronouns to refer to a ninth-grade student who had undergone a gender transition.

Transgenderism and homosexuality are too widespread to be attributed to a mix-up in hormones. Just as the esteemed writers of American Psychiatric Association's fifth edition of the <u>Diagnostic and Statistical Manual of Mental Disorders</u> surrendered to advocates for normalization of homosexuals and rejected the disorder classification of the parental alienation syndrome, they did likewise with transgenderism. Actually, according to the aforesaid manual, the great majority of those afflicted by gender confusion will outgrow this condition after passing through normal puberty.

True, there are biological abnormalities in a small minority of people with misperceptions of themselves, but such exceptions mustn't override normal sex distinctions. If the androgynous trend continues, man as unequivocally male and masculine will become as rare as the definitely female and feminine woman. On November 8, 2016, the National Center for Transgender Equality released a survey of 27,715 respondents from all 50 states, the District of Columbia, and three U.S. territories taken in 2015. Forty percent of the respondents said they had attempted suicide at some point. Examples are the suicide attempts by WikiLeaks "whistleblower" Chelsea Manning. The American Academy of Pediatrics claims transgender persons experience even more suicides than do homosexuals.

Bills have been proposed to outlaw what is commonly known as "conversion therapy" that aims to change the sexual orientation of gays and lesbians, to require insurance providers to cover sex reassignment surgery and to provide coverage for medications used to treat "gender dysphoria." The U.S. Supreme Court has repeatedly dismissed challenges against conversion therapy bans

Commonsense should tell us that men showering with girls is absurd. It might be appropriate for institutions and businesses to voluntarily build transgender bath and shower facilities, but foolish for government to coerce them to accommodate mixed sexes in their facilities.

In the Military.

Transgender people in the military are claimed to be in the thousands. June has been "Gay Pride" month in the military, wherein the Pentagon hosts something called the Annual Gay Appreciation Day, featuring Valerie Jarrett (who proclaimed, "Because we repealed 'Don't Ask, Don't Tell,' our military is stronger and our country is safer now that homosexuals may serve openly"). The entire farce made homosexual soldiers sound like supermen. President Obama, in a historic first for the Pentagon, has made Eric Fanning the first openly homosexual civilian secretary of the Army. [530] He lasted only 248 days. Chuck Hagel, the former Secretary of Defense, and Fanning heaped praise on a homosexual Marine Captain and said when he deploys in August, "he'll be taking his husband with him." Retired Brigadier General Tammy Smith and her "wife" were duly recognized. In London England, 31-year-old transgender Army Captain Hannah Winterbourne married 40-year-old actor Jake Graf — who used to be a woman.

President Obama's Defense Secretary Ash Carter banned the services from involuntarily separating people in the military who came out as transgender, and ordered the services to begin allowing such recruits to join the military, but provided the Joint Chiefs of Staff with a reprieve that they had requested to determine how to begin processing them. The order included provisions to pay for sex change operations and to allow male transsexual employees to shower in women's locker room. As it is, the military and prison systems are paying thousands of taxpayer dollars to perform transgender surgeries, and for "discrimination" relating to transgenderism.

Gender benders also wanted to ban the term "man" in military titles. Navy secretary Ray Mabus started the confusion by ordering his branch to review all job titles and consider removing any reference to "man" in them, a move that could force name-changes to nearly two dozen specialties, probably replacing seaman and airman with such as Seaperson, Airperson and Yeoperson.

President Trump has banned recruitment of the transgendered, but a court, hopefully temporarily, overturned that ban. A new policy will largely bar transgender troops and military recruits from transitioning to another sex, and will require most individuals to serve in their birth gender. According to News service reports, President Trump's Defense Secretary Jim Mattis delayed the Obama plan. On July 26, 2017 President Trump tweeted that they will no longer be allowed in the military. Coast Guard Commandant Adm. Paul Zukunft said he has no intention of applying that policy to the 13 Coast Guard members who have self-identified as transgender. Trump directed the Pentagon to extend indefinitely a ban on transgender individuals joining the military.

Homosexuality

Paul Popenoe, President of the American Institute of Family Relations, says, "Homosexuality and bisexuality are out of the closet to an unusual extent [531] — a sign of the times — although the Center for Disease Control informs us that less than 3% are so afflicted. When Gallup asked people to estimate how many Americans were homosexual in 2011, most guessed 25%. Gallup maintains the figure is about 3.4%, others say 2.5% — startling statistics for most people who just naturally assumed the media saturation was driven by a big population. Who can blame them? These numbers should be shocking to anyone who's lived through the deluge of homosexual policy, entertainment, school curriculum, and corporate capitulation of the past 10 years. [532] According to lore, this malady would attach to Walt Whitman, Frederick the Great, arguably to Alexander the Great and Julius Caesar, as well as Napoleon. Rush Limbaugh shocked politicians and the media for saying the country won't elect Democrat presidential candidate Pete Buttigieg president because he's been "kissing his husband" on stage after debates. [533]

I submit that homosexuality is antithetical to manhood, as well as to womanhood, and to marriage. For these reasons, the subject is germane to the theme of this book. While the terms 'real' men and 'manhood' are highly subjective and do not necessarily imply the deer-slayer type, they quite obviously exclude homosexuals. To those who say it is natural, Fred Reed replied, "So is hemorrhagic tuberculosis. So is sadism. So is genocide." Despite DSM-5 (The Diagnostic and Statistical Manual of Mental Disorders, published by the American Psychiatric Association) to the contrary, the Catholic Church teaches that homosexual acts are 'intrinsically disordered' based on the way in which our bodies are 'naturally oriented.' There are seven negative references to them in the Bible. The Adam and Eve coupling is normal, not Adam and Adam. Commonsense indicates the condition to be a hallmark of the deterioration of societies (however impolite to mention).

The "Student Non-Discrimination Act," called by some the "Homosexual Classrooms Act, is designed to indoctrinate an entire generation of American children with pro-homosexual propaganda and eliminate traditional values from American society. Its chief advocate in Congress is Rep. Jared Polis (D-CO), himself an open homosexual and radical activist. H.R. 998 has 147 co-sponsors in the House, and S. 555 has 34 co-sponsors in the Senate. Lawmakers in the state of California are proposing a law (SB 48) that would require schools to portray lesbians, homosexuals, transsexuals and those who have chosen other alternative sexual lifestyles as positive role models to children in all public schools there. [534] Not wanting to be left behind, the liberal former Minnesota former governor Dayton appointed a lesbian to the state Supreme Court.

The condition has become a cause for celebration, and "pride." San Diego firefighters were forced by lesbian Fire Chief Tracy Jarman to participate in the city's "Gay Pride" parade and subjected to "vile sexual taunts" by bystanders. The Thomas More Law Center sued the city on their behalf for sexual harassment, and won. [535] The 35 years sentence in Leavenworth given military transgender traitor Bradly Manning was commuted by former President Obama to 7 years. "She" is free now. He/she lived with his/her mother after its parents divorced, now calls his/herself Chelsea and desires a sex change at taxpayer expense. He/she was named Grand Marshal of the San Francisco Gay Pride parade (later rescinded). His/her condition may not be a sign of the times, but acceptance and celebration of the condition is such. The predilection toward pedophilia is equally objectionable, as is homosexual priests buggering altar boys.

The Boy Scouts of America's creed requires boys to be "morally straight." [fn46] That they opposed homosexual scoutmasters in protection of boys, offended homosexuals, atheists and the ACLU who have attacked the Scouts for over a decade. The Supreme Court upheld the Scouts' right to free association in the past, but the Scouts succumbed to the growing pressure to drop their "morally straight" claim, allowing open homosexuality among boys, and in July of 2015 allowed it among leaders also. Units sponsored by churches opposed to the change can maintain the ban if they choose. [536] Conclusion: homosexuality is now compatible with scouting values.

Frightened by warnings from the ACLU, the Pentagon warned military bases not to sponsor the Scouts. Fortunately, the Scouts have friends demanding a return to sensibility; the U.S. House passed by an almost unanimous vote, 418-7, a resolution (H. Con. Res. 6) urging the Defense Department to continue its long standing support of the Scouts (the 7 nay-sayers: Earl Blumenauer, D-OR; Barney Frank, D-MA; Dennis Kucinich, D-OH; Barbara Lee, D-CA; Jim McDermott, D-WA; Pete Stark, D-CA; Lynn Woolsey, D-CA, and former President Obama). The American Legion has also taken up the cause of the Scouts.

Many believe that the term "gay" and the associated term "pride" are misnomers, desperate cover-ups for a sad situation. Even the term "homosexual" was an earlier usage to sanitize the original — "sodomite." Not entirely without reason homosexuals used to be called queer. An old geezer [fn47] I worked with during a summer job on the highway department had a descriptive term for male homosexuals: "cocks---ers." Like ostriches, most people blind themselves to their actual disgusting behavior. Episcopal Bishop Gene Robinson had this to say, "Sticking your you-know-what up someone's rectum is ugly, gross, smelly, unhygienic, and nauseating..." Lesbians, hoping to form a resort called 'Lickalotta,' were evicted by outraged neighbors. [537] Most people don't care to visualize these spectacles. To dignify such behavior as an "alternate life style" is like equating bestiality with kindness to animals. When they parade it in the streets it is time to call a halt.

---

[46] Quite obviously, the Girl Scouts have no such strictures.

[47] Funny, I thought he was an old geezer then, but he was 25 to 30 years younger than I am now

The scene at left thanks to Australia's Endeavour Forum

Teasing homosexual children is insensitive and wrong, but calling it "bullying" or "hate crime" is mischaracterization. Bullying, properly defined, is the threat of physical violence. Anti-bullying measures are a slippery slope to criminalize free speech expressions of disapproval. Anti-homo-sexuals are castigated as bigots, and their attitudes are termed "homophobia." However, that hackneyed, faddish term is a misnomer because its denotation is *fear* of homosexuals. The feeling that homosexuality is wrong is not a phobia; it is an opinion — an understandable one. No one *fears* homosexuals; decent people are simply revolted by their deviant sexual practices. Antics of the misguided nincompoops at the Westboro Baptist Church of Topeka, Kansas, who picket funerals of fallen military personnel purportedly to demonstrate that "God hates fags," do their questionable cause far more harm than good.

A Pew Research survey showed homosexuals are generally unhappy with their condition, [538] and most of them understandably live lives of quiet desperation and self-hatred — contradicting prideful pretense. Studies, including Dr. Michael Bailey's, have shown that subjects are at high risk of suicide. Other research indicates very high levels of violence in homosexual relationships and of sexually transmitted disease. The National Institutes of Health is spending $438,699 to study why LGBTQs get drunk. That shouldn't be a mystery. According to Dr. Paul Cameron of the Family Research Institute, "married" homosexuals live about 24 years less than their married heterosexual counterparts do. Former *Liberator* columnist Muldoon X said AIDS sufferers are screwing themselves to death, and called that disease "A terrible swift sword."

It can be dangerous or costly to speak out against blatant homosexuality. Doing so is criminal in Sweden, Ireland and probably in Canada soon. [539] In California, homosexual mobs spewed hatred and destruction when Proposition 8 passed. [540] In 2009, the beauteous Carrie Prejean spoke against it, and become the new face of opposition, a modern Joan of Arc; her courage cost her the title of Miss USA. The wholesome Anita Bryant lost her sponsors and was driven into bankruptcy, The Benham brothers lost their HGTV show. Pat Buchannan was blacklisted at MSNBC. If objectors should sue me claiming to have been offended by this or other statements herein, I ask where is it written there is a right not to be offended? I should be able to counter-sue for being offended by such foolishness. I also rely on 1st Amendment rights.

I am admittedly no expert on the cause/s of homosexuality (who is?). Blogger J. Grant Dys argues that, with the death of genuine masculinity, an increasing number of young men are seeking to reclaim their manhood in homosexuality. Some, of both sexes, overcompensate by body-building. The undeniable talent and success of many homosexuals may be a reaction to or compensation for an unpleasant childhood. Democrat (presidential candidate, no less) Pete Buttigieg wished he were "straight." Even animals sense that homosexuality is unnatural. This affliction might be caused partially by rebellion against parents, or against society, or both. Almost without exception, they seem to come from dysfunctional families — either an overbearing mother or unreasonably harsh father, or no father, certainly not a normal, attentive father; and usually there is an unnatural fixation on their mothers. In view of the foregoing observations, it would appear that homosexuality could either be a "choice" or not. Whichever, psychiatry may be the cure.

No doubt, some will interpret these words as hating homosexuals. On the contrary, I feel sorry for them as well as for genuine transsexuals, and deplore the environment that caused their afflictions. Despite the appearance of some, they're not all freaks. Some I have met are very pleasant fellows. Some are not. Not much different than most people. Like hemophiliacs and persons with down syndrome, they are accidents of nature, but still God's creatures so should be treated kindly. I had friends and relatives who were victims of the malady.

Homosexual "marriage." It is axiomatic that marriage is the bonding of one man and one woman according to Natural Law. Calling a circle a square doesn't make it a square. Calling something a marriage does not make it a marriage. Same sex couples playing house are not conducive to procreation, therefore inimical to family, therefor germane to the theme of this book.

Children in same sex parent families fare significantly worse than those of opposite sex marriages. [541] Contrary to APA propaganda, scientifically rigorous studies show that children adopted by homosexual parents also do not do well in life. [542] That children of same-sex parents do as well as, or even better than, children from intact, two-parent married households is massively wrong according to a very large thorough study published by the journal *Social Science Research*. It was written by Mark Regnerus, a scholar at the University of Texas. [543] Catholic Pope Francis wisely regarded homosexual adoption as a crime against children.

Former Vice President Joe Biden gave his approval to these couplings by presiding over the "marriage" of Joe Mahshiue and Brian Mosteller at Biden's official residence in Washington, D.C. In a November 2017 postal survey 62 percent of Australians supported homosexual marriage, ensuring Parliament will consider legalizing such weddings.

In the Military.

Public Law 103-160 (10 U.S.C. § 654) mandated that the "Don't ask — don't tell" rule, a lesser-of-two-evils compromise, turns a blind eye to homosexuals in the service. In his State of the Union message on September 20, 2011, Obama strongly supported DADT repeal. The military's former Gay Exclusion law was rescinded. Defense Secretary Robert M. Gates relaxed enforcement of the rules and directed subordinates to come up with a plan for integrating homosexuals. Nevertheless, "Don't ask, don't tell" has served well; no change was needed, certainly not during danger of war. The Pentagon is also considering a legal change to its definition of sodomy. The office of the general counsel proposed decriminalizing consensual sodomy among adults, changing a 55-year-old policy. CNN reported that a waiver was granted a long serving Navy lesbian to remain serving under her (the media's term was "their") preferred gender. Pentagon chief Leon Panetta argued for costly benefits to the unmarried partners of homosexual military personnel, but not to unmarried partners of heterosexual military personnel. In an address to the Human Rights Committee at a large white tie gathering in Washington D.C. on October 10, 2009, President Obama promised to end "discrimination" against homosexuals in the military, and pushed for the U.S. Marine Corps to trade in their traditional covers for a "unisex" hat, giving them a look derided as "girly."

Such changes in policy were opposed by a majority of other military members including Army Gen. Casey, Marine Corps Gen. Conway and Air Force Gen. Schwartz and the heroic Oliver North. Most military members and veterans, people who know most about the issue, oppose integration of homosexuals. In a strongly worded letter, unearthed by the AP, dated April 30, 2010, Defense Secretary Robert Gates and Chairman of the Joint Chiefs of Staff Adm. Mike Mullen told the House Armed Services Committee that this integration policy would be a mistake. The American Legion fruitlessly called on the Justice Department to appeal a 7/6/11 ruling by the Ninth Circuit Court of Appeals to allow homosexuals to serve openly in the military. According to Lt. Colonel John Lewis Cook, USA (ret.) in his brilliant book on the subject, titled The New Golden Boys in the Military, this virus has the potential of killing the military from the inside. The thinking of opponents reflects the military's unique and vulnerable culture, and recognizes that military life is fundamentally different than civilian life. This about-face is bound to undermine morale and order. It has prompted reports that 10% would refuse to re-enlist. Gunnery Sergeant Harry Berres, USMC, said, "When I joined the military it was illegal to be homosexual, then it became optional, and now it's legal. I'm getting out before Obama makes it mandatory." General George Patton, Chesty Puller and their like. must be rolling over in their graves. Stay tuned.

Chapter 2. Social Issues

Marriage and Family — Godsend or Tender Trap?

As the song goes: "Woman needs man, and man must have his mate." Conjugal love is the most desirable and symbiotic relationship there is, "The worldly hope men set their hearts upon," says Omar Khayyam (They call him "the tentmaker," but he was much more than that). If their good natures collude, the relationship is marvelous, but if their bad natures collide, there is hell to pay. A loyal wife is the greatest asset a man can have, far greater than monetary riches, looks or intelligence. Attend to Shakespeare's Sonnet 116 below:

Let me not to the marriage of true minds
Admit impediment. Love is not love
Which alters when it alteration finds,
Or bends with the remover to remove;
Oh no; it is an ever fixed mark,
That looks on tempests, and is never shaken;
it is the star to every wandering bark,
Whose worth's unknown, although its height be taken.
Love's not time's fool, though rosy lips and cheeks
Within his bending sickle's compass come;
Love alters not with his brief hours and weeks,
But bears it out even to the edge of doom.
If this be error, and upon me prov'd,
I never writ, and no man ever lov'd.

The following is reproduced courtesy of D.A. Sears, Managing Editor — In Search Of Fatherhood(R) Forum For and About the Fathers of the World:

Children are a man's heart and soul. His children are his reason for being. They are the reason he rises early in the morning and heads off to a spirit-numbing, backbreaking and mind-bending job for eight, ten and sometimes twelve hours each day. And at the end of the workday, they are the reason he races home. Seeing their faces light up with a smile and hearing gleeful shrieks of "Daddy's Home!" as his children run to greet him when he arrives home makes him forget how tired he is. He nurtures his children. He disciplines them. He mentors them. He inspires them and yes, there are moments, when his children inspire him. Their laughter and sense of wonderment warms his heart and energizes his soul.

It is almost inevitable, and understandable, that attractions change, however ideal marriages are exclusive and permanent, requiring self-discipline. Society's strength is historically proportional to family stability. The natural family is the fundamental social unit, the 'cornerstone of society,' inscribed in human nature, and centered on the union of a man and a woman in the lifelong covenant and sanctity of marriage. The Bush's and Romney's are examples of good families.

Picture a family as a three-legged stool upon which the larger society rests. The legs of the stool represent mother, father and children. If any leg is removed or weakened, society has a precarious perch; fathers are the most vulnerable leg in modern times. Unfortunately, families, in the broad sense, are not the social influences they once were. Writer Mark Steyn said, "When the family dies, the nation follows." To preserve a marriage, it is necessary to choose reality and common sense over fantasy and glamor.

Despite possible drawbacks of marriage, a University of Michigan study finds that men are happier with marriage than women are by a two-to-one margin. According to a Gallup poll, one out of four women claims to be unhappily married; while only one out of 10 men make this claim.

Amneus:

> A man estimates his happiness in marriage relative to the eight hours he spends at a usually dull job. Coming home to be with his family is the high point of his day, after doing double entry bookkeeping, leaning over a drawing board or operating a jack-hammer. A woman has a steady diet of home and family and consequently estimates it lower. There is an optical illusion operating; just as someone who works at Disneyland finds it a rather tedious place, whereas someone who visits it only occasionally thinks it marvelous.

Avoiding the Tender Trap

Sharing life together is a huge commitment, not to be taken lightly. According to an 11/18/2010 study by the Pew Research Center in association with *Time* magazine, four in 10 people say marriage is becoming obsolete. The very terms, "married" and "divorced," are becoming irrelevant. Realistic terms to describe existing conjugal relationships according to their degree of vigor might be more appropriate.

This subchapter is reluctantly included for practical purposes. It is not to be mistaken as advocating completely free experiments in mating. Sometimes both sides of an issue can have merit. Every marriage and every baby born are not the dandy event naive little old ladies consider them. Real, deep love and marriage compatibility requires maturity. Arguments for morality and sanctity of marriage are fine; nevertheless, the realities of life, however stupid and unfortunate, sometimes get in the way.

Humans are always on the prowl for the opposite sex, either consciously or unconsciously. The strong urge to reproduce their kind is inherent in all living creatures, consciously or unconsciously. It has to be strong to entice men (and women) to put up with the perceived faults of the opposite sex. That is why God made pretty girls. Sexual attraction does not always, indeed maybe seldom does, equate to good matches. Divorcing morality from sex diminishes the associated pleasure. Sex and love are two different things. It would be better if they were not, but they are. Therein lies much of the domestic trouble in this world. Unfortunately, peak sexual desire doesn't comport with intellectual maturity. Most modern commentators on sexual issues fixate on the pleasure-receiving aspect of sex, seemingly unaware of the pleasure-giving aspect, which is more rewarding — to the mature. Opposite sex attractions between immature people can be catastrophic. The immensely pleasurable vaginal channel is tender bait to what can be a steel trap. If you take the bait, beware the trap; beware Dulcenia. A little honeymoon advice: When you're in the Garden of Eden, watch out for snakes. Hindsight is 20:20.

As they say, "There are women you marry, and women you screw (maybe when you're drunk); they are seldom the same women." It is important to distinguish between them. Since the triumph of feminism, there are more women to dally with and fewer ladies to marry. Although a man may be interested in a woman sexually (it's the nature of the beast), he might be foolish to marry her. Women of loose morals can be friendly, but not pleasant if you're married to one. On the other hand, I've seen several instances where 'town pumps' turned out to be fairly decent wives, usually with unsuspecting husbands. Most of us have something to hide. Both sexes lie to each other about many things, but women's claims of pre-marital virtue are certainly among the most common lies. Virginity is the greatest honeymoon present that can be bestowed, however seldom it is given these days.

Given the dangers, it might seem foolish to marry. If inordinate liabilities are placed on homeowners, people will prefer to rent rather than buy. So too with marriage. Fifty years ago living together was a daring thing to do; now, getting married is equally so. In view of the undeniable brevity of modern relationships, why pretend that marriage is permanent, and sign a contract to that effect? Why buy the cow when milk is cheap? Cynical though that is, it is hard to argue against. The most popular method to avoid the trap is to avoid marriage, usually by cohabitation, or in the vernacular "shacking up," at least until children arrive.

Common law marriages have been around for centuries. According to the 1970 census, the number of unmarried people living together in the U.S. had risen by 820 percent. About 60 percent of U.S. couples now live together before they first marry, compared with about 10 percent in the late 1960s. [544] Over ten million couples cohabit in the U.S. In view of present circumstances, that may be the best solution for some. But not for the children that forty percent of them have.

Many domestic and foreign intellectuals advocate cohabitation. Reportedly, a law in Yugoslavia requires a one-month period of living together before marriage may be formalized. There is much to be said for this option. Despite the statistics, some people have already evolved to the point where legal and ecclesiastic shackles, previously necessary to insure the marriage bond, can be replaced with personal integrity and discipline. Both social pressure, which modernism has largely removed, and desire can preserve the family unit; and of these, desire is more effective. Ties of love bind stronger than those of law. And, thanks to social engineering, there are tax advantages. [545]

Caveat Emptor! The legal dangers of marriage can apply almost equally to cohabitants. It is advisable to minimize dangers by obtaining a signed, notarized statement to the effect that both are aware that their arrangement is not an 'authorized' marriage. Informal unions cannot avoid all legal difficulties, but they do take a more realistic approach to the probabilities of termination, and permit the planning and conduct of one's affairs accordingly. If breakups occur, as they often do, this arrangement will at least spice its duration and ease the pain.

Arguments against cohabitation

While maybe fun, playing house does not augur well for marriage. Like homosexual marriage, cohabitation flies in the face of the stabilizing norms of marriage. Traditional marriage signifies a greater degree of commitment and a more positive attitude toward that commitment, as opposed to just a vehicle for sex. Maggie Gallagher says "Cohabitation not only undercuts marriage, but it also produces less stable marriages.

Axinn and Thornton found that "cohabiting significantly increases young people's acceptance of divorce." [546] David Hall: "Women who lived common-law before their first marriages have a 33 percent greater risk of divorce at any time in their marriage than... women who do not cohabit before their first marriage." [547] In 90 percent of cohabitations, at least one of the sex partners expects the arrangement to end in marriage. Almost half will be disappointed. A plain woman — plain outside or inside — might have to cohabit to obtain some of the benefits of marriage, but a beautiful woman — outside or inside — doesn't have to sell herself so cheaply. She can usually hold out for all the benefits. The formula for success in this world is Education, Job, Marriage, Babies — in that order. Self-evident to the mature but not necessarily to the young, this advice is supported by Sawhill and Haskins of the center-left Brookings Institution. We may yet discover that the families of the old-fashioned, conformist forties and fifties were not so dumb after all.

The law, as written, encourages unscrupulous women to lure sex-dumbed men into checkbook daddyhood." Condemning women who get pregnant intentionally and "turn casual sex into cash-flow sex," she notes, "in no other arena is a swindler rewarded with a court-ordered monthly cash settlement paid to them by the person they bilked..." A low class woman might seek out a guy with a decent job, get him to knock her up (him too dumb to use contraceptives; her too smart...). She expects marriage and a comfortable life, not otherwise in the cards for her.

There was a billboard somewhere in Kansas reading, "What do you call a guy who gets a woman pregnant, then abandons her?" Well, I ask what do you call a woman who intentionally (in this day and age) gets pregnant to trap a man into marriage? Gold digger? What do you call a guy who falls for it? Sucker? Penelope Leach, in her book <u>Children First</u>, poses an essential question: "Why is it socially reprehensible for a man to leave a baby fatherless, but courageous, even admirable, for a woman to have a baby whom she knows will be so?

Morality and Marriage
Marriage Depends on Morality

Moral breakdown may be as dangerous to civilization as military defeat. Immorality destroys marriage. Divorce destroys men, families and society itself.

We are engaged in a cultural war a war about values, some of which should be intuitively obvious. Moral admonitions may amount to little more than losing rear guard objections to encroaching hedonism; nevertheless, righteousness and saving marriage (therefore saving males) dictates that moral issues be addressed. The eminent philosopher James Q. Wilson said, "To defend morality is to defend the indefensible;" however I shall try — from my perspective, because restoration of traditional values is an integral part of salvaging the institution of marriage and restoring the great country that many of us grew up in.

Decadence took a steep plunge in the 60s, to the disadvantage of both sexes. An ideology propounded by Kinsey and Hefner abounds. In the modern idiom, conventional morality is "weird." The "new morality" now is simply the old immorality. Yesterday's tarts [fn48] are today's healthy, empowered young women; today's tarts are celebrities – exemplified in the "girls gone wild" phenomenon and college 'Spring Break' antics. Men hang around these women like dogs after a bitch in heat. Paraphrasing contemporary activist, Paul Elam, "women play the sex card, relying on pure blind human biology, the same way they did on the plains of Africa a million years ago." Feminist attorney Riane Eisler calls this atmosphere "the reclamation of nothing less than woman's ancient sexual power. Such women do not apologize; they flaunt it as a sacred right and glory in it as striking a blow for women's independence from patriarchy. Formerly they would have been condemned as bad women and unsuitable marriage material. The feminist revolution considers condemnation to be "sexist," hoping to obliterate the distinction between good and bad women.

The WE Fest is an annual "music" festival held in Northwestern Minnesota (before Covid). A knowledgeable person informed me that a nearby Walmart store sold pallets of condoms and morning-after pills in conjunction with the occasion. The head of the San Francisco Unified School District (SFUSD) proposed a policy that would hand out condoms to students as young as 12-years-old without their parents' knowledge. Teachers in Gervais, Oregon handed out condoms to students, sixth-graders on up. [548] A study published in the <u>Archives of Pediatric & Adolescent Medicine</u> suggests that abstinence education works well; [549] nevertheless the Obama administration cancelled funding for such programs. [550]

Nebraska Senator Ben Sasse perceptively describes many millennials as living in a state of perpetual adolescence. A respected social research team concluded that they are also confused and ignorant on moral matters. [551] No wonder sexually transmitted diseases are on the rise. When the Gallup polling company released its most predictable findings of the year asking if the state of moral values in America is, "getting better" or "worse," 72% of Americans responded "worse." [552] Aleksandr Solzhenitsyn concurs on the issue of current decadence. James Buckley says, "In recent decades "we have witnessed an erosion of moral standards and self-discipline that has given us among the civilized world's highest incidence of crime, abortion, pornography, drug abuse, [fn49] and illegitimacy, as well as some corporate scandals of Olympian proportions." Now, we inhabit a hyper-sexualized, coarsened culture. Miniskirts at funerals, my God! [fn50] Mimicking movies and TV, we have public cussing — sewage on parade.

---

[48] There are male sluts, but their image — understandably — isn't as bad as female ones. See Chivalry trade-offs under Normal Sex Roles in Chapter1.

[49] Drug overdoses kill more people in the U.S. than guns or autos.

[50] To me, long dresses can be sexier than short ones.

The half-time "entertainment" at the 2020 Super Bowl football game was straight SEX. Vulgar rap lyrics entertain a certain segment of society. Schoolkids are now tweeting nude pictures of themselves, calling it "sexting." New Hampshire had to ban high school dances because of things like "doggy dancing," "horizontal hulas," etc. I have heard of girls having sex with boys they don't even like. Engaging in sex without love is unrewarding and disgusting. There is no condom for the heart.

We have an age similar to that which Shakespeare described as nothing but stealing and fighting and "getting of wenches with child." The U.S. proportion of births to unmarried women is just over 40 percent. [553] Something must be terribly wrong when democrats boo mention of God in their 2012 convention platform, and Boy Scouts must declare bankruptcy due to numbers of scout leaders molesting young boys.

George Bernard Shaw said that America was the first country to pass from barbarism to decadence without passing through civilization. He may have been too pessimistic about the interim period. Charles Krauthammer (RIP) was the mentally toughest, smartest media personality I have ever observed. In a class by himself. If he said the moon was made of cheese, I would believe it. To paraphrase him, 'it will take mid-20th century thinking to save the 21st century from itself.'

Morality and manhood are evidently frowned upon in the social media: Facebook deleted videos on "masculine men" and "moderate Muslims" posted by the nonprofit conservative education site Prager U, and it "shadow banned" nine politically incorrect posts labeling them "hate speech." D. James Kennedy Ministries (DJKM) filed a lawsuit against the Southern Poverty Law Center (SPLC), the charity navigation organization GuideStar, and Amazon for defamation, religious discrimination, and trafficking in falsehood. The SPLC listed DJKM as a "hate group," while GuideStar also categorized it in those terms, and Amazon kept the ministry off of its charity donation program, Amazon Smile. [554]

Speaking to the World Congress of Families in Mexico City in March, 2004, John Howard, Senior Fellow at the Howard Center in Rockford, Illinois, stated an important truism: "The family and sexual liberation cannot co-exist... They are mutually exclusive." Promiscuity is self-damaging, especially for women. Nevertheless, our best hope would appear to be a resurgence of morality and probably patriarchy. It's worth a try.

Divorce: Background, Statistics, Criteria

The American family has become destabilized for well over four decades. Marriage, once called a sacrament, appears to be in serious jeopardy of relegation to the realm of ritualism, chastity belts, and other things anachronistic. Legal and social notions have reduced it to the status of an experiment, one of the games people play. The vow, "...until death do us part," has become almost a fairy tale. "As long as our love shall last" has replaced it in some modern ceremonies. The odds of survival are worse than those in Russian roulette. You can buy "Congratulations on your divorce" cards at drug stores.

Comprehensive, detailed statistics on marriage and divorce are difficult to determine. Coming from various sources, not all statistics agree with others. There was an accelerating curve of divorce from 7% of marriages in 1860 to the current expectation of around one-half. The rate increased 5.23 percent in the 100 years between 1867 and 1967 and 80 percent between 1960 and 1972. [555] For every 100 U.S. marriages, 49 are aborted by divorce. [556] According to the Centers for Disease Control, forty three percent of all first marriages end in divorce within 10 years. Dr. Wade Horn said 40 percent of first marriages end in divorce, contrasted with 16 percent in 1960. [557] In many areas, like San Mateo County, California, divorces consistently outpace marriages. The U.S. census bureau reports that single-adult households have replaced nuclear family households. In the year 2000, for every one hundred children born into this country, only forty reached maturity living with Mom and Dad. [558]

Stanley Kurtz writes that marriage is already destroyed in Scandinavian countries, where half of all children are now born out of wedlock. [559] Sweden leads the U.S. in divorces. Inese Šlesere, Secretary of the Latvian Parliament's Human Rights Subcommittee, informs us that the divorce rate there is 60 percent. [560]

The marriage contract, in addition to having a certain sanctity ("What, therefore, God hath joined together, let not man put asunder." — Mark 10:9), is a legal instrument specifying fidelity, "for better or for worse." Historically, one needed a good reason to divorce, i.e., fault in a partner. That is no longer the situation.

There are two basic divorce criteria — fault and "No-fault." The latter was first implemented in the Prussian General Code, of 1791-94. Lenin introduced it in Russia after the Communist Revolution. Later, U.S. "Progressives" brought it to these shores. It has now been adopted in some form in all states of the U.S. The reasons usually given are "growing apart" or "not feeling loved or appreciated." Fault and No-fault criteria have both good and bad facets, and generate many opinions both for and against, discussed below.

Fault divorce laws required a demonstration of fault against one of the parties. Even a couple whose only problem was incompatibility had to maintain that "grounds" existed. The system permitted, actually required, one protagonist to seize upon and magnify often average human imperfections into an inventory of divorce-justifying bad behavior. Guilt, with "guilty" and "injured" parties, had to be established or created. The claim was more important than its authenticity.

Divorce-bound persons, in need of an excuse to the courts, to themselves, to children, and to friends, are adept at invention and exaggeration. Obviously one should not believe everything derogatory one hears from a divorce litigant about the other. It must be taken with a big dose of salt. Typically, when fault criteria held sway men were almost universally considered the guilty parties and women the innocent parties, regardless of facts. Dr. Jessie Bernard, in her book Remarriage, reported that many former wives invented tales of cruelty, eccentricity, or sexual foibles to blacken their ex-husband's reputation.

Lord knows how many women were given divorces for frivolous reasons. One sixty-year-old California woman received a divorce on grounds of cruelty because her husband did all the work around the house, wouldn't even let her make the breakfast coffee. That, she told the judge, made her nervous and caused her "grievous mental suffering." Other such absurdities have included the husband not taking the wife for auto rides, and getting home at 10 p.m., then keeping her awake by talking. In Durham, England, Mrs. Eva Hovell got a divorce on grounds of cruelty because she didn't like the color her husband painted the house.

It was difficult to prove fault against women. They were generally always presumed innocent of wrongdoing. Courts usually squelched attempts to prove them guilty of anything serious. Adultery, like perjury, is a crime in most states, and punishable severely in some. Not so these days. A man who with a detective watched his wife have intercourse with another man was denied a divorce on grounds of adultery because of "entrapment." The court rationalized he could have stopped her. A married woman had a man other than her husband in her apartment from 9:30 p.m. to 5:30 a.m. They were both observed in the bathroom several times, nude or in nightclothes. The court believed her story that they were playing Chinese checkers, and the visitor was unable to leave due to illness — "Not guilty of adultery." [561] One man found gathering evidence to this end was ordered to cease "bothering" her.

Men who still have faith in justice still try proving these activities in divorce courts; neither favorable outcomes nor prosecutions are forthcoming. It is a waste of time even bringing these issues to the attention of a judge.

Men could be divorced for doing practically anything, or not doing the same thing. They were damned if they did and damned if they didn't. A sophistic curiosity called "constructive desertion" permitted a woman to leave a man under some pretext, and then divorce him on grounds of desertion. The New Jersey Superior Court for Union County decided that a wife could acquiesce in her husband's departure and still charge him with desertion. I no longer have that citation.

Often, one is actually more guilty of something than is the other; and often, but not more often, it is the male. Often the woman has been injured, but not more often than the man has been. There are very few innocent parties to divorce. If nothing else, they are guilty of poor judgment.

Fault grounds were implemented for the same reasons that fault was put into libel, slander, contracts, and other tort law: to protect both the injured and the injurer. As we frown on duels, vendettas, shooting of editors and 'collecting my money out of your hide' so do we also frown on outraged husbands killing adulterous wives and their lovers?

It is true, justice does not always require, nor dignity permit, the unnecessary ranging of individual against individual, making enemies of those who may not already be so. The presumption of fault, in the usual sense, can be wrong — terribly so. Dr. Levy, writing in, The Happy Family, said that he had never seen a case where the responsibility for conflict "could be laid exclusively, or even primarily, at the door to either partner." Mr. Justice Hofstadter said, "Generally family break-ups are not due to specific acts of either spouse, legal fiction notwithstanding. They result rather from a general malaise to which both have contributed." Fault usually comes after malaise has set in. It is the symptom, not the cause, of domestic discord.

The National Association of Women Lawyers claims credit for pioneering No-fault divorce, which it describes as "the greatest project NAWL has ever undertaken." As early as 1947, NAWL began promoting No-fault divorce to bar associations and state governments. I knew a prominent divorce reformer, nice fella, who favored no fault divorce laws because he was accused by his divorcing wife, accurately, of being alcoholic.

Arguments Against No-fault. The First Amendment either prohibits legislation of morality or it does not; we should not have a double standard. If the law can prohibit gambling, prostitution, and selling of merchandise on Sunday, it can recognize moral turpitude as a factor in divorce and custody. Separation of church and state should not require rejection of all moral considerations or hostility to religion. [fn51] Thomas Jefferson's phrase, 'wall between church and state,' does not appear in the Constitution; and even if it did, should not require rejection of morality.

---

51 Curiously, the ACLU does not demand separation of the state from Islamic practices.

Joseph D'Agostino, vice president for Communications at the Population Research Institute, says, "(N)o-fault divorce laws render a marriage compact less legally enforceable than a cell-phone contract." Writer David French says a marriage is less legally binding than a refrigerator warranty. Marriage contracts are now worth what Sam Goldyn thought verbal contracts were worth — nothing. In his exposé entitled Why No One Is Married, Ed Truncellito JD, describes marriages in the No-fault era as "registered cohabitation." Judy Parejko, a Wisconsin author with professional experience in divorce mediation, has written an intriguing book on this subject, Stolen Vows: The Illusion of No-fault Divorce and The Rise of the American Divorce Industry. Canada's *National Post* writer, George Jonas, had this to say:

If divorce reform reduced marriage from something made in Heaven to something made on earth, it took the concept of "No-fault divorce" to remove all value from it. When the law declared that it couldn't judge matrimonial disputes and would henceforth treat spouses who kept their marriage vows the same as those who repudiated them, it put a once-sacramental institution on the legal footing of a gambling debt... The coup-de-grace was delivered by giving common-law unions virtually the same legal standing as marriage. This, in effect, abolished the institution. Where all couples are "married," no couples are.

A social catastrophe that amounts to divorce on demand, it gives blessing to much sin at the expense of innocent parties. "No-fault" divorce laws are responsible for depriving families of the legal protections once offered by the institution of marriage. Hear Maggie Gallagher: "Marriage is one of the few contracts in which the law explicitly protects the defaulting party at the expense of his or her partner." [562] In Divorce Revolution, Lenore Weitzman writes, "the state becomes an ally of the spouse who wants to get divorced." This is true especially if that spouse is female. If the little woman wants out for even the poorest of reasons, that is all that's needed. When one's life and fortune have been premised on another's sworn word, should there not be a penalty for defaulting?

Unilateral No-fault divorce is not only a breach of (the marriage) contract, but creates an ex post facto situation. Article one, Section Ten of the United States Constitution states, "No state shall pass any ... law impairing the obligation of contracts." None may shed his contractual duties simply because he wants to. No business could operate without a well-defined law of contracts. Why should the marriage contract be less important?

Violation of these contracts by divorce courts is undermining our very society. No-fault would destroy Constitutional rights to petition the government for redress of grievances and would eliminate considerations of right and wrong. While the No-fault divorce basis was meant to eliminate unnecessary enmity, the airing of dirty linen and conflict, it could be even worse than the fault basis. Without fault (consideration of right and wrong), the only criterion left upon which to decide issues is sex: woman equals custody, man equals bills. Divorce, viewed through that prism bodes ill for men. No-fault, for a man, is like going from the guillotine to the gas chamber; it becomes simpler and less messy to kill him. Under it, a person could lose an ancestral farm worked by his family for generations to a tramp mate of a few years and not even be permitted to raise the issue of her conduct in the marriage.

No-fault seldom applies to men; allegations of abuse are still used for tactical advantage. This ploy is resorted to in an astonishing number of cases. An Illinois lawyer called the practice "Divorce gamesmanship," but dirty pool is not a game. In Hawaii, out of 5,455 divorces requested in 2004, all but 661 of them included allegations of domestic violence, precipitating temporary restraining orders. This nonsense triggered passage of Hawaii Senate Resolution 40 regarding the misuse of TROs (temporary restraining orders) in family law. Myrna Murdoch went to a judge and requested a restraining order against her cat named "Magic." The request was granted.

"The best-laid schemes o' mice an' men Gang aft agley" (With apology to Robert Burns). No-fault divorce and the subsequent practice of awarding mother custody demonstrate the Law of Unintended Consequences. It is empirically provable that the more No-fault divorce incentive there is the more divorce there is. There have been dramatic increases in divorce after passage of No-fault divorce statutes. [563], [52]

This is not what California Governor Ronald Reagan had in mind when he signed the first No-fault divorce bill into law. Some state officials are beginning to admit that they might have gone too fast in adopting No-fault legislation, notably Los Angeles County California's Superior Court Judge Nancy Wilson.

When moving in the wrong direction, any speed is too fast. We now sit, dazed, at the bottom of that slippery slope. Thanks, Legislators and Judges!

Health Matters

Why are men dropping like flies? A look at the 10 leading causes of death in 1996 reveals the reasons for the life span gender gap. For every one of the 10 leading causes of disease, men are at higher risk

---

[52] In New Hampshire "irreconcilable differences" (No-fault) became a legal ground for divorce on August 29, 1971. In the five-year period from 1969 to 1973, New Hampshire had a 740 percent increase in contested divorces without children, and a 187 percent increase in contested divorces with children.

than women are. For heart disease, men have a risk 82% higher than
women do. For four causes of death-injuries, HIV infection, suicide,
and homicide — men are at more than twice the risk.

Leading Causes of Death by gender/sex: (Figures below are age-
adjusted rates per 100,000 populations. Source: DHHS: Health, U.S.,
1998.

Cause of Death	Men	Women	Excess Male Mortality
Heart disease	178.8	98.2	82.1%
Cancer	153.8	17.9	41.4%
Injuries	3.3	17.9	141.9%
Stroke	8.5	24.6	-15.9%
Diabetes	4.9	12.5	-19.2%
Pneumonia/flu	16.2	10.4	55.8%
HIV infection	8.1	4.2	331.0%
Suicide	8.0	4.0	350.0%
Homicide	13.3	3.6	269.4%

Using the now-familiar "woman-as-the-greater-victim" strategy,
feminists alleged that women were being mistreated by the male-
dominated medical establishment. In 1990, Senator Barbara Mikulski
of Maryland accused the National Institutes of Health of "blatant
discrimination" for spending only 13.5% of its research budget on
women's health. It was known at the time that NIH also devoted 6.5%
of its research funds to afflictions unique to men, and the remainder of
the money went to study diseases that affect both sexes. Why Senator
Mikulski chose to ignore the latter figure is unknown.

In 1991, Bernadine Healy, MD, the first female director of the
National Institutes of Health, charged that "women have all too often
been treated less than equally" in health care. That same year, 83,340
more men than women died in the United States. By 1993, it had
become received wisdom that women were chronically short-changed in
their healthcare.

Numerous research studies refuted the feminists' allegations. For
example, an article by Andrew G. Kadar, MD in the August 1994 issue
of *The Atlantic Monthly* debunked the sex-bias myth that healthcare
services favored men. If anything, the reverse was true: Dr. Kadar
pointed out that from 1981 onwards, research funding for breast cancer
exceeded funding for prostate cancer by a ratio of about five to one
(More on this below).

As far as the "exclusion" of women from drug trials, this policy arose
from the 1962 thalidomide disaster, in which armless babies were born
to women who had ingested a dangerous drug during their pregnancy.

To claim that drug trials discriminated against women is akin to saying that women are discriminated against because they are not subject to the mandatory registration requirements of the Selective Service, which proves the point that a single false allegation can carry more weight than a hundred carefully reasoned denials.

To rectify the perceived mistreatment of women, a myriad of women's health initiatives were spun out, four of which have grave implications for men:

1. PHS Office on Women's Health. In 1993, the first Deputy Assistant Secretary for Women's Health was appointed to direct the Office on Women's Health. The Office was located in the fortress-like Hubert Humphrey Building in Washington, D.C. Five years later, the Office on Women's Health could boast the establishment of the following initiatives in the U.S. Public Health Service: PHS Coordinating Committee on Women's Health, Establishment of women's health coordinators in each of the 10 DHHS regions, Federal Breast Cancer Coordinating Committee, Federal Task Force on Women's Health and the Environment, Federal Multi-Agency Consortium on Imaging Technologies to Improve Women's Health, Establishment of 12 National Centers of Excellence in Women's Health, National Action Plan on Breast Cancer, Minority Women's Health Initiative, Compendium of DHHS Activities on Women and HIV/AIDS, National Women's Health Information Center, National Domestic Violence Hotline, National College Roundtables on Women's Health, Girl Power! to promote girls' self-esteem, Eating Disorders Task Force, National Osteoporosis Prevention Campaign, DHHS Resource Guide on Women's Health, Women's Health Curriculum, National Mentoring Program to promote women in academic medicine, National Directory of Women's Health Residency and Fellowship, Opportunities in Medicine, Menopause Resource Guide, Participation in international programs, including the WHO Global Commission of Women's Health, the Working Group on Women's Health of the US-Mexico Bi-national Commission, the Canada-US Forum on Women's Health, and the USA/Israeli Women's Health Conference. The price tag for these efforts: $4.4 billion in FY 1999.

Note, the foregoing list includes only department-wide women's health initiatives. Many other female-specific programs are found throughout the federal health bureaucracy. For example, the National Institutes of Health, which has its own Office of Research on Women's Health, has devoted considerable sums to disease-specific research on women's health, including breast cancer, cervical cancer, and reproductive health. The Health Resources and Services Administration (HRSA) operates a Maternal and Child Health Bureau. The Food and Drug Administration and Centers for Disease Control and Prevention have both established Offices on Women's Health. The U.S. Agency for International Development has devoted considerable resources to female reproductive control. The Department of Defense operates a major breast cancer research program. The list goes on and on.

2. Healthy People 2010. Every 10 years the federal government takes the pulse of the nation's health. Known as *Healthy People*, the gargantuan process includes a review of key health indicators and setting objectives for the upcoming decade. *Healthy People* serves as the blueprint for healthcare programs and funding.

In September 1999, DHHS Secretary Donna Shalala released the draft for the upcoming decade. *Healthy People 2010*, a four-pound paper behemoth, outlines health objectives for everything from food safety to tooth decay. And it has a great deal to say about women's health. It highlights the fact, due to their longevity, women are more likely to suffer from arthritis, osteoporosis, and other disabling conditions.

The *Healthy People* draft conveniently omits many key facts:
• Men are still dying of heart disease at almost twice the rate as women.
• Men are victims of 94% of occupational deaths.
• Men represent 30-35% of persons who require medical attention as a result of domestic violence.
• Men in community settings, are raped at a rate of 2/10,000 each year, and the problem is much greater in correctional settings.
• Men are victims of aggravated assault far more often than women (32.8/1,000 vs. 19.4/1,000)
• The 1.2 million men over 50 who suffer from osteoporosis need special attention because men are less likely to seek medical care

In fact, of 38 gender-specific objectives, 36 are directed to women. Only two are devoted to men. Over and over again, Healthy People 2010 downplays and ignores men's health.

3. The American Association of Health Plans (AAHP) represents the 1,000 health maintenance organizations (HMOs) and managed care plans that provide medical care to well over 140 million Americans.

What is the AAHP doing to advance women's health?
• Identification of exemplary models of women's health care in the areas of breast cancer, obstetrics, prenatal care, hormone replacement therapy, and (of course!) domestic violence.
• Fact Sheet on "Access to Specialty Care: Women's Experience in Health Plans"
• Bright Futures, a five-year cooperative agreement with the federal Maternal and Child Health Bureau
• Frequent articles in their monthly magazine on women's health

What is AAHP doing for men's health? Nada. Not a farthing.

Statistics, Disparate expenditures

Aron Kipnis, psychologist and author of <u>Knights Without Armor</u>, says that males account for 70% of all assault victims, 80% of all homicide victims, 85% of the homeless, 90% of persons with AIDS, and 93% of persons killed on the job (not to mention wars). Consequently, men currently die on average five years earlier than women do, and women are more likely to survive to collect social security than are men.

Despite the longevity statistics, there is an almost frantic obsession with women's health. Men are largely excluded from national health initiatives. Medical research expenditures demonstrate a strong preference for women. Gordon E. Finley, Ph.D. observes, "It seems that under 'Obama Care,' boys and men will lose." Harry Reid's (D-NV) behind-closed-doors-deal-busting bill established yet five more Offices of Women's Health throughout the federal government on top of at least five existing Offices of Women's Health, and further specifies that none can be combined. Nowhere in Reid's bill, nor in any federal agency, was there an Office of Men's Health."

Rarely has men's health become an issue. Senator Mike Crapo and former Congressman Randy "Duke" Cunningham, both Republicans — the former diagnosed with prostate cancer, introduced companion bills in the 109th Congress which would establish an Office of Men's Health at the U.S. Department of Health and Human Services. This office would mirror the work of the existing Office of Women's Health, which has helped to save thousands of women's lives and has improved the lives of many more. It would coordinate the fragmented men's health awareness, prevention, and research efforts being conducted by federal and state governments. It would promote preventative health behaviors, and provide a vehicle whereby researchers on men's health could network and share information and findings. It would be interesting to observe what opposition arose, and by whom. Granted, we spend more on experimental research for men. Warren Farrell says it is for the same reason we use rats in experimental research.

Veterans' health care is a scandal; not considered an entitlement, [564] it has been grossly under-funded according to former American Legion Commander Paul Morin. [565] Many veterans have died waiting long periods for treatment at veterans' hospitals, [566] another illustration of the government's incompetence to run things. I would like to see the V. A. cover private insurance.co-payments for veterans.

Obamacare epitomizes the ineptness of government involvement in health care. Reportedly this scheme gave people subsidies of more than $800 billion. The Obama Administration required insurance plans and/or taxpayers to provide free breast feeding equipment, breast implants (without even co-payments), abortion services and

contraceptives etc., etc. for women under the pretext of "health care." [fn53]
Vibrators are considered medical devices. Taxpayer-funded cervical
cancer shots are proposed for all females age 9 and upward, so as to
permit promiscuity without danger. A clamor arose to keep frequent
mammograms and cervix screenings in public health plans despite
statistics showing they are not cost effective. *The Huffington Post Live*
held a discussion about a topic in employment: whether women deserve
paid menstrual leave. [567] Women's migraine headaches are a larger
concern than men's migraines. [568]

Circumcision of both males and females are an attempt to improve
on God's design. When practiced on women in Africa, this procedure is
looked upon with horror, but raises few eyebrows when done to infant
boys in much greater numbers. Non-therapeutic circumcision of male
minors is a barbaric and generally unnecessary procedure, according to
the American Academy of Pediatrics. Akin to 1940s doctors singing the
praises of cigarette brands, it is recommended by doctors to earn extra
dollars (total cost is upwards of $1,750). Some claim it is primarily
subscribed to by mothers too lazy to clean their sons' penises. At some
sick psychological level, the practice may even be directed by mothers
at maleness per se. The Royal Dutch Medical Association and
related medical-scientific organizations in The Netherlands discourage
circumcision. Australia also seems to be emerging from the dark ages.
Australian Activist Alan Barron reports that non-therapeutic
circumcision is banned from public hospitals in that country.

Cancer, breast vs. prostate

Men are 20 percent more likely than women to contract cancer and
40 percent more likely to die from it. Breast and prostate cancer kill
almost equal numbers of men and women. Prostate cancer is the most
common cause of cancer deaths in American men after lung cancer.
Doctors tell us all men will get prostate cancer if they live long enough,
but no comparable recognition of or interest in prostate cancer exists.
Research funding is blatantly sexist. Warren Farrell's The Myth of
Male Power documents that 660% more money is spent on breast
cancer research — the one cancer that kills mostly women — than on
prostate cancer research. The September '96 issue of *Scientific
American* cited research showing almost 5 times as much money is
spent for breast cancer research as for prostate cancer research. It is
better in the U.K., where one fourth of monies spent on breast cancer
research is spent on prostate cancer research. [569]

Theresa Morrow of the organization Women against Prostate
Cancer, on May 28, 2008 stated to the Healthy People's Stakeholders

---

53 By a vote of 7-0, the city council approved a resolution recognizing March 10 as Abortion Providers Appreciation
Day in St. Paul, Minnesota.

meeting at the National Institute of Health Conference Center that, "women's health," including funding for breast, cervical and ovarian cancer, receives a little more than 13 times the funding that prostate cancer receives." The National Prostate Cancer Coalition [570] informs us that the U.S. Senate cut prostate cancer research. This means less hope for the over 2 million men living with the disease and their families, and the over 230,000 men who will be diagnosed with prostate cancer yearly. [fn54]

October being "Breast cancer awareness" month, pink accoutrements are the fad: the White House exterior was bathed in pink lighting on Oct. 24th, 2013, and the Empire State building was subsequently bathed in pink. The same with professional and college football stadiums, including officials uniforms and field decorations — ironic, inasmuch as participants are men (in contrast, the Minnesota Twins team has been donating to the Prostate Cancer Foundation). The Navy even painted a fighter jet pink. Additionally, there is a "Women's Health Day" during which the mainstream media on TV was seen wearing pinkish-red clothing. A campaign by Kentucky Fried Chicken featuring a pink-colored bucket was created to generate money.

To pretend fairness, the U.S. post office issued breast cancer and prostate cancer stamps. At the time, the breast cancer stamp cost 40¢ with seven cents going to breast cancer research. The first run of 200 million produced $14 million for breast cancer research. The prostate cancer stamp cost 33¢ with no proceeds for prostate cancer research.

To devote ever-increasing resources to women's health, when men are more vulnerable, is a violation of the basic public health principle of allocating resources to those at greatest risk. The lives of hundreds of thousands of men will continue to be threatened unless action is taken to combat this growing crisis. The popular attitude is, 'So what?' If it were the other way around, the outcry would be deafening, countless studies would be undertaken, and millions of dollars would be thrown at the disaster.

The crucial task is to develop a better test for prostate cancer — one that can distinguish between the slow-growing, non-threatening tumors and the more aggressive kind. On this score, there is some good news. Scientists at the Institute of Cancer Research announced that they had identified a gene — E2F3 — that could be the answer. "Now we know that the E2F3 gene is key in determining how aggressive the (prostate) cancer is," says Professor Cooper, "we hope to be able to develop such a test in the next five years." The latest promising test is the Oncotype DX Genomic Prostate Score. A new procedure, "MRI guidance" is

---

[54] I have lost several friends to that scourge.

showing promise. Abriaterone and Avastin are two newer medications in late trials that also show promise. A study published in *The International Journal of Oncology* found that a compound of natural ingredients suppressed prostate cancer by 27 percent. Provange is an effective prostate cancer treatment medicine. But because it is expensive, bureaucrats aspire to discontinue coverage under Medicare and Medicaid [571] Beneficial advances have also been occurring in imaging systems. It would help greatly if the imbalance of research funds were eliminated or even reversed.

Men with breast cancer are the only class of patients barred from Medicaid coverage by their sex. A South Carolina construction worker Raymond Johnson was denied Medicaid coverage for breast cancer treatments because he is a man. Finally, men's cancer issues are gaining attention, but not from government. Movember is an pitifully small annual charity event involving the growing of moustaches during the month of November to raise awareness of men's health issues, such as prostate and other male cancers. Check it out at Movember.com. More information here: [572]

Part III. Defences: reformation, dammit!

Chapter 1. Law and Policy

The central imperatives in sexual/gender fairness should be Equal Protection of Law and Due Process of Law. Any Equal Rights Amendment or Women's Equality Amendment should not be adopted without amendments permitting reasonable distinction between the sexes. This would save girls' sports from ruination by testosterone-advantaged boys, and prevent implementation of co-ed prisons. [573]

Reason demands consistency of law application. One set of litigants must not receive different treatment than another. Offenders must be held accountable. Simplistic suggestions for legal reform usually advocate changing law, but most law is fair on its face. Application of the law, sophistry and word parsing within it are problems. Confused, contradictory law must be examined in light of underlying moral issues. "Legal" and "illegal" must be made to more closely conform to right and wrong.

Income tax codes that discriminate against married persons should be abolished. According to a report by *PJ Media*, married couples can save thousands of dollars on healthcare premiums if they get a divorce and continue to live together. The nation-wide bluenose DUI laws declaring drivers drunk with blood alcohol levels as low as .08%, [fn55] are blatant violation of states' pushed by the prudish Mothers Against Drunk Driving organization — (MADD), and aimed primarily at men. The politically correct U.S. Senate voted 99 to 1 in favor of passage (The lone holdout was Fred Thompson). The federal government unconstitutionally coerced states into passing these laws. Even more preposterousness comes from the National Transportation Safety Board that now wants to decrease the legal driving limit to one drink, lowering the legal limit on blood-alcohol content to 0.05 "or even lower." [574] That could almost obtain by walking past a saloon (and there are probably bluenoses and pecksniffs who would like to jail us for that). A congressional proposal surfaced to tax cigars by as much as $10 apiece. Guess which sex mostly smokes cigars. Making laws and their applications more realistic, and severely punishing *actual* offenders would be more just and effective.

Litigants must be protected from barratry, exploitation, and aggravation. Judges should not be free to rewrite statutes to say what

---

[55] Any athlete, perhaps even ex-athlete, should be OK to drive at that level.

they would like, or what they believe to be better social policy. To avoid manipulation of records by judges, litigants should be permitted to record proceedings. One such worthy became livid when he saw me doing so.

Domestic Relations

Domestic relationships are too important, dignified, and delicate to be administered in the present manner. Unless marriage is permanent and sacred, it becomes an increasingly vulnerable and embattled institution that collapses before every temptation and crisis. The law must protect men from false paternity accusations, and permit their paternity inquiries.

Former president George W. Bush acknowledged his belief in the importance of marriage. His administration called for $360 million a year to be spent on pro-marriage research and activities as part of welfare reform, but the legislation became tied up in a quarrelsome senate. [575] President Trump believes people are taking advantage of the welfare system, and has instructed staffers to "work on a major reform proposal" and draft an executive order that would outline administration principles and direct agencies to come up with recommendations. In January 2018, the Trump administration rewrote the rules on health care for the poor, allowing states to require able-bodied Medicaid recipients to work, an order bitterly opposed by Democrats. Kentucky and Minnesota may already have this requirement. At least 10 states have proposed requiring some Medicaid recipients to work or participate in activities such as skills training, education, job search, volunteering or caregiving, with pregnant women and "medically frail" people exempted — though frailty is not defined. Those states, mostly Republican, include Arizona, Arkansas, Indiana, Kansas, Kentucky, Maine, New Hampshire, North Carolina, Utah and Wisconsin.

Iowa may set a good example for other states in national family politics. Its shared parenting legislation may have national implications. Though the Democrat party line had previously been against it, the bill passed the Iowa Senate unanimously, and was signed by Democrat Governor Thomas Vilsack. U.S. Senator Charles Grassley (R-IA), original lead sponsor of the Parental Rights and Responsibilities Act (PRRA), is reputed by many to be the most pro-family member of the US Senate.

Application of the elementary behavioral principles — positive and negative motivation — is necessary for divorce reform. Presently, women initiate many divorces because they are positively motivated to do so by assurance of obtaining custody, alimony, support and the lion's share of property, enforced by all the powers government can muster.

Conversely, men are coerced into supporting truant families by negative motivations.

A two-track reversal of these motivational factors is necessary. The first track provides positive motivations for men to carry out their genuine responsibilities. The best positive motivations are guarantees of paternal rights and prohibition of unreasonable alimony and support. The second track provides negative motivation for women to remain married by removing the positive motivations to divorce. Wild horses could not drag most women into divorce court if cases were judged solely on merit and they stood an equal chance of losing.

Proper use of motivation principles would result in:

- the incidence of divorce being greatly reduced:
- many more fathers having child custody, drastically reducing the need for public assistance and support collections,
- reduced juvenile delinquency and other aberrations due to reduced divorce and mother-custody problems,
- those men without custody, but who lost fairly, would be much more inclined to meet support obligations because they would pay only a fair amount of support and their visitation and other rights would be enforced, reducing even further the need for public assistance.
- Nearly all needed reform measures fall into a common category — fairness — which admittedly relies on interpretations of the term. Proper interpretation of fairness would require that:
- because marriage is a lifetime contract, spouses aspiring to terminate it unilaterally without very good cause be prevented from absconding with the fruits of marriage,
- merit, not sex, become the criterion for awarding custody, property and money,
- responsibility for support be reasonably and equitably shared,
- rights be enforced with equal vigor to that of responsibilities.

At peril to "romance," it might be preferable to have attorneys involved before a marriage rather than after. As it stands, a marriage license is easier to get than a drivers' license or a hunting license. A mandatory minimum marriage age is unlikely, but young aspirants ought to be warned of the obstacles. China recognizes the proper, almost mandatory ages as 25 for women and 28 for men. India's divorce rate proves that marriages arranged by adult parents work out better than those by hot-blooded 18-year-olds here. "Covenant marriages" prevent couples and judges from impulsively dissolving marriages without good cause. Incidentally, religion is a great antidote to divorce.

In dissolution, mediation is strongly recommended before proceeding to the law and lawyers, and requiring — where there are young children — counseling and a waiting period prior to divorce. The liberal (not neo-liberal) John Locke said that the state should make parents stay together until the children are raised. When two people bring children into the world, their primary responsibilities should shift from selves to their children.

Though marriage requires licensing, having children does not. The racist (actually more of an elitist) Margaret Sanger in her 1934 "Code for babies..." advocated for parental permits. [576] Of course that idea is also impracticable as well as fascistic. Mandatory premarital counseling to include the legal, sexual, financial, and other aspects should be required. It might help avoid the tragedy of mismatched marriages.

In May 2004, the California Supreme Court wisely acted to give courts the power to restrain proposed move-aways by custodial parents that are harmful to children. [577] At this writing about 20 states are considering measures that would change laws governing which parent gets legal and physical control of a child after a divorce or separation. The proposals generally encourage judges to adopt custody schedules that maximize time for each parent. Some of the measures, such as those proposed in New York and Washington state, take an additional step by requiring judges to award equal time to each parent unless there is proof that such an arrangement would not be in a child's best interests. According to Americans for Legal Reform a Durham County New York judge awarded more than 8 million dollars to a husband for "intentional infliction of emotional distress" from a man the husband said seduced his wife and ruined his marriage. Conceivably this model could also be applied for emotional distress and injury to children. Critics, the usual suspects, contend that these measures will risk giving leverage to abusive men.[578]

Because most temporary hearings are unnecessary, except in actual emergencies (their real purpose is usually to order several hundred dollars — at least — to one or both lawyers), they should be allowed only in emergencies. To be Constitutional, instead of chivalrous, rules of evidence must apply in evictions. Otherwise, there is too much abuse of process. Any party aspiring to shed a mate, and unable to prove that mate's presence to be dangerous, ought to be the party removed at a temporary hearing. If safety were the consideration, it would be more reasonable if the party feeling threatened voluntarily left.

The following policy statement was adopted by the Conservative Party of Canada on March 19, 2005 at their convention in Montreal:

A Conservative government will make the necessary changes to the Divorce Act to ensure that in the event of a martial breakdown, the Divorce Act will allow both parents and all grandparents to maintain a meaningful relationship with their children and grandchildren, unless it is clearly demonstrated not to be in the best interests of the children.

Any contract, including marriage, should ensure that each party has a legal and moral right to expect the other to comply with its terms, and that violators suffer consequences. Logically, a case could be made that persons being sued for divorce without good cause could sue the Plaintiff for breach of contract. Premarital contracts, generally honored by the courts only if the female litigant wishes them to be, should be more closely adhered to.

Hard cases make poor law. Sometimes there are no pleasant choices. The book, The Natural Family: A Manifesto, makes an excellent case for restoration of fault-based divorce. At the behest of DC-area based divorce reformer Mike McManus, [579] and Republican Senator Michelle McManus (no relation) introduced SB 1127 that would eliminate No-fault divorce in Michigan. Mike McManus claims that divorce is a significant factor in the state's economic problems, and that the bill could cut the divorce rate in half if passed.

Even the Catholic Church got it wrong; the lobbyist for the St. Paul/Minneapolis Archdioceses, a prominent local attorney named Mansour, argued for this law before the Minnesota Legislature back in the '70s, while I argued against it. After it passed, I complained to officials in the Vatican and to the Archdioceses about their official position on this law and their indifference regarding the damage it would do, and now has done, to marriage. With heads buried in the holy sand, they did not deign to respond. However, Mansour admitted privately to me a couple years later when we happened to pass on the street that he — and the Church — were on the wrong side of that issue. As long as No-fault divorce remains the law of the land and divorce-bound parents continue putting their own personal interests above the welfare of their children, the divorce rate will remain high.

An alternative: because the exclusively No-fault concept is even worse than the old fault system. Almost fifty years ago this writer devised a solution dubbed "fault option." The Minnesota Legislature ignored the proposal, but similar proposals later gained traction in other legislatures.

The idea of fault option is to alleviate instead of inflame basic conflict where possible, while preserving moral and legal rights. It utilizes the best, and eschews the worst, of both fault and No-fault modes. Under it, legislatures need not choose for citizens between the modes; it is presumptuous for them to do so. Today's citizens are not children; they have evolved sufficiently to participate in the conduct of their lives. This proposal would permit the principals themselves to decide under which mode to proceed. It would work thusly:

A. The No-fault mode would allow couples without children to avoid the destructive, mud-slinging and expensive atmosphere of adversary courts, obtaining their divorce from a court clerk on mutually consented terms, much as they got married. This mode would apply only if both parties agreed to it and to the terms.

B. If agreement could not be reached or if the couple had children, the fault mode would apply, and the parties could go to the mat in court. This would preserve the constitutional right of injured parties to redress grievances, and the right of children to the better parent if joint custody did not apply. Injury and culpability would be factors in determining custodial, financial and property awards. Either party could demand this mode apply.

By thus removing a large percentage of divorces from the courts, judicial workload would be cut sufficiently for the courts to function better. Lawyers, of course, would fight this reform tooth and nail.

Regarding Custody

Children have a right to a complete home, including father and mother, sustenance and guidance. It is a natural right deriving from the Laws of Nature and of Nature's God. It is my fundamental belief that the parental relationship is a God-given right, and that government must not deprive a parent of his children or his property, nor a child of his parent, without good and sufficient cause. Divorce courts must not be permitted to continue removing children from legally unimpeachable parents, just to be chivalrous, misandric or go-along-to-get-along.

Around the nation, lawyers and individuals have challenged state child custody laws, and hopefully will continue to do so. One example: on January 6, 2005 Pro Se attorney (a non-lawyer arguing on his own behalf) Harold Rosenberger argued a case, Rosenberger v. Pataki, Case #04-0312-CV, before the US Second Circuit alleging that New York's custody law is unconstitutional. Mr. Rosenberger's challenge addressed the fundamental rights of suitable parents to the legal and physical custody of their minor children where both parents are similarly situated. Rosenberger asserted, "The State cannot arbitrarily designate one parent a custodial parent and the other parent a non-custodial parent where there is no finding of unfitness..." The case was dismissed, as was a similar earlier one of mine, demonstrating again that the federal courts just do not give a damn.

The first rule of law in awarding custody should be the same as in medicine: First do no harm. Legitimate criteria (which sex — per se — is not) should determine custodial qualifications in divorce situations. The courts should resurrect their former principle that "It is not logical to assume that a woman can be a good mother and an adulteress at the same time. The primary duty of any mother (or father) is to educate her (or his) children in basic moral principles. One who does not possess these principles can hardly be expected to teach them to others." Meaningful criteria would help the image of the many good mothers, by demonstrating that they indeed deserve custody. The best custodial parent usually is the parent who remains loyal to the marriage agreement and the family.

It is generally accepted among authorities that, intellectually and morally, we are largely products of our environments, and that the imperfections of the custodial parent are mirrored in the child. It is imperative that the grossly unfit be eliminated from consideration. To these ends, objective tests, such as the Minnesota Multiphasic Personality Inventory and others, should be administered. Prospective stepparents ought also to be evaluated in the same way.

Going way back among many authorities who agree — some fully, some partially — with most of the foregoing are: Dr. Karl Menninger, world-renowned psychiatrist; Professor Urie Bronfenbrenner, Chairman of the White House Conference on Children; Dr. Starke Hathaway, Developer of the Minnesota Multiphasic Personality Inventory; Dr. David Goodman, child psychologist and author; Dr. Jessie Bernard, renowned sociologist and author; Dr. Richard Robkin, New York psychiatrist; Dr. Fredrick Wyatt, University of Michigan psychoanalyst and motherhood researcher; Dr. Stanley F. Yolles, Director, National Institute of Mental Health; Dr. Wm. Goode, President of the American Sociological Association; Dr. Edmund Bergler, psychiatrist/author; Dr. Anna Freud (the great man's daughter); Dr. Neil Rosser, University of North Carolina behavioral expert; Dr. Phon Hudkins, former lawyer/economist/sociological researcher with the U.S. Labor Department; Dr. Joan Aldous, University of Minnesota Family Studies Center; Dr. Everett S. Ostrosky, author; Professor Lawrence E. Fuchs, Brandies University; Professor Juan B. Cortes, PhD. Psychology, Georgetown University, Washington, D.C.; Psychologists Mark Reuter and Henry Biller; Frank Watz, M.D., Hagerstown, Ind.; and most anyone with a modicum of sense.

Writing in *The Family in America* (May 2004: 7), Professor Stephen Baskerville said:

An extensive body of state and federal case law, reflecting centuries of Common Law tradition, recognizes the right to parent one's children free from government interference. The United States Supreme Court noted that a parent's right to 'the companionship, care, custody and management of his or her children' is an interest 'far more precious' than any property right; May v. Anderson, 345 U.S. 528, 533; 73 S.Ct. 840, 843, (1952). The same Court stressed, 'the parent-child relationship is an important interest that undeniably warrants deference and, absent a powerful countervailing interest, protection. A parent's interest in the companionship, care, custody and management of his or her children rises to a constitutionally secured right, given the centrality of family life as the focus for personal meaning and responsibility;' Stanley v. Illinois, 405 U.S. 645, 651; 92 S.Ct. 1208, (1972).

"Our culture," says Wade Horn, "needs to replace the idea of the superfluous father with a more compelling understanding of the critical role fathers play in the lives of their children, not just as 'paychecks,' but as disciplinarians, teachers, and moral guides. The exiling of fathers from families in divorce is bad policy. Fathers must be physically present in the home. They can't simply show up on the weekends or for pre-arranged 'quality time.'" [580]

Dr. Lee Salk, director of pediatric psychology at the New York hospital Cornell Medical Center, said, "Males clearly have the same instincts, the same protective feelings toward children as females have... there is no scientific basis whatsoever to indicate that the female is superior in doing this" (sc. caring for children). There is even merit in the idea of Goldstein, Freud and Solnit — that drawing lots would be a better system of determining custody than what now operates.

The National Parents Organization [fn56] claims feminist organizations, family lawyers and state domestic violence establishments oppose presumption of equal parenting. These include the Nebraska State Bar Association and proponents of Measure 6 in North Dakota.

Advocating Paternal Custody

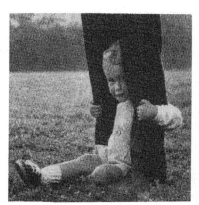

There is no better police force than millions of fathers — un-emasculated ones. As the old saw goes. "Father knows best." A poet said, "One father is a hundred school-masters."

Children who spend large amounts of time with their fathers have higher IQs, according to a British study. [581] Even non-resident fathers who are able to stay involved exert a strong positive influence on children, making them less likely to abuse drugs or alcohol, commit violence or property crime, or to have problems in school according to a Boston College study. [582] The evidence is empirical. How much proof of the proposition favoring father influence is needed, for Heaven's sake?

Because behavior patterns are formed in childhood, because authority and discipline are more vital to civilized development than

---

56 See nationalparentsorganization.org.

most other conditions and more lacking in father-deprived families, because males naturally and more positively project these images; therefore, in single-parent environments, the paternal may be more important than the maternal.

Hear how it used to be when there were fewer divorces: "The father owns the child against the mother, as well as against the world...of which no court is to disregard..." [583] Blackstone wrote that the father is the sole voice to speak for the infant. "The father also had a right of custody which was absolute as against the mother" — Jenny Teichman. "When divorce was rare, English common law automatically gave the children to the father." — Lorraine Dusky. Any action whereby a father attempted to divest himself of the custody of his legitimate children in order to give custody to the mother was void as contrary to public policy. Dusky said divorce was rare under that philosophy. According to Phyllis Chesler, "In Mauritania divorce is especially rare among those tribes where custody is retained by fathers." [584] A study from the National Bureau of Economic Research supports the foregoing. [585]

Although the idea may be shocking to some, routine paternal custody in divorce, as advocated by Prof. Amneus, would practically wipe out delinquency and eventually crime. It is imperative that all government officials recognize the self-evident stability that a father brings to a family and to society. Even if one could wave a magic wand and implement total father custody, it would take generations to undo the damage of past custodial practices.

Discipline is not normally a maternal quality. Generally, mothers are known to pamper children, while fathers are generally physically, emotionally, and reasonably more capable of maintaining order. A beautiful exception to that truism was caught on video during a Baltimore riot in defense of thugs with bad attitudes killed by cops. It depicted a heroic black mother, Toya Graham, dragging her 16-year-old son from the protesting mob and, berating him, admittedly using gutter language. [fn57]

Behavioral patterns apply even to animals; in Africa when poachers killed off older bull elephants for their tusks, the young males went wild, ganging up like the kids in *Lord of the Flies*, and embarked on killing sprees targeting rhinos. When rangers discovered the problem, they killed the young leader and flew in several bull elephants that soon restored order. As in this example, if fathers were empowered there would be more order and more peace, not just in Western countries, but across the world. The Ferguson, Baltimore, Charlotte, Minneapolis disturbances, and similar ones across the nation,

---

57 http://www.fox5dc.com/news/baltimore-mother-seen-smacking-son-participating-in-riots-honored-at-top-moms-luncheon

reminiscent of Watts almost 50 years ago, could probably have been avoided had fathers been in the picture to counter increasing drug and crime problems.

Both fathers and mothers spoil children terribly these days, but fathers probably less so. You can't even spank a misbehaving child these days without some busybody calling the cops. Too much TLC (tender, loving care) can create SLKs (spoiled little kids). A big problem with kids nowadays is that they have no work to do. It's hard to find a lad capable of doing the simplest of outdoor chores competently. Outside of sports, it's not easy these days to find a boy strong enough, or even ambitious enough, to push a lawnmower. A comprehensive 101-page report, Better Policies for a Healthier America — from the Trust for America's Health and the Robert Wood Johnson Foundation, claims, "70 percent of today's youth are not fit to serve in the military due to obesity or being overweight, criminal records, drug misuse or educational deficits." Dads are more likely to put them to work. The decline of manhood is probably a result of both mother custody and the triumph of style over substance. Of course, not all such kids are fatherless, but I'm betting a disproportionate number are so.

Why invest in juvenile prisons and 'early childhood programs' rather than protect the child from trouble and abuse by allowing his best mentor and protector, the father, to remain in his home? If fathers had more influence than do our demonstrably failing teachers unions, educational results should also improve. Fathers must accept these responsibilities, either voluntarily or otherwise. Society and courts must give fathers more authority and respect, AND they must learn to deserve it. Besides, awarding children to the parent more able to support them would greatly reduce our tax burden.

A big advantage of paternal custody is that it motivates both parents against divorce. Mothers do not want to lose children, and fathers need a housekeeper. It is true many current fathers are delinquent themselves, usually because they weren't socialized by *their* fathers. Amneus' argument for automatic father custody below illustrates why he may have been so far ahead of the pack that he was often considered to be behind it. Admittedly, his thesis may present new opportunity for abuse, but not nearly as bad as what happens now. Evidently, he anticipated that men would rise to the challenge if this responsibility were returned to them.

Amneus' 'Safe Drunk Driver Argument':

Opponents of father-custody will argue that even though delinquents are eight times more likely to come from matriarchal homes, still most father-deprived children do not become delinquents, so there can be no objection to mother custody. Of course, most father-deprived boys don't grow up to rob liquor stores and most father-deprived girls don't grow up to breed illegitimate children. Therefore, what? Therefore, we can ignore the increased probability that fatherlessness will create delinquency and illegitimacy? This might be called the "Safe Drunk Driver Argument": Most drunk drivers do not get in accidents. The overwhelming majority gets home safely and sleep it off. Drunks are, however, overrepresented among those who do get in accidents; and for this reason, society discourages drunk driving. The high crime areas of every American city are those with the largest numbers of fatherless children. No exceptions—though most of the citizens living on any ghetto street are not criminals.

The Safe Drunk Driver Argument is identical with the anti-patriarchal argument that defends the creation of fatherless households: Most father-deprived children do not become delinquents; therefore, creating father-deprived families is OK.

Most father-deprived children do not become teenage suicides, but most teenage suicides are fatherless children.

Most father-deprived children do not become educational failures, but most educational failures are fatherless children.

Most fatherless children do not become rapists, but most rapists were father-deprived children.

Most fatherless children do not become gang members, but most gang members are fatherless children.

Most fatherless children do not become child abusers or child molesters, but most child abusers and child molesters were fatherless children.

Most fatherless children do not become unwed parents, but most unwed parents were fatherless children. [586]

Sometimes one has to take matters into one's own hands. One method is "bicycle custody." Kids who are mature enough to know where they want to live, but ordered elsewhere by courts, can live where they darn well please despite the machinations of the entire legal system. After all, what can they do with a kid who keeps jumping on his bicycle and pedaling off to Dad's pad? Damn little! Years ago when I was an active divorce counselor, Ramsey County Minnesota Family Court Referee Kubes became hysterical when a friend of mine brought his thirteen-and-one-half year-old son to a temporary hearing to express his (ignored) preference for paternal custody. Next day I picked the boy up in front of his mother's house (He just "happened" to be out there hitchhiking) and delivered him to his father, where he remained into adulthood. He is now a well-adjusted man and good father.

When a mother and father are divorced or separated, and a child welfare agency removes the children from the mother's home for abuse or neglect, an offer of placement to the father, barring unfitness, should be automatic. Yet in the report, *What About the Dads?, Child Welfare Agencies' Efforts to Identify, Locate, and Involve Nonresident Fathers*, the Urban Institute presents a shocking finding: When fathers inform child welfare officials that they would like their children to live with them, the agencies seek to place the children with their fathers only 15% of the time. [587]

Judges must be made to realize that the biological marginality of the male role is not a reason for discriminating against males, not a reason for depriving them of their children, but a reason for strengthening their role. Judges must understand that fatherhood requires their support.

Joint Custody:

During the November 2004 election, 85 percent of Massachusetts voters supported joint physical and legal custody. In a paper presented at the 11th Annual Conference of the Children's Rights Council October 23-26, 1997, Richard Kuhn and John Guidubaldi, D.Ed. of John Carroll University (Cleveland, OH) and Kent State University (Kent, OH) contrasted divorce rate trends in the United States in states that encourage joint physical custody (shared parenting) with those in states that favor sole custody. Their conclusion was that states with high levels of joint physical custody awards (over 30%) in 1989 and 1990 showed significantly greater declines in divorce rates in following years through 1995, contrasted with other states. Divorce rates declined nearly four times faster in high joint custody states, contrasted with states where joint physical custody is rare. As a result, they say, states with high levels of joint custody have significantly lower divorce rates on average than other states. In addition, they say that states favoring sole custody had more divorces involving children. Their findings indicate that public policies promoting sole custody may be contributing to high divorce rates.

Others maintain that joint custody can be a cop out or Trojan Horse, awarded to fathers who might otherwise have gotten sole custody. As mentioned in Part I, Chapter I, joint *legal* custody is largely meaningless, a sop to make fathers think they have an equal say in the care of their children. Only joint *residential* custody is worthy of the name.

The American Coalition for Fathers and Children (ACFC) and others posited that Joint Custody or Shared Parenting is the cure to the custody problem, and is the closest thing to a two-parent family that we can give a child. The eminent Dr. Sanford Braver of Arizona State University says, "If we adopt a policy of presumption for joint legal custody, we will have better child support payments, we will have more contact with fathers, we will not have more conflict, we will not have worse parenting on the part of mothers, and most important of all, we will have better adjusted children." When fathers receive visitation, almost 80% pay all of their child support on time and in full. When fathers receive joint custody, the child support compliance rate jumps to more than 90%.

An opposing argument, hard to argue against, was posed by Professor Amneus:

> "Joint Custody is the cure," says Stuart Miller (of ACFC). No it is not; and Miller's reason for supposing it to be — "When fathers receive joint custody, the child-support compliance rate jumps to more than 90%" — is the worst possible "justification" for it. Miller is saying that joint custody makes the destruction of the family workable. Families ought not to be destroyed; they ought to be strengthened. Father custody will accomplish this; joint custody will not. Joint custody will only strengthen divorce.

Divided Custody (A modification of Joint Custody):

Most thinking people agree that a child needs both the maternal and paternal environment. While maternal qualities are important to very young children, paternal qualities are more important to older ones. Generally, young children need mothers most, and older children need fathers most. So, if one environment must be sacrificed due to divorce, that determination should be made with the intent of minimizing loss. The following suggestions would better serve children and justice by dividing parenting time closer to equally between mothers and fathers over the long run.

This writer has long proposed, where there is no clear disqualification of either parent, a rebuttable presumption of joint legal custody — with physical custody of boys less than 7 and girls before puberty to mothers; above those ages and upon reaching those ages, to fathers. The court would be required to submit written justification for deviation. Dr. Danilo Ponce, Professor of Psychiatry at the University Of Hawaii School Of Medicine, believed that, all other things being equal, fathers should have custody of boys after age three and of girls after age 11, mothers prior to those ages. Muslims have a sensible rule: women have custody of boys less than 7 years of age and of girls less than 15. That's eminently reasonable, far more so than the western tradition of almost total mother custody.

Financial
Alimony, Support and Property Awards

"No law can compel the enormous sacrifices, from working overtime, to taking a second job, to mortgaging the house to pay for college, that married fathers routinely make for their children, but which divorced fathers seldom do." [588]

There would be more good wives and fewer spurious divorces without alimony. A woman who fails to prepare for a career, promises to live with a man for life, has his children, throws him out, expects support from him or from taxpayers — and then pleads poverty — deserves little sympathy. Unlike the good professor Amneus' blanket condemnation of alimony, I would restrict it to reasonable amounts and to cases wherein the payor is grievously at fault.

Hear Judge Shepard:

> I believe that the facts of the case emphasize the need for re-examination of the entire concept of alimony and the continuing viability of that concept in contemporary society. Put another way, the question facing the Court is whether a judicially imposed system of involuntary servitude is to be continued wherein one human being is placed in bondage to another for what is effectively the remainder of his natural life. [589]

The cost of raising children is not nearly as high as we have been led to believe. A Wisconsin court found that state's guidelines "result in a figure so far beyond the child's needs as to be irrational." Because most "cost-per-child" figures used by courts to figure child support contain de facto alimony, cost estimates for foster care would be fairer. Alternatively, one could determine the percentage of welfare standard at which to sustain the children. It would vary from case to case; at least double that standard might be reasonable on average. Bill Gates' children, of course, would command considerably more than double the welfare standard.

Michael Dockery, an associate professor in the school of economics and finance at the Curtin University of Technology, claimed the cost of raising two children from birth to 21 was about $55,000. He said "People believe they'll be millions of dollars out of pocket if they have children... It's nonsense, children may even enhance their parents' wealth." If children were a "cost," parents would end up less wealthy than comparable couples without children. But his study, based on 3,168 couples, found this was not the case.

Because laws, practices and conditions vary from state to state it is impossible to propose universally applicable practices — only general principles. Many issues and parameters should properly factor into determination of reasonable child support awards: comparative wealth and obligations of parents, income of parents, age of children, location, etc. In the interest of fairness, the basic cost of children should be pro-rated between the parents, proportionate to their ability to pay, instead of having the father pay the entire cost. Incomes of custodial parents' second husbands or wives ought to be considered, although they seldom are unless it is to the advantage of mothers. Reportedly, Georgia's support guidelines will change to require consideration of both parents' incomes. Any child support assessment over 100 percent of actual cost of necessities should, at the option of the payor, be payable into a trust controlled by the payor.

Cracks are emerging in the rigidity of punitive Child Support Guidelines. In a Washington D.C. case, argued by Washington, D.C.

attorney Ron Henry, esq. [590] on behalf of the Children's Rights Council, [Fitzgerald v. Fitzgerald No. 87-1259 (D.C. Ct. App.)], the District of Columbia Court of Appeals overturned rigid guidelines over the vigorous objections of the Woman's Legal Defense Fund, which then proceeded to get most of the guidelines re-enacted by the DC City Council. In 2006, however, the DC City Council, realizing the harm being caused by its guidelines, enacted new guidelines that are far more flexible and less punitive toward fathers. At this point, only Massachusetts follows the method of the old District of Columbia guideline and, even there, the organization "Fathers and Families" has obtained limited reforms while continuing to work for more reform.

Realistic child support guidelines based on economic studies of child costs and consumer spending have been developed by economist R. Mark Rogers for use by states in developing reasonable standards. Called "Income Shares," they are available online at guidelineeconomics.com.

As explained earlier in this chapter, positive motivations work better than negative ones. So far, only the latter (extortion and jailing) have been employed. Why not try a more reasonable approach — fairness? Fairness would eliminate much bitterness and many refusals to pay.

It is parents' responsibility to provide children's needs, so long as their rights are honored. Often, failure to support results from questionable custody decisions. Disproportionate obligations are another cause of failure to pay. A survey by the Wisconsin Institute of Divorce revealed that arrearages in support and alimony are directly proportional to the severity of the "obligation."

Most non-complying fathers are willing to support, but under proper circumstances. Samuel W. Reid, of California is the 1st alimony/support resistor I'm aware of. Almost a century ago, this one-time prosperous young farmer announced, "I am perfectly willing to pay for the support of our 3-year-old child, if she is put in the proper kind of home. But no money for my ex-wife; I shall never pay. It's not the money; it's the principle. What if I am here for life? I'm the first martyr to a great cause." After 40 months in jail he was released on October 10, 1928, when he allowed his WW I army buddies to bail him out. [591]

In middle and lower income families there is seldom enough money left after divorce obligations for the evicted husband to live decently. An income just sufficient to support one household before divorce cannot be stretched to support two afterward. In determining a seasonal worker's ability to pay, his income should be figured on an annual basis, because projecting his earning capacity into the off-season as many courts do can result in unrealistic, dangerously high payments.

It is inherently unfair to take something away from people and then make them pay for it, that is — to ransom children. Unschooled farmers know donkeys must be fed and housed in order for them to be able to work, but officialdom would turn ex-husbands and fathers into donkeys if they stood still for it. According to the director of child support enforcement in Dade County, Florida, "Most men simply do not pay support until they are forced into it... If they don't pay for electricity, it's cut off... if they don't make car payments, the car is taken away... but if they don't make child support payments, nothing happens." [592]

Amneus responds:

> Nothing should happen. For paying his electric bill, he gets electricity. For making his car payment, he gets a car. For making support payments, he gets nothing but a reminder that his marriage contract was fraudulent, that the courts have destroyed his family and are trying to make him pay the costs of the destruction.

Hear Hon. Anne Kass. Presiding Family Judge, Albuquerque, New Mexico, Dist. Court:

> The time has come for someone to speak in defense of "dead-beat dads." Divorced or separated parents who do not pay support have been taking a beating from everyone, including the President. I have seen some parents who refuse to pay child support even though they have plenty of money to do so. . . However, I have seen far more parents who are ordered to pay child support who pay some support, but not all they are ordered to pay. Many of these parents are engaged in a financial struggle that the working poor cannot win. [593]

Un-married parents.   In view of the widespread availability of contraceptive devices, and except in the rare cases of actual rape, pregnancy results from voluntary choices by females; and therefore involuntary financial responsibility for these children should not devolve upon fathers. If a father has no abortion veto, logically he should have no support responsibility. Where fathers made conscious choices in initiating pregnancies (as opposed to just copulating), their responsibilities — and rights — should become equal to those of mothers, no more, no less.

Nationally syndicated advice columnist Amy Alkon believes that men, like women, should have reproductive rights. The Choice for Men movement seeks to give unmarried fathers the right to relinquish their parental rights and responsibilities within a month of learning of a pregnancy, just as mothers do when they choose to give their children up for adoption.

Property settlements should also be flexible, taking into account such factors as premarital ownership, respective contributions to the estate, and — lastly — needs of the parties. Some circumstances might justify a deferred, or post-marital, incremental settlement. An example is the case of a guiltless bride who sacrificed a career in order to work, thereby financing the husband's education, which paid off handsomely. Then it should not be called alimony, but her rightful share of a common investment, some of which has not yet accrued. Conversely, a divorced man might have something coming from a woman whose education or training he financed. There are mighty few circumstances wherein an erstwhile mate planning to abscond, that is — leave without good and sufficient reason, has any moral right to take common assets with him or her, certainly not those owned by the other prior to marriage.

Crime and Punishment

Due process requires fair notice and fair hearing, In crime deterrence, the eye-for-an-eye principle may never be surpassed; but punishment must be sex-blind. The death penalty is eminently appropriate in many cases; however, because of the haste to condemn males to death, maybe it ought to be suspended unless and until justice prevails.

DNA testing has been a boon to men. With its advent, many prisoners have been freed after wrongful convictions. Most of them are men with charges of rape against them. New Jersey resident Byron Halsey, who served more than two decades in prison for the rape and murder of two children, had his convictions thrown out on May 15, 2007 after an advanced DNA test showed that a neighbor might have been responsible. Superior Court Judge Stuart L. Peim vacated the verdict and granted a new trial because new evidence "would probably change the verdict." [594] In January 2003 Illinois Republican Governor, George Ryan, imposed a moratorium on executions in Illinois after DNA testing found that 13 prisoners on death row were innocent. Newspapers and the internet abound with such stories.

There have been well over 400 exonerations since 1989, and over half of those since 1999 were based on DNA evidence. The pace of exonerations jumped sharply, from about 12 a year through the early 1990s to an average of 43 a year since 2000, according to a study by the University of Michigan. A comprehensive 2/4/2016 *St. Paul Pioneer Press* article on exonerations revealed there were 149 in the U.S. in 2015. Innocence Projects — there are at least 41 — are constantly uncovering instances of wrongly imprisoned men, many having been incarcerated over 20 years. The Cardozo School of Law's Innocence Project, [595] among other efforts, used DNA evidence to exonerate one hundred and sixty-three innocent people (read men), [596] most over the objections of prosecutors.

Proposals to cap federal prison terms at 20 years with an option to extend them after scrutiny [597] except in unusual circumstances have been made; studies show most men mature out of lawbreaking age before middle age. Doing away with mandatory minimum sentences would ease the overload on prisons. Making laws and their applications more realistic, and severely punishing *actual* offenders would be more just and effective.

VAWA Reform. United States v. Morrison held the *Violence Against Women* act unconstitutional, but to no avail. A gesture toward balance did occur when former President Bush signed into VAWA the following non-exclusionary wording in Section 40002(b)(8): "Nothing in this title shall be construed to prohibit male victims of domestic violence, dating violence, sexual assault, and stalking from receiving benefits and services under this title." The final version includes text that for the first time recognizes male victims of domestic violence and sexual assault. Although the wording is weak and does not outline penalties for violation, it is better language than the previous law.

The foregoing was a step in the right direction, but only a cosmetic step. VAWA did not become sex-neutral. In blatant contradiction to President Bush's directive, the federal VAWA office was quoted on the Men's Health Network site as having written, "States must fund only programs that focus on violence against women..." The Justice Department went along, deciding that federal prosecutors should become involved in violence against men, but only if the victim is homosexual.[598]

Some decent women are not afraid to defend men's interests, and are often more effective at it than men. "VAWA does nothing for victims of domestic violence, and it's time to kill it," argues Janice Shaw Crouse, Ph.D., senior fellow of Concerned Women for America's Beverly LaHaye Institute, an international expert on cultural, women's, and children's issues — a commentator on major TV networks, a former presidential speech writer and author of <u>Children at Risk</u> and <u>Marriage Matters</u>.

Addressing False Allegations
Thou Shalt Not Bear False Witness.

I suspect there may be as many false accusations as true ones. It is this writer's oft-suggested opinion that persons who are found to have made a false accusation of crime, including sexual assault should receive the same jail sentence the falsely accused person would have received if he/she had been convicted. Legislators in West Virginia discovered that fewer than 20 percent of all child abuse charges in divorce and custody matters were legitimate; hence, they wisely passed a bill — House Bill 3065, also passed by the State Senate — that slaps criminal charges on those who falsely report child abuse or neglect in order to influence a custody case. The bill charges those who make a false abuse report with a $1,000 fine, or forces the plaintiff to pay for the defendant's legal fees. The misdemeanor crime would also carry a punishment of up to 60 hours of community service. [599] Oregon has joined the 21st Century: the Legislature passed legislation (419B.016) making the filing of false reports of child abuse in divorce, custody fight, or other domestic conflict a Class A violation resulting in a $750 fine. Bills to this effect have been proposed in several states, but have been successfully opposed by women's advocates.

Punishment was actually applied in England: Sally Henderson, from Woodmancote, was jailed for a year by Judge David Lane QC for making false rape allegations against former husband Richard Cooke in 2004. Henderson had earlier made similar claims against her live-in lover Mark Rowe. [600]

Expose Myths; determine inter-sex violence guilt
Cherchez la femme.

Former President Clinton told men they must never, ever raise their hand against a woman, which tells women they may be as provocative as they wish. Women must be disabused of the notion, admittedly instigated by men as per above, that they can get away with hitting men simply because they're female.

Contrary to popular fallacy, the majority of domestic assaults, between 55 and 57 percent, are initiated by women and not by men. While violence by men is decreasing, that by women is increasing. Let's look at the facts unearthed by unbiased scholars. An annotated bibliography examining [275] scholarly investigations, [214] empirical studies and 61 reviews and/or analyses was created by Martin S. Fiebert of California State University, Long Beach, which demonstrated that women are as physically aggressive, or more aggressive, than men in their relationships with their spouses or male partners. The aggregate sample size in the reviewed studies exceeded 365,000. [601]

Researcher R. L. McNeeley said wives and female companions are as likely to initiate family violence or murder a domestic partner as are husbands and male companions. [602] According to *Mother Jones* magazine, "Women report using violence in their relationships more often than men." "Women are doing the battering," wrote feminist Betty Friedan, "as much or more than men." Philip W. Cook has documented this extensively in Abused Men: The Hidden Side of Domestic Violence. It has been claimed that men are the victims of two to three times as much violence in this world as are women. [603] Women are more dangerous because they use weapons more often. [604]

A 2012 study by Bert H. Hoff, J.D. found "More men than women were victims of intimate partner physical violence, according to a national study funded by the Centers for Disease Control and U.S. Department of Justice." Hoff's research found that in the 12 months prior to the study's release, "an estimated 5,365,000 men and 4,741,000 women were victims of intimate partner physical violence." That's 53% and 47% respectively. [605]

According to a U.S. Department of Justice study, there are approximately 835,000 domestic assaults against men annually. A more recent Bureau of Justice Statistics study reports that the number of male victims 12 years of age and older is nearly 1.6 million per year. DHHS reports estimate that as many as 4,000 children, mostly male, are killed or maimed every year, mostly by women. [606] Recent statistics in Britain are similar to those in the U.S. *The Guardian* reports that "International research suggests that as much as half of domestic violence is committed against men, but in the UK, fewer than 7% of convicted perpetrators are female." A study in a 2000 *Guardian* piece showed that women were actually more likely to initiate violence in relationships. That study is based on an analysis of 34,000 men and women by British academic John Archer, professor of psychology at the University of Central Lancashire and president of the International Society for Research on Aggression. Archer analyzed data from 82 U.S. and U.K. studies on relationship violence, dating back to 1972. [607]

The British research firm Dewar Research found that, from 1995 to 2004, reported domestic violence against men as a percentage of total inter-sex violence ranged from 19% to 34%. The key word is 'reported.' It is common knowledge that men are reluctant to report abuse. Statistics on gender/sex violence are skewed by that reluctance [608] and by the fact that many reports are generated by "battered women's" shelters, spawning grounds for all sorts of feminist agitprop. A British government survey in roughly the same period revealed male victims to range from 39% to 49% of the total. In view of the skewed statistics, that survey may be more accurate. In England, the demand for newly opened battered men's shelters is greater than the supply.

The most recent, well-documented treatise on the subject of inter-sex violence is Domestic Violence: The 12 Things You Aren't Supposed to Know, by Thomas James J.D. [609] His book absolutely demolishes any argument that men are more guilty than women of perpetrating inter-sex violence. Other definitive studies show husband-battering to be at least as prevalent as wife-battering, if not more so. [610]

The data appearing below is from pages 48 & 49 of Advancing the Federal Research Agenda on Violence Against Women by Candace Kruttschnitt, Brenda L. McLaughlin, and Carol V. Petrie — editors, available from The National Academies Press:

Nonfatal intimate-partner violence victims	Female victims	Male victims
1985 National Survey of Family Violence	11.3% overall 3.0% severe	12.1% overall 4% severe

1992 National Alcohol and Family Violence Survey	9.1% overall 1.9% severe	9.5% overall 4.5% severe
2001 National Violence Against Women Survey	1.3%	0.9%
2001 National Crime Victimization Survey	0.43%	0. 08%
1993-94 Dunedin Multi-disciplinary Health and Development Study	40.9%	47.4%
1992 National Youth Survey	20.2% overall 5.7% severe	34.1% overall 13.8% severe

Despite feminist claims, self-defense is not the primary reason why women batter. Betty Friedan (RIP) said, "Perhaps it is the least understood fact of American political life — the enormous buried violence of women in this country today." [611] For such reasons, Laura Petracek, Ph.D., psychologist and anger expert, was moved to write her book The Anger Workbook For Women.[612]

Women are probably more likely than men to use verbal and psychological aggression, to create incidents or initiate fights. Arguably, there may be more psychologically battered men than psychologically battered women. Psychological battery includes threats of eviction and estrangement from children, etc.

Putting things in perspective: according to the "National Crime Survey," less than one percent of men or women are victimized by spouses. [613] Sibling violence is the most common form of family violence.

And putting things in racial perspective, what leftists mislabel as 'racism' (meaning by whites to blacks) is, in actuality an apprehension based on legitimate concern about the bad behavior of many blacks. It is evident in the newspapers. More than half of all homicides and robberies are committed by black offenders, even though blacks make up only thirteen percent of the population. Ditto with illegitimacy: seventy percent vs. thirty percent. Noticing such is termed "racist."

The legal profession
Shakespeare's character, Dick the Butcher, said, "The first thing we do, let's kill all the lawyers" (Get a rope!). If we cannot throw these moneychangers out of the temple, we must at least reform them.

Members of the legal profession must be servants of justice, not masters of it. The notion that the courts exist primarily for benefit of judges and lawyers must go. Tort reform is essential to bring health care costs down to reasonable levels, but tort reform is all but impossible with lawyers in control of governments. Americans for Legal Reform (ALR) [614] says, "We have been working for years to remove lawyers from public office outside the Judiciary, on the grounds that their presence in the other 2 branches constitutes an illegal breach of the Constitution's implicit prohibition against any 'single-hands' group or faction controlling all government..." ALR suggests that judges and lawyers be subject to mandatory psychological testing to determine if they are honest, ethical human beings. That is required to become a policeman or get a job in Home Depot; why not require judges and lawyers be tested? The non-profit Judicial Watch is probably the leading organization examining and exposing corruption in government.

Justice would be better served if the pay of its "servants'" did not depend so heavily on winning cases, right or wrong. As long as the profit motive exists, money, not justice, will be the primary end of lawyers. To admit the premise that justice is a birthright could be to accept the conclusion that the legal profession should be socialized. Government imposed a complicated system of laws and procedures on citizens, and therefore ought to provide for the free exercise and interpretation of them. The argument for socialized law is more logical than that for socialized medicine because proponents of socialized medicine can't claim that the government created disease. And the right to justice being at least as basic and desirable as the right to education and health, this same argument is at least as logical as that for a socialized teaching profession, which we have already.

Realistically we cannot expect lawyers to allow themselves to be socialized; so we should consider alternatives, however inadequate. A policing or government licensing agency perhaps, such as is required for other professionals, might be established — responsible to the people not to other lawyers. The right to counsel of one's choice, which predates even our Constitution, ought to mean what it says — that individuals can choose their own counsel whether or not their choice pleases courts or bar associations.

Welfare Reform

It is proper to distinguish between rights and privileges. The word "entitlements" is horribly misused. The giving of food, money and health care to indigents, undesirables and illegal aliens is disguised as "entitlement."

We must connect the dots between welfare and its many negative results, between cause and effect. Overall, welfare is inimical to marriage by promoting divorce, and greatly harms men and children.

It is only common sense that no-one, man or woman, has a right to bring children into this world unless they have the means to support them. The front page of a *St. Paul Pioneer Press* business section featured a weepy article deploring the plight of a 29-year-old single mother with a baby and no husband. She works part time for low pay and has a skimpy sick leave policy. There are many like her. Boo hoo. They are usually in bad circumstances by choice; either a government system — courts or welfare — bribed them into divorcing their husbands or they made a conscious choice to have children out of wedlock.

Where custodial parents are drawing welfare payments for childcare, the other parent should automatically be considered primary (non-paid) caregivers, as opposed to the present practice of government-funded childcare.

Welfare mothers brazenly complain about investigation of live-in men. If one is giving money on condition that the recipient has no other means of support, one should reserve the right to investigate that condition. Donors, not recipients or agents, should dictate the conditions. Gift horses should not be submitted to a tooth exam.

To paraphrase former Senator Jim DeMint: attacking recipients for accepting welfare's largess is like criticizing a 4-year-old for eating ice cream for breakfast. Proper targets are enablers acquiescing to their wants: obliging politicians, administrators and divorce court judges. True, some men cash in too, but mostly via women.

An objective congressional investigation into the correlation of divorce and AFDC/TANF ought to be undertaken, interviewing victims of these rackets, such as evicted husbands, as well as administrators. Some politicians with both feet on the ground occasionally propose legislation to reform the system. The Reagan welfare reforms, enacted in California in 1970-71, and the Republican welfare program (the PRWORA act), enacted in 1996 with bi-partisan support, reduced grossly inflated welfare rolls nationwide and caused a decline in illegitimacy. The Republican-led House narrowly passed a sweeping farm bill that would toughen work requirements for food stamp recipients. Democrats unanimously opposed the measure. [615]

According to U.S. Department of Agriculture (USDA) data on food stamp enrollment, more than 1.4 million households dropped off the program since President Donald Trump's first full month in office in February 2017. USDA data reveals that the number of households on food stamps in October 2018 dropped to 19,410,711, down by 1,428,558 from February 2017 when 20,839,269 households were enrolled in the Supplemental Nutrition Assistance Program.

However, the incessant battering of opposing forces demolishes most reform proposals like pieces of china in a bull shop. Meaningful reform has about as much chance of seeing the light of day as do Barak Obama's school records. Though bills appeared in Kansas and Missouri to limit TANAF and SNAP benefits to necessities, [616] TANF "reforms" amounted to little more than a fresh snowfall on the town dump. When the Obama administration tried to water down TANF requirements, GOP lawmakers and former presidential candidate Mitt Romney complained — to no avail it seems. Evidently, no one objected that the Constitution provides that Congress, not the Executive branch, has authority to make and issue waivers to law.[617]

It is nonsense to maintain that freebies should preempt national defense and repairing of the infrastructure. Poverty is better fought indirectly by eliminating its causes, one of which is divorce, than directly by doling out money and freebies. It seems patently obvious that we should spend our resources bolstering defenses instead of further subsidizing divorce and undesirables via welfare. Arguably, charity should not be the business of government, but of traditional charitable organizations and individuals. In his 1992 book The Tragedy of American Compassion, Marvin Olasky argued that government robbing Peter to pay Paul couldn't match the success of private programs with their spiritual and relational components.

Despite the gnashing of liberal teeth such benefits should be designated as charity or at least welfare. The embarrassment might encourage recipients to begin carrying their own weight. Negative incentives can be more practical. Captain John Smith, quoting the Bible (Second Thessalonians 3:10), admonished the Pilgrims, "If you don't work, you don't eat." What would John Smith say to today's recipients?

Because misandry is a causative factor in divorce, society probably should — and does — shoulder some of the financial burden of divorce (You break it, you own it). However, this is a limited obligation. Individuals have obligations to society also.

Welfare's Impact beyond Divorce

Though welfare's primary casualty is divorce, it causes social problems also in poverty, disproportionate illegitimacy, crime and indolence. It gives habitual social protesters the financing and leisure to pursue their fun and games. The food stamp program, administered by the Department of Agriculture, proudly reports that they "distribute free meals and food stamps to over 46 million people on an annual basis." Long ago President Franklin D. Roosevelt said "To dole out relief in this way is to administer a narcotic, a subtle destroyer of the human spirit. It is inimical to the dictates of sound policy. It is in violation of the traditions of America."

Being on welfare now pays the equivalent of $30.00 an hour for a 40 hour week, while the average job pays $24.00 an hour. Why work? The National Park Service, run by the Department of the Interior, warns us "Please do not feed the animals." Their stated reason for this policy: "The animals will grow dependent on the handouts, and then they will never learn to take care of themselves."

Government-sponsored welfare, including healthcare for the aged, infirm, and the honestly unemployed (those not responsible for their condition) can reasonably be justifiable by birthright. But that which encourages indolence, non-productivity and divorce should not. Moynihan said, "The issue of welfare is not what it costs those who provide it, but what it costs those who receive it."

Hear Cicero in 55 BC "The budget should be balanced, the treasury should be refilled, public debt should be reduced, the arrogance of officialdom should be tempered and controlled, and the assistance to foreign lands should be curtailed, lest Rome will become bankrupt. People must again learn to work instead of living on public assistance. . ." We have learned NOTHING over the past 2,075 years! Thomas Sowell said, "No society ever thrived because it has a large and growing class of parasites living off those who produce." No wonder that taxpaying residents of states with generous benefits, like New York, California and Illinois are moving out (shades of <u>Atlas Shrugged</u>).

The problems of criminality and poverty would be greatly lessened if generous benefits were not available to illegal immigrants. If eligibility were tightened, there would be plenty of unskilled labor to take jobs that Americans may find unpleasant or beneath them. Requiring work is only part of the cure. Restoring fathers to families is more important. Rampant fraud perpetrated by businesses should also be rooted out.

What social scientists and other sensible persons tell us about social issues today, 13-year-olds knew 60 years ago.

Private investigators could he hired, for a percentage of the money they save taxpayers. Paying tipsters a percentage should be reconsidered. Muldoon X suggested sterilizing habitual or prolific male and female AFDC/TANF recipients as a condition of eligibility. That measure has been employed for mothers to avoid murder charges.

Bleeding hearts will throw up their hands at the foregoing measures, but let's see what the voters say. We have brains as well as hearts. It is time to use them. Oren Cass wrote an excellent analysis of the situation in the October 14, 2012 issue of *National Review*. The brilliant philosopher and educator Thomas Sowell concurs with the suggested reforms above.

Part IV. The "Men's Movement," authentic and otherwise

To know where you're going, you have to know where you've been. Gender-sex problems facing men are worldwide. One might justifiably wonder why men and father victims haven't been able to confront and overcome them. There have been many attempts to do so; over time men have mobilized all over the world, and are loosely referred to as constituting "the men's movement." Individuals in and out of the movement have been butting heads against this massive wall of misandry for many decades, and getting bashed heads. Those expressing displeasure over their treatment in divorce are like hogs squealing while being led to slaughter, and are no more effective. See the complete movement history (also in need of update) at this website: http://mensdefense.org/.

Prof. Daniel Amneus   Reuben P. Kidd   Charlie Metz

Founding Fathers: Reuben Kidd (who died February 26, 2007 at age 94), George Partis, Jay Burchette and Charlie Metz (who died March 25, 1971 at age 51). These gentlemen, pictured below (except Jay), plowed fresh social and jurisprudential ground, only to see their insights unfortunately fall somewhat into disfavor. The men's movement has been wandering in the wilderness since their time. The situation is analogous to today's youth being unaware of this country's founders.

See the Dedication section, later, for more information on these wonderful gents.

Existing U.S. organizations

Years ago, when we were much better organized, we rallied and marched in Washington, D.C. No longer. Below is a rough summary of the current situation. In the United States the National Coalition for Men (NCFM.org), operates primarily out of the west coast, the American Coalition for Fathers and Children (ACFC.org), operates primarily out of the east coast, the Equal Justice Foundation (EJFI.org) operates primarily out of Colorado, and Jail for Judges (jail4judges.org), once operated out of the Dakotas, and the Men's Defense Association; all have or had agendas for reform. The much smaller Jail for Judges pursued judicial corruption; their "Judicial Accountability Initiative Law (J.A.I.L.)" was intended to create a special grand jury for the purpose of determining whether judges civilly sued as a result of blatant judicial offences should be stripped of immunity, and whether they should have been indicted for criminal violations. It was rejected by So. Dakota voters due to wording manipulation by state government officials. Peripheral organizations like the Children's Rights Council and Men's Health Network also pursued agendas for reform. There are activity spots also in Minnesota and Wisconsin. The National Coalition for Men (NCFM) seems to be most active currently, with a good website — NCFM,ORG. Their leader, Harry Crouch, is a good man. ACFC's David Roberts informed me that ACFC, like MEN International, is "minimally functional." The latter's non-profit status was canceled by the IRS due to failure to submit recent paperwork (Such annual red tape was too much for this 90-year-old widower).

There might be others; I've been out of touch in recent years. Of course there has always been numerous lone wolves advocating and counseling on various issues. Some of the aforesaid organizations may be able to provide attorney referrals for men in need. Google them.

Internal problems

"Little Platoons" in this movement have generally been too militantly independent and disorganized to contend with the systems arrayed against us. Bloggers tend to endlessly banter about this and that, seldom getting to basics. The sight of the forest is lost while examining individual trees. An analogy from Khayyam's time and place sums it up: "The dogs bark while the caravan moves on." Consequently men's defense has taken a back seat to feminism, and will continue to do so unless and until what's left of the movement gets its act together and begins singing from the same songbook. I'm not optimistic.

Past failures can be attributed to seemingly inherent male problems — largely egotistical — in activists and ignorance in followers, thus frustrating numerous efforts to consolidate into an effective counterforce. Some activists considered themselves the Messiah pioneering reform, fantasizing that they could go it alone — isolated from other groups. A few were reminiscent of Satan in Milton's *Paradise Lost*: "Better to reign in Hell than serve in Heaven." The analogy of lobsters in a bucket applied. Decades ago, one individual had thousands of dollars in grants lined up to support Men's Equality Now International, but an envious group was able to sabotage the scheme. A board member of one organization was able to get my criticism of homosexuality in a website article deleted (I wonder what a homosexual sympathizer would want in officership of a MEN's organization).

The gullibility of some groups has been breathtaking. The "National Fatherhood Initiative" holds or held rallies with celebrities, sells souvenirs and tells fathers how to have fun with their children. One might hope they would be more interested in helping fathers *have* their children. One quite prominent organization busies itself advocating for such things as baby-changing stations in men's' restrooms, campaigns to get cities to offer the same self-defense class to men as they offer to women (while claiming to be "warriors") and unrealistically advocates lawsuits to expand draft registration to women.

The "Promise Keepers" organization operated under the illusion that only men abandon families. Some groups hold wilderness retreats to "find the inner self" with drumming and poetic shtick; their guru was Robert Bly. Instead of fixating on psychological "wounds," they would be well-advised to cease liberal jabberwocky and put their big boy pants on or turn in their man card.

Anti-male males proselytized on such websites as consciousmen.com. Like feminists, some reek of self-hatred. Lately, in western countries, some groups have morphed into a sex-melding project, hung up on sexual and homosexual matters. A Montgomery County Pennsylvania group of men looked to help other men through the therapeutic power of ("non-sexual") cuddling. According to their Meetup page, the Men's Therapeutic Cuddle Group's goal "is to provide a safe, structured, and platonic environment for men to experience 'the three As': Acceptance, Affirmation and Affection." [618] A Twin Cities group had classes on masturbation. A front page article in their newsletter denounced white North American males.

Besides introducing new and strange philosophies into the cause, new age activists are barely aware that real issues of concern were addressed by their more legitimate predecessors long ago. In September 2014, *National Public Radio* hosted a gathering of activists proclaiming to hold the "1st Int'l Conference on Men's Issues." Actually they were about 46 years behind the times. There have been many such conferences, some much larger than theirs. What Santayana said is apropos, "Those who don't study history are doomed to repeat it." Those who do study history can do little more than warn about those who repeat it.

The University of Michigan has a "Changing Men" collection of movement literature. Though most material in it is representative of such groups, some of it is actually from the legitimate men's movement, including this book.

The grandstanding Democrat presidential candidate Joe Biden sponsored the virulently anti-male Violence Against Women Act (VAWA). Biden also supported Anita Hill's accusations against Clarence Thomas over 30 years ago, and blamed "a bunch of white guys" for refusing to believe her. One group today refuses to denounce him. Reminiscent of Lenin's "useful idiots, such nominal males suck up to feminists hoping to be eaten last. Men, choose which of these camps are yours.

Reform began on the West Coast with the above-pictured gentlemen, and now its demise may be commencing there in a 'woke' community. Yeats, you were right; the center did not hold. Pogo's expression is apropos, "We have met the enemy and he is us."

The author's suggested way forward

Everything that needs to be said has already been said. Since no one was listening, everything must be said again. — André Gide

I submit that reform must be more than a notion, that a modern crusade against the anti-male jihad must be mounted. The authentic men's movement has, or had, plenty of talent and resources – worldwide – to achieve success, if they could be properly marshaled and coordinated. A better way to demolish the wall would be to take a belt and suspenders approach — all back off, form up and hit it together. I believe it will come down no other way. Contrary to the adage, you *can* fight city hall, but one must be prepared to pay the consequences. Obviously, this "forming up" would require overcoming internal problems. Major groups must be persuaded to commence a policy of intra-movement cooperation. If large organizations seriously act in concert, and if movement writers take up the cause, smaller groups should be swept along like lifeboats in the wake of the Queen Mary. Such a combination of forces and resources (manpower) would be over-whelming, constituting a force equivalent to and potentially greater than that of feminism.

Anti-male elements in society can be defeated by only one thing: political clout on a national — or rather international — level. In theory, the best and most efficient construct to form up and develop clout would be to create a unified organization with democratically-elected leaders chosen from the most capable. Men's Equality Now (MEN) International, the last credible attempt to so unify the movement, came to naught. [fn58] So practically, in view of situational reality, the most that can probably be hoped for at present is a greater degree of cooperation among major — relatively speaking — existing groups. A juggernaut like this is more easily conceived than constructed. It may even be an "Impossible Dream." The cooperative approach requires a common philosophy, discipline and some mutual agreements. The discipline of British and German armies, however misguided and unfortunate at times to the rest of the world, was key to their successes. A common philosophy must be broad enough to include all reasonable approaches, and narrow enough to exclude approaches that are nominally masculinist but are actually harmful to a truly masculinist philosophy. Reformers must define who are legitimate members (and who aren't), and cooperate with allies. Endless arguments over trivialities and creation of ever new structures must be avoided.

Logically, it is imperative to determine philosophic Ends before addressing Means of achieving those Ends. Without such an understanding of Ends, the movement cannot know what it is – and what it isn't. As analogy, builders cannot build a long-lasting house without a foundation. The foundation of this movement must be built before the upper storey rooms. After long consideration, I believe that a common philosophic foundation should be the same as it is, or was, for Western civilization — the nuclear family. With that in mind, this writer has long proposed the following End: "To preserve the traditional nuclear family through restoration of equal dignity and equal (not identical) rights under the law for all persons across a broad spectrum of life, including divorce, employment, health, crime punishment and image." That or something essentially similar to it may be the only philosophy that all the disparate authentic elements of this poor "movement" can agree on. Until basic matters are agreed upon, achieving gender equality is impossible.

It seems that national political disputes have a minor parallel even in the men's movement. Members and organizations must distinguish between politics and politicians aligned with their interests and those which are not. I submit that the conservative philosophy is more in line with men's and families' interests than is the 'progressive' philosophy. For example, I am disappointed by the failure of modern organizations to understand the connection between welfare and family breakup (cause and effect), and to connect those dots.

---

58 Several decades ago, I drew up a proposed Constitution for it, and may still have it somewhere in a file cabinet.

We must keep things in perspective. While restoring fathers and fatherhood to their proper position is elemental, perhaps even primary, divorce discrimination is only one aspect of a larger anti-male phenomenon. Pursuing single issues such as divorce are unproductive approaches. Fathers are but a subset of men; alleviating their problems alone, like cutting off one head of a many-headed hydra, still leaves us with the underlying misandry. It will bite us again in another area. In order to correct injustice or inequality directed at fathers or at men in general, the entire hydra must be attacked; misandry itself should be the greater concern.

In the interest of broadening the base of the movement and making it more acceptable to the public at large, it may be necessary to include elements primarily concerned with issues of health and personal growth or introspection, elements that are not primarily concerned with external discrimination against men and fathers. I hesitate to include groups subscribing to the false premise that gender role change is necessary and good. In early days of the abortion debate, few men seemed to understand that a fetus was more than a blob of tissue, so merely advocated that fathers have equal right to determine the babies' fates. Modern groups don't seem to address the issue.

If those elements on the fringes – the introspective types – would focus upon more important issues confronting men and fathers, great strides could be taken. Along these lines, it might be advisable that the derisive term SNAGS be avoided. It might be better to have them on the inside pissing out than on the outside pissing in. Depending on intelligence level, it takes years to know who's who and what's what in this poor "movement." Such things, of course, are matters for consideration by the mainstream.

In order to know what's going on beyond their little circles, to know where to direct attentions and activities, movement members worldwide must be fully educated on issues. Early light on the issues circulated throughout the movement in the 1960s when I penned an article entitled 'A New Dimension in Prejudice.' It still exists somewhere in my files.

Printed forums such as NCFM's *Transitions* [fn59] and the (now defunct) *Liberator* are likewise important, reinstated if necessary. The internet is a potentially powerful resource, a high tech forum for communication and ecumenism. Websites and previous iterations of the *Men's News Daily*, could serve as a sounding board for advocacy of an ad hoc committee of recognized international leaders with unity or strong cooperation in mind. My God, even Al-Qaida's diverse groups reportedly agreed on a common web site! Some women have been more

---

59 I continue to wonder just what they are "transitioning" from and to.

effective at defending men's interests than have male activists. Karen Straughan is one such. Unfortunately, she refuses to recognize male activists who decades ago were saying the same things she thinks she invented. [619]

However, there is danger such forums could become nothing more than fancy Towers of Babel, befogged with tangential issues and introspection (now sometimes overdone to the point of confused speculation) and blather as has happened in the past.

It is imperative that the movement honor its founding fathers mentioned at the beginning of this section and theoreticians like Professor Amneus, all now deceased. History is full of lost opportunities.

Edmund Burke said, "The war of ideas is never fully won." True; it's battles must be fought anew by every generation. Samuel Adams said, "It does not take a majority to prevail ... but rather an irate, tireless minority, keen on setting brushfires of freedom in the minds of men." Margaret Mead said, "Never doubt that a small group of thoughtful committed citizens can change the world; indeed it's the only thing that ever has." Victor Hugo said, "There is nothing so powerful as an idea whose time has come." Right makes might. Reformers need more of what Tom Wolfe called "The Brotherhood of the Right Stuff," men with cajones. The great words of Gandhi: "First they ignore you, then they laugh at you, then they fight you, then you win." I encourage sincere reformers to run up the flag, sound the bugle and fight the good fight.

The legitimate men's movement can play a leading role in ensuring survival of civilization by supporting commonsense and traditional masculine attributes in gender relations.

Part V. Annex.

Civilization; Evolution, Devolution, Preservation

Writer Allen Brownfeld — quoting Justice Earl Warren — says we face civilizational decline. But, as one fella said, "We're still the best horse in the glue factory." [fn60] To understand how society arrived at its present state, we have to go back in history, way back — to view things from 30,000 feet so to speak, or higher. Such a perspective is important for the civic health of a nation. The early eons of human existence were savage. The sex urge, strongly inherent in both sexes and yet uninhibited, meant promiscuity was rampant. According to feminist attorney Riane Eisler, prehistoric society was one vast sex cult. In As It Was in the Days of Noah, author Jeff Kinley speaks of "pandemic unrestrained immorality." "Puritanism," says Alain Danielou, "is totally unknown in the primitive or natural world." [620] That is why it is primitive and natural. Writer Denise Noe said, "The simple truth is that monogamy is not a natural state for humans of either gender." Throughout millions of years of natural selection, the human male has been biologically programmed to spread seed, and the human female, biologically programmed to diversify and nurture it.

The female mammalian kinship system, which originated in the Mesozoic Era when the dinosaurs were young — some two hundred million years ago, held sway. "Families" (not societies) were matriarchal, composed of females and offspring fathered by predatory, comparatively better provisioned males. Each sex needed what the other had by nature; women could provide children, while men could provide food, shelter and protection. In the long arc of history, perceiving the advantages of mutual support and cooperation, probably around the Stone Age, the sexes gradually initiated exclusive relationships (much later formalized as marriages). Under this ages-old 'Sexual Contract' (if I may coin the term), each sex made necessary sacrifices to benefit both: females gave fidelity; males gave hard work, often resulting in death, injury and shortened lives. Being stronger, males ruled the roost. Females received security, and males received legitimate, inalienable children, and in its ideal form still do. Even today, men work exceedingly hard in exchange with women for sex and family.

Our ascent from the cave began; permanent families were created — monogamous and patriarchal in nature. Nevertheless, in some

---

[60] This will anger some America-haters, both external and internal. Nevertheless, there it is.

societies sexual promiscuity lasted into Biblical times (Sodom and Gomorrah) and beyond — especially the last five or six decades. Under the Sexual Contract, civilization — warlike though it often was — commenced. However imperfect, it has worked quite well through 5,000 years of recorded history.

The earlier matriarchal relationships were natural, and the later patriarchal ones were artificial, created by civilization and the laws of nature.

While Professor Stephen Goldberg wrote that the transition to patriarchy or civilized norms was inevitable, [621] Margaret Mead and Professor Amneus looked further into the matter; they recognized that the earlier matriarchal relationships were natural, and the later patriarchal ones were artificial, created by civilization and the laws of nature. The female role, says Mead, "is a biological fact, the male role a mere social creation..." Amneus agreed that the male role was contrived to prop up their weaker position, and carried Mead's insight far beyond what other philosophers had considered. He posited that patriarchy, the male kinship system, relative prosperity and the dawn of civilization emerged simultaneously, and are obviously mutually dependent.

Amneus understood that the male kinship system depends not on biological heredity but on social heredity. He showed that the great benefit of patriarchy was that sex could be put to work to create civilization by allowing men to be sociological fathers, that the very fabric of society depends on viability of this delicate structure — the Sexual Contract. He also suggested that the Judge Nolands of the world are destroying that vitally important contract.

Thus spake Amneus in The Case For Father Custody: A man wants a woman to marry him and he says to her, "If you will marry me, I will guarantee you that you will be the mother of your children." He is offering her nothing, since it is impossible that a woman should not be the mother of her own children.

A woman wants a man to marry her and she says to him, "If you will marry me, I will guarantee you that you will be the father of my children." She is talking sense. She is offering him a family. A family is made possible by a woman's agreement to share her reproductive life. The man's reciprocal offer is to be a provider for her and for their children.

A nubile young woman fulfills her dream of marrying a powerful and high-achieving man and bestowing her love freely and joyously on him. Each is accounted a winner if the marriage is stable. Society is a winner. The man works for the benefit of his wife and children, and the wealth he creates circulates through the productive and creative portions of the economy... It is highly advantageous to a woman to be a sex object and for society to have her be, for it is thus that men are motivated to be achievers and to create wealth and social stability and to benefit their children — and their wives. But the advantages can best be derived from a husband whose stable motivation (and therefore work performance) is assured. But society can use the woman as a sex object to motivate a man to support a family, to pay taxes, to buy real estate, to create a stock portfolio — to contribute to society rather than disrupt it.

Anthropologist Lewis Morgan's theory of marital evolution generally agrees with that of Amneus. He wrote that among civilized people one finds monogamy built on patriarchal rule, and on chastity and fidelity among women. Cornelia Skinner said, "Women's virtue is man's greatest invention. She is right; one might say civilization is premised upon women's virtue. Ronald Immerman of Case Western University agrees.

To Skinner's contrary, current feminism rejects most male "inventions" including women's virtue. Erosion of the Sexual Contract began with the recent ascendance of the feminine, the advent of androgyny, misandry and the modern sexual revolution. The modern, repeat modern, woman is high maintenance, practically unmarriageable. Amneus said she is not new at all; she is the autonomous, pre-patriarchal Stone Age woman, sexually emancipated, who refuses to form a permanent relationship with a man upon which he — or their children — can depend. Promiscuity is being promoted by "a new genre of women's writings about sex, writings that link sex with a full-bodied spirituality imbued with erotic pleasure." [622] Helen Gurley Brown (RIP) advocated such lifestyles in her 1962 book, <u>Sex and the Single Girl</u>.

Until fairly recently the modern family had been the means for imposing sexual discipline; but many women, seeing the family as their disciplinarian, their enemy, creator of the hated patriarchal system, have opted out.

Thomas Sowell warned against "replacing what worked with what sounded good." Kathleen Parker put it eloquently in her book: "When women no longer care about children, and men no longer care about women, we will have accomplished what millions of radical jihadists could only dream about: cultural suicide and an unraveling of the civilizing forces that millions of men perished to preserve." Writer Jigs Gardner says, "A nation that degrades its past has no future."

Urie Bronfenbrenner said, "American families and their children are in trouble, trouble so deep and pervasive as to threaten the future of our nation."[623] Monogamy and long-term marriage may be difficult at times, and unnatural to our species, but necessary to civilization.

It bears repeating: immorality destroys marriage, and divorce destroys men, families and society itself. Manageable society requires maintenance of the conditions of the pragmatic Sexual Contract. Where these conditions exist, society is stable and peaceful. Where they do not, they are not. We — at least ladies and gentlemen — must rise above our biological tendencies."

Of course we can't simply declare all men immediately in charge of their families; many may be incompetent or unmitigated low lifes. Correction must be a long term approach. Underlying causes of men's incompetence must be addressed. The concept of the inherently inferior male must be eliminated, in society as well as in law. This book addresses my views in that regard.

I believe society is curable, and like the Augean Stables can be cleaned up. Where is Hercules when we need him? If a human arose capable of doing that, he would probably be denigrated and ridiculed as so many have been throughout history. Our earthly savior may not be the individual, Hercules, but enhanced fatherhood. Fatherhood may be the most important part of manhood.

Judeao-Christian values could be the lamp that Omar Khyyham searched for to "guide our little children stumbling in the dark." And, God willing, may be the last hope for preservation of civilization.

Arnold Toynbee said, "Civilizations die from suicide, not murder." Considering the threats from radicals of all persuasions and from our deteriorating standards, it appears ours is in danger from both causes. Abraham Lincoln said, "America will never be destroyed from the outside. If we falter and lose our freedoms, it will be because we destroyed ourselves." News reports expose the unrest, to put it mildly, that is sweeping the world. Protest marches are proliferating, largely with no higher ideals than opposition to law and order.

Sociologists claim that the great civilizations of old — Rome, Greece, Persia, Babylonia, and others — became extinct because of family and moral breakdown. The old values are disappearing. In his A History of Marriage and Family, Australian Professor Willystine Goodsell posits that the causes of modern western social decline are identical to those that caused the fall of the Roman Empire, under siege not only from without but also from deterioration within. A *National Review* writer claims that in the U.S. 68,000 people die yearly from drug overdoses, 88,000 from alcohol abuse and 47,000 from suicide (and that was before Corona virus). These were mostly disillusioned men. Robert Bork warned we are "Slouching toward Gomorrah." In 1947, sociologist Carle Zimmerman showed how Greek and Roman decline was preceded by a renunciation of family life, first by educated elites and then others, and argued that our own civilization is on a similar trajectory. [624] Economist Thomas Sowell warned, "We are drifting down the Niagara river oblivious to the waterfalls up ahead. Once we go over those falls, we cannot come back up again." The 2020 presidential election could bring us face to face with the prophesized Armageddon.

In the end, given human stupidities, domestic and foreign undesirables, the future looks troubling. Exitus in dubio est. Tick, tick, tick.

The Author

Richard Doyle, retired military and civilian air traffic controller and commercial pilot, is President of the declining Men's Defense Association, founding father of Men's Equality Now International (MEN International) and author of <u>In Defense of Men, and of Civilization</u>.

Born December 3, 1930, un-pampered on the hard edge of the depression (the big one) in Rosemount, Minnesota, I escaped that zeitgeist of universal female sainthood that Westerners have been conditioned to accept. Active in athletics into young adulthood, I attended St. John's Prep. School, White Bear High School, and St. Thomas College in Minnesota.

Young, dumb, left wing (the Democrat mindset) and bewitched by the beauty of a wrong woman (My mother insisted I marry a good Catholic girl, she did not turn out to be such; her primary goal in life was to have fun. Nothing compared with that). I dropped out of college after two years to marry her during the Korean War. That unfortunate coupling produced babies. Loss of college deferment required that I serve in the military. Three years with the Marine Corps Reserve, including officer training school in Quantico, Virginia were followed by four years active duty with the Air Force, switching to the latter service in anticipation of a career that could support a family. In that service I was stationed at Offutt Air Force Base Nebraska (headquarters of the Strategic Air Command [fn61]) and Elmendorf AFB in Alaska. After discharge and already trained as an air traffic controller, I was hired by the Civil Aviation Agency, later re-named the Federal Aviation Agency (FAA). I took flight training on the G.I. Bill while working at the Topeka, Kansas tower. Later I transferred to the Minneapolis tower to be nearer my children.

My introduction to the gender/sex wars began in 1956 upon discharge from the Air Force when I returned home unannounced from a year and a half deployment in Alaska. It was unlike those heart-tugging TV scenes we see of loving wives and children greeting returning veterans (I tear up every time I see them). A babysitter let me in, and hurriedly left. I kissed the two sleeping little ones, and waited until my wife and what turned out to be an all but live-in boyfriend returned from a night out. Having received very little mail from home, I had suspected something like that. I heard the key in the door and opened it, motivating the guy to run down the apartment stairs not to be seen again (to my knowledge), though many others were. I called a cab, threw my wedding ring in a nearby swamp, paid

---

[61] where I had a top secret clearance no less (which I couldn't pass now), and had a very interesting encounter with General Le May.

the driver handsomely to get me a bottle of whiskey (it was after bar closing time) and take me to a sleazy hotel in downtown St. Paul. I drank the bottle and don't remember much after that. Thus began a decades-long nightmare.

I tried reconciliation, but my wife's continued preference for a non-marital lifestyle lead to a bitter divorce in 1957; she sued me alleging "cruel and unusual treatment." A custody fight followed, all the way to the state Supreme Court, which I lost of course — being male. Government agencies supported her at every turn with numerous adverse judicial and administrative rulings and decisions, ignoring copious evidence favorable to me. I rattled many bureaucratic cages to no avail giving me unique insight to domestic law and practices. Eventually there were no more cages to rattle. I felt like Abraham must have felt when God commanded him to sacrifice his son Isaac.

The situation negatively influenced my suffering children who paid a high price for their mother's choices, and are now thoroughly alienated from me. I doubt if any of them have even bothered to read this book. The cause is explained in Part I, Chapter 4, Parental Alienation Syndrome. My biggest regret is that I wasn't able to guide them. The Medea story literally materialized. As an old Irish territorial lament goes, "What's lost is lost and gone forever."

The whole catastrophe was a deeply shocking experience. The expression "gob smacked" sums it up. See Part I, Chapter 4 re. the *Effects of Divorce on Men*. Murder and suicide crossed my mind. Struggling with depression I was prescribed any number of anti-depressant and anxiety meds. I drank enough to float a battleship trying to drown sorrows. It didn't help, but the relaxing effect may have kept me alive. I nearly became one of those homeless vets on the street — 58,000 of them in the U.S. ("There but for the grace of God...") I consorted with less than marriageable women in those days —not exactly paragons of virtue and truth. Married two, one ended tragically. I plead guilty to stupidity. Mea culpa; Gomen-nasai (Google the Japanese translation). I could be much more specific, but don't care to; it would serve no good purpose. Further about these things deponent sayeth not. More from Kyyham: "The Moving Finger writes; and, having writ, Moves on: nor all thy Piety nor Wit Shall lure it back to cancel half a Line, Nor all thy Tears wash out a Word of it."

My Minneapolis tower work suffered. I was at fault in an almost catastrophic near miss between a landing Navy plane and a civilian jet loaded with passengers one night in instrument conditions. Pauperized by increases in my alimony/support obligation and thoroughly shaken by the near miss, I resigned from the FAA in 1966, throwing my ex-wife on welfare — a welcoming atmosphere for so many aspiring divorcees. Its easy availability, combined with misguided institutional chivalry, helps destroy many thousands of erstwhile families. That drives my strong dislike of it.

I placed an ad. in an aviation magazine seeking work as commercial pilot and flight instructor, and was offered a job in Gulfport Mississippi where I worked for several years, quitting to go into the shrimp business with the husband of one of my flight students; We moved in circles high and low. That enterprise had great expectations until Hurricane Camille's interference had other ideas — the venture failed. Our nets caught more trees and submerged cars than shrimp.

After the hurricane I moved to Elgin, Illinois to do divorce counselling for Charlie Metz's America's $ociety of Divorced Men until Charlie's death in 1971. I practically lived out of my car at times. While working with Charlie an epiphany came about that the treatment of men in and after divorce is but part of a broader pattern of discrimination. The popular preference and political support for women's concerns, and shock at the animosity directed at a male who dares buck the system were instrumental in converting me to a conservative. I became a card-carrying masculinist, color me macho, and in 1977 became a founding member of Men's Equality Now (M.E.N.) International, an international coalition of similar organizations.

After Charlie's death, I moved back to St. Paul, and in 1972, formed the Men's Rights Association (now Men's Defense Association), counseling many divorcing men. Among other things, we did surveillance on cheating spouses; that was when divorce courts disapproved of adultery. Phyllis Schlafly sent me several prospective members, but as I recall they were hopeless cases requiring extensive legal help.

Comes the good part: back in St. Paul I encountered, and married, an old high school girlfriend, Ritzy. Long ago — in high school, I took her to our first prom dance. But we went our separate ways. Half a lifetime later, she married me when I didn't have the proverbial pot or window. She evidently found something here worth salvaging. Divorced, she came with a colt as she so colorfully put it, a 9-year-old son (That kid now has a grandson). We both had made stupid first marriages. There is no need to tell the story of her divorce; it was similar to mine, so I am aware that blame is not confined to one sex. She inspired this sinner to change his ways and behave in a more adult manner. I was headed for homelessness before I met Ritzy again, so every day with her, regardless of her deteriorating medical condition, was a gift.

Motivated by Ritzy, I returned to the FAA; but, on strike, was fired during the great PATCO holocaust. I won an appeal, and was re-hired. Later retired we settled down here in Gopher Prairie (Sinclair Lewis' fictional Minnesota town), and where I boast Honorary Life

Membership in our local American Legion Post. Due to deteriorating health, Ritzy went on the hospice program in July 2019, and died in my arms on October 18th. I spoke my love in her ear as she drew her last breath. We had over 46 wonderful years together. My geographically nearest family are now my American Legion post members. Every day I bring a daisy to her urn in memory of a song she sung so well.

Epilogue

Active in the men's rights trenches for over 40 years, I edited and published *The Liberator*, [fn62] foremost newsletter in the men's movement, for over 30 years. The National Coalition of Free Men NCFM awarded me a plaque bearing this inscription: "With sincere gratitude for a lifetime of selfless service to the men's and fathers' rights movement..." It hangs proudly in my office. Then this from an autograph in Professor Daniel Amneus' book, Back to Patriarchy: "To Dick Doyle, who for years has been the backbone — & brain & muscle — of the Men's Rights Movement." Also this: "Keep up the good fight," Tom Martin, Philosophy Department, University of Nebraska at Kearney. New York men's movement writer Max Freedman dubbed me a "mensch," a high honor among those of Jewish persuasion.

A lightning rod, I was considered in some circles a social dinosaur and accused of advocating everything but suttee (Come to think of it...). I've been accused of everything from plotting overthrow of the government to demonic possession. The New York chapter of NOW dubbed me a "Male Chauvinist Pig" in the mid-70s. Oink. The Minneapolis chapter named me "Male Chauvinist Sleaze of the Year" (I still have the letter somewhere). I wear such tributes as a badge of honor. Slings and arrows come with the territory. Fifty caliber insults don't bother me. Rad-fems may want me burned at the stake or chemically altered for writing this book. George Orwell said, "The further a society drifts from truth, the more it will hate those that speak it." Opponents may bring charges of hate speech that I will dispute on 1st Amendment grounds, inter alia (after all, reading a book is a matter of choice). If the People's Revolutionary Tribunal, the UN or Canadian Human Rights Tribunals get wind of it the sharks will be circling. Hopefully, crusading attorneys and organizations with the right stuff will come aboard to defend these writings. Truth is a defense. Lynch mobs, take a number; I await the next release of the lions. Bring it on

However, accusations of misandry are erroneous. I believe women in general are no worse — or better — than men. Judgmental? Hell yes, I'm judgmental — as well as curmudgeonly. I don't suffer fools gladly. In the words of philosopher Harry Jaffa, spoken by Barry Goldwater,

---

62 I store most of the back issues in my basement

"...Moderation in the pursuit of justice is no virtue." Maybe I'm too strident or simplistic for sophisticated taste, and outside the mainstream of social consciousness, but that' does not equate to being wrong.

The anti-slavery cause was unpopular and shocking a century and a half ago, as were earlier voices crying in the wilderness. Attacking popular prejudices is treading on thin ice, as Galileo, Copernicus, Darwin, Freud, even Jesus Christ could attest, proving Voltaire's wisdom: "It is dangerous to be right in matters on which the established authorities are wrong." To quote Orwell, "In a time of universal deceit, telling the truth is a revolutionary act... To see what is in front of one's nose needs a constant struggle." An activist once told me I am pissing in (against) the wind. True; but I maintain many winds are blowing in the wrong direction.

One of the things veterans served for is freedom. It is true, freedom is not free. If it means anything, it means freedom of expression regardless of hurt feelings in others. Madison called free speech "the only effectual guardian of every other right." Having sacrificed too much in defense of freedom to walk away from it now, I'll continue that fight back in the courts if necessary. I was a distance runner in school, and this is a marathon

If I was put on earth for a purpose, it was to write this book. Someone besides William F. Buckley must stand athwart modern history yelling, "Stop!" There is an old saying, "Don't curse the darkness, light a candle. This is such a candle, a very small one lit in a dark night. Like the sound of one hand clapping or a tree falling in the forest, if these messages are not disseminated, will anyone hear them? If the message of this book becomes widely acknowledged, the sacrifice of my entire progeny will have been worth it. But so far that has not been the case.

Que sera, sera. As a wise old lady said, some fights are worth fighting even if you lose. If I should lose, this is a good hill to die on. Dylan Thomas said. "Do not go gentle into that good night, Old age should burn and rage at close of day; Rage, rage against the dying of the light."

Dedication and Thanks

Dedicated to the millions of children devastated, if not altogether ruined, by unfortunate aftermaths of divorce. Such children are collateral damage from usually stupid conflicts of personalities.

To my friends and mentors the late, great Charlie Metz and Professor Emeritus Daniel Amneus of the California State University, Los Angeles. Charlie is author of Divorce and Custody for Men (out of print) and founder of America's Society of Divorced Men, formerly in Elgin Illinois. Charlie pioneered the concept of advertising for and recruiting divorce victim members, then obtaining attorneys for them. After his death, I expanded that strategy greatly. Since we pioneered the tactic, lawyers themselves are advertising widely, but without the credibility we had. Both of their pictures have places of honor in my office.

Professor Amneus was one of the most learned and eloquent observers of social behavior of our time. A student of and writer about the classics, his soul lives on in this book with many brilliant insights from his marvelous tomes, especially <u>The Case for Father Custody.</u> He was not just educated, he was an intellectual. There can be a huge difference. That dear man would shudder if he read my poor scribbling here. I consider Professor Amneus to be the foremost theoretician in the legitimate men's/fathers' movement, intellectually head and shoulders above others. Dan'l instinctively understood, as all great philosophers do, what matters and what does not, what is right and wrong for the survival of civilization. In a sense, given today's realities, his reform prescriptions were impractical, but still much superior to current legal and social arrangements and mores. Often deemed a quixotic crusader, he was so far ahead of the times, some thought him to be behind them. As Thomas Aquinas would say, what is evident to the wise is not evident to all. "In the land of the blind, the one-eyed man is king." After this good man's death, his daughter urged me to carry on his work, and his son shipped cartons of his notes to me. His death made real the old saw that when an old person dies it is like a library burning down. I will not forget the many times accompanying Dan'l to the top of Mount Hollywood in Los Angeles' Griffith Park discussing many things. Dan'l and I would take a nip on occasion. In vino veritas. I fondly remember Dan'l performing "the Wine Mystique."

Dan'l and Charlie loved classical music. I spent many happy hours listening in both their homes. I telephoned Charlie's dear widow Millie every Christmas, but recently lost track of her. I consider myself a disciple of these two good men and their insights. We shall not see their likes again. Both are giants of the legitimate men's/fathers' movement (Requiescat in pace, both). I am reminded of F. Scott Fitzgerald's line to Jay Gatsby in <u>The Great Gatsby</u>: "They were a rotten crowd, sir. You're worth the whole damn bunch put together." That Gatsby line could refer to both my mentors.

To computer guru Lloyd Selberg, living a hermit-like existence in rural Missouri. He gave enormous technical help and suggestions.

I thank my good and loyal wife Ritzy for many years of unpaid work at the Men's Defense Association. Computer technology put end for her to type, re-type, and re-re-type my writings. She is one of the most decent women ever, and as the song goes, "a good old-fashioned girl with heart so true" — a Godsend literally. I have known other women, but she will always be Ichiban. [fn63] She put up with my many faults, and didn't object (much) to my drinking a few beers. Her singing entertained a huge audience at the 700-year anniversary celebration of the founding of my mother's small ancestral village of Uddersdorf, Germany. She sang the National Anthem at Tug-of-War championships, as it was meant to be sung, much better than faddish moderns render (trill) it before Super Bowl games. When songs she used to sing appear on the Lawrence Welk show I sensed her still singing them in her mind. A real lady, she; years ago while we were vacationing in the Bahamas a native band leader named Spurgeon Bowes would commence playing "Once, twice, three times a lady" when Ritzy and I entered the hall.

Ritzy was victim of a cruel stroke 14 years ago, and over five years ago broke her hip requiring surgery and temporary nursing home care. She had a myriad of other medical issues (old age is not for sissies). But half of her was better than the whole of most women. She was tough enough to handle her fate; I wouldn't be. Her deteriorating health required attention a nursing home couldn't give. For the last couple Memorial and Veterans' days (except this year) I should have been with other Legion Honor Guard members making the rounds of celebrations and cemeteries, as in previous years, but stayed home to care for her, "in sickness and in health, 'til death did us part.'"

We made the best of two previously shattered lives and, even considering Ritzy's poor health, had a wonderful marriage. Every day with her was a gift. Her condition, though terrible for her, has matured me. Best of all, she had the greatest asset any wife (or husband) can have: loyalty. It's so good to have had a decent wife!! I hope to meet up with her again after my slow crawl to the grave. Both holes in the ground are waiting patiently.

Semper Fi. Out.

---

[63] Japanese for Number One.

Endnotes

1 http://www.difi.org.qa/about/doha-call-to-action.   http://mensdefense.org/Qatar.htm

2 Shere Hite, Women and Love (New York, Knopf 1987) 459, and many other sources cited herein.

3 This is Dr. Lenore Weitzman's celebrated statistic, frequently quoted in feminist literature. See Chapter 8 of Professor Amneus' Garbage Generation for a discussion of it.

4 Zimmerman v. Zimmerman, USDC E. Pa. 5/16/75.

5 George Gilder, Family and Nation: Moynihan's Welfare Turnaround," Catholicism and Crisis. June 1986; reprinted in Human Events 26 July. 1986.

6 O'Reilly Factor 4/8/2016

7 ABC News reports.   http://seattle.cbslocal.com/2014/06/20/judge-orders-deployed-us-sailor-to-attend-custody-hearing-or-lose-daughter-face-contempt/.

8 American Retirees Association (for retired military personnel) newsletter. The organization is based in Redlands, California and Arlington, Virginia.

9 Cook County Illinois file # 69D11468, Kansas Chief Justice Prager

297 The results are published in Tim Groshens and J.J. Smith, A Report On the 2005 Survey of MSBA Family Law Section Members, 14 Family Law Forum, no. 2, pp. 21-32 (the Spring/Summer, 2005 issue).

11 Leon Koziol .com, Associated Press, 3/31/2010. http://leonkozioljd.wordpress.com/2013/04/24/more-family-court-inspired-violence-as-predicted/

12 http://www.divorcecorp.com/the-book/

13 Runge v. Runge: 212 S.W. 2d 275.

14 105 N.E. 2d 300.

15 Forman v. Forman, Fla Ct App., 3rd Dist., 5/27/75.

16 Cox vs. Cox; Utah Sup. Ct. 3/6/75.

17 Commonwealth ex rel. Edinger v. Edinger 5/12/53, Judge Musmanno, Penna. Sup. Ct.

18 In In re John A. v. Bridget M., 2005 WL 7290006 (N.Y.A.D. 1st Dept., 3/31/05)

19 http://deltabravo.net/custody/fay.php

20 New York Magazine, Nov. 18, 1985.

21 N.Y. Law Journal, 11/16/05.

22 London Daily Mail. Date missing

23 Melbourne, Australia Herald-Sun- March 1, 2009.

24 Civil Action File No. 2007-CV-1124 (contains Judge Nation's admission of being sexist).

25 http://www.miamiherald.com/news/politics-government/state-politics/article72042847.html

26 Basic Books, 1990

27 Father Facts, Dr. Wade Horn.

28 Rasmussen Reports. June 16, 2002.

29 PBS TV Frontline 2/25/86.

30 Dr. Wade Horn. April 13, 2004   speech in Melbourne, Australia

31 Industrial Abstract of the U.S. 2000.

32 The Family in America: New Research, December 1989.

33 Former Deputy Assistant Secretary of Health and Human Services during the Bush Administration.

34 Patrick Fagan and William Fitzgerald, The Child Abuse Crisis: The Disintegration of Marriage, Family and the American Community, 13, 17.

35 St.Paul Pioneer Press 8/14/2019

36 St. Paul Pioneer Press, 4/15/20

37 St. Paul Pioneer Press, 3/18/2015.

38 St. Paul Pioneer Press, 11/9/14, p 2B.

39 St. Paul Pioneer Press 7/7/2017.

40 St. Paul Pioneer Press 4/18/12.

41 AP 12/23/09.

42 Mom, boyfriend, St. Paul Pioneer Press, 9/2/11, p4b.

43 http://www.kare11.com/story/news/crime/2015/02/13/ -man-charged-in-beating-death-of-child/23376345/

44 St. Paul Press, 1/30/2020

45 According to Valerie Riches, Director of Family and Youth Concern, Oxford. London Daily Telegraph 28 Dec. 1996.

46 Carla Rivera, Los Angeles Times, 15 November 1996.

47 The Washington Times, July 5, 2004.

48 From "It's Personal for a Top NYC Divorce Lawyer", by Pranay Gupte, May 17,2005, the New York Sun, http://www.nysun.com/article/13956.

49 According to Myron Brenton, writing in The American Male.

50 Jed Abraham, Esq. The Divorce Revolution Revisited... Northern Illinois Univ. Law Review, Vol. 9, #2, 1989.

51 KhatKhat v. Hussein, New Jersey App. Div., April 18, 2008 and Davidson v. Davidson, New Jersey App. Div., April 25, 2008

52 AP. CNN.COM/Living. Undated.

53 Markowitz; NY Sup. Ct., NY Cty. 6/4/75.

54 House v. House, Calif. Ct App Dist. 8/11/75.

55 Thomas v. Thomas, Tx. Ct Civ App, 1st Dist. 5/22/75.

56 Wall Street Journal, Oct. 31, 2009

57 http://money.cnn.com/2015/01/06/luxury/billionaire-divorce-check/index.html

58 Wilson v. Wilson; 271 Ky. 631, 112 S.W. 2d 980.

59 http://money.cnn.com/2015/02/24/luxury/griffin-billionaire-divorce/

60 Associated Press March 19, 2009

61 National Post, http://fullcomment.nationalpost.com/2010/06/14/barbara-kay-first-kill-the-husband-second-claim-sympathy-as-a-widow/#ixzz0rDlwgNs5

62 http://www.nj.com/hunterdoncountydemocrat/index.ssf/2012/12/divorcee_sits_in_jail_while_ua.html

63 http://www.dailymail.co.uk/news/article-2255241/Sperm-donor-ordered-pay-child-support-lesbian-couple-despite-giving-rights-child.html

64 The Tennessean.com 07/22/07

65 Associated Press, Portsmouth Herald April 24, 2005

66 Oneonta Daily Star 10/23/07.

67 McAlester News-Capital, 10/13/07.

68 http://www.wxyz.com/news/region/detroit/detroit-man-fights-30k-child-support-bill-for-kid-that-is-not-his.

69 http://www.chron.com/news/houston-texas/article/Houston-man-must-pay-child-support-for-kid-that-s-11305261.php

70 Daily Record.Co.Uk, 4/ 19/2011.

71 Toronto Sun, 2/6/2013.

72 For a complete review of Title IV - D, see the B.N.A. Family Law Reporter, June 10, 1975, Monograph #8, Volume I, No. 30.

73 Las Vegas Sun, Feb. 8, 2010

74 Child Support Report, OSCE, U.S. Dept. of Health & Human Services. Sept. 2004.

75 Child Support Report Vol. XXVll, Sept. 2005

76 Wall Street Journal, 2 March 1995.

77 http://www.in.gov/judiciary/opinions/pdf/02111001tac.pdf

78 Foxnews.com. August 09, 2002

79 http://www.youtube.com/watch?v=3s_EF-3FA88

80 Office of Child Support Enforcement. U.S. Dept. of Health & Human Services.

81 http://www.fathersandfamilies.org/2012/07/27/feds-spend-499-in-child-support-enforcement-for-every-1-for-access-and-visitation/

82 Reason Magazine, June 2004. 13, 14.

83 1 FLR 2824.

84 http://www.msnbc.msn.com/id/44376665/ns/us_news-crime_and_courts/#.Tm4Yw9Rsw9I

85 http://www.post-gazette.com/pg/09192/983301-454.stm#ixzz0L9KnEdEa&D

86 South Bend Tribune, 3/7/08.

87 Gloucester, Mass. Daily Times, 3/21/73.

88 American Civil Liberties Union of Pennsylvania, Civil Liberties Record, February 1957.

89 http://www.cnn.com/2009/CRIME/07/15/georgia.child.support/ index.html

90 WBLT3 TV, Jackson, MS.

91 WSVN TV, Florida, 12/4/'06.

92 http://www.governing.com/topics/health-human-services/col-jailing-deadbeat-dads-effective-child-support-payments.html

93 The Intelligencer / Wheeling News-Register, 5/ 9/2011

94 http://www.aabb.org/sa/facilities/Documents/rtannrpt04.pdf.   esp. pp. 6-7

95 The Guardian, 28 November 2005.

96 Days of Tempest" The Liam Magill Story, Amazon.com, AAP, 17 March 2005. The Australian Gender Report for March 2005.

97 The Guardian, August 1, 2008

98 Kansas City.com, 7/7/09.

99 http://www.nytimes.com/2016/11/09/nyregion/rolling-dna-labs-address-the-ultimate-question-whos-your-daddy.htmlconsistent with an assault.

100 http://newyork.cbslocal.com/2012/08/15/whos-your-daddy-truck-offers-answers-with-dna-tests/

101 Men's News Daily, September 4, 2009

102 See The Marketing of Evil, by David Kupelian, pgs 133–142

103 cnsnews.com/news/article/terence-p-jeffrey/cdc-us-fertility-rate-hits-record-low-2nd-straight-year-407-babies#sthash.ayaBOZu3.a5w2i0wr.dpuf

104 From an article by Eleanor Hoover for the Los Angeles Times reprinted in the St. Paul Dispatch 9/2/75.

105 Heyn, The Erotic Silence of The American Wife 26, citing a survey by Playboy made in 1982.

106 https://www.ashleymadison.com/?c=1&lang=en_US&age_gate=0&utm_source=google&utm_medium=cpc&utm_term=ashley+madison&utm

107 Conservative Review 1/30/2020

108 See: The Effect of No-fault Divorce Law on the Divorce Rate Across the 50 States and its Relation to Income, Education, and Religiosity. Paul A. Nakonezny, Robert Shull, Joseph Lee Rodgers, Journal of Marriage and the Family 57 [1995]: 477-488.).

109 From Law Enforcement Administration study of 158,000 prisoners in 3,500 local jails, released May 15, 1980.

110 Daily Mail, 9/11/10.

111 The Seattle Times, 2/25/09.

112 http://www.foxnews.com, 01/29/2013 , 60 Minutes TV 7/22/2012.

113 https://apnews.com/fc93f552c97364fa1fd502c2c621a62f

114 http://www.cbs8.com/story/36855318/wilbert-jones-walks-free-after-46-years-in-prison-i-thank-god-for-my-family.

115 http://www.enumclaw.com/news/national-news/man-released-after-42-years-in-prison-for-innocence-in-arizona-fire-prosecutors-push-no-contest/ "60 Minutes" investigation, NBC News reports

116 http://www.nbcnews.com/news/crime-courts/ohio-men-wrongly-convicted-murder-after-39-years-released-n253356

117 http://abcnews.go.com/US/michael-morton-free-25-years-prison-exonerated-wifes/story?id=14663445

118 The Associated Press, 8/16/07

119 http://www.wral.com/judge-orders-new-murder-trial-for-darryl-howard-da-will-not-appeal/15975655/

120 The Little Black Book of Wisdom. Tony Lyons.

121 http://coloradocure.org/?p=284

122 St. Paul, Pioneer Press 6/6/2017.

123 http://www.infowars.com/man-faces-life-in-jail-for-recording-police/

124 http://dailysignal.com/2014/07/07/son-skips-church-father-arrested-child-endangerment/?utm_source=heritagefoundation&utm_medium=email&utm_term=headline&utm_content=1400712&utm_campaign=saturday

125 http://abcnews.go.com/US/prisoner-left-solitary-years-receives-155m-settlement/story?id=18677197

126 http://www.clickorlando.com/news/florida-man-sentenced-to-3-years-in-prison-over-dead-sick-cats/34030700

127 Chicago tribune 08/09/2009

128 South Florida Sun-Sentinel 9/25/07

129 killer of 4 cops in Washington State, whose sentence was shortened from 108 years to 47 years by then Arkansas Governor Mike Huckabee upon recommendation of his clemency board. He took full responsibility. 2 Washington State judges actually let him out of jail on minimal bail.

130 In November 2005, the Los Angeles Times published an article from one of the accusers in the notorious McMartin Pre-School molestation case, Kyle Zirpolo, now 30 years-old, admitting he had been pressured into lying that Ray Buckwey, a defendant, had touched him inappropriately.

131 See 'The Penile Plethysmograph, Abel Assessment for Sexual Interest, and MSI-II: Are They Speaking the Same Language?", The American Journal of Family Therapy, 35:3, 187—202.

132 State v. Marschall, 148 N.J. 89, 275-76, cert. den. 522 U.S. 850 (1997).

133 Rick Teague, Court Psychologist for five-county area of S.W. VA.

134 Margretta Dwyer, University of Minnesota Psychologist.

135 Alpha Publishing, 2002.

136 Huffington Post, 7/11/09

137 Ira Reiss, An End to Shame: Shaping our Next Sexual Revolution (Buffalo: Prometheus Books, 1990), p. 52.

138 R. L. McNeeley, The Truth About Domestic Violence: A Falsely Framed Issue, Social Work, Nov/Dec 1987, 488. (The definitive study. Heavily annotated).

139 Ibid. p 485; Marriage and Divorce Today, (Dec. 15, 1986).

140 Straus, M.A., Gelles R.J. & Steinmetz, Suzanne I., Behind Closed Doors: Violence in American Families (Doubleday NY 1980).
Dr. Murray Straus (R.I.P.) Professor of Sociology and founder and Co-Director of the Family Research Laboratory, University of New Hampshire.

141 Transitions, July/August, 1995.

142 Richard Gelles, The Book of David: How Preserving Families Can Cost Children's Lives, HarperCollins, 1996, 75f.

143 Wall Street Journal Online August 23, 2007; Page D1.

144 http://blog.independent.org/2012/03/19/violence-against-women-act-sanctions-rights-violations/

145 http://www.telegraph.co.uk/news/uknews/crime/11043785/Bullying-husbands-face-jail-under-new-proposals-by-Theresa-May.html

146 UK Daily Mail 1/5/2010. For a comprehensive video on DV, go to website http://www.youtube.com/watch?v=5lHmCN3MBMI&feature=youtu.be

147 Men's News Daily, November 9, 2009

148http://www.americanbar.org/publications/criminal_justice_magazine_home/crimjust_cjma
    g_16_1_chesneylind.html. http://www.liberalamerica.org/2014/05/29/watch-what-
    happens-when-a-woman-abuses-a-man-in-public-video/
149 CBS6 WRGB, July 31, 2008
150 St. Petersburg, FL Times September 13, 2006
151 http://variety.com/2014/tv/news/espn-suspends-stephen-a-smith-for-one-week-for-ray-rice-
    comments-1201271303/
152 St. Paul Pioneer Press 3/8/2012.
153 https://www.telegraph.co.uk/news/2018/11/22/growing-number-men-reporting-domestic-
    violence-police-ons-figures/
154   Chang and Smith vs. Office on Violence against Women (Civil Action No.   1:19-cv-01241
    TSC).
155 https://teapartypac.org/uh-oh-creepy-uncle-joe-biden-hit-with-metoo-allegations-its-about-
    time/
156 As reported by feminist Jessica Valenti, founder and Executive Editor of feministing.com,
    on Manumit Exchange 1/12/06.
157 http://www.govtrack.us/congress/bill.xpd?bill=s111-2982
158http://www.un.org/apps/news/story.asp?NewsID=35224&Cr=gender&Cr1=
159 St. Paul, MN Pioneer Press, 3/8/2013.
160 An analysis of the SAFE Act can be seen here:
    http://www.mediaradar.org/docs/RADARanalysis-HR739-SAFE-Act.pdf
161 Watch the clip. http://www.youtube.com/watch?v=BTc8X9AJpmE. Thanks Bruce Eden.
162   AOL News 7/25/07.
163 http://articles.nydailynews.com/2011-06-06/news/29648541_1_toddler-bunk-bed-florida-boy.
164 http://www.southstrandnews.com/news/andrews-high-student-charged-after-throwing-
    paper-airplane-at-teacher/article_42bcd2f8-d8e7-11e6-a478-f3a0ebe2c68b.html
165 St. Paul Pioneer Press, 3/10/16.
166 http://www.digitaljournal.com/article/315548
167 http://denver.cbslocal.com/2012/05/04/6-year-old-suspended-for-singing-im-sexy-and-i-
    know-it/
168 http://www.cnn.com/2013/12/12/us/six-year-old-kissing-girl-suspension/index.html.
169 http://sanfrancisco.cbslocal.com/2012/01/27/hercules-family-battles-playground-sex-
    assault-claim-against-6-year-old/
170 http://www.parentdish.com/2010/05/11/how-your-son-could-end-up-on-the-sex-offender-list/
171 The Phantom Epidemic of Sexual Assault, The Public Interest, Spring 1991.
172 Yahoo news. Nov 19.
173 http://www.nydailynews.com/news/crime/fbi-change-definition-rape-time-1929-article-
    1.988510
174 From the National Crime Survey, The Liberator August 1991.
175 St. Paul, MN Pioneer Press 8/29/13.
176 https://www.washingtonpost.com/local/public-safety/dc-police-framed-man-imprisoned-27-
    years-for-1981-murder-us-jury-finds/2015/11/18/7a454054-8e04-11e5-baf4-
    bdf37355da0c_story.html
177 Time Mag. 10/3/2005.
178 St. Paul Pioneer Press, 7/27/14
179 St. Paul Pioneer Press 6/6/2015.
180 AP. August 19, 2009
181 St. Paul, MN Pioneer Press, 7/1/2010.
182 St. Paul Pioneer Press, 11/14/2013.
183 St. Paul Pioneer Press, 6/18/2015.
184 Charles P. McDowell, et al, False Allegations, appearing as a chapter in Practical Rape
    Investigation: A Multidisciplinary Approach edited by Behavioral Science Unit, FBI
    Academy, Quantico, Virginia, 1985.
185 http://www.leatherneck.com/forums/showthread.php?t=82662
186 http://www.fillerfund.com/history.htm, http://www.saveservices.org/2013/07/e-lert-false-accuser-
    ligia-filler-why-hasnt-she-been-charged-with-perjury/

187 http://www.fillerfund.com/
188 In the Matter of the Marriage of SHAWN S. SUGGS Petitioner, and ANDREW O.
   HAMILTON Respondent No. 73892-1. Filed July 8, 2004
   http://pub.bna.com/fl/738921.htm
189 http://www.markbaeresq.com/Pasadena-Family-Law-Blog/2010/May/False-Allegations-of-
   Domestic-Violence.aspx
190 https://www.bostonglobe.com/metro/2015/05/29/amherst/4t6JtKmaz7vlYSrQk5NDyJ/story.h
   tml, and http://college.usatoday.com/2015/06/01/former-amherst-student-challenges-
   sexual-assault-conviction/.   http://reason.com/blog/2017/01/31/amherst-student-expelled-
   for-sexual-misc
191 https://www.rollingstone.com/culture/news/a-note-to-our-readers-20141205
192 http://www.esquire.com/news-politics/a33751/occidental-justice-case/.
193 http://www.foxnews.com/politics/2014/12/10/another-rape-ruckus-publisher-retreats-on-
   lena-dunhams-disturbing-claim/
194 http://www.mindingthecampus.org/2015/06/did-mattress-girl-tell-the-truth-not-very-
   likely/ http://www.breitbart.com/big-government/2015/05/20/fakerape-campaign-
   ridicules-mattress-girl-hoaxer/
195 http://www.avoiceformalestudents.com/list-of-lawsuits-against-colleges-and-universities-
   alleging-due-process-violations-in-adjudicating-sexual-assault/
   http://washingtonexaminer.com/section/campus-sexual-assault
196 http://www.thecollegefix.com/post/25736/
197 CBS 2 HD and wcbstv.com Sep 17, 2009
198 https://www.c-span.org/video/?425129-1/words-stuart-taylor.
199 http://www.latimes.com/local/politics/la-me-pol-bills-legislature-20140829-story.html
200 http://www.weeklystandard.com/why-campus-rape-tribunals-always-reach-guilty-
   verdicts/article/2010401.
201 https://www.nbcconnecticut.com/news/local/Woman-Sentenced-to-Jail-for-False-Rape-
   Accusation-Rolls-Eyes-in-Court-491565291.html
202 Durham NC Herald Sun June 8, 06
203 ABC News Law & Justice Unit, June 16, 2007
204 ABC News/The Law 2/18/2010.
205 St. Paul Pioneer Press, 1/28/2007.
206 St. Paul MN Pioneer Press 5/8/15, pg. 2A.
207 St. Paul Pioneer Press 10/11/13.
208 http://www.newsobserver.com/news/local/education/article24485476.html#storylink=cpy
209 St. Paul Dispatch 25 July 1975.
210 St. Paul Pioneer Press, 7/30/2010
211 St. Paul Pioneer Press,1/8/18.
212 State v. Barton; La. Sup Ct. 6/23/75.
213 Sarasota Herald-Tribune, March 25, 2008
214 The Columbus Dispatch, November 13, 2007
215 TheDenverChannel.com. July 6, 2007
216 http://www.foxnews.com/politics/2017/12/15/attorney-lisa-bloom-sought-to-line-up-
   paydays-for-women-accusing-trump-sexual-misconduct-report.html
217 https://www.grandforksherald.com/news/government-and-politics/4435807-proposed-
   sexual-harassment-policy-minnesota-legislature-would
218 St. Paul Pioneer Press, 7/24/13.
219 WorldNetDaily.com 13 Nov. 2004.
220 http://www.washingtontimes.com/news/2011/sep/18/lehman-rocks-navy-complaints-about-
   political-corre/?page=all

221 Army recruiting Commander Maj. Gen. Allen Batschelet claims that more than 71% of America's youth would fail to qualify for military service because of their physical, moral or cognitive shortcomings, and especially their weight; it's getting worse. http://www.usatoday.com/story/news/nation-now/2014/08/29/army-recruiting-obesity/14798757/

222 CNN.com/US

223 myfoxmemphis.com, 8/1/08

224 AP, 1/8/2010.

225 http://www.nytimes.com/2011/10/07/nyregion/barbara-sheehan-who-killed-husband-is-found-not-guilty-of-murder.html?_r=2&partner=MYWAY&ei=5065

226 National Review, Dec. 5, 1986. p 16

227 http://en.wikipedia.org/wiki/Office_on_Violence_Against_Women

228 http://fullcomment.nationalpost.com/2013/07/02/barbara-kay-nicole-doucet-is-innocent-by-reason-of-gender/

229 CBC

230 Telegraph Journal, 1/27/10

231 Daily Mail, 7/29/08.

232 CBC News, June 22, 2009

233 St. Paul Pioneer Press, 10/2/14. St. Paul Pioneer Press, 11-21-14.

234 Atlanta Journal-Constitution, AP., Yahoo news.com, 10 Feb. 2005

235 Appeal-Democrat.com August 18, 2008.

236 Santa Barbara Independent, Sept 18, 2008

237 AP, Yahoo News, 8/24/07.

238 St. Paul, MN Pioneer Press, 5/19/11.

239 CBS News Nov. 23, 2005. CNN Headline News March 21, 2006.

240 Associated Press (undated).

241 http://www.startribune.com/no-jail-for-former-champlin-park-high-coach-who-sexually-assaulted-boy-13/446558923/

242 WOWT-TV Omaha, NE January 28, 2010.

243 St. Paul Pioneer Press, 3/6/16.

244 NewsMax, March 2010, p14.

245 http://nypost.com/2017/09/26/oxford-university-stabber-avoids-jail-because-of-her-extraordinary-potential/Sex & gender, weak men) invertebrates.

246 https://www.nbcconnecticut.com/news/local/Woman-Sentenced-to-Jail-for-False-Rape-Accusation-Rolls-Eyes-in-Court-491565291.html

247 St. Paul Pioneer Press, 10/25/17.

248 Associated Press, August 07, 2013, www.foxnews.com/us/2013/08/07/woman-convicted-infamous-murder-spree-as-teen-critically-injured-in-car-crash/#ixzz2bN8ySl00

249 http://www.cbsnews.com/news/distracted-mom-found-innocent/

250 CNN.com/us, AP undated.

251 Associated Press, 9/4/07

252 Washington Post, 28 February 1998, p. B01.

253 St. Paul Pioneer Press, 6/6/2015

254 Fox News June 9, 2005.

255 ABC News Dec. 23, 2009.

256 https://www.fbi.gov/sacramento/press-releases/2015/folsom-naval-reservist-is-sentenced-after-pleading-guilty-to-unauthorized-removal-and-retention-of-classified-materials http://www.thedailybeast.com/articles/2015/08/14/hero-marine-nailed-for-sending-classified-report-from-personal-email.html

257 Andrew Hartman, U.$. Prisons Mean Money, Humanist, Nov/Dec. 6-10 Year missing.

258 Washington Times Weekly, Feb. 19, 2007.

259 Justice Department's Bureau of Justice Statistics, Washington (AP) 28 May 2004.

260 St. Paul Pioneer Press 5/25/15, pg. 12a.

261 60 Minutes, Feb. 11,2007.

262 St. Paul Pioneer Press, 5/2/17.

263 NCJ 228416, January 2010.

264 http://www.AKidsRight.org/arrests_jail.htm
265 St. Paul Pioneer Press 1/1/15, pg 1A
266 WKYC.COM, Jan. 31, 2008.
267 Canada National Post, September 2004.
268 Associated Press September 13, 2011
269 Mankind, Issue No. 59, p 6.
270 http://www.youtube.com/watch?v=2A8L59zw2ZQ
271 St. Paul Pioneer Press, 2/14/20
272 Phyllis Schlafly Report, Feb., 2020.
273 St. Paul Pioneer Press. 6/22/2018
274 Thinking Minnesota, Summer 2020, pg 49.
275 STP Pioneer Press, 1/9/2018.
276 Paul Pioneer Press, 2/14/20
277 http://abcnews.go.com/International/exclusive-interview-elian-gonzalez-
      us/story?id=31113975
278 AP 9/27/07.
279 Mensnewsdaily.com, October 11, 2009
280 http://www.independent.co.uk/life-style/love-sex/men-may-never-truly-get-over-a-
      relationship-breakup-says-study-10450413.html
281 American Legion Auxiliary Magazine, Aug 2013.
282 Washington Post, November 8, 2007; Page B01.
283 http://tbbf.org/22-veterans-commit-suicide-daily/08-
      2014#pk_campaign=GA2481?matchtype
      =b&keyword=22%20veterans%20a%20day&adposition=1t1
284 St. Paul Pioneer Press, 12/24/14.
285 Lynette Triere, Learning to Leave: A Woman's Guide (New York: Warner Books, 1982),
      285.
286 Quoted by Maggie Gallagher, Enemies of Eros, 200.
287 NBC TV News 9/24/96. Marriage and Welfare Reform, Wade Horn and Andrew Bush.
288 Figures confirmed by a 1970 Rehabilitation memoranda by the Florida Ocean Sciences
      Institute.
289 Prof. Daniel Amneus, Primrose Press,
      http://www.viaticumpressinternational.com/booksdir/primrose
290 Issue 27, September/October, 1997.
291 National Longitudinal Survey of Children and Youth, by Human Resources Development
      Canada, Statistics Canada, Catalogue no. 89-550-MPE, no.1, November 1996, p. 91.
      Available from StatCan. It is only available in hard copy. $25 +GST (1997 price). The
      table, reproduced as faithfully as possible, including relevant footnotes, is accessible at
      http://fathersforlife.org/fv/DV_news_letter_971223.htm#Children_in_SMHs.
292 Margaret Driscoll, The True Victims of Separation, The Medical Post, 5 April 1994.
293 Human Events, week of June 7, 2004, 21.
294 Henry Biller, Fathers and Families (Westport, CT: Auburn House, 1993), 1f.
295 David Popenoe, Life Without Father (New York: The Free Press, 1996), 62.
296 Popenoe, Life Without Father, 77, 156.
297 Maggie Gallagher, Enemies of Eros (Chicago: Bonus Books, 1989), 114f.
298 Requiem for the War on Poverty, Policy Review, summer, 1992.
299 Looking Forward: The Next Forty Years, ed. John Templeton, 132f.)
300 James Nelson, The Intimate Connection, Amazon.com, 119.
301 From Shakespeare's King Lear, 1605
302 Marital Conflicts, Divorce, and Children's Development, by professors José Cantón
      Duarte, Rosario Cortés Arboleda, and Dolores Justicia Díaz, from the Department of
      Evolutionary and Educational Psychology of the University of Granada. Science Daily
      (Jan. 23, 2008).
303 2005 Houston Chronicle, Feb. 13, 2005

304 At http://www.leadershipcouncil.org/1/pas/1.html

305 http://www.usatoday.com/story/news/nation/2015/07/09/judge-jails-kids-refusing-lunch-dad/29940397/

306 St. Paul, MN Pioneer Press 8/11/11 p9b.

307 Urban Institute and American University, July 2002. This paper was prepared for the U. S. Department of Health and Human Services' Office of the Assistant Secretary for Planning and Evaluation under HHS Grant Number 00ASPE359A. An earlier version of this paper was presented at the 23rd Annual Research Conference of the Association for Public Policy and Management, Washington, DC, November 1-3, 2001.

308 Address to the Commonwealth Club of California, 1992; quoted in FACE, August 1992.

309 Wikipedia.

310 AP & CBS News, June 13, 2005

311 Helen Alvare, Types and Styles of Family Proceedings, Report of the United States to the VII World Congress, International Association of Procedural Law (2003): 1.

312 ALR Review (April-June 1988): 4, 5.

313 New York Law Journal, 9/16/05, N.Y. Post 8/17/05.

314 Pat Robertson, PBS TV 25 Jan. 1988.

315 Murray v. Murray; Hill 1st Dist. Ct. 11/18/74. See also Jones v. Tyson; U.S. Ct. App (Ca) 9th Circuit 6/16/75.

316 NYTimes.com, Crime Prof Blog Feb. 16, 2007

317 Cook County, Illinois, file #369D13574.

318 Ramsey County Minnesota, file #362629.

319 NY Daily News, 12/10/17; Newsday,9/16/14.

320http://www.abajournal.com/weekly/article/lawyer_with_couch_of_restitution_disciplined_in_michigan

321 http://www.twincities.com/localnews/ci_22373043/burnsville-lawyer-suspended-after-affair-client.

323 La Crosse Tribune December 21, 2007

324 Chicago Tribune, St. Paul Pioneer Press 3/16/2012.

325 Time Magazine, Oct 3,'05.

326 By blogger Abusegate Bob, Men's News Daily, May 7, 2010.

327 http://articles.philly.com/2013-03-28/news/38073085_1_dcf-workers-firearms-police-department

328 http://freekeene.com/2011/06/16/thomas-james-ball-self-immolated-in-protest-of-the-justice-system/

329 http://losangeles.cbslocal.com/2016/06/24/woman-who-spanked-her-children-with-belt-after-she-caught-them-stealing-gets-arrested-and-sets-off-firestorm-of-debate/

330 Whistleblower, July 2015.

331 http://www.washingtonpost.com/politics/va-improperly-spent-6-billion-on-care-for-veterans-senior-agency-leader-says/2015/05/13/ab8f131c-f5be-11e4-b2f3-af5479e6bbdd_story.html, and Aljazeera TV News, 5/14/2015.

332 Wash Times Weekly, 12/24/'07.

333 STP. Pioneer Press, 12/17/14.

334 http://dailycaller.com/2014/02/02/wikipedia-is-very-masculine-so-feminists-pledge-to-fix-it/

335 So says The Declaration of feminism or The Document (an alleged secret feminist agenda).

336 https://www.heritage.org/marriage-and-family/commentary/new-report-shows-planned-parenthood-raked-15-billion-taxpayer-funds. The Patriot Post, 12/11/18

337 http://www.writing.upenn.edu/~afilreis/50s/friedan-per-horowitz.html

338 Endeavour Forum, March 2017

339 What civil rights have wrought, Townhall.com - Creators Syndicate. July 26, 2000.

340 Women of the Klan: Racism and Gender in the 1920s, Kathleen M. Blee. http://www.wnd.com/2014/10/feminism-todays-womens-ku-klux-klan/#Cv6RkitHfuRUxWJP.99

341 Foundations of Betrayal: How the Liberal Super Rich Undermine America. Phil Kent

342 CNSNews.com, 1/24/2011.

343 http://dailycaller.com/2012/12/05/womens-group-obamas-cabinet-clearly-needs-to-be-50-percent-female/

344 http://www.slate.com/blogs/the_slatest/2014/09/29/iceland_announces_u_n_men_only_gender_equality_conference.html

345 http://news.yahoo.com/feminist-government-green-tinge-sweden-105640149.html

346 Lynette Triere, Learning to Leave: A Woman's Guide (New York, Warner Books, 1982), 20f.

347 Beyond God the Father, 59.

348 It Changed My Life, 102, 153, 144.

349 Los Angeles Times, 1 August 1988.

350 Defense of the Family Survey of Christian Coalition (1996).

351 Quoted in Katherine Anthony, feminism in Germany and Scandinavia, pp. 248ff.

352 Phyllis Chesler, Mothers on Trial: The Battle for Children and Custody, 441.

353 http://www.huffingtonpost.com/reductress/8-sex-positions-that-will_b_3381552.html

354 http://www.youtube.com/watch?v=iARHCxAMAO0&feature=player_embedded

355 Whistleblower Magazine, September 2013

356 http://newsinfo.inquirer.net/inquirerheadlines/nation/view/20090124-185 270/Feminism-blamed-for-erosion-of-manhood.

357 https://www.wsj.com/articles/women-ceos-dont-get-paid-less-than-men-in-big-business-they-make-more-1496223001

358 Reuters, Nov 7, 2007.

359 ABC World News, May 12, 2010.

360 1984 Report, Bureau of Labor Statistics.

361 Human Events, Sept 10, 2007.

362 Research published in America's most prestigious peer-reviewed Economics journal and Reuters, 11/7/07

363 1150 Seventeenth Street, N.W. Washington, DC 200361150 Seventeenth Street, N.W. Washington, DC 20036.

364 Wall St. Journal, http://online.wsj.com/article/SB10001424052748704415104576250672504707048.html?mod=WSJ_hp_mostpop_read

365 According to ABC TV Nightly News on 7/12/2005.

366 Goldin noteshttp://www.intellectualtakeout.org/blog/harvard-professor-discrimination-not-cause-%E2%80%98gender-pay-gap%E2%80%99

367 St. Paul Pioneer Press 5/29/2013.

368 Understanding Women's Liberation, p70.

369 Feminism and Freedom, Michael Levin (New Brunswick, Transactions Publishers, 1994) estimates a loss in productivity of American business as high as 36%. Forbidden Ground, The Case Against Employment Discrimination Law, Richard A. Epstein, (Cambridge, Harvard Univ. Press 1995).

370 Published on an internet blog March 9, 2009 by Robert Franklin, Esq.

371 http://www.independent.co.uk/news/world/americas/american-cardinal-raymond-leo-burke-blames-paedophile-priests-on-radical-feminists-9973240.html

372 Phyllis Schlafly Report, July 2009

373 Women's Enews, 1/14/09.

374 Alan Carlson, Family Questions: Reflections on the American Social Crisis, (New Brunswick: Transaction, 1988): 116—125.

375 The Age, Weekender, 11/6/05 page 11.

376 The Sexual Paradox: Troubled Boys, Gifted Girls and the Real Difference Between the Sexes, by Susan Pinker

377 http://www.forbes.com/sites/maxjedeurpalmgren/2014/09/29/the-richest-women-in-america-2014/

378 An excellent article on this subject—worthy of Professor Amneus, but written by Harvard professor Harvey C. Mansfield—appeared in the June 2006 issue of Imprimis.

379 https://www.youtube.com/watch?v=OfPhq1JiETg.

380 NewsMax, May 2006

381 Nat. Rev., Oct 19, 2015, pg. 12.

382 http://www.iwf.org/

383 Eagle Forum Report Sept. 2017.

384 Human Events, week of 9/19/11.

385 https://www.washingtonexaminer.com/news/pricey-private-schools-to-teach-black-lives-matter-classes

386 Fox TV news 10/7/16.

387 N.R. 11/12/18

388 See this video, https://www.campusreform.org/?ID=9927

389 Dr. Richard Hise, The War Against Men (Elderberry Press) 81, 82.

390 http://www.gopusa.com/freshink/2014/09/10/men-arent-allowed-at-exclusive-all-womens-college-but-other-has-a-shot/?subscriber=1

391 http://connecticut.cbslocal.com/2014/09/22/wesleyan-fraternities-ordered-to-go-coed/

392 http://im41.com/archives/36277

393 http://www.thecollegefix.com/post/28540/

394 https://www.thecollegefix.com/post/32372/

395 Los Angeles Times, 9/2/18.

396 1/18/05 Boston Globe.

397 For further corroboration of Summers' thesis, see the article entitled "Editorial Board: Larry Summers gets his revenge on Harvard" in the National Post of July 30, 2008.

398 http://www.usatoday.com/story/money/business/2013/09/15/summers-fed-bernanke-analysis/2817101/

399 http://hypeline.org/professor-calls-police-on-student-over-dissenting-opinion/

400 http://www.breitbart.com/big-government/2016/03/30/university-moves-fire-conservative-professor-political-views/

401 Men's News Daily June 10, 2010

402 http://www.jccf.ca/wp-content/uploads/2013/01/2013CampusFreedomIndex.pdf

403 Http://www.telegraph.co.uk/men/thinking-man/11670138/why-are-our-universities-blocking-mens-societies.html

404 http://www.weeklystandard.com/the-end-of-men-in-literature/article/2002347

405 Los Angeles Times, 11/21/08.

406 https://www.theguardian.com/books/2016/oct/21/wonder-woman-un-ambassador-staff-protest

407 Boston Herald July 31, 2007

408 Dallas Morning News 3/13/08.

409 January/February 2010.

410 (AP) http://cnsnews.com/news/article/michael-w-chapman/duke-rape-accuser-got-160-tv-news-stories-accusation-3-murder

411 ABC, WCPO.com

412 http://www.theipinionsjournal.com/index.php/2010/01/copperfield-rape-victim-arrested-for-prostitution/

413 St. Paul Pioneer Press, 3/10/16.

414 http://gretawire.foxnewsinsider.com/2014/11/18/worst-journalism-prize-goes-to-newsweek-calling-president-bush-41-a-wimp-he-did-58-bombing-missions-over-the-pacific-and-was-shot-down-defending-our-nation-so-who-is-the-wimp-newsweek-or-preside

415 https://www.youtube.com/watch?v=rqIEePvPSoQ

416 NY Times 11/11/2009. The Obama Administration gingerly referred to the massacre as "workplace violence," instead of Islamist extremism. http://www.foxnews.com/politics/2011/12/06/military-growing-terrorist-target-lawmakers-warn/

417 http://www.cnsnews.com/video/national/oreilly-americas-race-problem

418 https://shorensteincenter.org/news-coverage-donald-trumps-first-100-days/ http://www.washingtonexaminer.com/pew-trump-media-three-times-more-negative-than-for-obama-just-5-percent-positive/article/2644448

419 Cartel, by Sylvia Longmire, Macmillan, ISBN 978-0-230-11137-0.

420 http://www.cnsnews.com/blog/sam-dorman/gay-columnist-calls-end-manhood

421 https://www.dailymail.co.uk/health/article-6845991

422 Available from the Council on Biblical Manhood and Womanhood. $22. Phone 888-560-8210.

423 http://www.cnsnews.com/news/article/sam-dorman/study-sex-hormones-account-genuine-difference-between-male-female-brains

424 Australia's Endeavour Forum July 2017.

425 Professor Willystine Goodsell, A History of Marriage and Family (Australia).

426 Male and Female: A Study of the Sexes in a Changing World, 173.

427 National Geographic magazine January 2018.

428 To see more from Fred, go to http://fredoneverything.net/SexualFuture.shtml

429 Gender and Society: Status and Stereotypes - a worldwide Gallup Poll about the roles of men and women in society.

430 Phyllis Schlafly Report, Nov 2011

431 http://www.telegraph.co.uk/news/worldnews/europe/9572187/Couples-who-share-the-housework-are-more-likely-to-divorce-study-finds.html

432 Dayton ch 22 ABC, 4/11/11. Judicial Watch, Aug. 2011.

433 http://denver.cbslocal.com/2015/11/10/female-springs-officers-win-lawsuit-no-longer-have-to-take-physical-fitness-tests/

434 Winnipeg Free Press 5/4/1992.

435 St. Paul Pioneer Press, 2/16/2012.

436 http://www.fox9.com/news/163067335-story

437 Citation: John R. Lott Jr., "Does a Helping Hand Put Others at Risk? Affirmative Action, Police Departments and Crime," Economic Inquiry, April 1, 2000.

438 Stp PP/ 6/27/2018.

439 http://nypost.com/2015/05/03/woman-to-become-ny-firefighter-despite-failing-crucial-fitness-test/

440 http://nypost.com/2013/11/24/unfireable-female-fdny-firefighter-quits/

441 National Review, 6/22/15, pg. 8.

442 New York Times 4/21/05

442 Phyllis Schlafly Report June 2011.

443 Forest Lake Times, 11/18/10, p5.

444 St. Paul Pioneer Press, 4/4/2013

445 Gloria Steinem described her as "violent and aggressive" with two lesbian daughters). Washington Post, December 7, 2007.

446 http://www.gopusa.com/theloft/2013/04/05/diversity-gone-wild-lifeguards-who-cant-swim/?subscriber=1

447 Press release 8-13-98, The U.S. Equal Employment Opportunity Commission Miami District Office.

448 http://www.csmonitor.com/World/Europe/2013/0715/More-women-in-the-boardroom-Europe-considers-forcing-the-issue?nav=87-frontpage-entryInsideMonitor

449 http://www.reuters.com/article/2014/11/25/us-germany-women-quota-idUSKCN0J92JI20141125

450 Parade Magazine 6/13/2010, pg. 10

451 http://thehill.com/policy/defense/228920-navy-halts-short-haircuts-for-new-female-recruits

452 CBS Evening News 16 Feb. 1976.

453 https://www.popsci.com/army-updated-physical-fitness-test?CMPID=ENE072418

454 https://news.clearancejobs.com/2019/10/05/army-combat-fitness-test-fiasco-slides-reveal-84-of-women-failing-acft/

455 http://freebeacon.com/blog/exclusive-two-more-female-marines-dropped-from-infantry-course.

456https://www.washingtonpost.com/news/checkpoint/wp/2015/09/08/marines-women-in-combat-experiment-gets-mixed-results/

457 http://www.mcclatchydc.com/news/politics-government/national-politics/article84983262.html
458 http://www.cnn.com/2016/08/15/politics/female-marine-infantry-course/index.html.
459 Townhall.com. Aug 11, 2007
460 https://ca.news.yahoo.com/pentagon-promotes-lean-groups-boost-women-leadership-122906058.html
461 http://abcnews.go.com/blogs/politics/2012/02/pentagon-to-lift-some-restrictions-on-women-in-combat/
462 http://apnews.myway.com/article/20130618/DA700L3O0.html

463 Brian Mitchell, Women in the Military: Flirting with Disaster (Washington D.C.: Regnery, 1998), 77f.
464 NY Daily News, January 14th 2010.
465 http://houston.cbslocal.com/2012/09/14/police-wife-stages-shooting-to-avoid-deployment/
466 http://www.gopusa.com/news/2015/01/26/feminizing-fort-leonard-wood/?subscriber=1
467 Huma https://ca.news.yahoo.com/pentagon-promotes-lean-groups-boost-women-leadership-122906058.html n Events, 15 June 1991.
468 http://www.militarytimes.com/story/military/2015/01/26/complaints-challenge-orders-
469 Reuters, Feb 23, 2010
470 http://news.blogs.cnn.com/2012/07/11/navys-new-gender-neutral-carriers-wont-have-urinals/
471 http://www.stripes.com/news/us/special-operations-troops-doubt-women-can-do-the-job-1.338486.
472 Brian Mitchell, Weak Link: The Feminization of the American Military, Regnery Gateway 1989.
473 www.wnd.com/2013/02/women-in-foxholes/#m7H8mPeP2MX0oaBb.99.
474 Whistleblower, January 2014.
475 Los Angeles Times, 28 July 1992.
476 American Legion magazine, January 2016, p 42
477 Washington Times, 21-27 June 2004, p. 1.
478 The American Legion Magazine, June 2012, pg. 56.
479 http://www.kgwn.tv/home/headlines/Warren-AFB-Commander-Relieved-of-Command-281388121.html
480 http://www.washingtontimes.com/news/2015/dec/17/army-women-hurt-more-often-in-combat-training-expe/
481 American Legion magazine, March 2007, p 38; and St. Paul Pioneer Press, 5/20/11.
482 http://wtkr.com/2012/09/21/culture-changes-at-va-hospitals-as-more-female-vets-seek-health-care/
483 The American Legion Magazine, Sept. 2016, pg 24.
484 http://www.fredoneverything.net/ WomenInCombat.shtml.
485 http://gynocentrism.com/2013/07/14/about/
486 http://thehill.com/blogs/floor-action/house/296679-%20dems-warn-climate-change-could-drive-women-to-transactional-sex
487 https://pjmedia.com/trending/university-of-texas-to-treat-masculinity-as-a-mental-health-
488 https://www.campusreform.org/?ID=9749
489 http://fullcomment.nationalpost.com/tag/domestic-violence/
490 http://www.foxnews.com/us/2012/06/04/arizona-man-claims-was-ejected-from-bookstore-for-being-alone-in-children/print..
491 http://www.docstoc.com/docs/22261242/Annual-Report-on-Embezzlement-Released/
492 http://www.huffingtonpost.com/2013/04/23/washington-state-gender-neutral-vocabulary_n_3135734.html
493 (New York Times, April 19, 1912) http://paperspast.natlib.govt.nz/cgi-bin/paperspast?a=d&d=EP19120511.2.113
494 http://www.nydailynews.com/news/national/aurora-shooting-died-bullets-sweeties-article-1.1119395
495 http://www.mirror.co.uk/news/world-news/mother-says-sex-son-incredible-7712560
496 http://www.theblaze.com/stories/2013/04/14/former-volleyball-star-model-gabrielle-reece-ignites-controversy-with-marriage-advice-being-submissive-is-a-sign-of-strength/
497 Available at http://www.viaticumpressinternational.com
498 Yuri Kageyama, Moderate Japan Recovery Expected. Website citation expired.
499 The Feb. 2010 Phyllis Schlafly Report

500 http://redalertpolitics.com/2017/10/11/american-sports-council-says-title-ix-keeping-qualified-athletes-competing/#RhvrBJetpqkgPUWO.99

501 Mansourian v. Regents of the University of California at Davis.

502 National Review, 12 July 2004, 48.

503 http://www.star-telegram.com/news/local/community/hurst-euless-bedford_news/article134761654.html#storylink=cpy

504 St. Paul Pioneer Press, 2/14/20

505 Daily Caller October 25, 2019

506 St Paul Pioneer Press, 2/13/20

507 Stephen E. Rhodes, Taking Sex Differences Seriously (Encounter), 374.

508 http://www.fox9.com/sports/100306733-story

509http://online.wsj.com/article/SB10001424053111904900904576554380686494012.html?mod=WSJ_hp p_editorsPicks_2

510 http://goo.gl/hXvK4j. http://www.abqjournal.com/830640/some-albuquerque-teachers-told-not-to-use-boys-and-girls.html

511 .http://www.endeavourforum.org.au/

512 http://www.nydailynews.com/life-style/cuny-bans-mr-ms-correspondence-article-1.2098225

513 https://www.breitbart.com/education/2019/09/13/bbc-tells-schoolchildren-there-are-over-100-genders/

514 http://www.foxnews.com/health/2015/02/01/nyc-health-dept-form-asks-parents-if-woman-giving-birth-is-male-or-female/

515 http://www...telegraph.co. uk/ news/worldnews/europe/france/9563543/France-set-to-ban-the-words-mother-and-father-from-official-documents.html. ,Sept 25, 2012

516 Reported by Carey Roberts in NewsWithViews, May 23, 2006

517 http://www.nytimes.com/2016/02/07/world/asia/wanted-in-china-more-male-teachers-to-make-boys-men.html?_r=0

518 St. Paul Pioneer Press, 6/29/16, p 11A.

519 Nat. Review, 12/7/'09

520 New Oxford Review, May '06

521 http://cnsnews.com/blog/dan-joseph/california-bill-would-allow-students-use-bathrooms-consistent-his-or-her-gender

522 http://www.cbsnews.com/8301-250_162-57598231/california-law-allows-transgender-students-to-pick-bathrooms-sports-teams-they-identify-with/

523 http://www.nytimes.com/2015/11/03/us/illinois-district-violated-transgender-students-rights-us-says.html?_r=0

524 http://dailysignal.com/2015/11/03/countdown-district-has-30-days-to-change-transgender-student-locker-room-policy-or-lose-federalfunds/?utm_source=heritagefoundation&utm_medium=email&utm_campaign=saturday&mkt_tok=3RkMMJWWfF9wsRouvaTIZKXonjHpfsX76uosXae3hYkz2EFye%2BLIHETpodcMTcFj MLzYDBceEJhqyQJxPr3NLtQN191pRhLiDA%3D%3D

525 Whistleblower Magazine, August 2013, p7.

526 http://www.breitbart.com/california/2015/04/21/poop-equality-students-hold-sht-in-at-public-california-university/

527 http://www.breitbart.com/big-government/2016/04/20/federal-court-sides-with-obama-forces-va-school-to-let-transgender-student-choose-bathroom/

528 https://www.frc.org/get.cfm?i=WA20B28&f=WU20B04

529 http://www.thesun.co.uk/sol/homepage/news/7089698/Parents-blast-council-after-kids-told-to-choose-their-gender.html

530 http://www.washingtonpost.com/politics/obama-to-nominate-first-openly-gay-service-secretary-to-lead-the-army/2015/09/18/d4b1aafe-5e30-11e5-8e9e-dce8a2a2a679_story.html

531 Phyllis Schlafly Report January 2010

532 http://www.frc.org/washingtonupdate/gallup-trots-out-surprising-new-stats

533 St. Paul Pioneer Press, 2/14/20

534 Patriot Update News 2/12/11.

326 CNSNews.com, August 6, 2007.

536 ABC, July 13, 2015

537 http://www.pridedepot.com/?p=1668

538 AP, St. Paul Pioneer Press 6/14/13Multiple

539 National Review March 2012 pg 26.

540 Washington Times, 11/24/08, p 34.

541 Heritage Foundation Issue Brief #4393.

542 National Review, July 2012, pg 28.

543 http://www.wnd.com/2012/11/my-2-dads-childhood-not-so-happy-and-gay/

544 A.P. St. Paul Pioneer Press 3/22/2012.

545 Washington Times, Oct. 1, 2012, pg 38.

546 Gallagher, The Abolition of Marriage, 170

547 Marriage as a Pure Relationship, Journal of Comparative Family Studies, xxvii (1996), 1-12;
      epitomized in The Family in America: New Research, April, 1996

548 http://koin.com/2014/05/28/condoms-to-be-given-to-sixth-graders-in-gervais

549 Human Events, 2/15/2010. P22

550 St. Paul, MN Pioneer Press, 3/4/2010.

551 St. Paul, Minn. Pioneer Press, 9/15/11, p8B.

552 http://www.gallup.com/poll/162740/americans-outlook-moral-values-
      pessimistic.aspx?utm_source=alert&utm_medium=email&utm_campaign=syndication&utm_conte
      nt=morelink&utm_term=All%20Gallup%20Headlines%20-%20Politics

553 https://www.cdc.gov/nchs/fastats/unmarried-childbearing.htm

554 https://pjmedia.com/faith/2017/08/23/d-james-kennedy-ministries-sues-splc-guidestar-and-amazon-
      for-defamation/

555 Marriage and Divorce July/Aug 1974, 36.

556 U.S. Census Bureau, Statistical Abstract.

557 The Family in America June 2004. Wade Horn was an adviser to President Bush and Assistant
      Secretary for Children and Families in the Department of Health and Human Services.

558 Judicial Watch, Washington, DC. newsletter July 2005.

559 Stanley Kurtz, The End of Marriage in Scandinavia, The Weekly Standard, 2/2/2004, 27.

560 The Family in America, May 2005.

561 Nelson on Divorce, 2nd Edition.

562 Gallagher, The Abolition of Marriage, 150)

563 See: The Effect of No-fault Divorce Law on the Divorce Rate Across the 50 States and its Relation to
      Income, Education, and Religiosity. Paul A. Nakonezny, Robert Shull, Joseph Lee Rodgers,
      Journal of Marriage and the Family 57 [1995]: 477-488.).

564 Fox News 8/21/07.

565 The American Legion Magazine, July 2007.

566 The American Legion Magazine, Jan. 2015.

567 http://www.breitbart.com/Big-Journalism/2014/05/20/Menstrual-Leave-Endorsed-by-HuffPo

568 ABC TV News 2/25/2012

569 Mankind, Dec. 2005

570 1154 15th Street, NW Washington, DC 20005. http://www.pcacoalition.org.

571 J.W Prostatecancer911.com.. Verdict, 6/20/11

572 Prostatecancer911.com.

573 Phyllis Schlafly Report, Feb., 2020.

574 http://freebeacon.com/issues/feds-want-to-lower-legal-driving-limit-to-one-drink/

575 Washington Times Weekly, May 10-16, (2004): 23.

576 Whistleblower, Aug. 20, 2015, pg 37.

577 In re Marriage of LaMusga.

578 http://www.wsj.com/article_email/big-shift-pushed-in-custody-disputes-1429204977-
      lMyQjAxMTI1NzE0NzYxNDc5Wj

579 http://www.marriagesavers.org/sitems/index.htm

580 Imprimis, June 1997.

581 Telegraph.co.uk, Oct 2008

582 January/February 2007 issue of the journal Child Development.

583 State v. Richardson, 40 N.H. 272, 277 (1890):

584 Phyllis Chesler, Mothers on Trial, 569.

585 http://www.cnsnews.com/news/article/sam-dorman/study-boys-affected-more-girls-family-disadvantages

586 See Amneus, 'Garbage Generation, 215-285 for documentation.

587 San Diego Union-Tribune, 7/11/07

588 Maggie Gallagher, The Abolition of Marriage: How We Destroy Lasting Love, (Regnery), 43.

589 Idaho Supreme Court Justice Shepard in Olsen v. Olsen, 98 Idaho 10 (1976).

590 Another of the nation's most knowledgeable authorities on Child Support guidelines.

591 Dec. 25, 1927, San Antonio Light. Discovered by Robert Franklin, Esq.

592 Miami Herald, 24 March 1980; cited in Triere, 157.

593 Family Law Quarterly Vol. 33 No. 1 1999, 1999 Child Support Symposium, Child Support at a Crossroads. Thanks Ronald K. Henry, Esq.

594 AOLNews.com 5/16/07

595 See www.innocenceproject.org.

596 Reason Magazine, Feb 05.

597 St. Paul Pioneer Press, 3/22/2015.

598 New York Times, June 10, 2010.

599 The Journal, 3/10/08

600 BBC News, 3 November 2006

601 http://www.csulb.edu/~mfiebert/assault.htm

602 R. L. McNeeley, The Truth About Domestic Violence: A Falsely Framed Issue 485-490.

603 Criminal Victimization in the U.S (1989).

604 Ibid. p 487.

605 http://www.theamericanmirror.com/u-s-navy-teaching-members-to-combat-male-privilege/

606 Transitions Magazine, Nov/Dec. 2004.

607 http://www.independent.co.uk/news/uk/home-news/women-are-more-violent-says-study-622388.html

608 Prof. Clifton Flynn, Family Relations, (April 1990) 194

609 Domestic Violence: The 12 Things You Aren't Supposed to Know, Tom James, J.D.Aventine Press, Chula Vista, CA, Amazon Books. ISBN 1-59330-122-7.

610 R.L. McNeely, Ph.D. & G. Robinson-Simpson, Ed. D, The Truth About Domestic Violence: A Falsely Framed Issue, Social Work, Nov/Dec 1987, 485, 490; Dr. Coramae Richey Mann, FL. State U.; Justice Quarterly Mar '88; Dr. Amneus, Garbage Generation, ps. 85,86.

611 It Changed My Life, p. 126.

612 New Harbinger Publications, CA.

613 Bureau of Justice Statistics and Uniform Crime Reporting. McNeeley, p 487.

614 POB 2679 Huntington Station, NY 1146

615 St. Paul Pioneer Press. 6/22/2018

616 St. Paul Pioneer Press, 4/15/2015.

617online.wsj.com/article/SB10001424052702303644004577525253742799344. html

618 https://philadelphia.cbslocal.com/2019/03/25/plymouth-meetings-men-only-cuddling-group-aims-to-heals-through-power-of-cuddling

619 http://www.youtube.com/watch?v=2LkYDpQQVJ0

620 Alain Danielou, Gods of Love and Ecstasy: The Traditions of Shiva and Dionysus (Rochester, Vermont: Inner Traditions, 1979), 17.

621 Stephen Goldberg, New York City University, The Inevitability of Patriarchy (Wm. Morrow & Co).

622 Sacred Pleasure, 284. ISBN 0062502832.

623 Nigel Davies, The Rampant God, pg. 277.

624 Family and Civilization, p. 146, Zimmerman.

Made in the USA
Las Vegas, NV
04 February 2021